PRINCIPLES of LEADERSHIP and MANAGEMENT in LAW ENFORCEMENT

PRINCIPLES of LEADERSHIP and MANAGEMENT in LAW ENFORCEMENT

Michael L. Birzer
Gerald J. Bayens
Cliff Roberson

CRC Press is an imprint of the
Taylor & Francis Group, an **informa** business

CRC Press
Taylor & Francis Group
6000 Broken Sound Parkway NW, Suite 300
Boca Raton, FL 33487-2742

© 2012 by Taylor & Francis Group, LLC
CRC Press is an imprint of Taylor & Francis Group, an Informa business

No claim to original U.S. Government works

Printed in the United States of America on acid-free paper
Version Date: 20120409

International Standard Book Number: 978-1-4398-8034-0 (Hardback)

This book contains information obtained from authentic and highly regarded sources. Reasonable efforts have been made to publish reliable data and information, but the author and publisher cannot assume responsibility for the validity of all materials or the consequences of their use. The authors and publishers have attempted to trace the copyright holders of all material reproduced in this publication and apologize to copyright holders if permission to publish in this form has not been obtained. If any copyright material has not been acknowledged please write and let us know so we may rectify in any future reprint.

Except as permitted under U.S. Copyright Law, no part of this book may be reprinted, reproduced, transmitted, or utilized in any form by any electronic, mechanical, or other means, now known or hereafter invented, including photocopying, microfilming, and recording, or in any information storage or retrieval system, without written permission from the publishers.

For permission to photocopy or use material electronically from this work, please access www.copyright.com (http://www.copyright.com/) or contact the Copyright Clearance Center, Inc. (CCC), 222 Rosewood Drive, Danvers, MA 01923, 978-750-8400. CCC is a not-for-profit organization that provides licenses and registration for a variety of users. For organizations that have been granted a photocopy license by the CCC, a separate system of payment has been arranged.

Trademark Notice: Product or corporate names may be trademarks or registered trademarks, and are used only for identification and explanation without intent to infringe.

Library of Congress Cataloging-in-Publication Data

Birzer, Michael L., 1960-
  Principles of leadership and management in law enforcement / by Michael L. Birzer, Gerald J. Bayens, and Cliff Roberson.
       p. cm.
  Includes bibliographical references and index.
  ISBN 978-1-4398-8034-0 (alk. paper)
  1. Law enforcement. 2. Management. 3. Personnel management. 4. Leadership. I. Bayens, Gerald J. II. Roberson, Cliff, 1937- III. Title.

HV7921.B527 2012
363.2068--dc23   2012011427

Visit the Taylor & Francis Web site at
http://www.taylorandfrancis.com

and the CRC Press Web site at
http://www.crcpress.com

For Joan, Gwynne, and Elena

Table of Contents

Preface	xix
Authors	xxi

1 Introduction to the Modern Police Agency — 1

Key Individuals, Concepts, and Issues	1
Definitions	1
Chapter Objectives	1
Introduction	2
Management and Leadership	3
Evolution of the Modern Police Department	5
Early Policing	5
Early English Law Enforcement	5
Development of Established English Police Forces	7
Policing in the American Colonies	9
Policing in Urban America	10
State Police	12
Police Reform Era	12
Progressive Era	12
Professionalism	13
Wickersham Commission	13
Policing in the 1950s and Early 1960s	15
War on Crime Era	15
Community Policing	17
How Does Community Policing Affect the Role of the Police Supervisor?	19
Policing Styles	21
Watchman Style	21
Legalistic Style	22
Service Style	22
Development of Police Management Theory	23
Traditional Management Model	23
Scientific Management	23
Bureaucratic Management	23
Administrative Management	24
Leadership	24

	Human Relations Model	25
	Behavioral Science Model	25
	Systems Theory	26
	Contingency Theory	26
	Human Resources Model	26
Organizational Culture		29
Questions in Review		29
Biggest Mistakes Police Leadership Makes and How to Avoid Them		31
	Lucky or Cunning and Resourceful	31
	What Is Your Opinion? And Your Justification for That Opinion?	31
End Notes		32

2 Introduction to Management Theory — 35

Key Individuals, Concepts, and Issues	35
Definitions	35
Chapter Objectives	36
Introduction	37
Management Theory	39
Scientific Management	40
Frederick Winslow Taylor	40
Henry Gantt	41
Frank and Lillian Gilbreth	43
Bureacratic Management	44
Max Weber	44
Administrative Management	48
Henri Fayol	48
Mary Parker Follett	49
Chester Barnard	50
The Humanistic Management Approach	50
The Human Relations Movement	50
Elton Mayo	50
Abraham Maslow	51
Behavioral Systems	53
Kurt Lewin	53
The Human Resources Perspective	54
Douglas McGregor	54
Rensis Likert	56
Systems Approach	57
Peter Drucker	57
W. Edwards Deming	59

Table of Contents   ix

Questions in Review	61
End Notes	61
Suggested Additional References and Links to the Web	62

3 Operational Management of a Police Agency   63

Key Individuals, Concepts, and Issues	63
Definitions	63
Chapter Objectives	63
Introduction	64
Basic Functions of a Police Agency	65
Patrol Operations	65
Directed Patrol	67
Split Force Patrolling	67
Differential Response to Calls	67
Investigation Process	68
Decoy and Sting Operations	70
Organizational Structure and Design	70
Differentiation	71
Spans of Management	71
Structural Design	72
Structure and Community Policing	73
Organizational Development	74
Personnel	75
Job Description	75
Job Design	75
Shifts	77
Commitment	78
Questions in Review	79
Biggest Mistakes Police Leadership Makes and How to Avoid Them	79
What Makes People Satisfied with the Police?	79
What Did the Researchers Find?	80
How Can the Police Increase Public Satisfaction with the General Perception of Police Performance?	80
End Notes	80

4 Leadership Approaches   83

Key Individuals, Concepts, and Issues	83
Definitions	83
Chapter Objectives	83
Introduction	85
What Is Leadership?	86

Leadership Approaches	87
Trait Approach	87
Sir Francis Galton	87
Ralph Stogdill and Cecil Goode	88
Situational Approach	89
Contingency Approach	90
Transactional Approach	92
Leadership Styles	93
Authoritarian (Autocratic)	93
Democratic (Participative)	96
Laissez-Faire	96
Charismatic Leaders	97
Which Leadership Style and When?	99
Questions in Review	99
End Notes	100
Suggested Additional References and Links to the Web	101

5 Planning, Implementation, and Evaluation — 103

Key Individuals, Concepts, and Issues	103
Definitions	103
Chapter Objectives	104
Introduction	104
What Is Planning?	105
Traditional Planning	105
Why Plan?	107
Evolving Themes	108
The Use of Research in Planning	108
Strategic Planning	109
The Applied Strategic Planning Model	111
Planning to Plan	111
Values Scan	111
Mission Formation	113
Strategic Business Modeling	113
Performance Audit	113
Gap Analysis	114
Integrating Action Plans	114
Contingency Planning	115
Implementation	115
Types of Plans	116
Operational Plans versus Strategic Plans	116
Short-Term versus Long-Term Plans	116
Single-Use Plans	117

Table of Contents   xi

	Other Miscellaneous Plans	117
	Personnel Allocation and Staffing Plans	117
	Personnel Plans	118
	Training Plans	118
	Budget Plans	118
	Factors in Planning	119
	Planning a Diverse Workforce	119
	Envisioning and Planning	119
	Evaluation	120
	Questions in Review	121
	Biggest Mistakes Police Leadership Makes and How to Avoid Them	122
	What Does Management Expect from Subordinates?	122
	End Notes	123

6 A Business Approach to Policing?   125

	Key Individuals, Concepts, and Issues	125
	Definitions	125
	Chapter Objectives	126
	Introduction	126
	Basic Elements of Total Quality Management	127
	The Plan-Do-Check-Act Cycle	128
	Historical Development of Total Quality Management	130
	A Brief on Deming, Juran, and Crosby	130
	Benchmarking	132
	Six Sigma	134
	Applying TQM Methods in Police Organizations	135
	TQM and Community Policing	136
	Reengineering	138
	Process Simplification	139
	Technology	140
	Applying Reengineering Principles to Police Organizations	140
	COMPSTAT	141
	Questions in Review	143
	End Notes	143
	Suggested Additional References and Links to the Web	144

7 Problem Solving   147

	Key Individuals, Concepts, and Issues	147
	Definitions	147
	Chapter Objectives	148
	Introduction	148

Discretion	150
Managing Discretion	152
Controlling Discretion through Professionalism	153
The Nature of Decision Making	154
Group Decision Making	155
Analytical Tools for Decision Making	157
Community Policing	160
Supervision and Management in Community Policing	163
Questions in Review	166
End Notes	166
Suggested Additional References and Links to the Web	167

8   Technology and Management   169

Key Individuals, Concepts, and Issues	169
Definitions	169
Chapter Objectives	170
Introduction	170
Police Technology	171
Historical View of Police Technology	171
The Current State of Police Technology	173
Computer-Aided Dispatch	174
Mobile Data Terminals	177
Automatic Vehicle Locator Systems	178
Automatic Vehicle Monitoring	179
Personal Locator Transmitter	180
Remote Control Information System	180
Crime Detection and Analysis Technology	180
Crime Mapping Technology	181
The Computer and Criminal Investigation	182
Evolving Weapon and Crime Control Technology	182
The Smart Gun	183
Fleeing Vehicle Tagging System	183
Disabling Net and Launcher	183
Mobile Video Recorders	184
Management and Technology	185
Human Resource Allocations	186
Training	186
Computer Crimes	187
Future Trends	188
Management Considerations	189
Organizational Issues	190
Questions in Review	190

Biggest Mistakes Police Leadership Makes and How to Avoid Them	191
Failure to Supervise a Police Lab in Houston, Texas	191
What Happened?	192
End Results	192
End Notes	192

9 Job-Related Issues — 195

Key Individuals, Concepts, and Issues	195
Definitions	195
Chapter Objectives	196
Introduction	196
Stress and the Police Occupation	196
A Portrait of Police Work	197
Police Stress	199
Levels of Stress	202
The Patrol Level	202
The Supervisor Level	203
Middle Management Level	203
Command Level	203
Special Case Stressors	205
Minority and Female Police Officers	205
Family Issues	206
Organizational Stressors	206
Critical Life Events	208
End Result of Police Stress	208
Substance Abuse	208
Danger Signs	209
Police Suicide	210
Managing Stress	213
Physical Exercise	214
Proper Diet	214
Social Affiliations	214
Relaxation Techniques	214
Other Approaches to Stress Management	215
A Healthy Work Environment	215
Critical Incident Stress Debriefings	215
Policing a Multicultural Community	216
Demographics and Diversity	217
Challenges and Opportunities for Law Enforcement	217
Hate Crimes	217
Building and Supporting a Multicultural Workforce	218

Training Officers to Work in a Multicultural Society	219
Questions in Review	222
Biggest Mistakes Police Leadership Makes and How to Avoid Them	222
Fighting Monsters	222
End Notes	224
Suggested Further References and Links to the Web	226

10 Training and Education   229

Key Individuals, Concepts, and Issues	229
Definitions	229
Chapter Objectives	229
Introduction	230
Why Train?	231
Legal Issues	232
Training Methods	236
Behaviorist Police Training	236
New Approaches to Police Training	238
Andragogy and Police Training	238
Training Applications	239
Cultural Diversity Training	239
Conflict Resolution and Mediation	240
Criminal Procedure	240
Community Survey	241
Experience and the Classroom	242
Training Curriculum	242
Historical Underpinnings	243
Evolving Police Training Curriculum	244
Caveats for Managers	248
The Environment of Police Training	249
Police Education	251
Questions in Review	255
Biggest Mistakes Police Leadership Makes and How to Avoid Them	255
City's Insurance Rates Rise: Suit over Police Chase Is Blamed	256
Oakland Considers Video Cameras in Police Cars in Reacting to Weight of Recent Lawsuits against City Cops	256
Supreme Court Examines Police Liability for Faulty Warrant	257
End Notes	258
Suggested Additional References	260

11 Recruitment and Selection — 261

Key Individuals, Concepts, and Issues — 261
Definitions — 261
Chapter Objectives — 261
Introduction — 262
Recruitment — 264
   Impact of Higher Education on Police Hiring Practices — 265
   Women in Policing — 271
   Minority Recruitment — 277
Selection of New Hires — 279
   Preemployment Standards — 280
   Americans with Disabilities Act — 283
   Drug Testing — 284
   Written Tests — 285
   Psychological Testing — 285
   Background Investigation — 286
   Polygraph Examinations — 287
   Interviews — 287
   Assessment Centers — 289
Questions in Review — 290
End Notes — 290
Suggested Additional References and Links to the Web — 291

12 Impact of the Courts and Legislation on Police Management — 293

Key Individuals, Concepts, and Issues — 293
Definitions — 293
Chapter Objectives — 294
Introduction — 294
Employment Discrimination — 296
   Scope of the Act — 296
   Title VII Suits — 297
   Types of Violations under Title VII — 297
      Disparate Treatment — 297
      Retaliation — 298
      Constructive Discharge — 298
      Disparate Impact — 298
      Religious Discrimination — 298
   Affirmative Action Programs — 299
Drug Testing of Police Officers — 299
Sexual Harassment — 301

Labor Relations	302
The Police Union Movement	304
Impact of Unionization on Professionalism	306
Impact of Unions on Pay and Working Conditions	307
Collective Bargaining	308
Police Strikes	309
Management Rights	310
Memoranda of Understanding	310
Off-Duty Employment of Police Officers	311
Conflicts of Interests	311
Other Limitations	312
Models for Off-Duty Employment	312
Police Response to Special Populations	312
Questions in Review	313
Biggest Mistakes Police Leadership Makes and How to Avoid Them	314
Do Police Officers Accused of Sex Offenses Get Only Slaps on the Wrist?	314
End Notes	315

13 Homeland Security and Policing — 317

Key Individuals, Concepts, and Issues	317
Definitions	317
Chapter Objectives	319
Acronyms Used in Homeland Security	319
Introduction	321
Homeland Security Act of 2002	322
Components of the DHS	323
Agencies of the DHS	323
Strategic Goals of the DHS	325
The DHS and Cyber Security	325
Law Enforcement and the DHS	327
Maritime Drug Interdiction	327
Treaty Enforcement	327
Living Marine Resource	327
National Incident Management System (NIMS)	327
Incident Command System (ICS)	328
Preparedness	328
Communications and Information Management	328
Joint Information System (JIS)	328
NIMS Integration Center (NIC)	329
General Police Duties after a Terrorist Act	329

Table of Contents　　xvii

　　Guide to Personal Emergency Preparedness　　330
　　Coping after a Terrorist Event　　330
　　　Reactions to a Terrorist Act　　330
　　　Practical Coping Ideas　　332
　　Questions in Review　　333
　　Biggest Mistakes Police Leadership Makes and How
　　to Avoid Them　　333
　　End Notes　　333

14　Ethics　　335

　　Key Individuals, Concepts, and Issues　　335
　　Definitions　　335
　　Chapter Objectives　　335
　　Introduction: What Is Ethics?　　336
　　What Constitutes Ethical Behavior?　　337
　　Ethics as a Restriction on Behavior　　338
　　Kantian Ethics　　339
　　Moral Development　　341
　　Values　　342
　　Law Enforcement Values　　344
　　　Departmental Values　　344
　　　Management Tools　　345
　　　Organizational Culture　　345
　　　Personal Gratuities　　346
　　　Individual Guidance　　346
　　　Leadership Roles　　347
　　Internal Affairs Unit　　348
　　Ethics in Review　　350
　　Ethical Exercises　　352
　　Questions in Review　　352
　　Biggest Mistakes Police Leadership Makes and
　　How to Avoid Them　　352
　　End Notes　　353

Index　　355

Preface

Principles of Leadership and Management in Law Enforcement is designed to serve as a comprehensive and readable textbook for a one-semester course that deals with management and leadership within a police agency. The authors' goal is to present a text that will open the readers' eyes to the fascinating concepts involving leadership and management as they are applied to police organizations.

The material covered is organized and presented in a logical fashion, with each chapter building on the previous chapters. In each of the chapters, our objective is to encourage the reader to think about and inquire into the development of new insights on the directions of police management concepts. While each chapter builds on the previous chapters, the text will be written in a manner to reduce the necessity of memorization by readers.

The authors would like to express their appreciation to the numerous individuals who helped contribute to the development of the text, including but not limited to our editor Carolyn Spence; Jennifer Stair, project manager for Taylor & Francis; and Katherine Grier, Cenveo Publisher Services.

Comments, corrections, and opinions regarding the text are appreciated and may be submitted to *cliff.roberson@washburn.edu*.

Authors

Michael L. Birzer is director of the School of Community Affairs and professor of criminal justice at Wichita State University. His research interests include police training, police behavior, the intersection of race and the criminal justice system, and qualitative research methods (ethnography, phenomenology, and ethnomethodology). His nonacademic criminal justice experience includes more than 18 years of service with the Sedgwick County Sheriff's Department in Wichita, KS, where he reached the rank of lieutenant. He earned his doctorate from Oklahoma State University.

Gerald Bayens is chair of the Department of Criminal Justice and professor of criminal Justice at Washburn University. His research interests include agroterrorism, judicial waiver laws, and the direct supervision philosophy of incarceration. His nonacademic criminal justice experience includes eight-plus years in law enforcement. His prior employment experience includes being director of Juvenile Corrections and director of Adult and Juvenile Community Corrections, Shawnee County, KS; Special Investigator, Kansas Bureau of Investigations; Criminal Investigator, Shawnee County Sheriff's Office; and military policeman, U.S. Marine Corps. Dr. Bayens has served as a professional consultant and trainer for many years in the area of quality management and human resource development. He has a PhD in criminal justice, with interdisciplinary emphasis in political science, research methods, and juvenile justice administration from Union Institute and University; an MS in criminal justice from The University of Alabama; and a BA in criminal justice with a minor in psychology from Washburn University.

Cliff Roberson is an emeritus professor of criminal justice at Washburn University. His previous academic experience includes professor of criminology and director of the Justice Center at California State University, Fresno; professor of criminal justice and dean of arts and sciences at the University of Houston, Victoria; association vice president for academic affairs, Arkansas Tech University; and director of programs for the National College of District Attorneys, University of Houston. His nonacademic legal experience includes Trial and Legal Services Supervisor, Office of State Counsel for Offenders, Texas Board of Criminal Justice; private legal practice; judge pro-tem in the California courts; trial and defense counsel and military judge as a Marine Corps judge advocate; and director of the Military Law Branch, U.S. Marine

Corps. Dr. Roberson is admitted to practice before the U.S. Supreme Court, federal courts in California and Texas, the Supreme Court of Texas, and the Supreme Court of California. His educational background includes a PhD in human behavior from U.S. International University; an LLM in criminal law, criminology, and psychiatry from George Washington University; a JD from American University; a BA in political science from the University of Missouri; and one year of postgraduate study at the University of Virginia School of Law. In 2009, a research study conducted by a group of professors from Sam Houston State University determined that Dr. Roberson was the leading criminal justice author in the United States based on his publications and their relevance to the profession (*Southwest Journal of Criminal Justice*, volume 6, issue 1).

Introduction to the Modern Police Agency 1

Key Individuals, Concepts, and Issues

Preservation of peace	Bobbies
Shire-reeve	Justice of the peace
Community policing	Supervisors
Styles of policing	Order maintenance
Traditional management model	Human relations model
Behavioral science model	Human resources model
Systems model	Rattlewatch
Wickersham Commission	August Vollmer

Definitions

Community policing: A decentralized model of policing in which officers exercise their own initiatives and citizens become actively involved in making the neighborhoods safer.

Leadership: The function of motivating others to perform those tasks that are necessary to the accomplishments of the agency's goals and objectives.

Management: The process of organizing, leading, planning, and controlling to accomplish the objectives and goals of an organization.

Police: An organized body of government officers representing the civil power of the governmental unit engaged in maintaining public order, peace, and safety and in investigating and arresting persons suspected of or accused of crime.

Chapter Objectives

After completing this chapter you should be able to:

1. Explain what constitutes a police agency
2. Outline the development of the modern police agency
3. Differentiate between leadership and management

4. Describe the general organizational design of police agencies
5. Describe the development of police management theory
6. Explain the concepts of organizational culture

Introduction

> The police at all times should maintain a relationship with the public that gives reality to the historic tradition that the police are the public and the public are the police.
> —**Sir Robert Peel**
> *1829*

The goal of this book is to provide the student with an understanding of the concepts and principles involved in leadership and management for law enforcement agencies. To do this, we need to examine how police organizations work, how people in them behave, and how individuals and groups may be effectively managed. As will be discussed later in this chapter, management and leadership are not interchangeable terms. For our purposes, police management is defined as police organizational practices undertaken for the purpose of producing knowledge that can be used continuously to improve satisfaction and organizational performance of the employees. The organizational practices include individual, group, organizational, and environment processes.

In the twenty-first century, the quality of management and leadership in most police departments and the quality of service provided the communities are higher than they have ever been. It appears, however, that police agencies will be pressed to even higher standards. Police work is in transition within our communities. Presently, our police are more frequently involved in creating and nurturing partnerships with the communities, schools, and neighborhood organizations (i.e., community policing).[1]

General theories of management and organizations and their application to police departments are examined in the text. In presenting these concepts and theories, we have attempted to provide a balance between theoretical and applied research on management and between conceptual and practical perspectives on police management and leadership.

We can narrow the many different purposes of the modern police agency into one broad function: the preservation of the peace within its jurisdiction in a manner consistent with the rights and freedoms secured by federal and state constitutions, judicial decisions, statutes, and regulations. As noted by many researchers, the preservation of peace is a complex process and includes more than simply preventing crimes, making arrests for law violations, and providing assistance in the prosecution of individuals charged with crimes.

The police normally spend more time in "peacekeeping" and "order maintenance" than in crime fighting. In fact, the police generally spend only about 15% of its activities enforcing the law.[2]

The majority of police agencies are a division of the local city, village, or county government. Local government is closer to the public than any other level of government, and as such generally it is the most trusted level.[3] The police agency is the "civil authority" that represents the civil power of the local government.[4] The word "police" is derived from the Latin word "politia," which literally means "civil administration." Local police departments employ approximately 535,000 full-time employees, including about 425,000 sworn personnel. Racial and ethnic minorities constitute approximately 21.5% of full-time sworn officers. Sheriffs' departments have an estimated 265,000 employees, including about 175,000 sworn personnel.[5]

Management and Leadership

Managers perform four essential functions in every organization: organizing, leading, planning, and controlling. The function of organizing includes making decisions about the purpose, structure, job design, and allocation of resources. Leading is the function of motivating others to perform those tasks that are necessary to the accomplishments of the agency's goals and objectives. The planning function consists of preparing for the future by setting goals and objectives and formulating courses of action to accomplish the goals and objectives. Planning involves the conducting of research, identifying strategies and methods, developing courses of action, and formulating policies and budgets. Controlling includes the ongoing assessment of how organizational systems and services are meeting the established goals and objectives. It is not based on fixing the blame and punishment, but on improving operations consistent with established plans.

In examining the roles of leadership and management in policing, the nature of the policing in America should be considered. The nature of policing in our society is shaped by the following principles:

- The prevention of crime is a proper role for the government.
- The best government is one that governs least.
- The authority of the government should be limited.
- Any use of police power must be regarded with grave suspicion.[6]

Leadership has two different meanings in our society. First, it refers to the process that helps direct and mobilize people or their ideas. Second, it refers to individuals in formal positions where leadership is expected (e.g., the chief of police). In this text, leadership is used in the first sense, the process that helps direct and mobilize people and or their ideas.

Leadership and management are not used as interchangeable terms in this text. They are alike in that both involve deciding what needs to be done, creating networks that can accomplish an agenda, and then trying to ensure that the job gets done. While they both are complete action systems, neither is simply one aspect of the other. To differentiate between leadership and management, the distinction developed by John Kotter, a professor of organizational behavior at the Harvard School of Business is used.[7] Kotter defines the functions of management as follows:

- planning and budgeting
- organizing and staffing
- controlling and problem-solving

On the other hand, Kotter defines the process of leadership as:

- establishing direction
- aligning people, motivating, and inspiring

As you will note from the above comments, leadership and management are distinct processes. For example, the planning and budgeting processes of management tend to focus on time frames, details, instrumental rationality, and eliminating risks. Leadership processes often focus on longer time frames, the big picture, strategies that take calculated risks, and people's values. As Kotter states, controlling and problem-solving (management) usually focus on containment, control, and predictability, whereas motivating and inspiring (leadership) focus on empowerment, expansion, and creating that occasional surprise that energizes people.[8]

Leadership and management also differ in terms of their primary function. Leadership can produce useful change. Management can create orderly results that keep something working efficiently. This does not mean that management is never associated with change, nor does it mean that leadership is never associated with order. As noted by Kotter: "Leadership by itself never keeps an operation on time and on budget year after year. And management by itself never creates significant change."[9]

The differences in function and form between leadership and management can create conflict. Strong leadership can disrupt an orderly planning system and undermine management hierarchy. Strong management may discourage risk taking and enthusiasm needed for leadership. An organization needs both strong leadership and management. If either is weak or nonexistent, the organization is like a rudderless ship. Both need to be strong. Strong management and weak leadership may create a bureaucratic and stifling environment, producing order for order's sake. Strong leadership and weak management can create an organization that is cult-like and producing change for the sake of change.

Evolution of the Modern Police Department

> America is a nation of small, decentralized police forces.
> *President's Commission on Law Enforcement and Administration of Justice, 1967*

Early Policing

Policing started as a private matter. Individuals were responsible for protecting themselves and maintaining an orderly community.[10] Organized police departments did not appear until the fourteenth century in France.

One of the earliest reported efforts in policing was in the sixth century BCE when unpaid magistrates in Athens were given the authority to adjudicate cases brought before them by citizens. It was the responsibility of the citizens to arrest the wrongdoer, bring him or her before the magistrate, and then to punish the offender. Citizens frequently banned together in towns and formed watches that operated during the hours of darkness. In addition, the citizen groups patrolled the town borders to protect the town against invaders.

About the fifth century BCE, *questers* (trackers of murders) were established as one of the earliest known specialized investigative units. Later, Emperor Augustus, who ruled the Roman Empire at the start of the Christian era, established the *praetorian guard*, considered by some as the first police force. The praetorian guard's duty was to protect the emperor and the palace. Augustus also established the *vigiles*, who patrolled Rome's streets both day and night. The vigiles were known for their brutality. They are considered by many as the first civil police force designed to protect citizens.

During the first century CE, public officials called *licors* were used in Rome to serve as the magistrates' bodyguards. They were also responsible for bringing prisoners before the magistrate and for carrying out the punishments imposed by the magistrates.

Early English Law Enforcement

Most European countries maintained professional police forces as early as the seventeenth century. England, however, fearing the oppression these forces had brought about in many of the continental countries and the cost involved in developing a force specifically for peacekeeping duties, did not begin to create professional police organizations until the nineteenth century.[11] The English believed that private citizens could do the job more cheaply, if given a few shillings in reward for arrests.

The use of private citizens, which was started by Alfred the Great (870–901), is the forerunner of American police agencies.[12] This system, which became know as the "mutual pledge" system, encouraged mutual responsibility among local citizens' organizations that were pledged to maintain law and order. Each man was responsible for his own actions and those of his neighbors. Each citizen had a duty to raise the "hue and cry" when a crime was committed, to collect his neighbors, and to pursue the offender. If the group failed to apprehend the criminal, all were subject to be fined by the king.

The first real police officer in England was the constable. The crown established groups of ten families. Each group was known as a "tithing." Later, ten tithings were grouped into "hundreds," and the constable was appointed to take charge of the weapons and equipment of the hundred. Next, the hundreds were grouped to form a "shire." A shire consisted of a geographical area equivalent to a county. A "shire-reeve" was appointed by the crown to supervise the shire. The shire-reeve was responsible to the local nobleman in ensuring that the citizens enforced the law. Later the shire-reeve's responsibilities changed from being a supervisory person to taking part in the pursuit and apprehension of criminals. The shire-reeve traveled on horseback throughout the shire, keeping the peace, holding court, and investigating crimes. The shire-reeve was the forerunner to the modern sheriff.

The first official police units were created in the large cities of England during the reign of Edward I (1272–1307). The units were generally known as "watch and ward" forces and were responsible for protecting the cities against fires, guarding the gates, and arresting criminals who committed crimes during the hours of darkness. During this time, the constable was the principle law enforcement officer in English towns.

To supplement the shire-reeve, in 1326, Edward II created the office of "justice of the peace." The primary responsibility of the justices, who were appointed by the crown, was to assist the shire-reeve in policing the county. Later they took on a judicial function by keeping peace in their separate jurisdictions.

The constable became an assistant to the justice of the peace and was responsible for supervising the night watchmen, inquiring into crimes, serving summons, executing warrants, and taking custody of prisoners. As law enforcement increasingly became the responsibility of the crown, the justice of peace, who was appointed by the king, assumed a greater degree of control over the locally appointed constable. By the end of the fourteenth century, the constable no longer was an independent official of the mutual pledge system and was now obligated to serve the justice of peace.[13] The justice of the peace remained the superior and the constable the inferior until the middle of the nineteenth century. It was also during this time that the formal separation between judge and police officer developed.

The use of the mutual pledge system declined. Community support languished. Fighting crime, which was everyone's business, became nobody's duty. The common practice of citizens hiring others to do the police work and allowing citizens to evade personal police service developed. Even constables used deputies or substitutes to take care of their duties. Accordingly, the earliest paid police officers were the individuals hired by citizens and constables to do their work. These officers were usually ill-paid and ignorant individuals who did not rank very high in community social standings. With the decline of the pledge system and low state of paid police officers, innovations in policing begin emerging in the English towns and cities in the seventeenth and eighteenth centuries.

Development of Established English Police Forces

Prior to the Industrial Revolution, England was essentially a rural nation with little opposition to the dominance of the justice of peace as the primary law enforcement machinery. By the end of the eighteenth century, however, England had become an industrial nation. Families left the farm and moved to the factory towns in search of work. As the towns and cities grew, patterns of social life changed, and an unprecedented social order developed. Accordingly, law enforcement became more complex.

Action was taken by both citizens and the English government to address the need for better law enforcement. The Bow Street Horse and Foot Patrol was formed by a civic association to patrol the streets and highways leading into and out of London. The government established public offices with law enforcement duties. The offices were later known as police offices. The police offices were generally staffed with three justices of the peace. Each justice of the peace was authorized to employ up to six paid constables. The offices helped to centralize law enforcement operations within cities and towns and other small geographical areas.

By 1800, there were nine police offices within the metropolitan area of London. There was little effort, however, to coordinate their independent law enforcement activities. In many cases, offices would refuse to communicate to other offices for fear that another office would take credit for detecting and apprehending an offender. Apparently because of their lack of coordination, the police offices were seemingly powerless to combat crime. The major problems included highwaymen on the roads leading into and out of London, daily bank robberies, and thieves lurking throughout the city. One major step taken during the early 1800s to reduce crime was the introduction of gaslights in the streets of London.

As noted by the President's Commission on Law Enforcement and Administration: "Many of the experiments in law enforcement before

1820 failed because no scheme could reconcile the freedom of action of individuals with the security of person and property."[14] In 1822, Sir Robert Peel contended that although better policing could not eliminate crime, the poor quality of policing contributed to social disorder and unrest. In 1829, Peel, while serving as the Home Secretary, introduced and guided through the English Parliament legislation that led to the establishment of the first organized metropolitan police force for London. The legislation, known as an "Act for Improving the Police in and near the Metropolis," provided for a police force of one thousand structured similar to a military unit. They were to be commanded by two magistrates, later known as commissioners, who had administrative but not judicial authority. The ultimate responsibility for equipping, paying, maintaining, and, to a certain degree, supervising the police was vested in the office of the Home Secretary. The Home Secretary was then accountable to the Parliament. The police later became known as "bobbies" because they were considered as Sir Robert's police. The bobbies were required to wear distinctive uniforms so that citizens could easily identify them and report any misconduct by the bobbies to proper authorities. The bobbies made their first appearance on the streets of London on Tuesday, September 29, 1829.[15]

Like many present-day police agencies, the bobbies discovered that finding competent individuals was an immediate problem. It was difficult to recruit suitable persons because of low pay. The radicals in Parliament were afraid of tyranny and therefore made it difficult to appropriate sufficient government funds to maintain the police force. The English Lords were willing to accept the protection of the police force but objected because the commissioners refused to use the traditional rules of patronage in making appointments to the force.

SIR ROBERT PEEL (1788-1850)

Robert Peel was born in Lancashire, England, the son of a middle-class manufacturer. His father, also named Robert, was a member of the British Parliament and received a baronetcy from the crown. This honor brought the title "Sir" to the family.

Robert Peel graduated from Oxford University in 1808 with a bachelor of arts degree. He was elected to the House of Commons in 1809. He was named Home Secretary in 1822. He succeeded in having the Metropolitan Police Act enacted in 1829. The act created the first modern police force in England. When his father died in 1830, Peel inherited his baronetcy. Peel later served twice as Prime Minister. Peel died in 1850 as the result of a riding accident.

Despite the problems, the London Metropolitan Police was a vast improvement over prior efforts of law enforcement. Within five years, other English towns and cities were asking Parliament for help. In 1839, Parliament empowered justices of the peace to establish police forces in the counties. In 1856, Parliament required all boroughs and counties to have a police force. With the establishment of regular police forces in the counties, justices of the peace relinquished their law enforcement duties. With the relinquishment of supervision by the justices and the lack of direction from Parliament regarding the investigative responsibilities of the police, the police officers were, by default, given broad discretion in performing their duties.[16]

The bobbies' strategy for crime prevention included the visible presence of uniformed officers throughout the city. While this was not a new strategy, since constables and watchmen had patrolled the streets for many years, the visible presence was more regulated and calculated to make more effective use of the show of force. Peel had devised a system of assigning officers to specific "beats." Uniforms also increased their visibility. To coordinate the patrols, a military command structure was adapted with ranks and an authoritarian chain of command. The quasi-military command structure continues to dominate present-day police administration.

Certain principles of policing were developed during this period that, for the most part, are still used in many police departments in the United States:

- The police are organized under military lines.
- The police must be under government control.
- The presence or absence of crime is a measure of police efficiency.
- The keeping of crime records by the police is necessary to determine the best distribution of police strength.
- Every police officer should be given an identifying number.
- Good appearance in a police officer helps command respect.
- Officers should first be hired on a probationary basis before becoming permanent officers.[17]

Policing in the American Colonies

When the colonists settled in America, they brought the English law enforcement structure with them. America was mostly rural and was policed by the offices of constable and sheriff. The constables under the mutual pledge system were responsible for law enforcement in the towns, and sheriffs were responsible for policing in the counties outside of the towns. Originally, the crown-appointed governors appointed the constables and sheriffs. After the revolution, these officers were elected by popular vote. In the larger cities, the English constabulary night watchman system was adopted. By 1636, Boston had a night watchman and a military guard. Soon both New York and

Philadelphia established similar night watch systems. The New York night watchmen system was referred to as the "Rattlewatch," because the men sounded rattlers during their rounds to announce their watchful presence.

Probably the first modern police forces in the United States were the slave patrols established in the South. The slave patrol was a distinctly American form of law enforcement intended to guard against slave revolts and to capture runaway slaves. The Charleston, South Carolina, slave patrol had over one hundred officers and at the time was probably the largest police force in America.[18]

Policing in Urban America

In the nineteenth century, the Industrial Revolution reached the colonies. American cities and towns grew in size, and constables were unable to handle the increasing social disorder caused by the migration to the urban areas. One historian described the lawlessness in America in the mid-1800s with the following words:

> New York City was alleged to be the most crime-ridden city in the world, with Philadelphia, Baltimore and Cincinnati not far behind....Gangs of youthful rowdies in the larger cities...threatened to destroy the American reputation for respect for law.... Before their boisterous demonstrations the crude police forces of the day were often helpless.[19]

Philadelphia was one of the first American cities to develop an organized metropolitan police force. In 1833, a wealthy philanthropist died and left in his estate funds to establish a competent police force in the city. Using these funds, the city government established a twenty-four-man police force for day work and a one hundred twenty-man night watchmen force. The force was disbanded less than two years later. Boston in 1838 created a day police force to supplement its nightwatch. Other cities soon established similar forces. The establishment of the police forces was not a break with the past. They were more like a consolidation and modification of existing institutions: day and night watches, constables, and sheriffs.[20]

In 1844, New York State passed legislation that established a unified day and night police force for New York City and abolished its nightwatch. In 1854, Boston consolidated its nightwatch with the day police. Other cities, using the New York model, developed their own unified police forces during the 1850s and 1860s. By 1870, all of the nation's largest cities had full-time, unified police forces. By the early 1900s, almost all cities had established unified forces. The police forces were generally under the control of a chief or commissioner who was appointed by the mayor, often with the consent of the city council. The mission of the early police departments was merely to "keep the city superficially clean and to keep everything quiet that was likely to arouse public ire."[21]

The salaries of the new police officers were among the lowest in local government service. The low salary precluded attracting sufficient qualified candidates. To meet staffing requirements, personnel standards were compromised. Many unqualified personnel were appointed as police officers. Illiteracy, poor health, chronic drunkenness, and criminal records were not barriers to police employment.

The chief requirement for appointment appeared to be the proper political connection. Promotions within the police forces were often based on politics rather than ability. For example, Chicago police officers in the 1850s were expected to kick back a regular portion of their salary to the local controlling political party. After the 1880 elections in Cincinnati, when a new political party gained control of city administration, 219 of the 295 police officers were summarily fired. Six years later, when a different political party assumed power, 238 of 289 patrolmen and 8 of the 16 lieutenants were fired.[22] Accordingly, the police officers were often objects of disrespect.

In the late 1800s, to eliminate politics from the police forces, many cities created police administrative boards that replaced the control once exercised by the mayors or city councils. The boards were given the responsibility of appointing police administrators and managing police affairs. Generally these boards were unsuccessful in removing politics from police forces. The boards were comprised of judges, lawyers, and local businessmen who lacked expertise in dealing with police problems. Another reason that the police boards were generally unsuccessful was the fact that they were not directly responsible to the local taxpayers that they served.

In some states, the state legislators assumed control over the police forces by requiring that police administrators be appointed by the state. The concept of state control was not uniformly applied and was directed mainly at the larger cities by state legislatures that were dominated by rural legislators. While the state controlled the police forces, they continued to be financed by local taxpayers. When the state-appointed administrator was not in harmony with the views of the majority of the city's citizens, friction more often than not developed. It was not until the 1900s that many cities regained control of their police forces.[23]

During the last part of the 1800s, police forces grew in size and expanded their functions. Sincere attempts of reform included the concept of merit employment, civil service, and, by 1900, the advent of police training schools on a modest basis. In 1895, Theodore Roosevelt, while a member of the New York City Board of Police Commissioners, attempted to raise recruitment standards and discipline corrupt officers. His efforts failed when the corrupt Tammany Hall political machine was returned to power in New York City in 1897.

State Police

The "Texas Rangers" were organized in 1835 to supplement the military forces of the new Texas government. When Texas was admitted into the United States in 1845, the rangers were reorganized as a state police, making them the first state police in America. They were disbanded during the post-Civil War reconstruction in 1874 and reorganized after the reconstruction period was over. In the early 1900s, the Texas Rangers and their counterparts, the Arizona Rangers (established in 1901) and the New Mexico Mounted Patrol (established in 1905), were primarily responsible for combating cattle rustlers and thieves along the Rio Grande.

The first modern day state police organization was formed in 1905 by the State of Pennsylvania. Its original focus was to be on the public dispute between labor and management. Later, the inadequacy of the sheriff-constable system in Pennsylvania and the inability or unwillingness of local police forces to pursue lawbreakers beyond their jurisdictional limits convinced the Pennsylvania legislature of the need for a statewide police force. Presently all states except Hawaii have a state police. In some states, the state police have only limited authority and are restricted to the functions of enforcing traffic and protecting the public on state and federal highways. In other states, the state police have been given general policing authority in criminal matters throughout the state.

Police Reform Era

The police reform era started about 1900 and lasted until the 1960s. As noted earlier, Theodore Roosevelt attempted to reform the New York Police Department in the 1890s. Although he raised police standards and was responsible for the discipline of corrupt and brutal police officers, his efforts failed when the Tammany Hall political machine was returned to power in 1897. The reform era resulted in increased military ethos of police and the first specialized police units such as traffic, juvenile, and vice.

Progressive Era

From 1900 to 1915, there were several attempts to reform police departments by middle-class, civic-minded reformers. Generally the attempts failed. During this period, police salaries continued to lag behind other civil-service employees. In 1919, the Boston Social Club, a fraternal association of police officers, voted to become a union and to affiliate with the American Federation of Labor (AFL). In September of that year, 70% of the Boston police officers went on strike. Governor Calvin Coolidge mobilized the state police to handle the rioting and looting that had broken out. The striking officers were fired and replaced by new recruits. The public turned against the striking officers. Coolidge, by firing them, became a hero, which may have helped him later get elected president.

Professionalism

In 1883, the federal civil service was founded by the Pendleton Act. Under civil service, covered federal employees were tested, appointed, and promoted based on merit rather than for political reasons. As local governments adopted their own civil-service systems, political influence in law enforcement agencies declined. While many individuals were pioneers in promoting professionalism of the police, two individuals stand out: August Vollmer and O. W. Wilson.

By the 1920s, under the leadership of the newly founded National Police Chiefs Union, police officers were generally under civil service control, and entry into the vocation was more restricted. The movement toward the professionalism of the police began under the leadership of August Vollmer. He contended that the first obligation of police was crime control and public protection. He consulted with other police agencies and wrote extensively about the need for and requirements of a professional police department. Vollmer urged the development of a national records bureau, which eventually became the Federal Bureau of Investigation.

O. W. Wilson, a former student and disciple of Vollmer, pioneered the use of advanced training for police. He also conducted the first systematic study of the effectiveness of one-officer squad cars. He developed workload formulas for police officers based on reported crimes and calls for service. This workload formula remained as the basic formula for police departments for years. Wilson developed management and administrative techniques for policing. He was the author of the first two textbooks on police management.

Other pioneers in the movement toward professionalism included Raymond Blaine Fosdick and Bruce Smith. Neither were police officers. Fosdick is credited with conducting the first scholarly research on policing when in 1915, he published *European Police System*, which examined the structures and practices of European police departments. Bruce Smith is noted for his efforts in surveying and researching police departments in eighteen states and the publication of his book on policing, *Police Systems in the United States*.

Wickersham Commission

The Volstead Act (National Prohibition) became law in 1920. Local police departments were unable to stop the alcohol operations of organized crime. Many law enforcement officers became corrupt and aided organized crime in its alcohol operations. As the result of police corruption, between 1919 and 1931, twenty-four states formed crime commissions to study crime and the ability of the police to deal with it.

President Herbert Hoover created the National Commission on Law Observance and Enforcement in 1929. The commission became known as the Wickersham Commission after its chair, Judge George W. Wickersham. The commission came into being because of the concern that organized criminal gangs and mobs were increasingly using violence to victimize and control major enterprises in the cities. The commission, however, chose to focus its broad mandate on the observance of law as well as its enforcement. Its report concluded that the Volstead Act was one of the roots of what they defined as a national problem and that it should be repealed.[24]

The Wickersham Commission was the first national commission on crime. It set a precedent by nationalizing the problem of crime in American society and the means of coping with crime. The Wickersham Report was issued in 1931. Two volumes of the report, Volumes 2 and 14, were concerned primarily with the police. In Volume 2, *Lawlessness in Law Enforcement*, the police were described as inept, inefficient, racist, and brutal. According to the commission, the police routinely practiced the use of pain, both physical and mental, to extract confessions or statements from suspects.

In Volume 14, *The Police*, methods were presented that the police could use to create a professional police force. This volume, primarily written by August Vollmer, stressed the need to increase pay and benefits for police officers and increase selectivity in the recruitment of officers. While the report upset citizens, police reform became less important as the nation experienced the economic problems of the Depression.

The Depression of the 1930s made employment as a police officer attractive to many individuals who in normal economic times would not have considered careers in policing. The job security aspects of policing encouraged better educated, middle-class individuals to apply for the police positions.

AUGUST VOLLMER (1876–1955)

August Vollmer was born in New Orleans. He was orphaned in childhood. After service in the Spanish-American War, he was elected in 1905 as town marshal in Berkeley, California. When the Berkeley police department was created in 1909, he was appointed as the first chief of police. He served as chief of police until 1932. Vollmer committed suicide in 1955.

Vollmer was a leader in the movement to professionalize police. He advocated university training for police officers, and the use of intelligence, psychiatric, and neurological screening tests for police officer applicants. He developed a unique approach in organizing the Berkeley Police Department. The uniformed field officer was established as a "criminologist" responsible for the performance of all police functions on the beat. Accordingly, each officer was required to be familiar with the resources on the beat and other resources available to deal with criminal and delinquency problems. The officer was responsible for resolving those problems without referral to other agencies unless absolutely necessary.[25]

Vollmer initiated scientific crime-detection and crime-solving techniques. He was a leader in the development of the School of Criminology at the University of California, Berkeley, and the use of the automobile in police patrol. He is considered by many as the father of modern American policing.

Policing in the 1950s and Early 1960s

In 1950, the U.S. Senate appointed a crime committee, chaired by Senator Estes Kefauver. The Kefauver Committee held the first nationally televised public hearings on crime. The hearing publicized organized crime and the fact that many law enforcement officers were controlled by organized crime. As a result of the hearings and the public's shock regarding police corruption, new attempts at police reform began. David R. Johnson described the 1950s as follows:

> The 1950s marked a turning point in the history of [police] professionalism. Following the major scandals, reformers came to power across the nation. Politicians had real choices between the traditional and new models of policing because a number of professional police reformers were available for the first time. With an enraged middle class threatening their livelihoods, the politicians opted for reform.[26]

The 1960s was a period of dramatic social change and involved one of the most unpopular wars in U.S. history. The struggle for racial equality and the anti-war protests were accompanied by marches, demonstrations, and riots. The police were caught in the middle between those who were fighting for civil rights and local government officials who were trying to maintain the status quo.

War on Crime Era

> The time will come when we will have to determine causal relations and consider the possibility that traditional methods of law enforcement produce more rather than less crime, particularly of a collateral character.
>
> *The Challenge of Crime in a Free Society*

James Q. Wilson describes the decade of the 1960s as follows: "It all began about 1963, that was the year, to over dramatize a bit, that a decade began to fall apart."[27] The civil unrest, the perceived inability of the police to handle the unrest, and the rising crime rates led to the creation of the President's Commission on Law Enforcement and Administration of Justice in 1965. The mandate of the commission was to study the nation's response to crime with a focus on the crime control effect of the administration of criminal justice. The commission differed from earlier crime commissions in that it focused on crime control issues rather than corruption and law observance, and it was expected to recommend new criminal justice initiatives to address the crime problem.[28] Unlike earlier commissions, this commission was staffed primarily by social scientists rather than lawyers.

The commission published the principal report in a volume titled *The Challenge of Crime in a Free Society* in 1967. This volume included a chapter on the police, which contained a series of recommendations regarding police practices. They also published numerous task force reports, including the *Task Force Report: The Police*. Police issues were also contained in two additional volumes: *Task Force Report: Science and Technology* and *Studies in Crime and Law Enforcement in Major American Cities*.

According to Samuel Walker, the most radical aspect of the commission's work was in undermining the traditional assumptions about policing and laying the foundation for a new approach to policing, the community policing approach. Walker also stated:

> The President's Crime Commission marks a critical period of transition between an old view of the police and a new one just being born. While the Commission embodied a traditional set of reform assumptions, it also set in motion new thinking that eventually undermined the traditional view. The full significance of the tensions between the old and new are evident only in retrospect.[29]

One of the major goals recommended by the commission was similar to one that had been advocated since the progressive era (i.e., achieving professional status for police). Recommendations of the commission included:

- The diversification of police forces by recruiting racial minorities and more women and assigning women to routine patrol
- Strengthening staff control
- Requiring supervisors to have higher levels of education
- Achieving social reforms through the intervention of government programs
- Consolidation and coordination of small police departments

- State-mandated personnel standards and required training
- Improving procedures for handling citizen complaints
- Adoption of special community relations programs

Many of the changes in policing since 1967 are attributed to the commission's report. The changes include higher recruitment standards, higher general level of education of police officers, and a more diverse police force. Many of the traditional barriers to women have been eliminated, and women are now assigned to routine patrol duty. The employment of minority police officers has increased significantly. As Walker noted, the commission marked the culmination of a half century of reform and the birth of a very different view of policing and police reform.[30]

Community Policing

> Community policing is not just a tactic that can be applied to solve a particular problem, one that can be abandoned once the goal is achieved.[31]

Jeremy Travis, the former director of the National Institute of Justice contends that there are three essential lessons that can be learned from the development of community policing:

- We should view the community as a full partner.
- We should focus on solving the problems that matter to the community.
- We should pay attention to little things.

Travis describes community policing as follows:

> Community policing is based on the notion that government and community should work closely together, that the police and the community are co-producers of safety.... In an operational sense, community policing engages the police and community in the art of "problem-solving," where the unit of work is a particular problem of crime and disorder, as identified by the police community partnership.... Within the policing organization itself, emphasis is placed on flexibility and innovation. Discretion is prized; risk-taking is encouraged; accountability is pushed downward within the chain of command.[32]

Most police and sheriff's departments have adopted community policing or are in the process of adopting some forms of it. The problem in this regard is that not everybody has the same definition of what constitutes community policing. In some departments, community policing consists of programs with specialists who work in one or more areas of the community. In others, it is a department-wide philosophy that influences all employees in terms of how they view their role in relation to the community. For purposes of this text, community policing is defined as an approach to policing that is based on meaningful interaction with community members in an attempt to define and solve problems related to crime, fear of crime, and social disorder. Community policing is based on the notion that government and community should work closely together and that the police and the community are co-producers of safety. As Travis noted, the police have learned three essential lessons from the development of community policing:[33] (1) view the community as a full partner, (2) focus on solving the problems that matter to the community, and (3) pay attention to little things. This definition of community policy requires that police officers and supervisors learn new skills and change the manner in which they assess problems, possible solutions, and behave.

To take the community as a full partner, the police must listen to the people they serve, ask them what they feel is important, value their priorities, and explore their capacities to provide solutions. To focus on solving specific problems that are important to the community represents a fundamental and powerful shift. Instead of looking at a crack house and seeing criminals who can be arrested, the police should be closing the place down. By not paying attention to little things, we signal our indifference or tacit acceptance. Our acceptance of low levels of disorder creates a hospitable environment for more egregious violations of social norms. As noted by George Kelling, a broken window left unattended invites other windows to be broken.

George Kelling lists twelve principles that should be considered in developing and implementing police guidelines for community policing.[34] While Kelling was examining the role of discretion in community policing, his principles provide an insight to the leadership and management aspects of community policing. Those principles are:

- Recognize the complexity of police work
- Acknowledge police use of discretion
- Recognize and confirm how police work is conducted
- Advance values
- Put police knowledge forward
- Undergo development by practicing police officers and citizens
- Understand clear and broad public promulgation
- Prescribe what officers may not do
- Emphasize police adherence to the process
- Establish accountability
- Receive recognition as an ongoing process

> **MISSION STATEMENT OF THE MADISON, WISCONSIN, POLICE DEPARTMENT**
>
> We believe in the dignity and worth of all people.
> We are committed to:
>
> - Providing high-quality, community-oriented police services with sensitivity
> - Protecting constitutional rights
> - Problem-solving
> - Teamwork
> - Openness
> - Planning for the future
> - Providing leadership to the police profession
>
> We are proud of the diversity of our workforce, which permits us to grow and which respects each of us as individuals, and we strive for a healthful workplace.[35]

How Does Community Policing Affect the Role of the Police Supervisor?

The traditional role of the police supervisor was concerned with control. Control was generally achieved through manipulating limited sanctions and offering even more limited incentives. Under community policing, however, the supervisor is expected to place more emphasis on supporting subordinates. Supervisors should help officers develop sound judgment, provide feedback on their performance, and help them work on problems in the neighborhoods they serve. No longer are disseminating information on departmental directives and monitoring officers' completion of reports primary functions of supervisors. Under community policing, supervisors may not be individually accountable for officers' performance.[36]

> **TRADITIONAL VERSUS COMMUNITY POLICING[37]**
>
> **Question:** Who are the police?
> **Traditional View:** A governmental agency that is principally responsible for law enforcement.
> **Community Policing:** The police are the public, and the public are the police. Police are paid to give full-time attention to the duties of the citizens.

Question: What should be the focus of policing?
Traditional View: The focus is on solving crime.
Community Policing: The focus is on a broader, problem-solving approach.

Question: How is police efficiency measured?
Traditional View: By detention and arrest rates.
Community Policing: By the absence of crime and disorder.

Question: What are the highest priorities for the police?
Traditional View: Crimes that are high value (e.g., bank robberies) and those involving violence.
Community Policing: The problems that disturb the community the most.

Question: What, specifically, do police deal with?
Traditional View: Incidents.
Community Policing: Citizens' problems and concerns.

Question: What determines police effectiveness?
Traditional View: Response time.
Community Policing: Public cooperation.

Question: How do the police view service calls?
Traditional View: Deal with them if there is no "real" police work to do.
Community Policing: They are a vital function of police work and a great opportunity.

Question: What is police professionalism?
Traditional View: Swift, effective response to serious crime.
Community Policing: Keeping close to the community.

Question: What kind of intelligence is the most important?
Traditional View: Crime intelligence regarding particular crimes or series of crimes.
Community Policing: Criminal intelligence about activities of individuals or groups.

Question: What is the essential nature of police accountability?
Traditional View: Highly centralized; governed by rules, regulations, and policy directives; and accountable to the law.
Community Policing: Emphasis on local accountability to community needs.

> **Question:** What is the role of headquarters?
> **Traditional View:** To provide the necessary rules and policy directives.
> **Community Policing:** To preach organizational values.
>
> **Question:** How do police regard prosecutions?
> **Traditional View:** As an important goal.
> **Community Policing:** As one of many tools.

Policing Styles

The history of American police administration is usually divided into three eras. Each era has its own particular administrative approach to policing. The first era was the political era, which began in the 1840s and lasted until the 1930s. The political era was characterized by the close ties between police and public officials. During this period, the police tended to serve the interests of the political group in power. The reform era is considered as beginning in the 1930s and lasting until the 1970s. This era was characterized by the police focusing on the solving of traditional crimes such as murder, rape, and burglary and on the arrest of the offenders. The final era, the community problem-solving era, started in the 1970s and continues to the present. This era takes a problem-solving approach to police work and stresses the need for a partnership between the police and the community.

Each historical period of police administration influenced and was influenced by policing styles. James Q. Wilson coined the concept of "police styles." He states that the style of policing describes how a particular police agency sees its mission and goals, and the methods and techniques used to accomplish its purpose. Wilson sees three styles of policing: watchman, legalistic, and service. According to him, nearly all police departments are now operating under one of the styles or a combination of two or more styles.[38] The watchman style is closely associated with the political era, the legalistic with the reform era, and the service era with the present era.

Watchman Style

The organizational form of the watchman style is flat and narrow: flat in that there is little opportunity for advancement and narrow because of limited differentiation in the types of work that each officer does. According to Wilson, this style exists in cities with heavy political patronage and little response to community needs. He also contends that this style tends to experience more police corruption than other styles. Promotion is a function of "who you know," and in-service training is almost nonexistent. The pay is generally low, and rewards for good service are limited. According to Wilson, there are few places in which the officer can be transferred in the department and few incentives to seek transfer there. Most of the officers will spend their careers on the patrol duties unless promoted to the rank of detective.

Under the watchman style of policing, the departments are concerned primarily with "order maintenance." Because not much is expected of the officers, they have a wide range of discretion and tend to handle matters informally rather than invoking the system officially. The common practice is to keep drunks off the streets and maintain a general appearance of order. In corrupt departments, discretion is often used as a weapon for shakedowns and bribes.

Legalistic Style

In departments using the legalistic style, a high degree of control is maintained over individual officers. The high degree of control is accomplished by handling every call as a law enforcement matter. Accordingly, for every response, the officer must make a report. For example, if an officer makes a traffic stop, the officer first calls in and reports the car, its license plate number, and the reason for the stop. If the officer does not issue a citation, the officer must explain the reasons for not doing so. In lieu of relying on the officer's assessment of the situation and judgment, there are numerous regulations and controls (often referred to as standards) to guide the officer. In this style of organization, the individual officer has little discretion. This style of policing is concerned with the strict enforcement of the law and often takes a "hands-off" approach to otherwise disruptive or problematic forms of behavior that are not violations of criminal law.

Service Style

The service style, according to Wilson, is an attempt to combine the efficiency of the legalistic style and the broad informal discretion of the watchman style. Under the service style, the police take seriously all requests for assistance or service but are less likely to respond by making an arrest or issuing a citation. The service-style organization is decentralized in order to maintain a sense of local community-oriented police. Community relations are a high priority with service-oriented police departments.

The service-style orientation does not measure an individual officer's performance on the number of arrests or citations issued, but on how appropriately the officer handles various situations. The individual officer has considerable personal discretion in responding to assistance or service requests. Service-oriented agencies are more likely to take advantage of community resources than the other types of police agencies. This style is marked by a concern with helping rather than strict enforcement of the law.

Development of Police Management Theory

In this section, a brief overview of the historical development of police management theory is presented. Management theory is discussed in depth in later chapters. There are five major management models that have been or are being used in policing: traditional management, human relations, behavioral science, human resources, and systems approaches to management. This chapter contains a brief introduction to each of the models. They are examined in depth in later chapters.

Traditional Management Model

The traditional management model is based on certain principles of management that promote efficiency. It developed from three separate management theories: scientific, bureaucratic, and administrative.

Scientific Management

Frederick W. Taylor was the central figure in the development of scientific management. Scientific management was one of the first models of organizational and management behavior developed.[39] The scientific management model emphasizes efficiency. For that reason, it is often referred to as the machine model. According to this model, work may be divided into subunits or specializations that may be performed more efficiently by individuals; that work could be scientifically studied to determine the "one best way" of performing the subunit or specialization. Scientific management sought to discover the best method of performing a specific task. There are four basic principles of this approach:

- Division of labor and specialization
- Unity of command and centralization of decision making
- One-way authority
- Narrow span of control

Bureaucratic Management

German sociologist Max Weber is credited with being the first person to outline the principles of organization. Weber studied the army and the church in an attempt to understand why those organizations were effective. As a result of his study, he developed six principles of organization that became the foundation of the traditional management model:

- Principle of hierarchy: each lower officer is under the control and supervision of a higher one.
- Division of labor: individuals are assigned a limited number of job tasks and responsibilities.
- Official policies: official policies should be promulgated to guide the activities of the organization.
- Written documentation: acts, decisions, and rules should be recorded in writing.
- Authority: authority of a person is associated with his position.
- Merit selection and training: candidates are appointed on the basis of their qualifications, and training is part of the selection process.[40]

The traditional management model for police agencies is based on the concept of centralized administration designed along the military organizational model. It is a more rigid model when compared to the more flexible approaches presently used. Officers hold military rank, and there is a definite chain of command. This model stresses strong leadership. The centralized administration refers to administration within local agencies. One of the principle components of the traditional model is the principle of local control.

Administrative Management

Administrative management emphasizes the broad administrative principles developed under scientific management and applied to higher management levels within the organization. Henri Fayol was one of the leaders of this movement. He defined fourteen principles of efficient management that were later applied to the coal and iron industry. Fayol used principles rather than "laws" to avoid any belief that the principles were inflexible.[41]

Leadership

Two of the leaders using the traditional management model in policing were O. W. Wilson and William H. Parker.[42] Wilson was a police officer under August Vollmer. Later he served as chief of police in the cities of Fullerton, California; Wichita, Kansas; and Chicago, Illinois. He also was a professor of criminology and dean at the University of California, Berkeley. His book on police administration became one of the most influential management textbooks used by police managers in the United States. His text was organized around three basic processes: planning, activating, and controlling.[43] Wilson's approach to police management included encouraging these main principles: (1) a professional police department separated from politics, (2) rigorous personnel selection and training process for police officers, and (3) maximum use of the latest technological innovations available to law enforcement.[44]

William H. Parker started with the Los Angeles Police Department (LAPD) as an officer in 1927. By 1939, he was a captain in the department.

Introduction to the Modern Police Agency 25

From 1950 to 1968, he was the chief. Under his leadership, the LAPD became a model of efficiency. Parker required recruits to have IQs of 110 or above and to undergo a one-year closely supervised apprenticeship and a thorough psychiatric examination. During Parker's period as chief, the LAPD was considered as the leader in standards of excellence for recruitment and training, sophisticated planning, and a solid image of professional law enforcement.

Human Relations Model

The human relations movement stemmed from the studies of Elton Mayo and Fritz Roethlisberger at Western Electric's Hawthorne plant near Chicago during the 1920s and 1930s. Where the scientific management theory focuses on efficiency, the human relations model focuses on the humanistic approach and in particular group behavior and relations among group members and management.[45] The human relations approach considers the police managers as team leaders who create a cooperative effort among officers through the use of management teams.

Behavioral Science Model

The behavioral science model is based on the works of Abraham Maslow and Douglas McGregor. Maslow developed his hierarchy of human needs in the early 1940s. According to his theory, the needs that motivate people fall into a hierarchy, with lower-level needs (physical and safety needs) at the bottom of the hierarchy and higher-level needs (esteem and self-actualization) at the top.[46] Douglas McGregor developed the concept of Theory X and Theory Y, which makes basic assumptions regarding human behavior. Theory X assumes that employees are lazy, have little ambition, dislike work, and must be coerced in order to perform satisfactorily. Theory Y assumes that people do not inherently dislike work and if properly rewarded will perform well on the job.[47]

The behavioral science model began to have an impact on police departments in the 1970s. This model, with its greater emphasis on employee participation, job satisfaction, and a more democratic approach, was in conflict with the traditional model of policing that emphasized hierarchical structure, authoritarian managerial practices, and a narrow view of the police role.

The behavioral sciences approach has three major components:

- An empirically stated goal that any person would be able to see, hear, taste, or feel something
- A criterion of success (normally less than 100%)
- A context in which to measure the goal developed in empirical terms

Contemporary approaches stress the integration of knowledge. They include the systems of human resources management and are influenced by the increased sophistication of behavioral science and by attempts to build on that knowledge.

Systems Theory

The systems theory is based on the concept that all parts of a system are interrelated and interdependent to form the whole. The system is composed of elements or subelements that are related and dependent upon one another. When the subsystems interact with one another, they form a whole. Managers must be aware of the actions of other subsystems and that any changes they make in their own subunits will have an effect on the other subunits.[48] Systems may be viewed as "open" or "closed" systems. A system is open if it interacts with its environment and closed if it does not. The concept of open and closed systems is not an absolute but a relative matter because all systems interact with the environment, but the degree of interaction varies.

Contingency Theory

The contingency theory is based on the concept that there is no single form of organizational structure or style that is appropriate for all situations. While both the systems and the contingency theories recognize the importance of the interrelationship between the parts of the organization and the organization and the environment, the systems theory is more abstract and does not attempt to define the relationships. The contingency theory developed as researchers discovered that certain methods and practices that were effective in one situation might not be in another situation. Accordingly, contingency theorists contend that there are no universal principles that may be applied in all circumstances. The task for managers is to determine which methods are more effective in their specific situations.

Human Resources Model

The human resources model, like the behavioral sciences model, recognizes the importance of human resources in police administration. In this section, we introduce two current management philosophies that were developed for corporate management and have been used by police chiefs in the United States: management by objectives (MBO) and total quality management. More in-depth coverage of these philosophies is covered in other chapters. MBO was developed by George S. Odione in 1965.[49] MBO is based on the concept that the best way to ensure success is through planning. First, there is an agreement as to the goals to be achieved. Then there is planning for how to achieve those goals. MBO is more concerned with general organizational planning than the system and contingency philosophies. It also de-emphasizes the role of specific personnel in the planning process.

Total quality management philosophy is given credit for turning the Japanese from a low-tech, substandard industrial nation to one of the world's industrial leaders.[50] Total quality management attempts to create a culture that encompasses workers, feedback, cooperative teamwork, and customers as critical considerations in the organizational enterprise. It is customer-oriented and sees the production system as a supplier-customer chain. It involves pro-active problem-seeking and the concentration on work-process control and improvement.

HISTORICAL TIME LINES IN POLICING

1631: Boston establishes the "night watch," the first system of law enforcement in America.
1712: Boston hires the first full-time paid law enforcement officers in the United States.
1776: The Declaration of Independence is written.
1789: Congress creates the position of U.S. Marshall, the first federal law enforcement agent.
1789: U.S. Customs Service is established.
1794: U.S. Marshall Robert Forsyth is the first officer in the United States to be killed in the line of duty.
1806: The first African American police officer is appointed in New Orleans.
1829: The London Metropolitan Police is established.
1835: The Texas Rangers are established. This is the oldest statewide law enforcement agency in the United States.
1846: The first detective unit is organized in Boston.
1858: The Boston and Chicago police departments become the first in the United States to issue uniforms to their officers.
1862: The U.S. Bureau of Alcohol, Tobacco and Firearms is established.
1863: The Boston police department is the first to issue pistols to its officers.
1865: The U.S. Secret Service is established.
1870: Thomas J. Smith, of Abilene, Kansas, is the first U.S. police chief killed in the line of duty.
1870: The U.S. Department of Justice is established.
1871: John Wilson of Portsmouth, Virginia, is the first African American police officer killed in the line of duty.

1881: Gunfight at the O.K. Corral occurs.
1889: The first police strike occurs in Ithaca, New York.
1891: The National Chiefs of Police Union is established. It is the first national police group established and later became the International Association of Chiefs of Police.
1902: Fingerprints are first used in the United States.
1908: The FBI is established.
1910: The first police car is used by the Akron, Ohio, Police Department.
1910: Alice Stebbins of Los Angeles is appointed the first female police officer with the power to arrest.
1912: The first police wagon is used in Cincinnati.
1913: The first police motorcycles are used by police departments in the Northeast.
1919: Boston police strike.
1924: Mary T. Davis is the first female police officer killed in the line of duty.
1931: The Wickersham Commission is established.
1935: The Texas Negro Peace Officers' Association, the first formal police association organized by African American officers, is founded.
1952: Dotson Sutton became the oldest policeman killed in the line of duty. He was 80 years old.
1959: This is the last year in which less than one hundred police officers are killed in the line of duty in the United States.
1965: The President's Commission on Law Enforcement and the Administration of Justice is established.
1972: The Knapp Commission is established to investigate police corruption in New York.
1973: The U.S. Drug Enforcement Administration is created.
1974: Police begin to wear soft body armor for protection.
1976: The National Organization of Black Law Enforcement Executives is founded.
1988: The FBI is the first law enforcement agency to use DNA evidence to solve crime.
1991: The Rodney King incident occurs in Los Angeles.
1991: The National Law Enforcement Officers Memorial is established in Washington, DC.
1994: The U.S. Violent Crime Control and Law Enforcement Act is signed into law.
1995: The Alfred P. Murrah Federal Building in Oklahoma City is bombed.
2002: The Department of Homeland Security is created.

Organizational Culture

An organization's culture is important when assessing the quality of leadership and management within the organization. Organizational culture refers to sum of the matrix of values that exist within an organization. The matrix consists of the individuals and groups present within an organization. Each individual in an organization has his own set of values. Individuals belong to groups. Most individuals belong to more than one group. For example, the officers in one division may be considered as one group. The officers who are veterans compose another group. The officers who belong to a racial minority form another group. Officers who are detectives constitute another work group. One officer may be a member of several of these groups. Each group has its values. Many of the values overlap. Some values may also conflict. Accordingly, the police organization is pulled in a number of different directions as the values compete for dominance. Collectively, the values form a culture that defines what the environment is and how the organization should respond to it. Culture helps guide individuals in defining the proper courses of action and in making the decisions as to which behaviors are appropriate and which are not.

Historically, a department's organizational culture evolved around how the individuals within the organization defined their roles. If the police in a department perceive their role as law enforcement, then they will tend to make more arrests than officers who perceive their role as order maintenance.

Questions in Review

1. Managers perform four essential functions in every organization: organizing, leading, planning, and controlling. Explain the functions of each.
2. A traditionally accepted mission of the police department is the preservation of peace. How is that mission accomplished under the community policing approach? Under the traditional approach?
3. The nature of policing in the United States is based on the concepts that the prevention of crime is a proper role for the government, the best government is one that governs least, the authority of the government should be limited, and any use of police power must be regarded with grave suspicion. How would these concepts limit your actions as chief of police in your hometown?
4. Leadership and management are not interchangeable terms. Kotter defines the functions of management as planning and budgeting, organizing and staffing, and controlling and problem solving. What does he see as the functions of leadership? What are the differences

in function and form between leadership and management? How can those differences create conflict?
5. The early forms of policing considered it to be a private matter. Individuals were responsible for protecting themselves. The traditional approach to policing sees the police as the protectors of society. In community policing, the police and the community are partners in protecting the community. Has community policing moved back toward the concept that individuals are responsible to a large extent for protecting themselves?
6. As the mutual pledge system declined and community support languished, fighting crime, which was everyone's business, became nobody's duty. How did this situation develop?
7. As England became an industrial nation in the latter part of the eighteenth century, families left the farm and moved to the factory towns in search of work. As the towns and cities grew, patterns of social life changed, and an unprecedented social order developed. What effects did these changes in society have on policing?
8. As Sir Robert Peel's bobbies developed strategies for crime prevention, certain principles of policing were evolved that are still used in the United States. What are some of those principles?
9. In the 1850s, New York was described as the most crime-ridden city in the world. What was the status of policing at that time? Was the lack of an effective police force one of the major factors?
10. The police reform era started in the 1930s and lasted until the early 1970s. The history of police administration is usually divided into three eras, with the political era beginning in the 1840s and lasting until the 1930s. If the police reform era started in the 1900s, why did the political era of police administration last until the 1930s?
11. James Q. Wilson's three styles of policing are the watchman style, which was concerned primarily with order maintenance; the legalistic style, which was concerned primarily with law enforcement; and the service style, which attempts to combine the efficiency of the legalistic style and the broad informal discretion of the watchman style. What is the principle style of policing used by your hometown police department?
12. In the historical development of police management, six different management theories have been used. First was the traditional model, which was based on the concept of centralized administration designed along the military organizational model. Next was the scientific management model, which emphasized efficiency. The human relations and participative management approach considered police supervisors as team leaders who create a cooperative effort among the officers. Then there is the behavioral approach

model, which attempted to establish a criterion for success, and the systems approach, which uses a number of systems for accountability, forward planning, and fiscal organization. The last management theory is the proactive one, which has a strong commitment to community involvement. During what different time spans were each of the management theories considered as viable theories?

Biggest Mistakes Police Leadership Makes and How to Avoid Them

Lucky or Cunning and Resourceful

Many Americans, including police officers, consider that the terrorists who carried out the carnage on 9/11 were extremely lucky. Question: Were they lucky or were they cunning and resourceful? Robert Matti concluded that the terrorists performed and carried out a brilliant blow against America and freedom-loving people throughout the world on 9/11. He concluded that the attackers studied and figured out our weakness and brought the world's strongest nation to its knees.[51]

What Is Your Opinion? And Your Justification for that Opinion?

Matti contends that many of us underestimate terrorism, and he is concerned that many professional law enforcement officers who should know better also have this point of view. According to him, underestimating the enemy is highly dangerous. Terrorists are far from being stupid, and to prevail in this conflict we must think and act one step ahead of our foes. The 2004 train bombing in Madrid, Spain, is considered by most as a well-coordinated attack with multiple bombs exploding at approximately the same time.

Probably opinion will be evenly divided on the first question regarding whether the terrorists were lucky or cunning and resourceful. A more important question is: Does it make any difference as to how you plan countermeasures to hopefully prevent future attacks on your city? Should the possibility that the terrorists were cunning and resourceful change your defense measures?

A similar situation occurred in the 1960s when President Kennedy was assassinated. If you accept the official view, it was a lucky shot that killed JFK. But in planning for the future protection of a president, does it make any difference if you have a well-trained sniper or an average shooter who connects with a lucky shot?

The one possible result is the opinion that it was luck and will never happen again. Can we afford to take that attitude?

End Notes

1. George L. Kelling, "Broken Windows and Police Discretion," *National Institute of Justice Research Report*, NCJ 178259 (October 1999).
2. John S. Dempsey, *An Introduction to Policing*, 2nd ed. (Belmont, CA: Wadsworth, 1999), p. 2.
3. Wayne Hanson, "Wanted Transformational Leaders," *Supplement to Government Technology* (November 1999), p 4.
4. Dempsey, p. 1.
5. Executive Summary, NCJ 178934 (October 1999).
6. Paul Chevigny, *Edge of Knife: Police Violence in the Americas* (New York: The Free Press, 1995), p. 6.
7. John P. Kotter, *A Force for Change* (New York: The Free Press, 1990).
8. Kotter (1990), pp. 7–8.
9. Kotter (1990), p. 7.
10. Charles Reith, *The Blind Eye of History: A Study of the Origins of the Present Police Era* (London: Faber, 1912).
11. The President's Commission on Law Enforcement and Administration of Justice, *Task Force Report: The Police* (Washington, DC: GPO, 1967), p. 1. President's Commission on Law Enforcement and Administration of Justice, Task Force Report: Science and Technology (Washington, DC: GPO, 1967) and President's Commission on Law Enforcement and Administration of Justice, Task Force Report: Studies in Crime and Law Enforcement in Major American Cities (Washington, DC: GPO, 1967)
12. This section is based on William G. Bailey, ed. *The Encyclopedia of Police Science* (New York: Garland, 1989); Charles Reith, *The Blind Eye of History: A Study of the Origins of the Present Police Era* (London: Faber, 1912); and S. G. Chapman and T. E. St. Johnston, *The Police Heritage in Europe and America* (East Lansing, MI: Michigan State University, 1962).
13. Royal Commission on the Police, *Royal Commission on the Police Report, 1962* (London: Her Majesty's Stationery Office, 1963).
14. Royal Commission on the Police, note 4 at p. 4.
15. T. A. Critchley, *A History of Police in England and Wales*, 2nd ed. (Montclair, NJ: Patterson Smith, 1972), p. 58.
16. Edward Barrett, Jr., "Police Practices and the Law: From Arrest to Release or Charge," *California Law Review* (March 1962), Vol. 50, pp. 17–18.
17. Clemens Bartollas and Larry D. Hahn, *Policing in America* (Boston: Allyn and Bacon, 1999), p. 5.
18. Samuel Walker, *Popular Justice: A History of American Criminal Justice* (Oxford: Oxford University Press, 1998), p. 22.
19. Arthur Charles Cole, "The Irrepressible Conflict, 1859–1865" in *A History of American Life*, Vol. 8, Arthur M. Schlesinger, Sr. and Dixon Ryan Fox, eds. (New York: MacMillan, 1934), pp. 154–155.
20. Walker (1998), p. 52.
21. Arthur M. Schlesinger, Sr., "The Rise of the City, 1878–1898," in *A History of American Life*, Vol. X, Arthur M. Schlesinger, Sr. and Dixon Ryan Fox, eds. (New York: MacMillan, 1934), p. 115.

22 Samuel Walker, *A Critical History of Police Reform: The Emergence of Professionalism* (Lexington, MA: Lexington Books, 1972), pp. 40–43.
23 It is noted that some states still exercise some control over local police agencies.
24 Albert J. Reiss, Jr., "An Evaluation and Assessment of the Impact of the Task Force Report: Crime and Its Impact—An Assessment," in *The 1967 President's Crime Commission Report: Its Impact 25 Years Later*, John A. Conley, ed. (Cincinnati, OH: 1994).
25 G. Douglas Gourley, *Effective Municipal Police Organization* (Beverly Hills, CA: Benziger, Bruce and Glencoe, 1970), p. 41.
26 David R. Johnson, *American Law Enforcement: A History* (St. Louis, MO: Forum Press, 1981), p. 121.
27 James Q. Wilson, *Thinking About Crime* (New York: Basic Books, 1983), p. 3.
28 John A. Conley, "Introduction," in *The 1967 President's Crime Commission Report: Its Impact 25 Years Later*, John A. Conley, ed. (Cincinnati, OH: 1994).
29 Samuel Walker "Between Two Worlds: The President's Crime Commission and the Police, 1967–1992," in *The 1967 President's Crime Commission Report: Its Impact 25 Years Later*, John A. Conley, ed. (Cincinnati, OH: 1994).
30 Walker (1967), p. 33.
31 Robert Trojanowicz, Victor E. Kappeler, and Larry K. Gaines. *Community Policing: A Contemporary Perspective*, 2nd ed. (Cincinnati, OH: Anderson, 1998), p. 5.
32 Jeremy Travis, "Lessons for the Criminal Justice System from Twenty Years of Policing Reform." Keynote address to "New Beginnings," the first conference on the New York Campaign for Effective Crime Policy, March 10, 1996.
33 Travis.
34 Kelling.
35 M. A. Wycoff and W. K. Skogan, *Community Policing in Madison: Quality from the Inside Out* (Washington, DC: National Institute of Justice, 1993).
36 National Institute of Justice Research Preview "Community Policing in Action: Lessons from an Observational Study" (June 1998).
37 Adapted from: Malcolm K. Sparrow, *Implementing Community Policing* (Washington, DC: National Institute of Justice, 1988), pp. 7–9.
38 James Q. Wilson, *Varieties of Police Behavior* (Cambridge, MA: Harvard University Press, 1968), p. 155.
39 James McCalman and Robert A. Paton, *Change Management: A Guide to Effective Implementation* (London: Paul Chapman, 1992).
40 T. Burns and G. Stalker, *The Management of Innovation* (London: Tavistock, 1961).
41 H. Fayol, *General and Industrial Management*, translated by C. Storrs (London: Pitman & Sons, 1949).
42 Edward A. Thibault, Lawrence M. Lynch, and R. Bruce McBride, *Proactive Police Management* (Englewood Cliffs, NJ: Prentice-Hall, 1985).
43 O. W. Wilson, *Police Administration* (New York: McGraw-Hill, 1950).
44 Thibault (1985), p. 13.
45 Daniel A. Wren, *The Evolution of Management Thought*, 4th ed. (New York: Wiley, 1994).
46 Abraham H. Maslow, *Motivation and Personality* (New York: Harper & Row, 1954).

47 Douglas McGregor, *The Human Side of Enterprise* (New York: McGraw-Hill, 1960).
48 F. Luthans, *Introduction to Management: A Contingency Approach* (New York: McGraw-Hill, 1976).
49 George S. Odione, *Management by Objectives* (New York: Pitman, 1965). It is noted that the term "management by objectives" was first used by Peter Drucker in *The Practice of Management* (New York: Harper, 1954).
50 Larry K. Gaines, Victor E. Kappeler, and Joseph B. Vaughn, *Policing in America*, 2nd ed. (Cincinnati: Anderson, 1997).
51 Robert Matti, quoted in *Police Magazine* (March 2004), p. 10.

Introduction to Management Theory

2

Key Individuals, Concepts, and Issues

Frederick Winslow Taylor	Scientific management
Henry Gantt	Gantt chart
Frank and Lillian Gilbreth	Human relations movement
Max Weber	Weberian bureaucracy
Henri Fayol	Administrative science
Mary Parker Follett	Functional relating
Chester Barnard	Theory of organization
Elton Mayo	Hawthorne Studies
Abraham Maslow	Hierarchy of needs
Kurt Lewin	Force field analysis
Douglas McGregor	Theories X and Y
Rensis Likert	Linking pin model
Peter Drucker	Management by objectives
W. Edwards Deming	Total quality management

Definitions

Bureaucracy: An organizational structure characterized by regular procedure, division of responsibility, hierarchy, and impersonal relationships.

Division of labor: The division of a complex production process into a number of simpler tasks, each one of which is undertaken by a different individual who typically specializes in one task on a permanent basis.

Force field analysis: A framework for weighing the pros and cons of factors (forces) that influence a situation. Forces are either driving movement toward a goal (helping forces) or blocking movement toward a goal (hindering forces).

Gantt chart: A popular project management charting method in which a schedule is displayed graphically. It consists of a horizontal bar chart with time as the horizontal axis and either resources, jobs, or orders as the vertical axis. Individual operations are displayed as horizontal bars in the chart, indicating the time at which the job begins and ends.

Hawthorne Effect: A form of reactivity whereby employees' motivation and productivity improve simply in response to the fact that some interest is being shown in them.

Linking pin: A number of overlapping work units in which a member of a unit is the leader of another unit.

Management by objectives: A systematic and organized approach to increasing performance by aligning goals and subordinate objectives throughout the organization.

Principle of exception: Lower-level managers should handle routine matters, and higher-level mangers should only receive reports of deviations above or below standard performances.

Chapter Objectives

After completing this chapter you should be able to:

1. Explain Taylor's scientific management theory
2. Explain how Gantt charts are used to determine a project schedule
3. Outline the principles of Weber's bureaucratic model of organizations
4. Explain how the Hawthorne Effect can affect employee behavior
5. Identify the levels of Maslow's hierarchy of needs and relate their importance to employee motivation
6. Describe the use of force field analysis for managing organizational change
7. Differentiate among Theory X and Theory Y organization

Case Study 2.1

In November 2011, at the direction of the command staff, you presided over a committee of managers (i.e., lieutenants and sergeants) to study the need for a new policy on the use of social networking sites by members of the police department. A survey of department employees conducted earlier in the year found that a high percentage of patrol officers use social networking sites on duty and off duty for professional reasons including investigations and training, as well as for personal communications. At that time, the overwhelming majority of managers saw no need for a new policy, with most citing they would use disciplinary action deemed suitable for conduct unbecoming an officer for any behavior violations found through Internet posts. With this information, the managers of the police department recommended against a new social networking policy.

Recently though, embarrassing national headlines of inappropriate postings on Facebook, Twitter, and LinkedIn by police officers in other parts of the country have cast doubt on police professionalism and the abilities of police officers to make good judgments. In one case, a patrol officer admittedly made inappropriate and offensive Twitter postings over department pay issues and perceived favoritism. In another case, an officer posted pictures from a homicide crime scene.

Although problems have not surfaced at your agency, the chief of police has remarked that a policy on employee social networking use is necessary to ensure the public's trust in the professionalism of the police department. He maintains that an officer's behavior both on and off duty is a direct reflection of the entire department's integrity. The chief has instructed you to convene the agency's managers and draft a policy that governs the use of social networking sites by employees.

1. What guidelines would you consider to ensure that social network use on the job is not counterproductive to management and team productivity?
2. When drafting the department's policy, will you consider whether managers will be required to monitor an employee's social networking activity? Why or why not?
3. What will be the repercussions from not following the policy?

Introduction

No man in the history of American industry has made a larger contribution to genuine cooperation and juster human relations than did Frederick Winslow Taylor by his *Principles of Scientific Management*. He is one of the few—very few—creative geniuses of our times.
—**Ida M. Tarbell**
October 25, 1924

Modern police operation in the United States is the result of various organizational management approaches that have been tried and tested in police agencies over the last century. Often pressured to deal with critical social issues of the times (e.g., escalating crime problems), police leaders face constant demands to develop strategies in the areas of planning, problem solving, and police tactics. When critical issues tended to be more aligned with political pressures (e.g., public accountability), police leaders have found ways to implement better practices in the areas of budgeting, staffing, and resource utilization.

Police management has a healthy history of reform efforts by many leaders in the police field. The development of the civil service examination in the early 1900s, for example, provided that police personnel would be selected and promoted based on merit rather than political patronage. In the period of 1900–1925, police departments in the largest cities in the United States began placing greater emphasis on making arrests for crimes against property (theft and burglary) and crimes against persons (i.e., assault and robbery). Arrests for victimless crimes (i.e., public drunkenness and other public order violations) decreased during the same time period.

In the 1930s, Orlando W. Wilson, the chief of police in Wichita, Kansas, advocated using technological innovations (e.g., two-way radios and computerized record keeping) to improve law enforcement's capabilities in the community. During the 1960s, while serving as chief of police in Chicago, Wilson continued to advocate police management reforms. His book, *Police Administration* became an instrumental part of the police reform effort, as police managers in law enforcement agencies throughout the United States began to make use of many of Wilson's management principles.

During the 1950s and 1960s, under the direction of Police Chief William Parker, the Los Angeles Police Department became a model for organizational reform, emphasizing the importance of careful planning, economic efficiency, and rigorous personnel selection and training standards.

In the 1970s, community policing efforts gained widespread acceptance in the field of policing. Proactive management approaches to policing became popular as police leaders began to place greater emphasis on crime prevention strategies. A problem-oriented policing approach to crime reduction advocated by Herman Goldstein placed great emphasis on "team policing," a process whereby police managers focus resources on problems rather than waiting to react to problems. A strong commitment to community involvement and making optimal use of modern technology are viewed as two of the key elements to proactive policing.

The community policing approach gained additional support in the 1980s. "Broken windows" is a metaphor coined by James Q. Wilson and George L. Kelling and used in the title of several publications in the 1980s and 1990s; it asserts that neighborhood disorder is a source of public fear and that broken windows invite social disorder and criminal activity into the neighborhood. Accordingly, to reduce crime and social disorder, police must bring the community together to restore civility, which will result in lowering citizens' fear of crime and the crime rate.

Throughout the history of police management, when particular strategies emerged and showed positive benefits, they were quickly advanced in the police field. The successes of many police organizations are often touted as having been the result of good management practices, good leadership people, or both.

In the next two chapters, we explore the differences between management and leadership from a theoretical point of view. The terms management and leadership are sometimes used interchangeably, because most of the people who are in positions of leadership today are called managers. The "general manager," for example, is a common job title used in business to designate the top person in authority within the organization. However, management and leadership are not the same. Management is an operational function used to guide an organization. Management involves adherence to established policies and practices to get the job done. Leadership is a people-oriented concept that operates outside and beyond the perimeters of rules and policies. Leadership permeates all levels of an organization from the line staff to the chief executive. It has nothing to do with job titles and everything to do with relationships.

We begin first by exploring various management theories and their application within the police organization. In Chapter 4, we will turn our attention to leadership theory, discussing factors affecting police administration and decision making.

Management Theory

Modern management practices are the result of significant increases in large, complex organizations that arose in the twentieth century. The history of management can be divided into two broad perspectives: classical and humanistic management. Within each of these perspectives, there are several divisions, each having their own unique qualities and rationale. Exhibit 2.1 provides an illustration of several management perspectives and the contributing theorist. These management philosophies were developed by twentieth-century inventors and other pioneers, who were trying to produce consistent results on key dimensions expected by customers, employees, and other organizational constituencies, despite the complexity caused by large size, modern technologies, and geographic dispersion. They created management to help keep a complex organization on time and on budget.[1]

As industrial management theories began to penetrate government thinking, many law enforcement agencies implemented change based on these theoretical concepts. Moreover, the role of policing was evolving, with managers being required to perform many more roles within the

I. Classical Management	II. Humanistic Management
A. Scientific Management	A. Human Relations
Frederick Taylor	Elton Mayo
Henry Gantt	Abraham Maslow
Frank and Lillian Gilbreth	B. Behavioral Systems
B. Bureaucratic Management	Kurt Lewin
Max Weber	C. Human Resources
C. Administrative Management	Douglas McGregor
Henri Fayol	Rensis Likert
Mary Parker Follett	D. Systems Approach
Chester Barnard	Peter Drucker
	W. Edwards Deming

Exhibit 2.1 Management perspectives and theorists that dominated the twentieth-century management movement.

organization. How they handled various situations was largely dependent on the management philosophy of the agency. Let us review the contributions of several pioneers in management science and consider their application to law enforcement.

Scientific Management

Frederick Winslow Taylor

Frederick Winslow Taylor (1856–1915) is considered the father of scientific management. He was raised in an upper-class, liberal Philadelphia family and at age twenty-five earned an engineering degree at the Stevens Institute of Technology in New Jersey. Even though he excelled in math and sports, Taylor chose to work as a machinist and pattern maker in Philadelphia at the Enterprise Hydraulic Works.[2]

After his apprenticeship at the hydraulic works plant, Taylor became a common laborer at the Midvale Steel Company. He started as shop clerk and quickly progressed to machinist, foreman, maintenance foreman, and chief draftsman. Within six years, he advanced to research director, then chief engineer. While working there, Taylor introduced piecework in the factory. His goal was to find the most efficient way to perform specific tasks. He observed how work was actually done and then measured the quantity of production.[3]

During his early shop experience, Taylor observed that much of the blame for low production and inefficiency rested with management. Thus, as a fellow worker, his attention was first attracted to the problem of improving working conditions and raising the standard of living of the individual workman. At Midvale, he used time studies to set daily production quotas. Incentives would be paid to those reaching their daily goal. Taylor doubled productivity using time study, systematic controls and tools, functional foremanship, and his new wage scheme.

At age thirty-seven, Taylor became a consulting engineer, and his most important client was the Bethlehem Iron Company, later known as Bethlehem Steel. In 1901, he made Bethlehem "the world's most modern factory and potentially a prototype for manufacturers and engineers in other industries" by installing production planning, differential piece rates, and functional foremanship.[4] A major component of Taylor's system was determining a time for each step in a work process and then using a strict management system to keep the workers on that timetable. Taylor's precision stopwatches could time a task to a hundredth of a second, but his ability to measure the duration of a task was far in excess of any true value that data had in reorganizing workplace practices. Among Taylor's other contributions to Bethlehem in 1901 were a real-time analysis of daily output and costs, a modern cost accounting system, reduction of yard workers' ranks from 500 to 140, doubling of stamping mill production, and a lowered cost per ton of materials handled, from eight cents to four cents. He successfully implemented cost saving techniques even though he added clerks, teachers, time-study engineers, supervision, and staffing support positions.

In 1906, Taylor presented his now famous paper, *On the Art of Cutting Metals*, before the American Society of Mechanical Engineers as his presidential address. It was the result of nearly three decades of experimentation, during which time some thirty to fifty thousand recorded experiments were carried out. Taylor estimated the cost of these experiments at between $150,000 and $200,000. He further stated that they were undertaken "to obtain a part of the information necessary to establish in a machine shop our system of management" and were designed to answer three recurring questions:

1. What tool shall I use?
2. What cutting speed shall I use?
3. What feed shall I use?

In 1911, Taylor published *The Principles of Scientific Management*.[5] The importance of this work is that it established a foundation from which other management perspectives grew. Taylor also made other contributions, including the **principle of exception**, which meant that lower-level managers should handle routine matters, and higher-level mangers should only receive reports of deviations above or below standard performances.

The application of Taylor's theory may appear to be a natural fit for policing. Based on its appearance, scientific management makes sense if we consider its fundamental principles call for simplifying job responsibilities by breaking them down and dividing them among employees and then for controlling employees' in order to eliminate inefficiency. However, as we will see in our ongoing discuss of management theory, very rigid top-down management may impose many problems within the organization if police officers feel unmotivated. That is, failing to include line police officers in the decision-making process in the ever-changing police organization may leave the primary workforce to carry out policies that they had no say in. Lorne Kramer, former police chief in Colorado Springs, Colorado, argues that police managers need to push everyone in the organization to have and to express an opinion. "It's always the quiet ones who will kill you," he said. "If they are silent, they don't own it. By their silence they will undermine what you are trying to do."[6]

Henry Gantt
Henry Gantt (1861–1919) was an associate of Frederick Taylor and a pioneer in the area of scheduling and rewarding employees. He is most noted for the development of the **Gantt chart**, which emphasized time rather than quantity, volume, or weight as the key factor in planning production. Gantt

viewed production inefficiency as the result of management's inability to formulate realistic standards. He believed that work needed to be effectively scheduled and that workers needed to be motivated through offers of production bonuses. Exhibit 2.2 illustrates a Gantt chart used by a police agency

Tasks	Week 1	Week 2	Week 3	Week 4	Week 5	Week 6	Person assigned
Assemble community policing task force, address objectives, and determine necessary resources.	■	■					Officer W. Kiel, Officer J. Lee, Officer A. Loren, Sgt. T. Nicole
Request approval of police administration and local governmental authority to proceed.	■	■					Sgt. T. Nicole
Review surveys used in other jurisdictions and develop appropriate survey to assess attitudes of citizens regarding community policing.		■					Officer A. Loren, Sgt. T. Nicole
Re-assemble task force team and provide update.			■				Sgt. T. Nicole
Develop plan for administering community policing survey.			■	■			Officer A. Loren, Sgt. T. Nicole
Pretest plan and revise as necessary.				■			Officer W. Kiel, Officer J. Lee
Implement plan.				■	■		Officer W. Kiel, Officer J. Lee, Officer A. Loren, Sgt. T. Nicole
Analyze survey responses and prepare report document.						■	Officer W. Kiel, Officer J. Lee, Officer A. Loren, Sgt. T. Nicole
Evaluation and recommendations.						■	Sgt. T. Nicole, Officer W. Kiel, Officer J. Lee, Officer A. Loren

Exhibit 2.2 Illustration of a Gantt chart to assess citizen attitudes.

that is interested in assessing the attitudes of citizens regarding community policing practices. Note that the three key elements of the Gantt chart include tasks to be performed, timetable to accomplish the tasks, and personnel assigned to perform the tasks.

Today, law enforcement managers have access to several project management software programs including well-designed, easy-to-use Gantt charts that measure and report a project's progress. Gantt chart software is easy to install on a computer, is simple to use, and comes with unique features that allow managers to:

- Create task lists and link tasks together with a schedule
- Assign resources and track time spent
- Monitor actual versus planned progress
- Set baselines and monitor delivery

Frank and Lillian Gilbreth

Frank Bunker Gilbreth (1868–1924), a bricklayer by trade, and his wife, Lillian Moller Gilbreth (1878–1972), a psychologist, devoted themselves to efficiency. They studied the movement and motions of baseball players, physicians, disabled veterans, and workers. By observing and analyzing how repetitive tasks were performed, the Gilbreths believed they could discover the single best way of performing any job. The time then saved through a more efficient use of the body's movements would allow for the creation of "happiness moments." In *Fatigue Study*, published in 1916, the Gilbreths describe their goal:

> The aim of life is happiness, no matter how we differ as to what happiness means. Fatigue elimination, starting as it does from a desire to conserve humanlife and to eliminate enormous waste, must increase "Happiness Minutes," no matter what else it does, or it has failed in its fundamental aim.[7]

The work of the Gilbreths in analyzing motion and movement was part of the manufacturing revolution in the United States. During the early twentieth century, new technologies were changing the ways in which factories operated. The widespread introduction of electricity, for example, had a tremendous effect on how factories were designed and built, enabling manufacturers to construct plants that emphasized the handling and movement of materials using conveyor belts, cranes, and other devices. Breakthroughs in industries like iron and glass were eliminating many of the steps in the process previously done by skilled craftsman. While manufacturing technology continued to determine the social relations within the factory, the advances also increased the presence of management in day to day, and hour to hour, operations.[8]

They used still photography first and then motion pictures to break down movements of the body into their basic elements. After analyzing hundreds of workers, the Gilbreths claimed to discover the existence of sixteen "therbligs" (Gilbreth spelled backwards), which they considered the basic units of movements. All human motion and movement, no matter how complicated, was the result of various combinations of therbligs. Thus by dividing any activity into smaller and smaller discrete steps and then reassembling those steps in a "better" way, more efficient work could be done. The Gilbreths' roles within this factory revolution were as consultants, hired by factory owners to improve the efficiency of the plants. The Gilbreths felt what they were doing would benefit both the factory owner as well as the worker. In a plea to factory owners to recognize the necessity of eliminating fatigue in typical working conditions, the Gilbreths wrote:

> Have you reason to believe that your workers are really happier because of the work that you have done on fatigue study? Do they look happier, and say they are happier? [If yes,] then your fatigue eliminating work has been worthwhile in the highest sense of the term, no matter what the financial outcome. Naturally, the savings that accrue must benefit everyone, but saving lies at the root of fatigue elimination, and if every member of the organization, including the manager and the stockholders, is getting more "Happiness Minutes," you are surely working along the right lines.[9]

Police work is regarded as an extremely stressful occupation. The public expects officers to perform flawlessly, but constant exposure to the full spectrum of street violence and other negative interactions with the public can affect police officers on a chronic basis. In addition to the stressors inherent in police work, numerous studies have shown that factors related to organizational structure and climate can be an even greater source of stress for the police officer. Exhaustion caused by shift work, mandatory overtime assignments, seemingly endless hours waiting to testify in court, and management expectations of doing more with less, combined with family responsibilities, puts the modern law enforcement professional at serious emotional and physical risk.[10] So understanding and eliminating fatigue is essential to countering the potential negative consequences of physiological, psychological, and behavioral stresses associated with the work.

Bureacratic Management

Max Weber

> Man is dominated by the making of money, by acquisition as the ultimate purpose of his life. Economic acquisition is no longer subordinated to man as the means for the satisfaction of his material needs. This reversal of what

we should call the natural relationship, so irrational from a naive point of view, is evidently as definitely a leading principle of capitalism as it is foreign to all peoples not under a capitalist influence.

—**Max Weber**
The Protestant Ethic and the Spirit of Capitalism, 1904

Max Weber (1864–1920), the founder of modern sociology, was the first to observe and write on the bureaucracies that developed in Germany during the nineteenth century. He considered them to be efficient, rational, and honest, a big improvement over the haphazard administration that they replaced. Weber suggested that well-established organizations functioned according to six principles:

- Fixed and official jurisdictional areas that are ordered by rules, laws, and administrative regulations.
- Hierarchy and levels of graded authority where the lower offices are supervised by the higher ones.
- Management is based on official documents.
- The officials have thorough and expert training.
- It requires the full time work of the official.
- Management follows established rules.

Max Weber was the first to use the term **bureaucracy**, as well as the first to analyze it comprehensively. Analysts today speak of a "Weberian bureaucracy," meaning one that fits his ideal type closely. He did not see bureaucracy in the negative light in which we tend to think of it today. He saw it as the most logical and rational form of organizational structure for large organizations. His bureaucracies were based on authority, and he analyzed the bases of authority and found three basic types:

1. Legal or rational authority: Based on law, procedures, rules, etc. Authority in this structure is based on purposeful reasoning and formally defined, accepted structures of rules and procedures. The power of those in authority depends on their acceptance of due legal process and qualification. Some characteristics include:
   - ownership according to purposeful, agreed rules
   - appointment on technically defined grounds (merit and technical expertise) election
   - membership of a decision-making group and adherence to the rules of decision-making

2. Charismatic authority: Based on the personal qualities of an individual. The organization is based on the leader. His special qualities

attract the support of followers who value the benefits that association with the leader brings. The leader organizes, directs, and distributes rewards. Organizational success depends on the single-mindedness and expertise of the leader and his inspired followers. Charismatic influence may live on if the leader's values and doctrines are integrated by followers. Weber studied and wrote extensively on religion. His concept of charisma derived from theology. His best known book is *The Protestant Ethic and the Spirit of Capitalism.*
3. Traditional authority: Based on family relationships. Roles, customs, and practices have become accepted into the ritual of life. Things happen because they have always happened that way (precedent). Authority and position is an inherited commodity vested in those who for reason of birth or selection represent the traditional customs (i.e., dynasties).

The environment in which police operate is very unique, composed of political, economic, and social forces. Policing systems operate within a hierarchical structure characterized by several layers of management bureaucracy. A large police agency, for example, is likely to have five clear layers of authority: the executive of the agency (police chief, sheriff, etc.), top managers (commanders, majors, etc.), middle managers (captains, lieutenants, etc.), line supervisors (sergeants, corporals, etc.), and line staff (patrolmen, deputies, etc.).

In many police agencies, the executive and top managers make the decisions, and middle managers develop procedures for implementing those decisions. Line supervisors strive to ensure consistency of the line staff—those who actually do the work involved.

An important idea about police organizations is that bureaucratic characteristics, such as rules, **division of labor**, written records, hierarchy of authority, and impersonal procedures, become important as the agency grows large and complex. Bureaucracy is a logical form of organizing that lets the executive use resources efficiently. However, bureaucracies are not very responsive to their customers. This is due largely to the layers one must go through to get a message communicated to the top. Many large police agencies have attempted to decentralize authority, flatten organization structure, reduce rules and written records, and subdivide into small divisions in an effort to be more responsive to the community.

In Exhibit 2.3, we offer a police organizational chart to display how levels within the organization are linked together into a coherent whole. In simple terms, it reflects what police officers and other personnel should do and what their responsibilities are within the agency. The purpose of the organization

Introduction to Management Theory

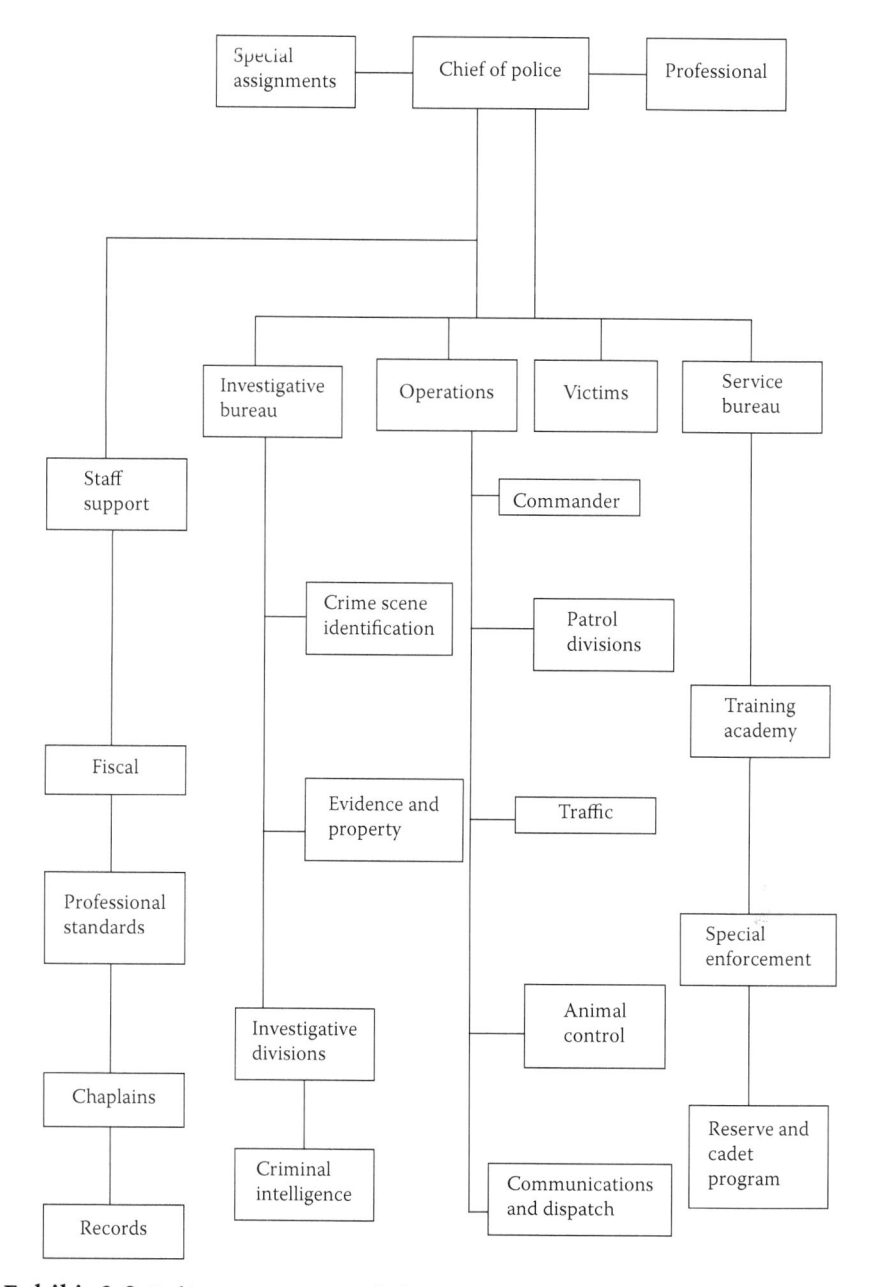

Exhibit 2.3 Police organizational chart.

chart is to encourage and direct employees into activities and communications that enable the organization to achieve its goals. The organization chart provides the structure, but the employees provide the behavior. The chart is a guideline to encourage employees to work together, but management must implement the structure and carry it out.

Administrative Management

Henri Fayol

Henri Fayol (1841–1925) remained comparatively unknown outside his native France for almost a quarter of a century after his death. Then, Constance Storrs published *General and Industrial Management*, a translation of Fayol's (unfinished) work *Administration Industrielle et Générale: Prevoyance, Organisation, Commandment, Controle*, and he posthumously gained widespread recognition for his work on administrative management. Fayol was a key figure in the turn-of-the-century classical school of management theory. Today he is often described as the founding father of the administration school.

Fayol spoke of "administrative science" and identified five functions of management:

1. Forecast and plan: examine the future and draw up plans of action.
2. Organize: build up the structure, material, and personnel of the undertaking.
3. Command: maintain activity among the personnel.
4. Coordinate: bind together, unify, and harmonize activity and effort.
5. Control: ensure that everything occurs in conformity with policy and practice.

Notice that most of these activities are very task-oriented, rather than people-oriented. This is consistent with the philosophies of Frederick Taylor and the ideology of scientific management.

Fayol identified fourteen principles of management that are common to all organizations seeking to constructively do work. He laid down the following principles of organization (he called them principles of management):

1. Specialization of labor: Specializing encourages continuous improvement in skills and the development of improvements in methods.
2. Authority: The right to give orders and the power to exact obedience.
3. Discipline: No slacking or bending of rules.
4. Unity of command: Each employee has one and only one boss.
5. Unity of direction: A single mind generates a single plan, and all play their part in that plan.
6. Subordination of individual interests: When at work, only work things should be pursued or thought about.
7. Remuneration: Employees receive fair payment for services, not what the company can get away with.
8. Centralization: Management functions are consolidated, and decisions are made from the top.

9. Scalar chain (line of authority): There is a formal chain of command running from the top to the bottom of the organization, like the military.
10. Order: All of the materials and personnel have a prescribed place, and they must remain there.
11. Equity: Equality of treatment (but not necessarily identical treatment).
12. Personnel tenure: Limited turnover of personnel. Lifetime employment for good workers.
13. Initiative: Think out a plan, and do what it takes to make it happen.
14. Esprit de corps: Harmony, cohesion among personnel.[11]

A refinement of the concept of functional management was made by Luther Gulick, who is perhaps best known for the functions of the executive represented in the acronym POSDCORB. The letters stand for planning, organizing, staffing, directing, coordinating, reporting, and budgeting. These elements of POSDCORB are described in detail in Chapter 5. Suffice it to say here, POSDCORB won immediate acceptance in the law enforcement community, which saw in it a concise rendition of the essential element of the managerial process. It promptly held a noticeable place in police training programs as well as police literature. It was offered as a partial panacea for the reformation of police administration and held a prominent place in consulting reports recommending the reorganization of police departments.[12]

Mary Parker Follett

Mary Parker Follett (1868–1933) was a political scientist, social worker, speaker, and advisor to leaders concerned with labor-management relations. While still in college, she published her first book, *The Speaker of the House of Representatives* (1896), in which she researched the methods used by the effective holders of that position in Congress. In a review for the *American Historical Review* that same year, Theodore Roosevelt declared that it was indispensable reading. In 1918, she reenergized her interest in government by publishing her second book, *The New State: Group Organization the Solution of Popular Government*. The premise in this book was that group networks that took responsibility for discovering and implementing the solutions for social problems should replace bureaucratic institutions as the primary form of governance in the United States. The ideas about participation advanced in this book proved to be the primary underpinning for her later theories on management.[13]

Mary Parker Follett was considerably more attentive to the practical realities of relationships in organizations than any of her contemporaries in management studies. She referred to "functional relating" and "coordination" within organizations and their impacts on the dynamics of the whole. Her efforts earned her a place in the pantheon of pioneers in the field of management.

Chester Barnard

Chester I. Barnard (1886–1961), enjoyed a forty-year career in the communications industry, including a presidency of the New Jersey Bell Telephone Company. Beginning in the early 1920s, Barnard wrote several articles on the functions of the organization and the effectiveness of the executive process.

Barnard's approach to organization and management was philosophic, focusing on social reality. He seized upon the concept of an organization as a social system, elaborated it in original definitions of formal and informal organization, worked out the awkwardly designated but vital difference between effectiveness and efficiency, incorporated noneconomic motivation into a theory of incentives, and developed a controversial concept of authority. Barnard revolted against the classical idea that command is the essential condition of obedience.[14]

Barnard received recognition for his treatment of communication because he recognized that by it management maintains its authority in organizations. Barnard acknowledges communication principles in *Functions of the Executive*, which reflected his experience and thinking. These principles included the following ideas:

- It is important that channels of communication are well known and defined.
- Objective authority requires leadership to channel communication to every member of the organization.
- Lines of communication must be as direct and short as possible.
- A complete line of communication should be used.
- Competence of persons within the communication processes must be adequate.
- Lines of communication should not be interrupted.
- Every communication should be authenticated.[15]

The Humanistic Management Approach

The Human Relations Movement

Elton Mayo

George Elton Mayo (1880–1949) guided a famous series of experiments known as the Hawthorne Studies. These studies grew out of preliminary experiments at the Western Electric Hawthorne Works plant in Chicago, from 1924 to 1927, on the effect of light on productivity. In short, those experiments showed no connection between productivity and the amount of illumination. However, from this work, researchers began to wonder what kind of changes would influence output. The work of Mayo and his research colleagues has contributed to organization development in terms of human relations and motivation theory.

In one of the studies, Mayo wanted to find out what effect fatigue had on the productivity of workers. He took five women from the telephone relay assembly line, segregated them from the rest of the factory, and made frequent changes to their working conditions. Mayo changed the hours in the workweek, the hours in the workday, the number of rest periods, and the time of the lunch hour. On occasion, the workers were returned to their original, harder working conditions. Throughout the experiments, an observer recorded the actions of the workers and informed them about the experiment.

The results of the experiments showed that even when the conditions changed unfavorably, production increased. Rest periods were given and taken away, yet the production of telephone relays continued to rise gradually. Mayo and his colleagues concluded that the workers exercised a freedom that they did not have on the factory floor. They had formed a social environment that also included the observer who tracked their productivity. They socialized both at work and eventually outside the workplace. In short, when they were allowed to have a friendly relationship with their supervisor, they felt happier at work. When they were allowed to discuss changes prior to them occurring, they felt part of a team and were extremely loyal to the plant.[16] In another study, Mayo took a group of fourteen men and segregated them from the work force. The men were given the opportunity to earn more money if they produced more. The assumption of the researchers was that the workers would adopt a new role apart from the soldiering that existed among plant employees and produce more since it was in their best interest. The workers' productivity did not increase, however, and it became apparent that the values of the informal group appeared to be more powerful than pay incentives.[17]

The power of the social setting and peer group dynamics became known as the **Hawthorne Effect**. The studies themselves produced the human relations school of management and subsequent ideologies of democratic management, such as participatory decision making, quality circles, and team building.

Abraham Maslow

Abraham Maslow (1908–1970) was a psychologist and leading exponent of humanistic psychology. Born in Brooklyn, New York, and educated at the City College of New York and the University of Wisconsin, Maslow spent most of his teaching career at Brandeis University. Maslow developed the need hierarchy, provided in Exhibit 2.4, suggesting that there are five sets of goals that may be called basic needs. These are:

- Physiological or basic needs: oxygen, food, water, and shelter.
- Safety needs: safety from physical harm, financial security, and secure employment.

- Belonging needs: a sense of being accepted by others and being loved by one's family.
- Self-esteem needs: a stable, firmly based, high level of self-respect, and respect from others in order to feel satisfied, self-confident, and valuable.
- Self-actualization needs: described by Maslow as a person's need to be and do that which the person was born to do. It is their "calling."

Maslow arranged these into a series of different levels or the order of importance of these basic needs, which is visually displayed in Exhibit 2.4. Man's basic needs are physiological, for example, hunger, thirst, sleep, etc. When these needs are satisfied they are replaced by safety needs, reflecting his desire for protection against danger or deprivation. They in turn, when satisfied, are replaced by the need for love or belonging to, which are functions of man's desire to belong to a group, to give and receive friendship, and to associate happily with people. When these needs have been satisfied, there are then esteem needs (i.e., the desire for self-respect), which are affected by a person's reputation and the need for recognition and appreciation. Finally, individuals have a need for self-actualization or a desire for self-fulfillment, which is an urge by individuals for self-development, creativity, and job satisfaction.

Maslow's concepts were originally offered as general explanations of human behavior but quickly became a significant contribution to workplace motivation theory. They are still used by managers today to understand, predict, and influence employee motivation.

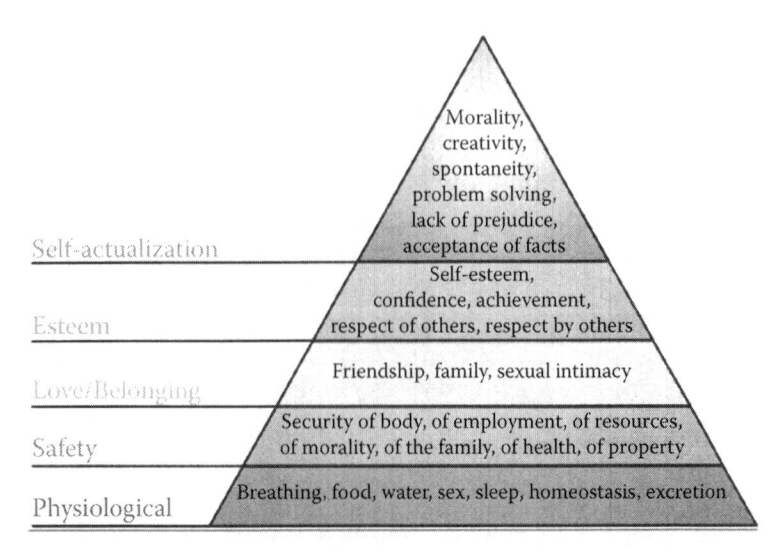

Self-actualization	Morality, creativity, spontaneity, problem solving, lack of prejudice, acceptance of facts
Esteem	Self-esteem, confidence, achievement, respect of others, respect by others
Love/Belonging	Friendship, family, sexual intimacy
Safety	Security of body, of employment, of resources, of morality, of the family, of health, of property
Physiological	Breathing, food, water, sex, sleep, homeostasis, excretion

Exhibit 2.4 Maslow's Hierarchy of Needs.

Maslow was one of the first people to be associated with the humanistic, as opposed to a task-based, approach to management. As people have increasingly come to be appreciated as a key resource in successful companies, Maslow's model has remained a valuable management concept.[18]

Behavioral Systems

Kurt Lewin

Kurt Lewin (1890–1947) was born in Germany and received his formal training in psychology in Berlin. During World War I, Lewin served as a lieutenant in the German army and was wounded in action. After the war, he returned to the Psychological Institute in Berlin but eventually came to the United States in 1932 as a visiting professor at Stanford University. Lewin left Stanford for Cornell and eventually settled down at the University of Iowa from 1935 to 1944. After Lewin moved from Iowa, he established and directed the Research Center for Group Dynamics at the Massachusetts Institute of Technology.

Lewin is most noted for his development of the field theory. The field theory is the proposition that human behavior is the function of both the person and the environment. Behavior is related both to one's personal characteristics and to the social situation in which one finds oneself. Lewin thought of motives as goal-directed forces. He believed

> that our behavior is purposeful; we live in a psychological reality or life space that includes not only those parts of our physical and social environment that are important to us but also imagined states that do not currently exist.[19]

Lewin developed **force field analysis**, a technique often used in decision making. Force field analysis is a management technique for diagnosing situations. It may be useful when looking at the variables involved in determining effectiveness of and when planning and implementing a change in management program. Lewin assumes that in any situation there are both driving and restraining forces that influence any change that may occur.

Driving forces are those forces affecting a situation that are pushing in a particular direction; they tend to initiate a change and keep it going. In terms of improving productivity in a work group, pressure from a supervisor, incentive earnings, and competition may be examples of driving forces.

Restraining forces are forces acting to restrain or decrease the driving forces. Apathy, hostility, and poor maintenance of equipment may be examples of restraining forces against increased production. Equilibrium is reached when the sum of the driving forces equals the sum of the restraining forces. This equilibrium, or present level of productivity, can be raised or lowered by changes in the relationship between the driving and the restraining forces.

For illustration (Exhibit 2.5), let us consider the dilemma of a new police sergeant who takes over a traffic unit of six deputies and finds that productivity is high but the human resources have been drained. The former shift sergeant had upset the equilibrium by increasing the driving forces (that is, keeping continual pressure on the subordinate patrolmen to write more tickets) and thus achieving increases in output in the short run. By doing this, however, new restraining forces developed, such as increased hostility and antagonism. At the time of the former sergeant's departure, the restraining forces were beginning to increase, and the results manifested themselves in turnover, absenteeism, and other restraining forces, which lowered productivity shortly after the new sergeant arrived. Now the new sergeant faces a new equilibrium at a significantly lower productivity.

Let us assume that our new sergeant decides not to increase the driving forces but to reduce the restraining forces. The sergeant may do this by taking time away from the usual production operation and engaging in problem solving and training and development.

If commitment to objectives and technical know-how of the group are increased, they may become new driving forces and, along with the elimination of the hostility and the apathy that were restraining forces, will now tend to move the balance to a higher level of output.

Police sergeants and lieutenants are often in a position in which they must consider not only output but also intervening variables and not only short-term but also long-term goals. It can be seen that force field analysis provides a framework that is useful in diagnosing these interrelationships.

The Human Resources Perspective

Douglas McGregor

Douglas McGregor (1904–1964) in his book, *The Human Side of Enterprise*,[20] examined theories on behavior of individuals at work. He formulated two theoretical models that are referred to as Theory X and Theory Y.

Driving Forces	Restraining Forces
Autocratic control of shift sergeant pressures patrolmen to produce more traffic tickets. →	← Police officers develop animosity toward shift sergeant
	← Absenteeism increases, productivity decreases.
New sergeant places less emphasis on increased production of traffic tickets. →	
New sergeant places more emphasis on public safety training. →	

Exhibit 2.5 The use of force field analysis regarding the decision to issue more traffic citations.

Theory X Assumptions

- The average human being has an inherent dislike of work and will avoid it if possible.
- Because of their dislike for work, most people must be coerced, controlled and directed, and threatened with punishment to get them to put forth adequate effort toward the achievement of organizational objectives.
- The average human prefers to be directed, dislikes responsibility, has relatively little ambition, and wants security above all.

Theory Y Assumptions

- The expenditure of physical and mental effort in work is as natural as play or rest.
- External control and the threat of punishment are not the only means for bringing about effort toward organizational objectives. People will exercise self-direction and self-control in the service of objectives to which they are committed.
- Commitment to objectives is a function of the rewards associated with their achievement.
- The average man learns, under proper conditions, not only to accept but to seek responsibility.
- The capacity to exercise a relatively high degree of imagination, ingenuity, and creativity in the solution of organizational problems is widely, not narrowly, distributed in the population.
- Under the conditions of modern industrial life, the intellectual potentialities of the average man are only partially utilized.

McGregor's assumptions have great implications for the operations of police agencies. Police managers who consider their subordinates as lazy and unmotivated may view their primary function as one needing to exercise constant authority over personnel. They may perceive coercion as the only method of achieving desired results because Theory X subordinates do not agree that end goals are desirable. Other police managers, however, may see promise in the application of McGregor's Theory Y in practices such as decentralization and delegation, job enlargement, participation in decision-making in organizations, consultative management, and innovative approaches to performance evaluation that involved self-appraisal.

McGregor's theories persuaded managers at the Pulaski, Tennessee, police department to videotape employees at their daily work as they performed routine law enforcement activities. It was believed that a media portrayal of the "work itself" would serve as a powerful internal motivational force that the department could capitalize upon for widespread, long-term organizational benefit. Over a nine-month period, a reserve officer took video of police department personnel actions, ranging from field events to office work, from actual operations to organized events of fellowship.

The final production was shown to the police department employees and their families at the annual holiday party. The employees immediately displayed positive reactions as the tape played. Afterwards, managers presented all officers with a personal copy of the "video yearbook" and told them that it served as tangible proof of their significance and importance to the agency. In essence, the tape provided motivational support from the managers and reaffirmed the employees' importance to the agency.[21]

Rensis Likert

Rensis Likert (1903–1981) conducted research on human behavior within organizations, particularly in the industrial situation. He examined different types of organizations and leadership styles, and he asserted that to achieve maximum profitability, good labor relations, and high productivity, every organization must make optimum use of their human assets.

Likert contended that organizations that make the greatest use of the human capacity were those in which effective work groups were linked together in overlapping patterns. This **linking pin** pattern occurs when one person serves simultaneously in two groups: a member of one group (a higher group in the hierarchy) and the leader of another group (a lower group in the hierarchy).

In his book *New Patterns of Management*,[22] published in 1961, Likert identified four different management systems or climates: (1) exploitive-authoritative, (2) benevolent-authoritative, (3) consultative, and (4) participative groups.

1. The exploitive-authoritative system exists in organizations where:
    - Decisions are imposed on subordinates
    - Motivation is characterized by threats
    - High levels of management have great responsibilities, but lower levels have virtually none
    - There is very little communication and no joint teamwork

2. The benevolent-authoritative system occurs where:
    - Leadership is characterized by a condescending form of master-servant trust
    - Motivation is mainly by rewards
    - Managerial personnel feel responsibility, but lower levels do not
    - There is little communication and relatively little teamwork

Introduction to Management Theory 57

3. The consultative system refers to:
   - Leadership by superiors who have substantial but not complete trust in their subordinates; where motivation is by rewards and some involvement
   - A high proportion of personnel, especially those at the higher levels, feels responsibility for achieving organization goals
   - Some communication and a moderate amount of teamwork.
4. The participative group system exists in organizations where:
   - Leadership is by superiors who have complete confidence in their subordinates
   - Motivation is by economic rewards based on goals that have been set in participation
   - Personnel at all levels feel real responsibility for the organizational goals
   - There is much communication and a substantial amount of cooperative teamwork

This fourth system is ideal for the profit-oriented and human-concerned organization. Likert suggests that all adopt this system to achieve the maximum rewards for the organization. When converting an organization, four main features of effective management must be put into practice:

- The motivation to work must be fostered by modern principles and techniques and not by the old system of rewards and threats.
- Employees must be seen as people who have their own needs, desires, and values, and their self-worth must be maintained or enhanced.
- An organization of tightly knit and highly effective work groups must be built up that are committed to achieving the objectives of the organization.
- Supportive relationships must exist within each work group. These are characterized not by actual support, but by mutual respect.

Systems Approach

Peter Drucker

Peter Drucker (1909–2005) was born in Vienna, Austria, and educated in Austria and England. In 1937, with the outbreak of World War II, Drucker left Europe and came to America where he worked in several places including banking and academic fields. From 1950 to 1971, Drucker was professor of management at the Graduate Business School of New York University. From 1971 to 2002, he served as Clarke Professor of Social Science and Management at Claremont Graduate School in Claremont, California. In 1987, the Claremont Graduate Management Center was renamed after Drucker.[23]

Drucker introduced the phrase **management by objectives** (MBO) in 1954, and American businesses began embracing the notion with what often amounted to evangelical dedication. During the 1960s and 1970s, MBO was the most fashionable of all management practices. Many police agencies adopted some form of MBO, which, as Drucker originally proposed, asks managers to focus on results or outputs.

MBO was viewed as an effective planning, control, and development system. MBO is a bottom-up, process-oriented, and team-oriented planning system. Objectives are defined as being relatively few and long term in their focus. Goals are defined as being relatively more numerous and short-term in their focus (Exhibit 2.6).

The first phase of the MBO process is planning in order to identify a few critical result areas that will produce the vast majority of results. Some examples of key result areas include staff development and training, staff morale, anticipation of competition, and customer relationships.

The second phase of MBO is execution. The process for implementing bottom-up MBO is: people in the smallest units, usually teams, initiate a set of written performance objectives. The team objectives are process oriented (identify what is to be done to improve the way jobs are performed) The objectives are discussed by associates (among themselves in self-managing teams), followed by agreement on the objectives to which everyone can then become

Steps in the MBO Process

- Describe roles and missions: "Who does what?" Goals are established jointly and agreed upon in advance.
- Define key result areas.
- Identify indicators of effectiveness: "What is good performance?"
- Set objectives with a bottom-up process, as described above.
- Decide on task-oriented and process-oriented action plans.
- The team monitors progress: information, reports, conversations, communication (constant, open, informal).
- Communication is the grease for the MBO wheel; it keeps everyone running smoothly. Teams must continually communicate to everyone (management included) on progress toward achieving their objectives, and management must communicate with everyone on how the station is doing in meeting its objectives (financial and rating information included). Use newsletters, wall charts, memos.
- Everyone (management and teams) evaluates results, makes necessary adjustments, and sets new objectives. MBO must be a continuous process; it must be part of an on-going system.
- A final mutual review of objectives and performance takes place. This sets the stage for the determination of objectives for the next time period. The objectives in an MBO system must be inextricably linked to the company's mission statement. Every objective must help accomplish the overall mission, then managers must "manage to the mission."

Exhibit 2.6 Adapted from Peter F. Drucker, *The Practice of Management*. HarperCollins Publishers, 2006.

Introduction to Management Theory

committed. Then there are periodic reviews by the team itself to determine to what extent the objectives have been met or exceeded, and the results are communicated to management.

MBO is best used as a system that assists people in an organization plan their objectives for an upcoming period. Managers can use the system with their supervisors, and supervisors can use the system with their associates. Objectives are set for the coming year and then updated and reviewed on a quarterly basis. Goals (short term, relatively more numerous, and activity oriented) are reviewed at least monthly. Objectives and goals are prioritized and performed accordingly. Finally, objectives and goals must be flexible so that they can be changed when conditions change.

Drucker points out that the purpose of a business is not properly defined as making a profit but as creating a customer. If an organization sets its objectives in such a way that it continually creates customers, then profits will come. If people are given time to get accustomed to using an MBO system and use it properly for planning and control, the system can serve any size organization well.

W. Edwards Deming

Dr. W. Edwards Deming (1900–1993), born in Sioux City, Iowa, earned his bachelor's degree in physics from the University of Wyoming and his doctorate in mathematical physics from Yale University. From 1928 to 1939, Deming worked as a mathematical physicist for the U.S. Department of Agriculture. This work first exposed Deming to the theories and practices of statistical control. From 1939 to 1945, Deming worked extensively with the Bureau of Census and the U.S. weapons industry. During this period, he developed his basic quality management system.

Deming developed his "system of profound knowledge" as a comprehensive theory for management by which every aspect of life may be improved. He encouraged the Japanese to adopt a systematic approach to problem solving, which later became known as the plan-do-check-act cycle. Repetitive completion of the plan-do-check-act cycle keeps the organization constantly moving on the path of continuous quality improvement.

Deming suggested that every organization should promote continuous quality improvement by implementing fourteen management principles:

1. Create constancy of purpose toward improvement of product and service, with the aim to become competitive, to stay in business, and to provide jobs.
2. Adopt the new philosophy. We are in a new economic age. Western management must awaken to the challenge, must learn their responsibilities, and take on leadership for change.

3. Cease dependence on inspection to achieve quality. Eliminate the need for inspection on a mass basis by building quality into the product in the first place.
4. End the practice of awarding business on the basis of price tag. Instead, minimize total cost. Move toward a single supplier for any one item, on a long-term relationship of loyalty and trust.
5. Improve constantly and forever the system of production and service, to improve quality and productivity and thus constantly decrease costs.
6. Institute training on the job.
7. Institute leadership. The aim of supervision should be to help people and machines to do a better job. Supervision of management is in need of overhaul as well as supervision of production workers.
8. Drive out fear, so that everyone may work effectively for the company.
9. Break down barriers between departments. People in research, design, sales, and production must work as a team to foresee problems of production and use that may be encountered with the product or service.
10. Eliminate slogans, exhortations, and targets for the work force asking for zero defects and new levels of productivity. Such exhortations only create adversarial relationships, as the bulk of the causes of low quality and low productivity belong to the system and thus lie beyond the power of the work force.
11. a. Eliminate work standards (quotas) on the factory floor. Substitute leadership.
    b. Eliminate management by objective. Eliminate management by numbers, numerical goals. Substitute leadership.
12. a. Remove barriers that rob the hourly worker of his right to pride of workmanship. The responsibility of supervisors must be changed from sheer numbers to quality.
    b. Remove barriers that rob people in management and in engineering of their right to pride of workmanship. This means, *inter alia*, abolishment of the annual merit rating and of management by objective.
13. Institute a vigorous program of education and self-improvement.
14. Put everybody in the company to work to accomplish the transformation. The transformation is everybody's job.[24]

Deming is considered the father of total quality management (TQM). TQM is an organizational approach to customer satisfaction involving customers, people, and the continuous improvement of processes. In Chapter 6, we will exam quality management in depth and explore how TQM characteristics have been implemented in police agencies in order to improve service to the community.

Questions in Review

1. Why is Frederick Taylor considered the father of scientific management?
2. What is the purpose of a Gantt chart?
3. What are the three types of authority noted by Max Weber?
4. Explain the "Hawthorne Effect."
5. Describe Abraham Maslow's hierarchy of needs.
6. Prepare a force field analysis for the case study provided at the beginning of the chapter.
7. Would you prefer to work for a Theory X or Theory Y organization? Why?

End Notes

1 John P. Kotter, *A Force For Change* (New York: Free Press, 1990).
2 Marvin R. Weisbord, *Productive Workplaces* (San Francisco: Jossey-Bass, 1987).
3 Robert Kanigel, "Frederick Taylor's Apprenticeship," *The Wilson Quarterly* (Summer, 1996).
4 Daniel Nelson, *Frederick Taylor and the Rise of Scientific Management* (Madison, WI: University of Wisconsin Press, 1980).
5 Elizabeth G. Hayward, *A Classified Guide to the Frederick Wilson Taylor Collection* (Hoboken, NJ: Samuel C. Williams Library, Stevens Institute of Technology, 1996).
6 Chuck Wexler, Mary Ann Wycoff, and Craig Fischer. *Good to Great Policing: Application of Business Management Principles in the Public Sector* (Washington, DC: Police Executive Research Forum, June 2007).
7 Frank and Lillian Gilbreth, *Fatigue Study* (Easton: Hive Publishing, Co., 1973; reprint of 1916 ed.), p. 149.
8 Nelson, p. 11.
9 Gilbreth, p. 150.
10 Dennis Lindsey, "Law Enforcement Organizations Must Learn to Manage Fatigue and the Risks Associated with It," in *FBI Law Enforcement Bulletin*, Vol. 76, No. 8 (August 2007), pp. 1–7.
11 Henri Fayol, *General and Industrial Management*, translated by Constance Storrs (London: Sir Issac Pitman, 1949).
12 Rose Dunn, *Haiman's Healthcare Management*, 7th ed. (Chicago, IL: Health Administration Press, 2002).
13 Pauline Graham (ed.), *Mary Parker Follett: Prophet of Management* (Boston, MA: Harvard Business School Press, 1995).
14 William R. Wolf, *The Basic Barnard* (New York: New York State School of Industrial and Labor Relations, Cornell University, 1974).

15 Chester I. Barnard, *The Functions of the Executive* (Cambridge, MA: Harvard University Press, 1968).
16 Fritz J. Roethlisberger and William J. Dickson, *Management and the Worker* (Cambridge, MA: Harvard University Press, 1939).
17 Roethlisberger and Dickson (1939), p. 522.
18 Abraham Maslow, *Motivation and Personality*, 3rd ed. (New York: Harper & Row, 1987).
19 Abraham Tesser, *Advanced Social Psychology* (New York: McGraw-Hill, 1995).
20 Douglas McGregor, *The Human Side of Enterprise* (New York: McGraw-Hill, 1960).
21 John White, "The Work Itself as Motivator," *FBI Law Enforcement Bulletin*, Vol. 70, No. 2 (February 2001), pp. 7–10.
22 Rensis Likert, *New Patterns of Management* (New York: McGraw-Hill, 1961).
23 Peter F. Drucker, *Adventure of a Bystander* (New York: Harper & Row, 1979).
24 W. Edwards Deming, *Out of Crisis* (Cambridge, MA: M.I.T. 1986).

Suggested Additional References and Links to the Web

1. *The Goal of Management: From MBO to Deming to Project Management and Beyond* is a 2004 white paper prepared by Rodney Brim, PhD, CEO Performance Solutions Technology. This document provides an excellent detailed examination of the history and evolution of management by objectives and Deming's quality improvement. http://www.managepro.com/pdfs/FromMBOtoPM.pdf
2. *Managing Innovation in Policing: The Untapped Potential of the Middle Manager* is a 1995 National Institute of Justice Research Preview prepared by Jeremy Travis, Director NIJ, which concludes that middle management's power to affect change can be harnessed to advance community policing objectives by including those managers in planning, acknowledging their legitimate self-interests, and motivating their investment in long-range solutions that enhance community safety and security. http://www.ncjrs.gov/pdffiles/midman.pdf
3. MindTools.com is a Web page that provides information about leadership, team management, problem solving, personal productivity, and team-working skills. For this chapter on management theory, we suggest you check out the following: Force Field Analysis, http://www.mindtools.com/pages/article/newTED_06.htm and the Plan-Do-Check-Act, http://www.mindtools.com/CXCCorporateTour/PDCA.php

Operational Management of a Police Agency

3

Key Individuals, Concepts, and Issues

Citizen advisory board
Kansas City Study
Differential response to calls
Decoy and sting operations
Spans of management
Community policing
Job design
Workplace culture

Robert Peel
Directed patrol
Marvin Wolfgang
Vertical differentiation
Structural design
Organizational development
Job enrichment

Definitions

Differential response to call: Calls to police are responded to based on how they are classified.

Directed patrol: Patrol officers are given specific directions to follow when they are not responding to calls.

Organizational development: An emerging applied behavioral science discipline that seeks to improve organizations through planned, systemic, long-range efforts focused on the organization's culture and its human and social response.

Span of management: The number of persons that a manager directly supervises.

Split force patrolling: A portion of the patrol division is designed to handle all calls dispatched to patrol units. The remaining units are given directed patrol assignments that are not interrupted except for serious emergencies.

Undercover operations: A form of investigation where the officer assumes a different identity in order to obtain certain information.

Chapter Objectives

After reading this chapter your should be able to:

1. Explain the science of organizational development.
2. Explain the concept of span of management.

3. Discuss the differences between directed patrol and differential response to calls.

Case Study 3.1

You are appointed the chief of police of a midwestern city. The department has experienced high personnel turnover and high absenteeism, and generally the department morale is very low. What would be your first steps to change the department?

CITIZEN INPUT ON POLICE MANAGEMENT

In an effort to better understand the community, Police Chief Michael of Portland, Maine, in 2000 formed a citizen advisory board that was an extension of the community policing initiative established by the Portland Police Department in 1994. Since then, community policing centers have been created with civilian coordinators and officers assigned to specific neighborhoods. Portland has grown in its diversity in the past few years. For example, there are at least twenty-eight different languages spoken by students in the Portland public schools.

The chief's purpose in establishing the board was to have more community involvement in the day-to-day operations of the police department. Unlike citizen review boards, which focus on allegations of police misconduct, the new board was to provide input on the day-to-day operations of the department. None of the appointed members had any prior police experience. During the first six months, the members were taken through the department's budget process, its organization chart, recruitment policies, and internal affairs. The chief stated that the members of the board could provide input to any information and were free to discuss their impressions with the public. The chief stated: "We have opened the door to civilian review."[1]

Introduction

In this chapter, we will examine the operational management of a police agency. One of the primary goals of the chapter is to acquaint the readers with the recent innovations in the operational management of a police agency. Included are recent innovations that examine alternatives to the traditional random routine police patrols and rapid response to 911 calls, alternatives to shift work, and the movement based on job design and enrichment.

Basic Functions of a Police Agency

The traditional functions of a police agency include random patrols, rapid response to citizens' 911 calls, and retroactive investigation by detectives of past crimes. These functions are being replaced or implemented by proactive tactics that involve the use of tactical operations, decoy operations, undercover operations, sting operations, and code enforcement teams. One of the basic assumptions of policing since the days of Robert Peel has been that the presence of police deters crime. The related assumption is that increasing the number of police officers on patrol will decrease crime. As will be noted later in this chapter, beginning in the 1970s, researchers have questioned the validity of those two major assumptions.

Patrol Operations

Police patrol operations are often referred to as the backbone of policing. Patrol operations involve the activities and role of officers assigned to patrol duties and the various methods of doing patrol work including motorized, bicycle, mounted, and foot patrols. Traditionally, the police officer at the beginning of his or her shift receives the keys and patrol car from the officer who used it on the previous tour. The officer then patrols a designated geographic area as part of a random routine patrol, also known as a "preventive patrol." During the patrol, the officer receives response calls from a police dispatcher. Normally the calls will require the officer to go to a specific place within the patrol area and perform police work as required. The police work generated by the calls usually involves making an arrest, providing first aid, breaking up a fight or disturbance, or taking a crime report. If the calls concern a reported crime, the officer will generally make a preliminary investigation and then refer the case to a detective, who conducts a follow-up investigation. When the officer is finished with the call, he resumes patrol until requested to respond to another call.

How effective is preventive traditional policing using the random routine patrol, rapid response to 911, and retroactive investigation of past crimes? It is difficult to evaluate the effectiveness of police work. If a city has a low crime rate, it may mean that it has an effective police force, less criminogenically inclined citizens, or an ineffective police force that does not have the ability to detect crime and whose citizens fail to report crime because of their lack of confidence in the police force. In addition, the police do not control all the variables that produce or reduce crime (e.g., social disorganization of the communities, poverty, and economic problems). Despite the problems in evaluating police effectiveness, the systemic research on the issue has influenced major changes in the manner in which police departments operate.[2]

The Kansas City Study was the first major research project aimed at evaluating the effectiveness of random routine patrolling. With the support of the Police Foundation, the Kansas City Police Department, in 1972 and 1973, conducted a year-long experiment to test its effectiveness. The experiment was both influential and controversial.

Prior to the start of the experiment, researchers collected data on reported crimes, arrests, traffic accidents, response times, citizen attitudes, and victimization for each of fifteen patrol beats in the South Patrol Division in Kansas City. There were twenty-four beats in the South Patrol Division, but nine were eliminated as unrepresentative of the area. Of the fifteen beats under the study, five (control beats) were assigned to a control group with no changes in normal patrol staffing or tactics. In five other beats (reactive beats), all preventive patrolling was eliminated. Outside patrol units handled calls in those beats and left the beat once the calls were handled. In the final five beats (proactive beats), the level of preventive patrolling was increased two to three times the normal level. If random routine patrolling is effective in reducing crime, you would expect to see little or no change in the control beats, an increase in crime in the reactive beats, and a reduction in crime in the proactive beats.

The Kansas City Study failed to demonstrate that adding or taking away police patrols makes any difference regarding crime within the community. The researchers concluded that decreasing or increasing routine preventive patrol within the range tested had no effect on crime, citizen fear of crime, community attitudes toward the police on the delivery of police service, police response time, or traffic accidents.[3] George Kelling, director of the research, stated that it would be a mistake to conclude that patrol was completely unnecessary or that police departments could manage with fewer resources.[4] According to Samuel Walker, the study seems to indicate that possibilities exist for more flexible and creative approaches to the use of police.[5] The Kansas City Study created questions regarding the most effective ways to use police officers and set the stage for the academic study of policing.

Using a design similar to that used in Kansas City, the Newark Foot Patrol Experiment was conducted in 1978–1979.[6] Some beats received additional foot patrols, other beats received less, and a third group of beats was used as control beats. The researchers concluded that additional foot patrols did not reduce serious crime and that generally crime levels are not affected by foot patrols at a significant level. The different levels of foot patrol did, however, have a significant effect on citizen attitudes. Citizens were aware of the different levels. Residents in beats with increased foot patrols consistently opined that crime problems diminished more in their neighborhoods than in other neighborhoods. The reduced fear of crime was also associated with more positive attitudes toward the police, including police activities that were not related to foot patrol. Foot patrol officers also reported more positive attitudes about citizens. As noted by Samuel Walker, foot patrol officers ranked helping the public as the second most important part of their job, whereas motor patrol officers ranked it fifth.[7]

Directed Patrol

Directed patrol is an alternative to traditional random routine patrolling. In directed patrolling, the patrol officers are given specific directions to follow when they are not responding to calls. For example, the precinct commander may prepare a list of directed patrol assignments that the officers can concentrate on when they are not responding to calls. The list is compiled based on a review of the precinct's crime statistics, complaints from the community, and other data.

Split Force Patrolling

One of the problems with directed patrolling is that calls for service often interrupt the performance of directed patrol assignments. Under split force patrolling, a portion of the force is designed to handle all calls dispatched to patrol units. The remaining portion of the patrol unit is assigned to directed patrol assignments, and those assignments are not interrupted except for serious emergencies. The Houston, Texas Police Department adopted a form of split force patrolling with their high-intensity patrols. The high-intensity patrol officers conduct highly visible patrols in specific areas to emphasize police presence. They do not respond to 911 calls except in serious emergencies.[8]

Differential Response to Calls

The differential response to calls approach rejects the traditional approach that the police should respond as quickly as possible to all calls. The differential response approach involves the screening of 911 calls and responding differently to each type of call. Generally, the calls are classified into three categories: (1) those that require immediate response, (2) those in which the response may be delayed, and (3) those that require no officer response. In the third category, the follow-up may be by telephone, by mail, or by having the caller come to the station or substation.

An evaluation experiment was conducted in Greensboro, North Carolina. Slightly over half of the calls (53.6%) required immediate response by a police officer and about 20% did not require an officer response. The Greensboro citizens expressed a high degree of satisfaction with the differential response.[9] Researchers generally agree that citizen expectations are not entirely fixed but are dependent to a great degree on what the police tell them to expect.[10]

Another alternative method of handling low-priority calls is to use non-sworn personnel to handle those calls not requiring the presence of a sworn officer. Community service officers are used in many departments to handle many of the routine assignments. The use of community service officers frees sworn officers for more critical tasks. As noted in the section discussing job design, there are some negative effects in removing the sworn police officer from these duties.

Investigation Process

After patrolling, the next major crime control process is the investigation of reported crimes by detectives. Under traditional policing operations, patrol officers complete initial reports, and then the cases are assigned to detectives who are expected to conduct follow-up investigations. The traditional assumptions are that the detectives, by virtue of their expertise and lack of responsibility for responding to citizen calls, will be able to solve cases.

The Rand Institute evaluated the effectiveness of the criminal investigation process. The researchers surveyed one hundred and fifty large police agencies and made site visits to twenty-five police departments. The researchers concluded that the most important determinant in identifying the offender was based on information obtained by the patrol officer, not the detective. If the patrol officers did not identify the offenders, the detectives were not likely to identify them either. The researchers concluded that detectives spent the majority of their time on tasks that were unrelated to the solving of crimes. Detectives, however, were important to the preparation of the cases for trial by ensuring that proper reports were completed, witnesses were interviewed, and other tasks were performed.[11]

When the National Advisory Commission on Criminal Justice Standards and Goals published their report, they recommended that detectives be assigned only to very serious or complex preliminary examinations and that most preliminary investigations be accomplished by the use of patrol officers.[12] In 1977, the Law Enforcement Assistance Administration proposed the managing criminal investigations (MCI) concept. Under MCI, the role of patrol officers would be expanded to include investigative responsibilities, and a new method would be used to manage police investigations by including solvability factors, case screening, case enhancements, and factors regarding police and prosecutor coordination.

The MCI concept also established a system to grade cases as to their solvability. This system includes (1) availability of witnesses, (2) any named or known suspects, (3) whether a suspect can be identified, and (4) whether the complainant will cooperate in the investigation and later prosecution. Each of four factors is given a numerical grade. The total score is used to make an estimation of the solvability of the crime. One goal of the MCI is to maximize investigators' time by assigning them only to those cases that are important and that they have a high probability of solving.[13]

Marvin Wolfgang's research on predatory street crime revealed that only a small percentage of the population is responsible for most of the predatory street crime in the United States. Based on this research, many police agencies have adopted repeat offender programs that identify individuals who have committed similar offenses in the past and that are considered as career offenders. Next, the police consider those individuals as possible targets of investigations when new offenses are committed.[14] In addition, police agencies have established special career criminal investigative units that can enhance the investigation of offenses considered to have been committed by a career criminal.

AN ANALYSIS OF VARIABLES AFFECTING THE CLEARANCE OF HOMICIDES

In a recent study released by the National Institute of Justice, researchers concluded that police practices and procedures when investigating a murder can have a greater impact on whether the case gets closed rather than the circumstances of the crime.[15] The researchers examined the percentage of murders that end in arrest in four unidentified large American cities. The lead researcher, Charles Welford, noted that despite the plummeting homicide clearance rates for criminal homicide in the past thirty years (from 94% in 1961 to 67% in 1996), the level of clearance in some departments remained stable. He concluded that the stability suggests that other, persistent factors are affecting police ability to clear homicide cases.[16]

The findings demonstrating that the police make a difference run counter to the Rand study in the 1970s that indicated that clearances by detectives seemed to be related more to case characteristics than to things the detectives did. The researchers singled out fifty-one characteristics that were closely associated with clearance in homicide cases. Fourteen of the characteristics were factors that the police had no control over such as the victim's race, the location of the murder, and the presence of witnesses. The remaining thirty-seven characteristics were related to investigative practices. For example, the case is more likely to be solved if three or four detectives are assigned to it rather than just one and if the investigators arrived at the scene within thirty minutes of being notified of the crime. In addition, following up on witness information made it twice as likely that the case would be cleared. Listed below are some of the fifty-one characteristics:

- number of detectives assigned to the case
- time detectives arrived on the scene
- crime scene described in case report
- witness information followed up
- weapon found at scene
- crime scene measured

Decoy and Sting Operations

One of the primary purposes of patrolling is to prevent crime through the visible presence of police. Decoy operations, however, attempt to hide the presence of police. Decoy operations by the police have increased in the past few years. The operations may take several forms including blending and decoy. Blending occurs when the officers are dressed in civilian clothes and try to blend into an area and patrol it on foot or in unmarked police cars. Blending operations generally target an area where a significant amount of crime occurs or involve following particular people who appear to be potential criminals. In decoy operations, the officers dress and assume the roles of others. For example, an officer plays the role of a drunk or other defenseless person in order to apprehend a criminal trying to take advantage of the defenseless person.

In recent years, sting operations have also become a major law enforcement technique. One of the most popular types of sting operations involves the police renting a storefront and putting out the word that they were willing to buy any stolen property. Stakeout operations generally involve the practice of a group of heavily armed officers hiding in an area or a store or building waiting for an impending holdup. Stakeouts are extremely labor intensive and are also controversial.

An undercover operation is a form of investigation in which the investigator assumes a different identity in order to obtain information or achieve another investigatory purpose. Generally, the undercover investigator plays the role of another person.

Organizational Structure and Design

In studying the formal structure of an organization, we tend to focus on: (1) the formal relationship and (2) duties of personnel in the organization and (3) the set of formal rules, policies, procedures, and controls that serve to guide the behavior of its personnel.[17] Organizations are generally characterized as open or closed systems. While there are probably no entirely open or closed organizations, the labels open and closed are used to describe the extent to which an organization approximates one or the other. A closed organization sees little need for interaction with the external environment. The closed system view is that the organization has complete rationality, optimizes performances, is predictable, and exhibits internal efficiency and certainty.[18] Because the closed system view assumes that the organization is functional and all outcomes are predictable, the organization can ignore external changes such as political, technological, and economic. The open view is that the organization is not a closed system, but an open one that has many dynamic interactions with the larger society in which it is embedded. Generally, the open system seeks and continuously imports sources of energy. The open view or the interactive nature of policing is at the core of community policing. Organizational design generally focuses on two spatial levels of differentiation, vertical and horizontal.

Differentiation

Vertical differentiation is based on levels of authority or positions holding formal power within the organization. For example, an organizational chart that shows the chief at the top and the officers at the bottom would be an example of vertical differentiation between the chief and the officers. Horizontal differentiation may be based on activity (e.g., patrol division and detective division) by clientele (e.g., senior-citizen detail and gang squad) by geography (e.g., Precinct 1 or 2) by time (e.g., day and night shifts) or by process.

The level of complexity within a police agency is determined by the amount of horizontal and vertical differentiation that exists within the organization.[19] In police agencies, the differentiation process generally occurs in two basic ways. The first is the synthesis approach, which focuses on combining tasks into larger and larger sets of tasks. This approach is often referred to as the "bottom-up" approach. The synthesis approach is often used by agencies that are declining in size with the need to consolidate jobs or units.

The second approach, the analysis approach, considers the overall work of the agency from the top and splits the work assignments into increasingly more specialized tasks as one moves down the organization from the top to the bottom. The latter approach is often referred to as the "top-down" approach. The top-down approach is often used in growing organizations because it is easy to visualize the sets of tasks to be accomplished and to break those sets into subsets.

Spans of Management

Under traditional management concepts, the principle of hierarchy requires that each lower level of an organization be supervised by a higher level. The term "span of control" is a concept that recognizes that there are limitations on potential and the importance of the principle of hierarchy. The span of control is the number of subordinates an administrator can personally supervise effectively. Decisions regarding span of control directly influence the required levels of management in an organization. Generally, seven is accepted as the maximum number of persons that one person may effectively supervise. The term span of management is currently being used to replace the span of control. Span of management is broader than span of control and considers factors that relate to an individual's capacity to directly supervise the activities of others (e.g., the manager's experience, ability, and level of energy).

Some police agencies have narrow spans of management, which result in tall structures and many levels of management. Others are relatively flat, with wider spans of management. Taller organizations tend to be more complex and generally are slower to react because of the number of different levels present within the chain of command. To be successful, tall organizations must develop policies and procedures that will overcome problems caused by the complexity of the organization.

Flat organizations will have shorter lines of communication between the top and bottom levels of the organization. Accordingly, the communications are more likely to be faster, and less chances for distortion are available. In addition, individuals working in organizations with flat structures tend to have higher morale and job satisfaction when compared to those in organizations with taller structures. Organizations with flat structures, however, tend to place more stress and pressures on supervisors and require high-caliber managers.

Structural Design

There are four basic structural designs or combinations thereof used in police agencies: line, line and staff, functional, and matrix. The oldest, simplest, and clearest form of organizational design is the line structure. With the line structure, authority flows from top to bottom in the organization, in an unbroken line. The term line comes from the military and is used to refer to units that were to be used to engage the enemy. Line is also used to refer to those police units that perform the work of the agency (e.g., patrol, traffic, and investigation). The line structure lacks supporting elements such as personnel, public relations, training, scientific analysis, or fiscal management. The line structure is typically found in small police departments.

The line and staff structure is the line structure with the addition of support elements such as personnel, public or media relations, training, etc. The addition of the staff elements provides expert advice to the line units in areas requiring special knowledge. It also relieves the line managers from performing some of the tasks such as training. Often the staff functions will be subdivided into support and administrative staff services. Support services would be services such as communications and crime laboratories. Administrative staff services would include services such as personnel.

The functional structure is a line and staff structure that has been modified by the delegation of management authority to supervisors outside of their normal span of control (e.g., the captain in charge of the intelligence gathering may be in charge of intelligence officers in different units). The authority is organized along functional lines rather than by operational units. Each unit is responsible for some function or purpose of the police mission. Difficulties often arise when purposes overlap or conflict. For example, a patrol unit and a robbery task force may be responsible for the reduction of robberies in the same high crime area. In some cases, to prevent any conflict of authority, the officers in the special units are responsible to a variety of unit commanders.

The most complex form of organizational design is the matrix or grid structure. The essence of the matrix structure is in the assignment of members of functional areas to specific projects such as task forces. The matrix structure greatly increases the complexity of the organization and has only been successful in the short-term delivery of police services such as the 1981 task force in Atlanta that was responsible for the arrest of Wayne Williams for the murders of young males in that city.

Structure and Community Policing

As noted elsewhere in the text, community policing requires department-wide commitment to involve the citizens as partners in the crime control process and in efforts to improve the overall quality of life in the community. Community policing requires organizational restructuring. Where traditional structures of police organizations have historically followed the principles of hierarchy that are designed to control subordinates, community policing requires decentralization and shorter and flatter organizational structures.

Because community policing tends to empower the police officer with more discretion and more responsibility, the organization should be structured to provide for participatory decision-making and a collegial atmosphere. In addition, the organization must be designed to be open and sensitive to the environment.

In some police agencies, the restructuring for community policing was confined to only some bureaus (e.g., decentralization of the patrol process). Other departments opted to adopt community policing in all aspects of the agency.

EVERY OFFICER A LEADER?

Community policing and problem ownership strategies are presently the dominant operational themes of most police departments.[20] What type of organization will be needed to support those dominant operational themes? Terry Anderson contends that police, justice, and public safety agencies should first build the "leadership organization" and then build the "learning organization." The learning organization refers to community policing and problem ownership strategies. Anderson stresses the importance of the organization and how the culture must develop its employees before it can move on to being a quality organization and developing transforming leaders.

The present dominant operational themes of most police departments, according to Anderson, require that every officer be a leader in order for the organization to reach its maximum effectiveness. He defines the transforming leader as one who with vision, planning, and communications has a positive unifying effect on individuals around a set of clear values and beliefs in order to accomplish a clear set of measurable goals. Transforming leaders are individuals who seek to better themselves and improve for the future. They are active agents of positive change. Without transforming leadership, he contends that organizations will suffer and fail to reach their full potential. Most of all, communities will suffer from their ill-trained police. He considers culture and human resources issues as areas of vital concern to a strong organization and believes that they provide vital links to the making of a transforming leader.[21]

Organizational Development

Organizational development (OD) is the name given to the emerging applied behavioral science discipline that seeks to improve organizations through planned, systematic, long-range efforts focused on the organization's culture and its human and social process.[22] OD generally has the following objectives:

- Improvements in the interpersonal competence of managers
- Changes in values so that human factors and feelings are considered as legitimate
- The reduction of tensions between and within groups by increasing understanding
- Developing more effective team management, resulting in an increased capacity for groups to work together
- Development of better conflict resolution procedures
- Development of open, organic management systems that are characterized by trust, mutual confidence, wide sharing of responsibility, and the resolution of conflict by problem solving

Organizational development is often accomplished with the assistance of a consultant, either from outside the agency or from within. The consultant, also referred to as the change agent, facilitates the change process by structuring learning experiences, diagnosing problems, and encouraging certain types of interaction processes. The actions of a change agent are often referred to as interactions because the changes are designed to prevent the erosion of the organization's effectiveness by modifying the ways in which its members function. Although the OD intervention may cause visible changes in the organization, such as in its structure, formal authority relationships, policies, and technology, more often the focus of OD is on the hidden or more subtle features of an organization.

Determination of whether to use an external or internal change agent depends on several factors. An internal agent will have valuable insight into both the formal and informal organization, as well as possible sources of support and sources of resistance. If the selected agent has a good reputation within the organization, this may provide the agent with instant credibility. One of the biggest disadvantages of using an internal agent is the possible lack of acceptance of the agent by the organization as an expert. In addition, the internal agent must be relieved of his or her present duties to act as a change agent, thus creating a need to shift the agent's prior duties to someone else. The biggest disadvantage of an outside change agent is the absence of knowledge regarding the organization. The biggest advantage is the tendency to accept outside change agents as experts in the field, especially when the outside agent has a national professional reputation.

Personnel

Job Description

A job description should describe what a person holding that position actually does. It should be a detailed, formally stated summary of duties and responsibilities for a position. Under traditional management concepts, each position should have a job description. It should not be limiting or restrictive. It should be a statement of the minimum requirements of the position. Job descriptions also identify the expectations and standards for evaluation of individuals.

A good job description usually contains the position title and identifies the person's supervisor (by position, not name), education and experience requirements of the position, salary level, duties, responsibilities, and job task details. Job task details are the functions of the position that make it different from all other job positions in the organization. They should be broadly stated and thus leave room for growth, change, and expansion. Job descriptions should change as the requirements of the position change.

Job Design

The concept of job design is broader than a job description. It includes the traditional elements of a job description and more. It has been described as the deliberate, purposeful planning of the job including all of its structural and social aspects and their effect on the employee.[23] Job design is often linked with job efficiency, with job efficiency being the most important function. This can be attributed to Frederick Taylor's influence and his research involving increasing efficiency of labor through the fragmentation of work and the use of time and motion studies.[24] As noted in Chapter 2, Taylor worked on the assumption that most employees are unmotivated by work and are motivated by leisure and pay.

Taylor's influence has been prominent in policing. As noted by one researcher, policing is a "Taylorized occupation."[25] For example, because of concern over productivity and efficiency, many police administrators fragmented the roles of police officers by removing many tasks from sworn officers and giving them to nonsworn personnel (e.g., traffic control, bus monitoring, and parking). Thus, the regular police officer was no longer the Florence Nightingale. A similar movement, until recently, has also been toward decreased discretion and increased control over individual officers. This movement has been referred to as the deprofessionalization syndrome.[26] As one group of researchers noted, the irony behind the syndrome was that it was created by management in an attempt to increase professionalization.[27]

Many researchers have described what should be considered in developing a job design by formulating lists of criteria that should be included. Some of the recent interest in job design developed out of the movement to increase job satisfaction. The concern over job satisfaction is caused in part by studies indicating that many police officers would not recommend policing as a career to a friend, and many reported that their enthusiasm for policing had diminished after time on the job.[28] The concern for job satisfaction is also fostered by the job enrichment concepts that can be traced to the human relations school and the works of Maslow, McGregor, and Herzberg that were discussed in Chapter 2.

As the human relations school replaced Taylor's concept of workers as motivated generally by money and leisure to one in which workers were also motivated by social attachments, job designing took on more importance. Job satisfaction and job enrichment were accepted as key motivators. Contemporary job designs incorporate the increasingly complex theories of employee motivation.

The job enrichment movement began in the 1950s when Herzberg developed his motivation-hygiene theory in his critical incident research where he asked workers to describe the high and low points of their employment. Two sets of factors were developed as motivation factors. The first factors, hygiene factors, are external to the work being performed and include pay, supervision, physical conditions at the work site, and interpersonal relations. Herzberg contended that these factors do not motivate, but they prevent dissatisfaction. The second set of factors, the motivators, were intrinsic to the work itself and include responsibility, recognition, and opportunities for growth and achievement. Accordingly, job design is concerned not only with job efficiency but also with motivating employees by meeting their higher-order needs.

Listed below are the psychological job requirements noted in one popular list of items that should be considered in developing a job design. Note the concern for job satisfaction that is built into the list.

1. Adequate elbow room that promotes a sense that the employees are their own bosses
2. Reasonable challenges that give the employee chances to learn on the job and to continue learning
3. Satisfying rhythm of work that eliminates or reduces boredom and provides an optimal level of work
4. Respect and help from fellow associates
5. A feeling that the work is meaningful
6. Room for personal growth; not a dead-end position[29]

One of the leading job enrichment models was developed by J. Hackman and R. Oldman.[30] In their theory, they describe the job characteristics that they regard as the most important for employee motivation:

- Variety: the degree to which the job requires a variety of activities, skills, and talents
- Significance: the degree to which the job has a meaningful impact on others or the importance of the job
- Autonomy: the degree of freedom, independence, and discretion that the individual has when performing the job
- Feedback: the degree to which the individual receives direct and clear information about the effectiveness of his or her performance

Generally, job design efforts incorporate the "job analysis" process. Job analysis refers to the process of studying the work assignments with the goal of specifying the precise skills and training needed for the position. Job analysis is often limited to the technical dimensions of the job and is used to help develop job descriptions and set appropriate levels of compensation.

Shifts

According to a 1999 Police Executive Research Forum, the most popular schedule for police officers is the 3/12 schedule (a three-day week of twelve-hour days).[31] What effect does a 3/12 schedule have on the physical and mental health of officers? In recent years, police agencies, in addition to trying new police tactics, are also examining officer working conditions.

James Carpentier and Dr. Pierre Cazmian concluded in their 1977 study, *Nightwatch*, that night work always causes fatigue and in many cases a psychosomatic occupational disorder. In a 1991 Police Executive Research Forum, Chicago Police Lieutenants James L. O'Neill and Michael A. Cushing strongly recommended that agencies discontinue rotating shifts in police departments and change to steady tours. They contend, along with many other researchers, that the practice of rotating tours has damaging effects on the officers' physical and psychological health. The lieutenants contend that the body is not a machine that can be turned on and off and that the body needs to follow a normal, natural pattern to function properly.

Nassau County, New York, started a pilot program in 1995 to test the effects of steady tours on police officers. The agency had been on eight-hour rotating shifts prior to the study. In March 1995, two of the department's eight precincts established steady nonrotating tours. In August 1995, the two experimental precincts were compared with two similar precincts that were still using rotating tours. The researchers concluded that in the experimental precincts, absenteeism and sick time were less, and employee satisfaction was higher.

Later in August 1995, two more precincts were added to the experimental group. The researchers concluded that the use of steady tours brought down sick time and absenteeism while raising employee satisfaction. In November 1995, the entire department went on steady tours. In a 1999 follow-up report, the researchers concluded that the Nassau County Police Department's average number of sick days taken because of line-of-duty injuries had declined from a high of 7,436 in 1995 to a low of 2,183 in 1998 (last year available).

The use of steady tours, however, does have some disadvantages. One of the problems noted by Ed Nowicki, a thirty-two-year police veteran and a member of the Police Advisory Board, is that you have may have experienced officers working day shifts and brand new officers working night shifts; frequently shifts are loaded one way or another with experienced or inexperienced officers. Others contend that officers who work on steady tours do not see the community in all its aspects because communities change and are different according to the time of day, and a police officer needs to understand the community from all aspects.

Commitment

Many police management scholars contend that organizational commitment is critical to the organizational effectiveness of a police department. Organizational commitment refers to the strength of an individual's identification with and involvement in a particular organization. It is characterized by three factors: a strong belief in, and acceptance of, the organization's goals; a readiness to exert effort on behalf of the organization; and a strong desire to remain a member of the organization.[32]

The attitudes of police officers toward their work and their organization have been the subject of extensive research in the last thirty years. One of the earliest and most frequently cited studies on organizational commitment and policing was conducted in 1975 by Van Maanen.[33] The study is unusual in that it also examined the developmental trend of organizational commitment. He surveyed a group of police recruits during their training and probationary employment, which lasted up to thirty months. According to his findings, at the start of their training, the organizational commitments of the subjects were higher than similar employees in other occupations. The commitment, however, decreased with time and experience. He attributed this decrease to the "powerful character of the police socialization process" and the desire to get and keep the approval of their supervisors.

Questions in Review

1. Explain the differences between directed patrolling and split force patrolling.
2. Explain the process of organizational development.
3. What are the traditional functions of a police agency?
4. Why is an understanding of the Kansas City Study helpful to police agencies? What did the study establish?
5. How does the MCI grade cases as to their solvability?
6. Explain how the primary purposes of decoy operations differ from traditional police patrolling.
7. Explain the differences between the "top-down" approach and the analysis approach to police organizations.
8. What are the basic structural designs used in police agencies?
9. Is it important that every officer be a leader? Support your opinion.
10. What are the psychological job requirements that should be considered in developing a job design?

Biggest Mistakes Police Leadership Makes and How to Avoid Them

What Makes People Satisfied with the Police?

Too often, police management fails to take the necessary steps to ensure that the citizens are satisfied with their police department. The biggest factor, according to a research project funded by the National Institute of Justice, is people's perceptions about the quality of their lives—their sense of safety, for example.[34]

What Did the Researchers Find?

- A person's personal experience with police is nearly as important as the person's impression of the neighborhood and quality of life in determining his satisfaction with the police.
- Citizens who have a high sense of safety and favorably rate their neighborhoods are more likely to have a positive opinion of their police department.
- Caucasians and nonblack minorities were more satisfied with police than were blacks and younger residents.

How Can the Police Increase Public Satisfaction with the General Perception of Police Performance?

The researchers recommended that police executives take the following steps to foster the public's perception of the effectiveness of their police department:

- Identify each type of police–public encounter they would like to address.
- Specify the behavior residents should rightfully expect in each type of encounter with a police officer.
- Implement the appropriate officer training and field supervision to meet or exceed those expectations.
- To monitor results of such efforts, departments can conduct encounter-level surveys, which should solicit respondents' assessments of their encounters or experiences with police officers.

End Notes

1 *Law Enforcement News* (February 14, 2000), p. 7.
2 Joan Petersilia, "The Influence of Research on Policing," in *Critical Issues in Policing: Contemporary Readings*, Roger G. Dunham and Geoffrey P. Albert, eds. (Prospect Heights, IL: Waveland Press, 1989), pp. 230–247.
3 George L. Kelling, Anthony Pate, Duane Dieckman, and Charles E. Brown. *The Kansas City Preventive Patrol Experiment: A Summary Report* (Washington, DC: Police Foundation, 1974).
4 Kelling et al., pp. v–vi.
5 Samuel Walker, *Police in America: An Introduction*, 3rd ed. (New York: McGraw-Hill, 1999).

6. Anthony M. Pate, "Experimenting with Foot Patrol: The Newark Experience," in *Community Crime Prevention: Does It Work?* Dennis P. Rosenbaum, ed. (Beverly Hills, CA: Sage, 1986).
7. Walker, p. 87.
8. *Law Enforcement News* (December 15, 1991), p. 3.
9. J. Thomas McEwen, Edward F. Conners III, and Marica Cohen, *Evaluation of the Differential Police Response Field Test* (Washington, DC: GPO, 1986).
10. Eric J. Scott, *Calls for Service: Citizen Demand and Initial Police Response* (Washington, DC: GPO, 1981).
11. P. Greenwood and Joan Petersilia, *The Criminal Investigation Process: Volume I. Summary and Policy Implications* (Washington, DC: GPO, 1975).
12. National Advisory Commission on Criminal Justice Standards and Goals, *Police* (Washington, DC: GPO, 1973).
13. Donald F. Cawley, ed., *Managing Criminal Investigations Manual* (Washington, DC: National Institute of Justice, 1977).
14. Stephen Goldsmith, "Targeting High-Rate Offenders: Asking Some Tough Questions," in *Law Enforcement News* (July 1991), p. 11.
15. *Law Enforcement News* (February 29, 2000), p. 1.
16. Charles Wellford and James Cronin, *An Analysis of Variables Affecting the Clearance of Homicides: A Multistate Study* (Washington, DC: National Institute of Justice, 2000).
17. D. A. Tansik and J. F. Elliot, *Managing Police Organizations* (Monterey, CA: Duxbury Press, 1981), p. 81.
18. Stephen Robbins, *The Administrative Process* (Englewood Cliffs, NJ: Prentice-Hall, 1976), p. 259
19. B. J. Hodge and W. P. Anthony, *Organizational Theory: An Environmental Approach* (Boston: Allyn & Bacon, 1979), p. 249.
20. *Law Enforcement News* (February 29, 2000), p. 9.
21. Terry D. Anderson, *Every Office Is a Leader: Transforming Leadership in Police, Justice, and Public Safety* (Boca Raton, FL: CRC Press, 1999).
22. Wendell L. French and Cecil H. Bell, Jr., *Organizational Development* (Englewood Cliffs, NJ: Prentice-Hall, 1973), p. xiv.
23. D. Hellriegel, J. W. Slocum, and R. W. Woodman, *Organizational Behavior*, 4th ed. (St. Paul, MN: West, 1986).
24. Frederick W. Taylor, *Scientific Management* (New York: Harper & Row, 1947).
25. J. Frye, James Fyfe, Jack Greene, William Walsh, O.W. Wilson and R. C. McLaren, *Police Administration*, 5th ed. (New York: McGraw-Hill, 1997).
26. E. B. Sharp, "Street-Level Discretion in Policing: Attitudes and Behaviors in the Deprofessionalization Syndrome," in *Law and Policy Quarterly*, No. 4 (1982), pp. 167–189.
27. Stan Stojkovic, David Kalinich, and John Klofas, *Criminal Justice Organizations: Administration and Management*, 2nd ed. (Belmont, CA: Wadsworth, 1998), pp. 138–139.
28. G. P. Alpert and R. Dunham, *Policing Urban America*, 3rd ed. (Prospect Heights, IL: Waveland, 1997).
29. Stan Stojkovic, David Kalinich, and John Klofas, *Criminal Justice Organizations: Administration and Management*, 2nd ed. (Belmont, CA: Wadsworth, 1998).

30 J. R. Hackman and G. R. Oldham, *Work Redesign* (Reading, MA: Addison-Wesley, 1980).
31 *Police Magazine* (April 2000), p. 46.
32 R. T. Mowday, L. W. Porter, and R. M. Steers, *Employee-Organization Linkages: The Psychology of Commitment, Absenteeism, and Turnover* (New York: Academic Press, 1982), p. 27.
33 J. Van Maanen, "Police Socialization: A Longitudinal Examination of Job Attitudes in an Urban Police Department," in *Administrative Science Quarterly*, Vol. 20 (1975), pp. 207–228.
34 Michael D. Reisig and Roger B. Parks, *Satisfaction with Police: What Matters?* U.S. Dept. of Justice, Office of Justice Programs, NCJ 194077 (October 2002).

Leadership Approaches 4

Key Individuals, Concepts, and Issues

Francis Galton
Ralph Stogdill and Cecil Goode
Paul Hersey and Ken Blanchard
Fred Fiedler
Edwin Hollander
Robert House
Autocratic
Democratic

Great-man theory
Trait theory
Situational leadership theory
Contingency theory
Transactional approach
Path-goal theory
Laissez-faire
Charismatic

Definitions

Chain-of-command: A system whereby authority passes down an organization from the top through a series of positions in which each is accountable to the one directly superior.

Eugenics: A theoretical concept of social and biological improvement of the human race through the application of the study of heredity to human affairs.

Leadership: The function of motivating others to perform those tasks that are necessary to the accomplishments of the agency's goals and objectives.

Legitimacy of position: A perception that the leader has the authority to exert influence.

Situational variables: Situational variables describe characteristics of a situation or environment that have the potential to influence our communicative behavior.

Chapter Objectives

After completing this chapter you should be able to:

1. Distinguish between leadership and management

2. Describe trait, situational, contingency, and transactional theories of leadership
3. Discuss several ways in which leadership style differs in individuals

Case Study 4.1

Sergeant William Kearney is a nine-year veteran of the Pine County Sheriff's Office, having been hired when the current sheriff took office in 2003. He was promoted to his present rank three years ago and supervises ten deputies on the evening shift. Sergeant Kearney has had the opportunity to work in many of the various divisions at the sheriff's office. He has a good idea of the overall police operations.

The organizational structure at the Pine County Sheriff's Office places great emphasis on middle management. In effect, the eight sergeant positions and four lieutenants are midmanagers and serve as intermediates between the administration and the line staff. They represent department administration to their subordinates and at the same time represent their deputies to the administration. Currently, the upper management consists of the sheriff, under-sheriff, and three watch commanders. A total of fifty-two deputies and fifteen civilian staff comprise the remainder of the work force.

In this police agency, all employees are given the opportunity to participate in the planning of agency goals, make suggestions to improve police services in the community, and submit ideas to make the job more efficient and enjoyable. The sheriff challenges employees to think of new ways of improving service, and the sergeants play a key role in facilitating ideas into action within the organization. Sergeant Kearney openly asserts that employee participation has greatly benefited both the sheriff's office and the community over the years. He cites as examples the low attrition rate at the sheriff's office, which is less than 5% annually, and sick leave usage, which is at an all time low. In support of Sergeant Kearney's claims, a recent citizen poll conducted by the local media found that the community was highly satisfied with the performance of the police. Also, citizen complaints against the police have been virtually nonexistent for the past eighteen months.

The sheriff's office will, however, see a change in administration at the end of the year. Both the sheriff and under-sheriff have decided to retire and not run for re-election. At present, the leading candidate for the sheriff position is a Captain Max Bernard, a local city policeman. Prior to becoming a police officer, Captain Bernard served twenty years in the U.S. Marine Corps. He is known to possess a great deal of knowledge about police tactics and has a reputation of being direct with his subordinates. His political campaign slogans include "criminals are our enemies" and "when the streets become battlegrounds, the public expects a strong police response."

1. How would you describe the leadership style of the current sheriff? What are the advantages and disadvantages of this approach?
2. What problems might surface when the administrative leadership at the Pine County Sheriff's Office changes?
3. How can attitudes of the organization's leader affect the work behavior of the line staff?

Introduction

> Let's Get Rid of Management
>
> People don't want to be managed. They want to be led.
> Whoever heard of a world manager?
> World leader, yes.
> Educational leader.
> Political leader.
> Religious leader.
> Scout leader.
> Community leader.
> Labor leader.
> Business leader.
> They lead.
> They don't manage.
> The carrot always wins over the stick.
> Ask your horse.
> You can *lead* your horse to water, but you cannot *manage* him to drink.
> If you want to manage somebody, manage yourself.
> Do that well and you'll be ready to stop managing.
> And start leading.
>
> *United Technologies Corporation, 1986*

In the previous chapter, we noted that successful application of management theory is greatly dependent on the ability of managers to ensure the consistent application of established protocols within the organization. Because most police agencies are paramilitary-structured organizations, supervision responsibilities fall within the spectrum of its managers, namely sergeants and lieutenants. The extent to which these managers are successful in getting the job done is greatly influenced by the level of support from the organization's administration—its leaders.

Leadership does not simply happen. It has to be learned, developed, and refined over time. Leaders do exhibit certain distinct practices when they do extremely well. In *Leadership Challenges*, James Kouzes and Barry Posner tell us that leaders engage in five specific practices when they are getting extraordinary things done in the organization. These include:

1. Modeling behavior they expect of others
2. Inspiring a shared vision for an exciting future
3. Challenging the process to create opportunities to innovate, grow, and improve
4. Fostering collaboration and trust that enable others to act
5. Encouraging the heart of their constituents to carry on[1]

In this chapter, we identify several leadership approaches. We start by highlighting traits that a person should possess in order to gain employees' trust so that they willingly follow, accept change, and improve to achieve the goals of the organization and those whom the organization supports. We follow with a discussion of other theoretical assumptions of leadership including situational, contingencies, and transactional approaches. We end our discussion of leadership with a brief description of leadership styles. Let us begin by defining leadership.

What Is Leadership?

There is no single agreed upon definition of leadership. Warren Bennis, distinguished professor and founder of the Leadership Institute at the University of Southern California, states that "there are more than 350 definitions, with more coined by the dozens each month."[2] For our purposes here, we define leadership as the function of motivating others to perform those tasks that are necessary to the accomplishments of the agency's goals and objectives. It essentially is a process of influencing group activities toward the achievement of organizational goals.

Leadership has been described as an influence relationship among leaders and employees who intend real changes and outcomes that reflect their shared purposes.[3] So, leadership can exist at all levels of an organization from the executive to line staff and all levels in between. However, the very nature of this description indicates that leaders must have followers to influence. Definitions of lead and leadership all point to this relationship. Lead is "to guide or conduct by showing the way" and "to induce; to prevail on; to influence." Leadership is "the position or guidance of a leader" and "the ability to lead."[4]

Another way to describe leadership is to distinguish it from management. Exhibit 4.1 provides a few characteristics of the role of the manager versus that of the leader. It is important to note, however, that in every formal leadership position, there is a need to manage organizational tasks and processes. Therefore, managing can be considered a subset of leadership. In other words, in order to be an effective leader, you must necessarily be an effective manager first.[5]

MANAGERS	LEADERS
Function to maintain an efficient work process.	Primarily serve to produce useful change.
Depend on the system for success.	Rely on people for success.
Plan, budget, and establish timetables.	Create a vision and sell others on that vision.
Assign subordinates to perform tasks.	Empower and develop personnel.

Exhibit 4.1 Characteristics of managers and leaders.

Leadership Approaches

Several leadership perspectives have evolved over time, each having its own merit. These theories attempt to explain the factors and conditions associated with the emergence of leadership or the general nature of leadership.[6] Of the more noted leadership theories, we have selected four approaches that have greatly influenced law enforcement. They include trait, situational, contingency, and transactional theories. A brief explanation of each theory follows.

Trait Approach

Few would dispute that "great leaders" have had tremendous influences on the course of history. Consider the significant impact of General Dwight D. Eisenhower, Dr. Martin Luther King, Jr., and Prime Minister Margaret Thatcher. Each were great leaders endowed with exceptional qualities that captured the imagination of the public and whose effect on society can only be described as profound.

In early leadership studies, the characteristics of leaders were the primary focus of many researchers.[7] Initial investigations of leadership considered leaders as individuals endowed with certain personality traits that furthered their abilities to lead. These studies investigated individual traits such as intelligence, birth order, socioeconomic status, and child-rearing practices. One researcher that we highlight is Sir Francis Galton, who developed a theory that human intellect, and for that matter most human abilities, were innate. That is, leaders are born, not made.

Sir Francis Galton

Sir Francis Galton (1822–1911) was a scientist and explorer, born in Birmingham, England. He studied at Birmingham, London, and Cambridge, but left the study of medicine to travel in north and south Africa. Most of Galton's research focused on hereditary matters, which led him to the study of anthropometry and, later, fingerprints (Exhibit 4.2). Galton was a pioneer in **eugenics**, coining the term itself and the phrase "nature versus nurture."

Galton believed that leaders are the product of genetics. Several of his ideas are referred to in the works of his cousin Charles Darwin. He felt that an impulsive decision by a great man could change the course of history. Similar theorists believed that certain types of leaders could set off global developments and prohibited others from leading society down a different path.[8] For decades, this trait-based perspective dominated empirical and theoretical work in leadership. Researchers conducted many studies proposing a number of characteristics that distinguished leaders from nonleaders. Eugene Jennings, for example, submitted a comprehensive assessment and examination of the great man theory of leadership, which assumes that great leaders possess certain traits that are inherited and that they will arise when

---

Francis Galton and Fingerprinting

A British anthropologist and a cousin of Charles Darwin, Francis Galton began his observations of fingerprints as a means of identification in the 1880s. In 1892, he published his book, *Fingerprints*, establishing the individuality and permanence of fingerprints. The book included the first classification system for fingerprints.

Galton's primary interest in fingerprints was as an aid in determining heredity and racial background. While he soon discovered that fingerprints offered no firm clues to an individual's intelligence or genetic history, he was able to scientifically prove that fingerprints do not change over the course of an individual's lifetime, and that no two fingerprints are exactly the same. According to his calculations, the odds of two individual fingerprints being the same were 1 in 64 billion.

Galton identified the characteristics by which fingerprints can be identified. These same characteristics are still in use today and are often referred to as Galton's Details. This system of classification was improved upon later by Sir Edward Richard Henry, who founded what is widely known today as the Henry System of Classification.

Exhibit 4.2 From *The Fingerprint Sourcebook* by Scientific Working Group on Friction Ridge Analysis, Study, and Technology (SWGFAST), et al. March 2011. Accessible at http://www.nij.gov/pubs-sum/225320.htm

there is a great need. He concluded that fifty years of study had produced nothing to distinguish leaders from nonleaders.[9]

Ralph Stogdill and Cecil Goode

Other works in the development of trait theory include the research of Ralph Stogdill and Cecil Goode. They believed that studying leaders and comparing them to nonleaders could identify a leader. The idea was to identify which traits only the leaders possessed. Stogdill and Goode noted that leaders differ from followers in definite characteristics including:

- A strong drive for responsibility and task completion
- Vigor and persistence in pursuit of goals
- Venturesomeness and originality in problem solving
- A drive to exercise initiative in social situations
- Self-confidence and a sense of personal identity
- A willingness to accept the consequences of decision and action
- A readiness to absorb interpersonal stress
- A willingness to tolerate frustration and delay
- An ability to influence other persons' behavior
- A capacity to structure social interaction systems to the purpose at hand[10]

Moreover, the following traits were determined to be important for successful leadership:

- The leader is somewhat more intelligent than the average of his followers. However, he is not so superior that those who work with him cannot readily understand him.

- The leader is a well-rounded individual from the standpoint of interests and aptitudes. He tends toward interests, aptitudes, and knowledge with respect to a wide variety of fields.
- The leader has an unusual facility with language. He speaks and writes simply, persuasively, and understandably.
- The leader is mentally and emotionally mature. He has come of age mentally and emotionally, as well as physically.
- The leader has a powerful inner drive or motivation that impels him to strive for accomplishment.
- The leader is fully aware of the importance of cooperative effort in getting things done, and therefore understands and practices very effectively the so-called social skills.
- The leader relies on his administrative skills to a much greater extent than he does on any of the technical skills that may be associated directly with his work.[11]

While trait theory was very popular in the 1950s, it has been generally discredited as an oversimplified approach to leadership. That is, personality is just one element of effective leadership and often not the decisive one. In successful organizations, the leader scrutinizes the business situation, determines what the organization requires, and chooses the approach that best meets those requirements. Sometimes the approach fits the leader's personality; sometimes it does not. Until scientists discover a gene for leadership, the debate about personality will persist.[12]

Situational Approach

Finding that no single trait or combination of traits fully explained leaders' abilities, researchers have examined the influence of the situation on leaders' skills and behaviors. Situational theories propose that leaders choose the best course of action based upon **situational variables**. Different behavioral styles of leadership may be more appropriate for certain types of decision making. According to this focus, a person could be a follower or a leader depending upon circumstances. Attempts were made by researchers to identify specific characteristics of a situation that affected leaders' performance.

The ideas of situational leadership theory unveil the complexity of leadership but still prove to be insufficient because they do not predict which leadership skills would be more effective in certain situations. Similar attempts to examine leadership have yielded information regarding behaviors of effective leaders. These behaviors have been categorized along two dimensions: initiating structures because of concern for organizational tasks and consideration for individuals and interpersonal relations. Initiating structures include activities such as planning, organizing, and defining the tasks and work of people. In other words, how work gets done in an organization. Consideration for individuals and interpersonal relations addresses the social, emotional needs of individuals including their recognition, work satisfaction, and self-esteem influencing their performance.[13]

Perhaps the best-known work in the area of situational leadership theory is that of Paul Hersey and Ken Blanchard. According to Hersey and Blanchard, there are four main leadership behaviors:

- Telling: Leaders tell their people exactly what to do, and how to do it.
- Selling: Leaders still provide information and direction, but there's more communication with followers. Leaders "sell" their message to get the team onboard.
- Participating: Leaders focus more on the relationship and less on direction. The leader works with the team and shares decision-making responsibilities.
- Delegating: Leaders pass most of the responsibility onto the follower or group. The leaders still monitor progress, but they are less involved in decisions.

According to Hersey and Blanchard, knowing when to use each style is largely dependent on the maturity of the person or group being led. Maturity is broken down into four different levels:[14]

- Lowest maturity level: People at this level of maturity are at the bottom level of the scale. They lack the knowledge, skills, or confidence to work on their own, and they often need to be pushed to take the task on.
- Second maturity level: At this level, followers might be willing to work on the task, but they still do not have the skills to do it successfully.
- Third maturity level: Here, followers are ready and willing to help with the task. They have many skills, but they are still not confident in their abilities.
- Highest maturity level: These followers are able to work on their own. They have high confidence and strong skills, and they are committed to the task.

In Exhibit 4.3, we provide a rendering of the Hersey-Blanchard model that maps each leadership style to each maturity level.

Contingency Approach

Although situational leadership theory contains an underlying assumption that different situations require different types of leadership, the contingency approach attempts to specify the conditions that moderate the relationship

Leadership Approaches

Maturity Level Style	Most Appropriate Leadership
M1: Low maturity	S1: Telling/directing
M2: Medium maturity, limited skills	S2: Selling/coaching
M3: Medium maturity, higher skills, but lacking confidence	S3: Participating/supporting
M4: High maturity	S4: Delegating

Exhibit 4.3 Hersey-Blanchard model of maturity level and leadership style.

between leader traits or behaviors and performance criteria.[15] Contingency theory suggests that appropriate behavior in a given situation depends on a wide variety of variables and that each situation is different. What might work in one organization or employee group might not work in a different organization with its own set of issues and employee concerns. This methodology acknowledges that no one best way exists to manage in a given situation, and those situational variables, from both the internal and external environments, impact leadership practices.

In 1976, Fred Fiedler published *A Theory of Leadership Effectiveness*, which introduced his famous contingency theory, classifying leaders according to the extent to which they are relationship-or task-oriented. Relationship-oriented leadership is predicated on the desire to achieve personal acceptance. Task-oriented leadership is generated by effective task accomplishment. Fiedler then classifies situations in terms of the task structure for subordinates and the power position of the leader. Task structure is the extent to which a task is defined and understood as compared to an ambiguous and poorly outlined task. For example, police organizations rely on policy and procedure manuals to define tasks that are to be performed by police officers. In Chapter 7, we will discuss the use of policy and procedures by police agencies. The power position of the leader refers to the degree to which the status confers authority and the level at which others accept and comply with directions.

The question then becomes: Can we change our leadership styles to suit the situation? It is difficult, but studies have shown that leadership styles can indeed be learned. The best example of this is the path-goal theory proposed by Robert House, which includes the interaction of leadership behaviors with situation characteristics in determining the leaders' effectiveness. According to House, to be effective, a leader must select a style that enhances employees' satisfaction with their jobs and increases their performance levels.

House identifies four leader behaviors (achievement-oriented, directive, participative, and supportive) that are contingent to the environment factors and follower characteristics. A description includes:

- Achievement-oriented leadership: Challenging goals are set, and high performance is encouraged while showing confidence in the groups' ability.

- Directive leadership: Specific advice is given to the group, and ground rules are established.
- Participative leadership: Decision making is based on group consultation, and information is shared with the group.
- Supportive leadership: Good relations exist with the group, and sensitivity to subordinates' needs are shown.[16]

Supportive behavior increases group satisfaction, particularly in stressful situations, whereas directive behavior is suited to ambiguous situations. It is also suggested that leaders who have influence upon their superiors can increase group satisfaction and performance. House also identified two situational variables: subordinates' personal characteristics and environmental demands (such as the organization's rules and procedures) that most strongly contributed to leaders' effectiveness. He suggests that the leader in a number of ways can affect the performance, satisfaction, and motivation of a group by offering rewards for the achievement of performance goals, clarifying paths toward these goals, and removing performance obstacles.[17]

An example of the path-goal theory in the law enforcement setting is the chief of police's relationship with mid-managers such as lieutenants. The chief that successfully applies the path-goal theory will match a lieutenant's individual needs to the needs of the organization. The chief will also adjust his or her leadership style to match the lieutenant's tasks, personality, and leadership characteristics. Lastly, the chief should develop clear career paths and goals for mid-managers to enhance their motivation toward task completion. The lieutenant that is intrinsically and extrinsically motivated will likely experience higher job satisfaction, benefiting the entire organization and setting a positive example for subordinates.

Although contingency models further our understanding of leadership, they do not completely clarify what combination of personality characteristics, leaders' behaviors, and situational variables are most effective. Newer studies investigating organizational change have rediscovered the whole issue of organizational leadership on a broader level. One such approach is transactional leadership, which we review next.

Transactional Approach

Edwin Hollander's transactional approach proposes that the interaction between a particular leader and a particular follower will change over time based on such things as the changing confidence level of the leader and of the follower and other environmental changes that may be subtle and difficult to document.[18]

Hollander's primary focus is to show leadership to be something that is dependent on many different forces, few of which any leader may have control over. In the transactional approach, Hollander explores characteristics of the followers and the situation. He emphasizes the importance of a complete understanding of the situation and one's subordinates in order to accomplish a goal. Though he stresses the importance of the realization of all these aspects by the leader, Hollander also further develops the role the follower plays in affecting the leader and the situation. For example, a new hire requires more supervision than an experienced employee. A person who lacks motivation requires a different approach than one with a high degree of motivation.

Along with the interaction among these three properties (leader, follower, and situational characteristics), it is important to understand how the leader originally obtained the position, how the leader has kept the position, and what factors have had what effects on the situation. Hollander stresses the importance of having **legitimacy of position** not through hierarchy but by competency. He also stresses the importance of being able to recognize change happening within the situation. Whether planned or not, change will take place to some extent, and a good leader should be able to recognize the change, how it could affect the situation, and what therefore should be done.

Now that we have reviewed a few important leadership assumptions, let us turn our attention to behavior styles of leadership.

Leadership Styles

Leadership style is the manner and approach of providing direction, implementing plans, and motivating people. Early researchers identified two basic types of leadership styles: autocratic and democratic. Others expanded these concepts over the years to suggest there may be as many leadership behaviors as there are leaders. Still others have stressed that organizational behaviors are for the most part, more closely aligned with decision-making processes that occur within the organization rather than leadership styles. Because we will explore decision making in Chapter 5, we limit our discussion here to four general behavioral styles of leadership: authoritarian, democratic, laissez-faire, and charismatic. A quick reference to these styles is provided in Exhibit 4.4.

Authoritarian (Autocratic)

The autocratic leader is the commander and chief, who tells the employees what is to be done and how it is to be done, without getting the advice of others. Authoritarian leaders are often people who were previously supervised by someone who relied upon this very strict style of leadership.

The autocratic style of leadership is widespread in police organizations. It occurs in both large and small police agencies where the police chief or sheriff has set the tone by virtue of position power. In other words, the tone starts at the top and then permeates the entire organization. A highly structured

Autocratic Leader:
- I am the leader by virtue of my power position within the organization.
- I determine the policies because I have been chosen the leader based on my knowledge of what needs to be done.
- I determine all techniques, procedures, and activities.
- I appoint all committees and determine the work tasks and timetables.
- I command respect and expect unwavering loyalty.

Democratic Leader:
- I encourage and assist the group in discussions to determine agency policies.
- I assist the group with discussions relating to the formulation of agency goals.
- I supply technical advice or facts when needed but permit group choice.
- I permit members' freedom to work with whom they choose and to divide the tasks as they see fit. However, I urge members to work toward achievement and against disorder.
- I try to be "objective" and "fair" in praise and criticism and to not hold myself up as the final judge or "all wise" being.

Laissez-Faire Leader:
- I allow complete freedom to the group to formulate its own policies. I maintain a "hands-off" approach.
- I offer advice and resources only when I am asked. I take no part in discussion, or decision-making.
- I take no part in assigning work or allocating time.
- I maintain no pressure toward achievement and enter into disorder only when there is personal danger involved. I believe in freedom.
- I am passive toward judgments of praise or criticism.

Charismatic Leader:
- I am sensitive to an ever-changing environment. I criticize the status quo and propose radical changes in order to achieve organizational goals.
- I am sensitive to employees' needs.
- I formulate a strategic vision for the organization and constantly present it to employees in an inspiring way.
- I walk with self-confidence, always demonstrating my belief in the potential outcome of the vision.

Exhibit 4.4 Four general styles of leadership.

chain-of-command is followed, and absolute obedience is required of subordinates.

There are times when this type of leadership style is the desired approach. It is likely that authoritarian leadership is always warranted under the following conditions:

- When an emergency situation occurs and time is of the essence.
- When external forces (e.g., political influence) render pressure on the leader.
- When the decision is grounded on facts of law, rules, or regulations.

However, in all of these cases, the leader is required to possess the knowledge of the situation and the best possible solutions available before giving the directive.

The authoritarian style of leadership may have a stronghold on the police organization when subordinates feel they do not possess the authority to make the certain decisions. This is especially true of patrolmen who,

Leadership Approaches

for whatever reason, come to heavily rely on the supervisor or manager to provide direction.

Finally, there are times when subordinates need to be controlled. When it is apparent that a police officer is becoming ineffective in the field, for example, it requires the leader to take an immediate and direct approach. If an employee purposely fails to follow established procedure, then intervention by the leader is expected.

NATIONAL INSTITUTE OF JUSTICE RESEARCH FOR PRACTICE: HOW POLICE SUPERVISORY STYLES INFLUENCE PATROL OFFICER BEHAVIOR

A study sponsored by the National Institute of Justice examined three research questions relating to the way in which police supervisory styles influence patrol officer behavior within the community:

1. What types of supervisory styles are prominent in the field?
2. How do supervisory styles influence patrol officer behavior?
3. What are the resulting implications for departmental policy and practice?

Field observations of the Indianapolis, Indiana Police Department and the St. Petersburg, Florida Police Department, as well as interviews, identified four types of supervisory styles: traditional, innovative, supportive, and active. None of the four styles was noted as ideal; each had its drawbacks and limitations. The report details aspects of each style and then identifies the active supervisory style as the most influential on patrol officer behavior.

The most important finding was that style or quality of field supervision can significantly influence patrol officer behavior. Researchers found that an active supervisory style resulted in patrol officers who were twice as likely to use force against suspects. Patrol officers who had an active supervisor were also more likely to be proactive in their policing activities and spend more time per shift engaged in problem-solving and community-oriented activities. Overall, the research revealed that police supervisors best lead by example, which is the hallmark of the active style. However, supervisors must take care to present a positive example and avoid negative behaviors, like the unlawful use of excessive force. Study limitations include the fact that data were generated from only two police departments in urban areas.

The complete report can be accessed electronically at https://www.ncjrs.gov/pdffiles1/nij/194078.pdf.

Democratic (Participative)

The democratic style of leadership encourages the organization's employees to become involved in the decision-making process. It is a proactive style of leadership in which employees determine what to do and how to do it. This type of leadership necessarily means that the leader has confidence in the abilities of subordinate personnel. However, the leader maintains the authority to make the final decision.

The goal of democratic leadership is to tap into the skills and talents of employees working for the organization. As such, leaders and subordinates alike participate in the decision-making process. This ultimately benefits the agency when personnel work to achieve their highest potential and thereby increase productivity.

Moving from autocratic to democratic leadership is a complex and difficult process. It requires efforts by all personnel in the organization. Employees must also understand that while their ideas may be solicited, there are no guarantees that their ideas will always be implemented. There also may be obstacles that are encountered when changing from autocratic to democratic leadership. These obstacles include:

- Some personnel may hesitate to speak up or take on additional responsibilities. If they do not trust the motivation of the leader or do not understand how their personal needs fit the organization's agenda, they will be reluctant to volunteer in a more participatory environment.
- Some personnel may be more inclined to give their opinions than their committed action. It is easy to describe what is wrong, but it can be challenging to find personnel who are willing to truly become part of the solution.
- The emphasis on participation may open up a number of troublesome issues that personnel are not sure how to resolve. Some leaders perceive questions about their style and decisions as attacks or a lack of support.
- A democratic environment can feel like unstructured chaos with no one providing leadership. When everyone is providing input, the decision-making process can become tedious and burdensome.
- Some personnel may use a democratic environment to pursue their own agenda or protect their own turf. When personal ambition confounds sincere attempts at developing participation, conflicts develop, and efforts can be unproductive.

Laissez-Faire

The third style of leadership is laissez-faire, which is best described as a conscious attempt to avoid influencing the work of subordinates. It basically

Leadership Approaches

amounts to leaders who shirk their management duties by delegating everything. Such leaders instill no confidence in their ability to supervise, manage, or lead. They leave too much responsibility with subordinates, set no clear goals, and do not help their group to make decisions. Instead, things are left to simply drift, while the leader stays submersed in paperwork—to look busy.[19]

A study of adults who were instructed how to lead boys' clubs compared democratic and authoritarian leadership with laissez-faire leadership. Laissez-faire leaders gave group members complete freedom of action, provided them with materials, refrained from participating except to answer questions when asked, and did not make evaluative remarks. This behavior was in contrast to that of autocratic leaders, who displayed a much greater frequency of order giving, disrupting commands, praise and approval, and nonconstructive criticism. It also contrasted with the democratic style leaders, who gave suggestions and encouraged subordinates to guide themselves.[20] Under laissez-faire conditions, the groups were not well-organized, less efficient, and less satisfying to members than under democratic conditions. The work was of mediocre quality, and less work was done. There was more play, frustration, disorganization, discouragement, and aggression under laissez-faire than under democratic leadership. When groups of boys were required to carry out various projects under a high degree of laissez-faire leadership, they felt a lack of organization to get things done and did not know where they stood. When a laissez-faire leader followed an autocratic leader, the group exhibited an initial outburst of aggressive, uncontrolled behavior. This form of behavior subsided during the second and third meetings. Similar outbursts were not observed after the transition from laissez-faire to other forms of leadership. Although it did not stimulate as much aggression as did the autocratic condition, laissez-faire leadership was disliked because it was accompanied by less sense of accomplishment, less clarity about what to do, and less sense of group unity. The investigators concluded that laissez-faire leadership resulted in less concentration on work and a poorer quality of work than did democratic and autocratic leadership. There was less general satisfaction than from the democratic style but still somewhat more satisfaction than from the autocratic style that was employed in their study.[21]

Charismatic Leaders

Our final leadership style to discuss here is related to charisma, a term coined by sociologist Max Weber to describe someone with extraordinary power. Weber defined it thus: "The term 'charisma' will be applied to a certain quality of an individual personality by virtue of which he is considered extraordinary and treated as endowed with supernatural, superhuman, or at least specifically exceptional powers or qualities. These are such as are not accessible to the ordinary person, but are regarded as of divine origin or as exemplary."[22]

Charismatic leaders are distinguished from other leaders by possessing an unusual capacity to experience passion, extraordinary self confidence, persistence, determination, and optimism. In theory, these personality characteristics are required of charismatic leaders because the visions that they articulate call for significant change in the status quo.[23] Charismatic leaders strongly appeal to the values and self-concepts of followers by articulating radical solutions to their problems.[24] Research on charisma in organizational settings often focuses on leaders who found new organizations or transform organizations in crisis.[25]

Charismatic leaders are different from other leaders in their use of personal power—it is manifest in their elitist idealized vision, their entrepreneurial advocacy for radical change, and their depth of knowledge and expertise. In "Behavioral Dimensions of Charismatic Leadership,"[26] Jay Conger and Rabindra Kanungo provide a number of behavioral components that distinguish charismatic from noncharismatic leaders. We have listed five of these components in Exhibit 4.5. These components are interrelated, rarely appearing in isolation. It is this collection of behavior components that distinguishes charismatic leaders from other leaders.[27]

Historically, charisma has most often been associated with careers in politics, the military, or entertainment, which require playing to large audiences; but in the past several years, charisma has become important for law enforcement executives as well. Police leaders realize that central to the success of the police agency is the leader's ability to create a positive image in which the community willingly embraces a relationship with

	Charismatic Leaders	Noncharismatic Leaders
Relations to status quo	Opposed to status quo and strives to change it	Agrees with status quo and strives to maintain it
Trustworthiness	Passionate advocacy by incurring great personal risk and cost	Disinterested advocacy in persuasion attempts
Expertise	Uses unconventional means to transcend the existing order	Uses available means to achieve goals within the existing order
Behavior	Unconventional or counter-normative	Conventional, conforming to existing norms
Articulation	Strong and inspirational articulation of future vision and motivation to lead	Weak articulation of goals and motivation to lead

Exhibit 4.5 Distinguishing attributes of charismatic and noncharismatic leaders. (Adapted from Jay Conger and Rabindra N. Kanungo, "Behavioral Dimensions of Charismatic Leadership," in *Charismatic Leadership: The Elusive Factor in Organizational Effectiveness* (San Francisco, CA: Jossey-Bass Publishers, 1988).)

the police. Police leaders are also expected to be community leaders and catalysts on matters considered to be outside the primary scope of law enforcement.

Which Leadership Style and When?

Depending on the dynamics involved among the followers, the leader, and the situation, a good leader makes use of all of the four behavioral styles of leadership. For example, a police commander is likely to employ an authoritarian style if he or she has all the information to solve a particular problem, time is of the essence, and the patrol officers are well-motivated. On the other hand, a participatory style is most desired when teamwork is required for problem-solving, and the employees are very knowledgeable about their jobs. Here are a few examples of forces that influence the style to be used by the leader:

1. Time availability: the less time, the more likely a leader will use an authoritarian style of leadership
   Example: When emergency situations arise and quick decisions are necessary, they are most likely going to be made by the highest-ranking police on the scene.
2. Experience of the employees: the less experienced the employee, the more likely a leader will use an authoritarian style of leadership
   Example: Police agencies use an authoritarian style when new recruits begin on-the-job training.
3. Trusting relationships: the more respect and trust within the police agency, the more likely a leader will use a participatory style of leadership
   Example: Allowing all employees to have input into the development of employee handbooks or policy manuals can lead to well-thought-out guidelines and can head off potential trouble during the course of regular business.

Questions in Review

1. What qualities distinguish a skilled manager from a good leader?
2. Compare and contrast trait, situational, contingency, and transactional theories of leadership.
3. Explain the behavioral styles of authoritarian, democratic, laissez-faire, and charismatic leadership.

End Notes

1. James Kouzes and Barry Posner, *Leadership Challenge*, 3rd ed. (San Francisco, CA: Jossey-Bass Publishing, 2002).
2. Warren Bennis, *On Becoming a Leader* (Cambridge, MA: Perseus Books, 2003).
3. Richard Daft, *The Leadership Experience* (Mason, OH: Thomson South-Western, 2005).
4. *Webster's New Universal Unabridged Dictionary* (New York: Simon and Schuster, 1983).
5. Mitch Weinzetl, *Acting Out: Outlining Specific Behaviors and Actions for Effective Leadership* (Springfield, IL: Charles Tomas Publisher, 2010).
6. Ralph M. Stogdill, *Handbook of Leadership: A Survey of Theory and Research* (New York: Free Press, 1981).
7. William R. Lassey, ed., *Leadership and Social Change* (San Diego, CA: University Associates, Inc., 1983).
8. Bernard M. Bass, *Stogdill's Handbook of Leadership* (New York: The Free Press, 1981).
9. Eugene E. Jennings, *An Anatomy of Leadership: Princes, Heroes, and Supermen* (New York: Harper, 1960).
10. Stogdill, p. 18.
11. Cecil E. Goode, "Significant Research on Leadership," in *Personnel*, Vol. 25, No. 5 (1951), p. 349.
12. Charles Farkas, and Suzy Wetlaufer, "The Ways Chief Executive Officers Lead," in *Harvard Business Review*, Vol. 74, No. 3 (1996), pp. 110–112.
13. Gary Johns, *Organizational Behavior: Understanding and Managing Life at Work* (Glenview, IL: Addison-Wesley Publishers, 1995).
14. Paul Hersey, Kenneth Blanhard, and Dewey Johnson, *Management of Organizational Behavior*, 9th ed. (Upper Saddle River, NJ: Prentice-Hall Publishing, 2007).
15. Fred E. Fiedler, *A Theory of Leadership Effectiveness* (New York: McGraw-Hill, 1967).
16. Robert J. House, "A Path-Goal Theory of Leader Effectiveness," in *Administrative Science Quarterly*, Vol. 16 (1971), pp. 321–338.
17. House.
18. Edward P. Hollander, *Leaders, Groups, and Influence* (New York: Oxford University Press, 1964).
19. Leland Bradford and Ronald Lippitt, "Building a Democratic Work Group," in *Personnel*, Vol. 22, No. 3 (1945), pp. 142–148.
20. Ronald Lippitt, "An Experimental Study of the Effect of Democratic and Authoritarian Group Atmospheres," in *University of Iowa Studies in Child Welfare*, Vol. 16 (1940), pp. 44–195.
21. Ralph White and Ronald Lippitt, "Leader Behavior and Member Reaction in Three Social Climates," in *Group Dynamics: Research & Theory*, Dorwin Cartwright and Alvin Zander, eds., 2nd ed. (New York: Harper & Row, 1960).
22. Max Weber, *Economy and Society: An Outline of Interpretive Sociology*, Guenther Roth and Claus Wittich, eds., translated by Ephraim Fischoff, Hans Geth, A.M. Henderson, Ferdinand Kolegar, C. Wright Mills, Talcott Parsons, Max Rheinstein, Guenther Roth, Edward Shils, and Claus Wittich (Berkeley, CA: University of California Press, 1978).

23 Robert House and Jane Howell, "Personality and Charismatic Leadership," in *Leadership Quarterly*, Vol. 3, No. 2 (1992), pp. 81–108.
24 Boas Shamir, Robert House, and Michael Arthur, "The Motivational Effects of Charismatic Leadership: A Self-Concept Based Theory," in *Organization Science*, Vol. 4 (1993), pp. 577–594.
25 Janice Beyer and Larry Browning, "Transforming an Industry in Crisis: Charisma, Routinization, and Supportive Cultural Leadership," in *The Leadership Quarterly*, Vol. 10 (1999), pp. 483–520.
26 Jay Conger and Rabindra N. Kanungo, "Behavioral Dimensions of Charismatic Leadership" in *Charismatic Leadership: The Elusive Factor in Organizational Effectiveness* (San Francisco, CA: Jossey-Bass Publishers, 1988).
27 Conger and Kanungo.

Suggested Additional References and Links to the Web

1. "Shared Leadership: Can Empowerment Work in Police Organizations?" is an article by Todd Wuestewald & Brigitte Steinheider published in *The Police Chief*, April 2011.
   The authors discuss how scientific management theories have gradually given way to more participative approaches that stress employee empowerment and job involvement. http://policechiefmagazine.org/magazine/index.cfm?fuseaction=display&article_id= 789&issue_id=12006.
2. "Leadership during Difficult Budget Times" is an article by John L. Gray, Chief of Police (Retired) in Arlington, Washington published in *The Police Chief*, August, 2011.
   The article contains several tips for providing effective agency leadership during difficult times.
   http://policechiefmagazine.org/magazine/index.cfm?fuseaction=display_arch&article_id=1819&issue_id=62009
3. *On Leadership: How Video Games Build Leaders* is a three-minute video featuring Stanford University Professor Byron Reeves, who discusses how online multiplayer games are creating the next generation of leaders. http://www.washingtonpost.com/wp-dyn/content/video/2010/04/07/VI2010040701157.html
4. MindTools.com is a Web page that provides information about leadership, team management, problem-solving, personal productivity, and team-working skills. For this chapter on leadership approaches, we suggest you check out the following:
   Leadership Skills: Become an Exceptional Leader http://www.mindtools.com/pages/main/newMN_LDR.htm
   The Hersey-Blanchard Situational Leadership Theory http://www.mindtools.com/pages/article/newLDR_44.htm

Planning, Implementation, and Evaluation

5

Key Individuals, Concepts, and Issues

O. W. Wilson	Values
Strategic planning	Mission
Operational planning	Goals
Luther Gulick	Business modeling
POSDCORB	Performance audit
Divisions of labor	Gap analysis
Community policing	Integrating action plans
Ronald Lynch	Contingency planning
Evaluation	Implementation
Short term plans	Long-term plans

Definitions

Community policing: A decentralized model of policing in which officers exercise their own initiatives and citizens become actively involved in making neighborhoods safer.

Goals: Measurable and desirable outcomes for individuals, groups, or the organization that work toward accomplishing the organizational mission.

Long-term plans: Plans with a time frame of usually three or more years.

Mission: A definition of the purpose that the organization is attempting to fulfill in society.

Operational plans: Plans that specify how the goals of the organization are to be achieved.

Planning: A function that involves visualizing future situations, setting goals and deciding upon the best way to achieve them.

Short-term plans: Plans that are put into place for duration of one year or less.

Strategic planning: Establishes the overall purpose and results of an organization and how those results will be achieved.

Principles of Leadership and Management in Law Enforcement

Chapter Objectives

After reading this chapter, you should be able to:

1. Explain the purpose of police planning
2. Describe traditional police planning
3. Describe evolving police planning methods
4. Identify and discuss the nine components of the strategic management model
5. Differentiate between short-term and long-term plans
6. Identify and discuss the various factors involved in planning
7. Explain the evaluation process

Introduction

Alice: Which way should I go?
Cat: That depends on where you are going.
Alice: I don't know where I'm going!
Cat: Then it doesn't matter which way you go!!

—Lewis Carroll
Through the Looking Glass, 1872

The planning, implementation, and evaluation of police strategies and programs are important yet cumbersome endeavors. In order to effectively plan and control their destinies, police agencies must develop sound planning processes. In 1958, O. W. Wilson in his landmark text *Police Planning* wrote that

> Police objectives are achieved most effectively and economically through the efficient operation of three interrelated processes: viz., planning, doing, and controlling. Of these, planning is basic. Without it, effective direction, coordination, and control are impossible.[1]

It is undeniable that Wilson's thesis is just as important today as it was in 1958. Planning is the bedrock of a police organization, without it, police operations would be quite haphazard.

Today, police executives find themselves in the unenviable position of increased demand for services while at the same time working within limited fiscal resources. In essence, the police are increasingly asked to do more with less. They are expected to address crime concerns in their communities coupled with the important mandate of providing criminal investigations that in many cases require sophisticated technologies. It is for these very reasons that police agencies must engage in thoughtful and effective planning. Effective planning is a necessity in that it is geared to accomplish police tasks and goals in the most economic fashion. Moreover, planning brings the organization's present state into line with its goals for the future.

What Is Planning?

Planning has been presented in various fashions in the general management literature. If we take the word planning literally, we may view it as a process that assists a person or an organization in accomplishing a task. Planning is primarily the process of deliberately linking present actions to future conditions.[2] Moreover, planning is the process that defines the organization's goals and establishes the overall strategy for achieving those goals.[3] Thus, planning entails the establishment of a protocol that will guide the organization in both the short and long term.

Planning also serves another important purpose. It provides direction to the police rank and file of what has to be done and how it is to be done in order to accomplish the organization's goals and objectives. Planning is a complex process. In order for police executives to be effective planners, they must be willing to receive input from personnel throughout the organization regardless of rank. Planning establishes a coordinated effort within the police organization. It provides a sense of direction to both command staff and those police officers in the field performing the delivery of services to the general citizenry. When police officers know the direction of their organization and what they must do to contribute to and accomplish organizational goals and objectives, they are more prone to coordinate their activities, cooperate with each other, and work as a team for a common purpose.

Traditional Planning

The administrative management system developed in the 1930s advocates that within organizations there should be a unity of command and a clearly defined division of labor. Most police organizations today follow the tenants from the administrative management theory. For example, they are organized along clearly definable divisions of labor. These divisions of labor include patrol, investigations, warrant service, and traffic functions. There is also a clear unity of command, with each line police officer knowing the supervisor to whom he is accountable in a given situation. Classical management theorists argued that planning was an insurmountable process. This classical thought is the underpinning of the administrative management theory. This can best be illustrated by Luther Gulick, who coined the acronym POSDCORB, which has become well known in the management literature:

- P for planning: working out in broad outline the things that need to be done and the methods for doing them to accomplish the purpose of the enterprise.
- O for organizing: the establishment of the formal structure of authority through which work subdivisions are arranged, defined, and coordinated for the defined objective.
- S for staffing: the whole personnel function of bringing in and training the staff and maintaining favorable conditions of work.
- D for directing: the continuous task of making decisions and embodying them for specific and general orders and instructions and serving as the leader of the enterprise.
- CO for coordinating: the all-important duty of interrelating the various parts of the work.
- R for reporting: keeping the subordinates for whom the executive is responsible informed through records, research, and inspections.
- B for budgeting: including all that goes with budgeting in the form of fiscal planning, accounting, and control.[4]

Police planning is in no way uniform or consistent among police agencies. Some agencies spend a great deal of time on planning, while others do just enough to get by. The scope of planning is generally dependent upon the size of the police organization. Larger agencies will typically spend more time and resources on the planning process when compared with smaller agencies.

We take as a starting point O. W. Wilson's 1958 classic text: *Police Planning*. Wilson was one of the first to actually address the issue of police planning to the point of writing a virtual cookbook approach for planning that targeted police executives. For Wilson, the role of the police chief was to prevent crime, repress criminal activity, protect life and property, preserve peace, and ensure public compliance with countless laws. According to Wilson, the chief of police is supplied with personnel and equipment to assist in the attainment of these objectives. Wilson pointed out that in light of these awesome responsibilities encumbering the police, the chief must organize, direct, coordinate, and control in a manner that will assure the most effective and economical accomplishment of his purpose.[5] The foundation for police planning has changed little through the years and involves five basic steps:

1. The need for the plan must be recognized.
2. A statement of the objective must be formulated.
3. Relevant data must be gathered and analyzed.
4. The details of the plan must be developed.
5. Concurrences must be obtained from organizational units whose operation may be affected by the proposed plan.[6]

O. W. Wilson and Roy C. McLaren advocated that planning should be an essential part of the administrative and management process. They believed that the act of planning is an inseparable part of the administrative process and that planning is essential to the successful conclusion of any serious police undertaking.[7]

Similarly, Ronald Lynch offered the notion that police planning can actually be organized into four models: purposeful planning, traditional planning, crisis planning, and entrepreneurial planning.[8] The purposeful model weighs both risk and opportunity within the context of the entire organization and would include a thorough analysis of the organization and its purpose. Analyzing future trends, looking for the best ways to implement new programs, and looking at potential problems would be within the constructs of the purposeful model.

The traditional planning model seeks to maintain the status quo by minimizing risk and threats to the stability of the organization. This model is common in American police organizations in part because of the bureaucratic arrangement; this is especially the case in medium and larger agencies. Police organizations are said to be rational bureaucracies because they have many people performing many different functions at different levels within the organization. For agencies desiring to change traditional protocol, the very nature of a bureaucracy may serve to slow the change process.

The crisis model is directed toward specific events or issues affecting the police organization. In this model, management closely monitors subordinates and moves from one crisis to another. This model is found in many police organizations. The very nature of police work is conducive to this planning model. One of the authors of this book, a former law enforcement manager, knows that much of a police manager's job is dealing with a vast amount of crises within the organization itself. The crisis model tends to be reactive in nature. Often managers wait for problems to arise rather than anticipating and preparing to deal with them.

The entrepreneurial model is high risk in orientation. With this model, managers may be seen as moving from one roll of the dice to another.[9] The entrepreneurial model has been utilized in private industry for many years, where taking a fair amount of risk is not as critical as taking risks in the policing profession.

Why Plan?

Planning is an important function of police management, and it involves much more than just a process of envisioning. Planning requires setting clear-cut goals and objectives and working to attain those goals and objectives during specified periods of time in order to reach a planned future state. The goals and objectives developed during the planning process should provide the police organization with its core priorities and a set of guidelines for virtually all day-to-day management decisions. Forward thinking police administrators should view planning as an intricate part of their administrative function.

Planning provides a framework for police commanders and others within the organization to assess situations similarly, discuss alternatives in a common language, and decide on actions based on shared understandings. Moreover, planning provides an opportunity on at least an annual basis to constantly adjust to current events and actions. This is critical in the policing profession. The planning process allows for the improvement and revaluation of policies and procedures.

Evolving Themes

There are a host of factors that will impact the manner in which police agencies plan for the future. One such factor is community policing. Community policing strategies will have an impact on police planning. Community policing has been presented in the contemporary literature as constituting a viable way for the police to reduce and control crime. This strategy represents a change in a police tradition that was largely based on the police reacting to incidents of crime. With the strategy of community policing, officers are expected to not only to respond to the full range of problems that the public expects the police to handle, including peacekeeping, but also to take the initiative to identify a broad range of community problems.[10] Community policing has sparked many changes in the policing profession. Under the axiom of community policing, police will be required to work in partnership with citizens in order to solve problems and improve the quality of life in neighborhoods. The ideas of community policing are relatively simplistic in that the police take on a role of being more involved with assisting the community with information.[11]

Plans to implement community policing will vary depending on the size of the department and the extent of community policing strategies within the department. Some police agencies will plan for a special unit approach to community policing, whereas others will take on a holistic implementation throughout the entire organization. Regardless of the approach, the very nature of community policing will require much planning.

The Use of Research in Planning

Ideally, police planning should include a review of the research in the field. Research has played an invaluable role in shaping the manner in which police operate today. It is important that a protocol for the transition of theory to practice be established. Research has shaped and influenced policing in such areas as patrol methods, patrol deployment, and criminal investigations. Moreover, research findings have shed light on many other important issues including the importance of citizens reporting crime to the police.

Research should drive fundamental policy in policing. There is a clear dichotomy between sound practice and the benefit of research. In some cases, police organizations function and make major decisions based on haphazard approaches. For example, a police administrator may survey rank-and-file police officers in an effort to determine job satisfaction levels. This is an admirable task on the part of police administration, but it is all too often done with no clear-cut protocol of how the data will affect fundamental practice. The goals and objectives of the survey should clearly specify how the data will be utilized.

Research and practice together compose a vital process that allows ideas to be progressively generated and refined as they evolve from concepts to practices and from practices to concepts. Applied research can assist in more effective planning. Consider this: Would it not, for example, be advantageous for police administrators to have knowledge of citizen perceptions of the fear of crime prior to developing staffing patterns for the patrol division? Furthermore, it may be beneficial for police administrators interested in continuing foot patrol initiatives in a specific area of the community to examine pertinent data centering on crime decreases and increases in specific areas monitored by foot patrol during the planning process for further foot patrol initiatives.

Planning is a partnership process that ideally should involve academics and practitioners, and in some cases private agencies and citizen groups.[12] Police executives may find it beneficial to form partnerships with colleges and universities to provide technical support for the collection and analysis of data. The data and findings gleaned from research should be studied prior to implementing the planning process. Historically, there has been a gap between research conducted at colleges and universities and the manner in which police organizations practice. When theory, research, experimentation, and practice intersect, the final product should be more effective policing.[13]

Strategic Planning

As discussed in this chapter, planning has been presented in various fashions in the literature. Oftentimes planning is presented as a process of anticipatory decision making and deciding on the appropriate response before action is taken. This section presents strategic planning as an improvement to the more traditional methods. Strategic planning may prove to offer police organizations a more effective way to meet the demands of providing the most effective services to the citizenry. Strategic planning is the process by which the guiding members of an organization envision its future and develop the necessary procedures and operations to achieve that future.[14]

Strategic planning allows police organizations to envision and anticipate the future. This is in contrast to organizations that engage traditional short- and long-term planning. Short- and long-term planning is primarily an extrapolation of current trends. Strategic planning is a process designed to anticipate future trends. Strategic planning can assist in determining what the police organization intends to accomplish and how the organization and its resources will be used in accomplishing these goals in the future.

The advantage of strategic planning for the police organization is that it allows the organization to build momentum and sharpen its focus. It is not uncommon in police work for police rank-and-file members to become so focused on daily pressures that their organizations lose momentum. Strategic planning forces future thinking while at the same time building commitment to agreed upon goals.

One other advantage of strategic planning, which is in line with the goals of community policing strategies, is that it improves the organization's ability to solve problems. Planning focuses on the organization's most pressing and critical problems, choices, and opportunities. Problem solving is a crucial element of community policing.[15] The problem-solving process entails looking beyond the initial incidents that are the result of some underlying cause. For example, it may be that total acceptance of the community policing strategy within an organization is lacking. Or it may be that the chief and command staff has not created an environment within the organization for community policing changes to take place. Examples of this may be evaluating rules, regulations, policies, and procedures of the organization to ensure that the culture of problem solving and community policing are readily apparent. Or it may be discovered that there is a gap in the line level supervision. Line supervisors may not support the philosophy of community policing fostered by the chief. In this case, corrective action must be taken on the part of line level supervisors, thus removing the gap in performance. The chief must further make sure that line level supervisors understand the values of the organization.

Strategic planning allows for the enhancement of teamwork, learning, and commitment throughout the organization. Everyone should be involved with the strategic planning throughout the organization. In discussing the organization's history, current situation, future direction, and future options, everyone within the organization learns from each other. Section and unit commanders must be made aware of how each entity within the police organization is dependent on the other. Often, divisions and sections within police organizations tend to suboptimize and only concern themselves with their own small operating environments without much consideration of how they are interrelated with the larger organization.

The Applied Strategic Planning Model

Strategic planning is the process of defining the overall purpose, direction, and end goals of the organization, and creates a road map of sorts of how the organization will get there. The applied strategic planning model presented by Leonard D. Goodstein, Timothy M. Nolan, and J. William Pfeiffer provides a guide for those police managers preparing for applied strategic planning. These authors present a nine-step model of the applied strategic planning process: (1) planning to plan, (2) values scan, (3) mission formation, (4) strategic business modeling, (5) performance audit, (6) gap analysis, (7) integrating action plans, (8) contingency planning, and (9) implementation.[16] Each of these steps will be briefly discussed.

Planning to Plan

The planning to plan stage involves the strategic planning team evaluating and answering several questions as well as making some important decisions prior to initiating the planning process. The following questions should be asked in the planning to plan stage:

- How much commitment to the planning process is present?
- Who should be involved?
- How will we involve the absent stakeholders?
- How does the organization's fiscal year fit the planning process?
- How long will it take?
- What information is needed in order to plan successfully?
- Who needs to develop the data?[17]

These questions will set the tone for the planning process. For example, commitment levels within the police organization should be established prior to initiating the strategic planning process. Once commitment is secured from the chief of police and command staff, then the strategic planning team should be formed. Ideally, the planning team should not exceed ten to twelve permanent members who broadly represent the organization.

Values Scan

The values scan is an examination of the values of the organization. Simply put, core values are what the organization believes in and are committed to. They are enduring beliefs that a specific mode of conduct or end state of existence is personal or socially preferable to an opposite or converse mode of conduct or end state of existence.[18] Values can also be described as expressions of the organization through the actions of the employees.

A review of the history of the American police reveals that many police chiefs of the past established a set of core values for their organizations.[19] In fact, many chiefs made their value statement public. O. W. Wilson, while chief of police in Wichita, Kansas (1927–1939), made a set of values public when he coined the Square Deal Code. Much of Wilson's code, although written in the 1930s, is still relevant today.

> To Serve on the Square: to be a friend to man; to protect citizens and guests, safeguard lives, guarantee liberty, and assist in the peaceful pursuit of happiness; to be honest, kind, strong, and true, and always proud of our department and city; to give friendly aid in distress; to be gentlemen [sic], practicing courtesy and weaving a daily thread in the habit of politeness, always thoughtful of the comfort and welfare of others; to keep our private lives unsullied, and example for all; to be honorable that our charter many be strengthened; to bear malice or ill will toward none; to guard our tongues lest speak evil; to act with caution lest our motives be questioned; to be courteous and calm in the face of danger, scorn, or ridicule; to ignore unjust criticism and profit by good; to be alert in mind, sound in body, courteous in demeanor, and soldierly in bearing, a comfort to the distressed, a protector of the weak, and a pride to our city; to practice self-restraint, using no unnecessary force or violence; to intimidate no one nor permit it to be done; to take appropriate action whenever an offense is committed; to have moral courage to enforce the law; to be unofficious, firm, but mindful of rights of others; never permit personal feeling, animosities, nor friendships to influence decisions; never to act in the heat of passion; to assist the public in their compliance with regulations; to save unfortunate offenders from unnecessary humiliation, inconvenience, and distress. With no compromise for crime, to be relentless toward the criminal, our judgment charitable toward the minor offender; never to arrest if a summons will suffice; never to summons if a warning would be better; never to scold or reprimand but inform and request. All this to make Wichita a better place to live. For we stand for RIGHT, JUSTICE, and a SQUARE DEAL.[20]

When the values scanning stage is initiated, the organization's purpose, philosophy, and assumptions should be clearly identified. Ideally, during the values scan, the planning team moves from an individual focus to the broader examination of the organization. Organizational values will be consumed in the future behavior of the organization and will represent a shared sense of purpose for all within the police organization.

Mission Formation

The mission formation of an organization defines the business of the organization. The mission statement is a concise definition of the purpose that the organization is attempting to fulfill in the community. It is through the mission statement that police administrators must ensure that rank-and-file police personnel work toward the overall goals and objectives of the organization. The mission statement should answer four primary questions:

1. What function(s) does the organization perform?
2. For whom does the organization perform this function?
3. How does the organization go about filling this function?
4. Why does the organization exist?[21]

Strategic Business Modeling

Strategic business modeling is the path by which the police organization will accomplish its mission. This is a fairly succinct process that establishes the specific direction of the organization. In this stage, the planning team may be asked to examine and analyze several future scenarios. The planning team will address the pertinent steps for achieving those scenarios, who will be responsible for the steps, and when can the steps be accomplished. The strategic business model should reflect the mission, goals, and objectives of the organization. For example, the police organization may conceptualize the incorporation of a community-oriented policing strategy. Therefore, the steps necessary to accomplish this should be identified, including those personnel who will be responsible for accomplishing those steps. Quantifiable organizational objectives are also established during the strategic business modeling stage. One objective may be to have all patrol officers trained and practicing community-oriented policing strategies within a specified time. The key here is that the objective must be measurable.

Performance Audit

The performance audit is an examination of the organization's current performance. Some questions asked may be what does the police department currently do, and how do they do it? During this stage, the internal (within the organization) strengths and weakness are examined, and the external operating environment (outside of the organization) is examined. During the external environment examination, strengths, weaknesses, opportunities, and threats should be identified. The analysis of these factors is one way to corroborate the strategic business model.

Internally within the organization, it is important to examine the recent performance of the police organization in terms of staffing patterns, technology, tactical considerations, budget considerations, and service quality. The performance audit should ideally provide information for the next step: the gap analysis.

In short, the strengths and weaknesses of the organization must be examined from an objective and critical point of view. The external environment should be examined for strengths, weaknesses, opportunities, and threats. This will become increasingly important for those police organizations that are evolving into community-oriented policing strategies. The underlying question that police planners should be prepared to answer here is, does the organization possess the capability to implement its strategic business plan, successfully fulfilling the mission of the organization?

Gap Analysis

Taken literally, gap analysis is the process of examining the gaps in the current performance of the organization and the desired performance specified in the strategic business model. Gaps that may prohibit the successful obtainment of goals and objectives are identified during this stage. The gap analysis is the comparison of the data generated during the performance audit with that which is necessary for executing its strategic plan. Specific strategies should be tailored to close any gap that is identified.

The gap analysis in a police organization, for example, may identify gaps in implementing department-wide community-oriented policing strategies. These gaps should be addressed prior to implementing community-oriented policing, or the implementation may prove to be quite haphazard and lack the central commitment and support needed to carry out this important police mandate. If for some reason the gap cannot be closed out, the planning team must return to the strategic business modeling stage and rework the model, until a time when the gap can be closed.

Integrating Action Plans

Once the gaps in the gap analysis stage have been closed, two important issues remain: (1) the grand strategies or master business plans must be developed for each of the lines of business (what services the organization offers); and (2) the various units of the organization must be functional, and businesses need to develop detailed operational plans based on the overall organizational plan. These unit plans must reflect the grand strategy and must include budgets and timetables.[22]

Operational plans ideally should be written to reflect the mission of the organization. If a police department is planning for the implementation for community-oriented policing, then each division and section within the department should write operational plans to reflect the change to community policing. For example, if the training division reflects these changes through comprehensive curriculum, but the patrol division subsequently does not practice or follow through with community policing, then the implementation of the strategy will fail. Operational plans must reflect the overall mission of the organization.

Contingency Planning

Police planners should develop a specific set of contingency plans. Contingency planning is based on the assumption that the ability to accurately forecast significant factors in the environment is somewhat limited, especially in terms of variations in those factors. These factors would include external threats to the organization. Can you think of external environmental factors that may force the police organization to utilize contingency plans? The fact is that there may be many factors in the external operating environment that impact the applied strategic planning model. One example of this may be the unemployment in a community, which may spark increases in specific crime-related activities. One other example is the rise or projected rise in the number of young persons in a community, which may also increase the demand for police activity. The amount of neighborhood decay within a community may increase the utilization of police resources in those areas. These are just a few examples of projected trends in which the police should be prepared and have contingency plans in place to deal with these unexpected events.

Contingency plans are also beneficial for unanticipated internal environmental opportunities. For example, if budget cuts occur within the police organization this may affect staffing tables and the number of police officers assigned to specific areas. Contingency plans may also anticipate attrition, that is, police officers who resign or retire in close time proximity during a short period of time.

Implementation

The implementation of the strategic plan involves the concurrent initiation of several operational plans designed at the unit and functional level plus the monitoring of these plans at the operational level. It is important that all sections and divisions within the organization have knowledge that the strategic plan has been initiated. Thus, each section and division should begin to live and integrate the strategic plan into daily operations. The strategic plan becomes a living and breathing document. Decisions that are made at all levels of the organization should reflect the strategic plan. When this occurs, the strategic plan truly assimilates into the organizational culture.

Strategic planning provides direction for police agencies to look into the future and develop the necessary protocol to accomplish their objectives. Such planning involves choices about the mission the organization will pursue as well as its role in the larger environment. Strategic planning may be beneficial for police organizations that are making the transition to community-oriented policing strategies.

Types of Plans

There are several types of plans in most police departments. Many of these plans are designed to direct and offer guidance to specific functions within the police organization. The very nature of the policing profession and the mandate required of the police make it imperative that specific plans are in place. The following section will describe a few of the more common plans that are used in police organizations.

As a foundation, the most specific way to describe organizational plans is by their latitude. Police organizations use plans that are based on a specific time frame (e.g. short-term versus long-term plans), and police organizations use plans that are labeled single-use plans. These are sometimes called operational plans.

Operational Plans versus Strategic Plans

As discussed previously in this chapter, plans that apply to the entire organization, establish the police organization's primary objectives, and attempt to position the organization in terms of its environment are called strategic plans. On the other hand, plans that detail how the overall objectives are to be achieved are called operational plans. Strategic plans include an expanded time span, usually three or more years. Strategic plans and operational plans differ somewhat. They primarily differ in terms of time frame, scope, and whether they include a known set of organizational objectives.[23]

Operational plans usually cover shorter periods of time. Most police organizations have standard operating procedures in place that provide direction in specific situations. For example, standard operating procedures provide guidelines for the police response to given situations in the field, (e.g., robbery calls, burglary calls, traffic accidents, and major crime scene incidents).

Short-Term versus Long-Term Plans

As indicated by the title, short-term plans are considerably different in time frame when compared to long-term plans. Short-term plans are usually designed with a time frame of usually one or two and in some cases three years. Long-term plans are usually those plans beyond three years. Police departments operate in a dynamic and constantly changing society; this makes it important that police operational plans be reviewed and refined as needed. Long-term plans should be written with the flexibility to change, as required, with the changing external environment.

Single-Use Plans

Police organizations have a great need for single-use plans. These plans provide direction for specific events. For example, suppose a police organization receives information that there will be a strike at a large manufacturing plant within their jurisdiction. A single-use plan is developed to provide specific direction and assignments for police officers assigned to work the strike. In essence, single-use plans are designed to meet the needs of a unique situation and are created in response to nonprogrammed decisions that police executives make.

Other Miscellaneous Plans

There are a number of other planning endeavors carried out within police organizations. Personnel allocation, staffing, personnel, training, and budget plans all fall within the category of management plans.[24] In general, management plans impact the entire organization as a whole and not just specific sections or units.

Personnel Allocation and Staffing Plans

The most important and the most expensive police resource is personnel. Thus, the allocation of personnel becomes not only a very important planning issue but also imperative. The number of personnel that are assigned to the various sections and divisions within the police organization should be based upon need. Personnel allocation plans should not be written at random, haphazardly, or in reaction to some event. They should be based on data related to the demands for police service.

There are several factors that should be considered in personnel allocation plans. Actual and projected workload requirements should be determined. Trends occurring in the community should be studied. For instance, a large amusement park that has recently opened in the community and is projected to attract thousands of persons each week may result in an increased need for police services. This information should be factored and considered when determining staffing patterns. Patrol activities should be carefully studied to ensure that increases or decreases in the number of police for specific areas are met. Actual and projected personnel attrition should be studied, projected, and accounted for in the personnel allocation plan.

Personnel Plans

The recruitment and selection of police officers is one of the most important responsibilities of police executives. It is through the process of recruitment and selection that future investigators, supervisors, commanders, and chiefs enter into the police service. Personnel plans should be developed to provide the proper direction from the initial recruitment through the final selection. The entire recruitment and selection procedure should be outlined. Appropriate forms should be developed, and an applicant data-tracking system should be in place.

Not only should recruitment and selection plans be developed, but also career development plans for veteran officers must be put in place. The career development plan should list opportunities for police personnel and the requirements for advancement within the organization. The plan should specify years of experience needed for advancement, college education, and specialized schools or training. Police employees should know exactly what they must do to advance within the organization.

Training Plans

Training plans not only ensure that recruits are trained correctly but also provide directions at the in-service level so that police officers can stay abreast of the current legal trends, technological advancements, and new skills and competencies required of police officers. Plans should provide a guide for curriculum in order to ensure consistency and to protect the police organization from failure-to-train liability. Likewise, curriculum and protocol should be developed for field training officers who train recruits after they have graduated from the formal academy classroom setting.

Budget Plans

Budget plans detail financial and budget considerations for current and future situations. Budgeting includes such broad areas as fiscal planning, accounting, and control measures within the organization.[25] Projected personnel costs, equipment, and any improvement desired in the agency should be planned following budget guidelines. For example, a police organization may desire to secure mobile data computer terminals for patrol vehicles or replace worn out equipment. Such items require a sound justification and need, which should be thoroughly detailed within the plan. A well thought-out budget plan addresses the justification for each budgetary item, particularly any increases in funding. The police organization that anticipates and plans their budget and financial future is a more fiscally effective organization.

Factors in Planning

There are a number of factors involved in planning that should be given consideration. One such factor is who should be involved in the police planning process. Should it be only command personnel? Or should line level personnel be involved? Progressive organizations involve personnel at all levels of the organization in the planning process. In the traditional police organization, planning decisions were generally made by police management with little or no input from the officers in the field delivering police services to the community. It makes good sense that police officers from all levels within the organization be involved in the planning process. At times, line officers are in the best position to provide insight into real problems faced in the field. If the organization forms a planning team, which is recommended, it is imperative that a large cross-section of the organization be represented.

Planning a Diverse Workforce

The composition of the workforce is changing ever so drastically. The American labor force will become somewhat more brown and black in the next twenty years, but its most pervasive new tint will be gray. America's baby boomers share the hopeful prospect of living decades past the traditional retirement age. Many of them will want to keep working and will have much to offer.[26] America's racial composition is changing more rapidly than ever, and the number of immigrants in America is the largest in any post-World War II period.[27] Police planners play an important role in ensuring a diverse workforce that is representative of the changes in their communities. Planning provides the foundation for developing organizational policies and practices that nurture an environment and commitment to employee diversity. Planning should play a key role in guiding organizational activities such as employee recruitment to meet diversity goals.

Envisioning and Planning

Envisioning is the process by which individuals or groups develop a vision or dream of a future state for themselves or their organizations.[28] A dream or a vision is a precursor to the planning process. It is by the initial vision that the organization is then in a position to create plans that help shape that vision.

Historically, police organizations have been very effective at expressing their vision to the police rank and file. The process of envisioning is critical with the evolving community policing strategies. A vision provides members of the organization and the planning team with an anticipated view of the future and will help to shape the processes used to obtain that future. The process of establishing a vision can also establish a clear sense of direction and a mobilization of energy, as well as nurturing a sense of involvement among rank-and-file police employees. A vision provides an organization with a forward-looking, idealized image of itself and its uniqueness.[29] Plans are developed around the vision and mission of the organization. The following questions will assist the organization in establishing a vision.

1. Where do we want to be? This is the process of strategically setting goals.
2. Where are we now relative to the strategically set goals?
3. What is the current position? What resources do we have? What limitations or barriers are we facing?
4. How do we get there from here? What programs and policies will allow us to achieve the goals?[30]

Evaluation

A critical part of the planning process is the evaluation and assessment stage. Evaluation assists the planning team in examining deficiencies within the plan. The evaluation indicates whether plans have proven to be correct and effective.

During the planning process, goals were developed as guidelines to ensure that the organization is working toward fulfilling the plan and vision. A goal is an achievable end state that can be measured and observed. Goals provide direction for all organizational decision making. Thus, goals provide the criterion against which actual accomplishments can be measured.

Each division and section within the police organization sets goals so that the mission of the organization can be met. For example, the patrol division may set a goal to expand neighborhood crime prevention programs by 10% during the next planning year. Suppose that the police department had a mission statement that fosters the creation of a crime prevention culture within the department. In order to accomplish the mission, every division within the department will develop goals with the underlying premise of crime prevention. The investigations division may set goals to increase dialogue with, for example, the victims of burglary on what prevention steps to take in the future in order to lessen their chances of victimization. The detective division in this example has established goals to work toward the department mission to create a crime prevention culture.

It should be noted that the goals illustrated above could easily be evaluated. For example, the goal of the patrol division to expand neighborhood crime prevention by 10% can be measured by simply calculating the addition of neighborhood crime prevention programs. In the case of detectives, establishing a goal to increase dialogue with the victims of burglary can also be evaluated. Here data would be collected on those burglary victims that received an assessment session with a detective.

Evaluation involves comparing what actually happened with what was planned for. Not only do goals have to be evaluated and assessed in order to measure whether they have been accomplished, but feedback must also be obtained concerning the results of the planning cycle, the efficiency of the implementation process, and the effectiveness of new procedures, projects, or programs.[31] This is important in the planning process where it is desired to know what, if anything, happened as a result of implementing the plan. Evaluation can also serve as a road map for the planning team during the next planning cycle. With that said, it is important to note that a plan should be a living and breathing document that provides an opportunity for police executives to continually assess the progress of the organization in meeting the planned future state. The planning document should be open for change in the event the organization needs to adapt to changes in the operating environment. As part of the evaluation process, police executives have an opportunity to gain insight into needed improvements or what alternatives may work in future situations.

Today's policing profession requires effective planning. The police profession has become very complex. Haphazard planning can be disastrous for the police organization. Police organizations will increasingly be required to evolve beyond gearing planning with a focus on crime fighting as their main mission to planning the community-oriented department. Police organizational planning must be proactive and continuous, not reactive, intermittent, or expedient.

Questions in Review

1. What is organizational planning?
2. Why is the process of planning in police organizations important?
3. What are the underpinnings of the traditional planning models?
4. What are the planning models as described by Robert Lynch? Discuss each of these planning models.
5. How will police planning change under the evolving philosophy of community-oriented policing?

6. How can research assist in effective police planning?
7. What is strategic planning? Identify the elements in the applied strategic planning model.
8. What is a vision and why is this important in police planning?
9. What are appropriate ways to evaluate the success of the police organizational plan?
10. What are organizational goals?
11. How can planning be used as a mechanism to improve the diversity of the police organization?

Biggest Mistakes Police Leadership Makes and How to Avoid Them

What Does Management Expect from Subordinates?

Sergeant Richard Forsyth of the Buena Park, California Police Department contends that it is essential for effective management that subordinates are aware of what management expects of them.[32] Sergeant Forsyth sets forth an insightful way to look into the subject of management from the view of a subordinate. He looks at what considerations are important in the M-A-N-A-G-E-M-E-N-T of employees:

- M for management: Management means bringing about, accomplishing, and conducting. Forsyth contends that employees want to work for managers "who gets things done in the right way."
- A for accountability: Accountability is important to all levels of an organization. Forsyth states that managers should demonstrate a willingness to be held accountable by getting out from behind their desks and becoming personally involved with their subordinates, bonding with them by speaking and listening to them, observing them, and sharing experiences.
- N for nobility: Nobility means being morally sound, superior in character and nature. Forsyth contends that subordinates want to follow managers who model such qualities, but unfortunately, many managers seem to think that two standards exist in the way people act—one for professional conduct and one for private conduct.
- A for action: Action defines leadership, according to Forsyth. He contends that leaders make decisions about where they want to go, what they want to do, and how they will get there. And they do what they said they would do.
- G for guiding principle: Forsyth contends that people generally follow a guiding principle that tells them to treat others as they would

like to be treated. He lists three ways that supervisors can do this: (1) managers should only employ supervisory tactics that they would consider appropriate if their own bosses used them; (2) managers should lead by example; and (3) managers should treat employees with dignity, kindness, caring, and compassion.
- E for education: Managers must facilitate education of their employees.
- M for mentoring: Mentoring constitutes another important aspect of management. Because the best learning comes from doing, Forsyth advocates that sergeants can gain insight into a lieutenant's decision-making process and lieutenants can assist with staff work generally done by captains.
- E for ethics: Managers must set the example for their subordinates. Their words, attitudes, emotions, thoughts, and actions all reveal their personal ethics. Forsyth contends that supervisors are held to a higher standard and that, fair or unfair, the higher an individual climbs the "ladder of success," the more people expect him or her to uphold the ethical standards of law enforcement.
- N for notice: Managers should "notice" the quality work done by their personnel. According to Forsyth, people depend on the evaluations of others, particularly in the work place.
- T for trustworthiness: The first ideal of the Boy Scouts of America is that "A scout is trustworthy." Supervisors must remain honest with their employees. Managers, according to Forsyth, must treat their words as their bond.

End Notes

1. O. W. Wilson, *Police Planning*, 2nd ed. (Springfield, IL: Charles C. Thomas, 1958).
2. John K. Hudzik and Gary W. Cordner, *Planning in Criminal Justice Organizations and Systems* (New York: Macmillan Publishing Co., 1983).
3. Stephen P. Robbins and Mary Coulter, *Management*, 6th ed. (Upper Saddle River, NJ: Prentice Hall, 1999).
4. Luther Gulick, "Notes on the Theory of Organization," in *Papers on the Science of Administration*, L. Gulick and and L. Urwick, eds. (Reprint, New York: August M. Kelley, 1937).
5. Wilson (1958), p. 3.
6 Wilson (1958), p. 14.
7 O. W. Wilson and Roy Clinton McLaren, *Police Administration*, 4th ed., (New York: McGraw Hill, 1977), p. 157.
8 Ronald G. Lynch, *The Police Manager: Professional Leadership Skills*, 2nd ed. (Boston, MA: Allyn & Bacon, Inc., 1978).
9 Hudzik and Cordner, p. 17.

10 Herman Goldstein, "Toward Community Oriented Policing: Potential, Basic Requirements, and Threshold Questions," in *Crime and Delinquency*, Vol. 33, No. 1 (1987), p. 6–30.
11 Willard Oliver, *Community Oriented Policing: A Systematic Approach to Policing*, 2nd ed. (Upper Saddle River, NJ: Prentice Hall, 2001).
12 Victor G. Strecher, *Planning Community Policing: Goal Specific Cases and Exercises* (Prosepect Heights, IL: Waveland Press, Inc., 1997).
13 Strecher, p. 62.
14 Leonard D. Goodstein, Timothy M. Nolan, and J. William Pfeiffer, *Applied Strategic Planning: A Comprehensive Guide* (New York: McGraw-Hill, Inc., 1993) p. 3.
15 Michael L. Birzer and Cliff Roberson, *Police Field Operations: Theory Meets Practice* (Boston, MA: Allyn and Bacon/Pearson Publishing, 2008).
16 Goodstein, Nolan, and Pfeiffer, p. 8.
17 Goodstein, Nolan, and Pfeiffer, p. 9.
18 Milton Rokeach, *The Nature of Human Values* (New York: Free Press, 1973).
19 Michael L. Birzer, "Organizational Change and Community Policing," in *Community Policing: A Policing Strategy for the 21st Century*, Michael J. Palmiotto, ed. (Gaithersburg, MD: Aspen Publishing Co., 2000).
20 William J. Bopp, *O. W. Wilson and the Search for a Police Profession* (1977), pp. 138–139.
21 Goodstein, Nolan, and Pfeiffer, pp. 17–18.
22 Goodstein, Nolan, and Pfeiffer, pp. 29.
23 Robbins and Coulter, p. 214.
24 James J. Fyfe, Jack R. Greene, William F. Walsh, O. W. Wilson, and Roy C. McLaren, *Police Administration*, 5th Edition (New York: McGraw-Hill Inc., 1997).
25 Luther Gulick, "Notes on the Theory of Organization," in *Classics of Organizational Theory*, J. M. Shafritz and P. H. Whitbech, eds. (Oak Park, IL: Moore Publishing Co., 1978), pp. 52–61.
26 Richard W. Judy and Carol D. Amico, *Workforce 2020: Work and Workers in the 21st Century* (Indianapolis, IN: Hudson Institute, 1997), p. 22.
27 Farai Chideya. *The Color of Our Future* (New York: William Morrow and Company, 1999), p. 102.
28 Goodstein, Nolan, and Pfeiffer, p. 38.
29 J. M. Kouzes and B. Z. Posner, *The Leadership Challenge: How to Get Extraordinary Things Done in Organizations* (San Francisco, CA: Josse Bass, 1987).
30 Charles R. Swanson, Leonard Territo, and Robert W. Taylor, *Police Administration: Structures, Processes, and Behaviors* (Upper Saddle, NJ: Prentice-Hall Inc., 2001).
31 Swanson, Territo, and Taylor, p. 519.
32 Richard Forsyth, "M-A-N-A-G-E-M-E-N-T Defined: Subordinates' Expectations," in *FBI Law Enforcement Bulletin*, Vol. 73, No. 3 (March 2004), pp. 23–26.

A Business Approach to Policing?

6

Key Individuals, Concepts, and Issues

Evidence-based practices
Continuous process improvement
Principle-centered leadership
Empowered employees
Team environment
W. Edwards Deming
Joseph M. Juran
Philip B. Crosby

Zero defects
Benchmarking
Reengineering
Process simplification
Total quality management
PDCA cycle
Six Sigma
COMPSTAT

Definitions

Benchmarking: A continuous process of comparing an organization's systems and services to the best in the field.

COMPSTAT: A police managerial accountability mechanism involving four principles: timely and accurate intelligence, effective tactics, rapid deployment, and relentless follow-up and assessment.

Process improvement: A management strategy that systematically applies the principles and tools of quality to assure that, individually and collectively, processes continuously evolve to meet customer and business needs.

Reengineering: The fundamental rethinking of business processes to achieve improvements in measures of performance, such as costs, quality, and service.

Total quality management: A management process and set of disciplines that are coordinated to ensure that the organization consistently meets and exceeds customer requirements.

Chapter Objectives

After completing this chapter, you should be able to:

1. Explain the meaning of total quality management (TQM)
2. Explain how the plan-do-check-act (PDCA) cycle is used to obtain continuous improvement
3. Identify key leaders in the field of quality and their contributions
4. Explain how reengineering differs from TQM
5. Define the core principles of COMPSTAT

Case Study 6.1

Max Harley is the newly elected sheriff of a large urban county. The total population of the county is nearly five hundred thousand citizens, with one-quarter of the population residing in rural areas. Sheriff Harley is responsible for operating the county jail, serving warrants and civil process papers, court security, and patrol in the rural areas outside the city limits. The county encompasses a metropolitan area, and municipal law enforcement services are provided by a medium-sized city police department. It has long been common knowledge that the rural residents receive less patrol services than persons who reside within the city.

Sheriff Harley is considered a progressive leader who is interested in upgrading the level of patrol. A primary goal of the sheriff is to increase citizen satisfaction in this area. He has suggested that his agency incorporate some of the same community policing strategies being used by the city police departments.

1. Why should customer satisfaction be important to law enforcement leaders?
2. How should the sheriff decide what other services need to be provided by his agency?
3. What can the sheriff do to gain support for community policing initiatives?

Introduction

The currently fashionable language of economics and management used by command personnel to describe police functions, command obligations, and planning conjures a metaphoric imagery: policing as a hard-driving, profit-making business, a lean machine, that competes for market share and profits while carefully monitoring and modifying strategies and tactics to enhance its advantage.

—**Brian Forst and Peter Manning**
1999

It has been suggested that if law enforcement agencies are to function properly in the twenty-first century, they must operate much the way that the business sector operates in America. That is, policing must employ contemporary management philosophies involving process-oriented and customer-driven strategies to help attain agency objectives of higher quality, lower cost, customer satisfaction, and employee motivation. Police management and supervision practices do attempt to meet these goals when community policing strategies are implemented that aim to get police closer to the citizens in their jurisdictions and thereby create a problem-solving collaborative. As police leaders realize the benefits of this cooperative, they are more apt to continue and expand upon community policing initiatives. This in turn can lead to greater interest in successful strategies found in the business sector.

One contemporary line of business management that meshes well with policing in modern times is reengineering. The basic premise of this concept requires that leaders consider the extent to which the police organization's structure, deployment practices, and personnel assignments can be altered to accommodate the organization's objectives. For example, if community policing deployment practices are being reviewed, a reengineering approach might address the question: To what extent can officer work schedules be altered so that they can meet with citizens who could help solve crime problems? This approach is contrary to traditional mandates that organize the police department's manpower around ridged shift schedules that maximize blanketed 24-hour, around-the-clock coverage.

Another management philosophy that law enforcement agencies can incorporate to make policing a more complete package is total quality management. The day-to-day focus of quality management is to prevent errors by doing the right things right the first time. When quality is evident, it takes less time to accomplish objectives, and lower costs can naturally occur. Quality processes focus on both long- and short-term objectives rather than traditionally short-term, reactive ones. Errors are thought to be caused by process problems and not by the labor force. The responsibility for quality, however, belongs to all persons in the organization.

Because political and legal mandates increase and police agencies are required to be more fiscally responsible, law enforcement managers are increasingly embarking on new directions in police management and operations. In this chapter, we discuss total quality management and reengineering and question whether these business practices are really useful to police managers. We begin by examining quality management and describe TQM characteristics that have been tried in police agencies to improve service to the community. Next, we illustrate how reengineering principles may be useful to management and supervision processes in contemporary police organizations.

Basic Elements of Total Quality Management

TQM has become increasingly important in the modern law enforcement agency in recent years. TQM is a set of principles, tools, and processes for managing and improving the quality of police service. TQM is a productivity improvement strategy that is characterized by a commitment to meeting the needs of customers and constituents. Key characteristics of the TQM process are continuous process improvement, principle-centered leadership, empowered employees, and a team environment. These concepts and their main ideas are summarized in Exhibit 6.1. A popular tool in the TQM process is the plan-do-check-act cycle, which encourages a methodical approach to problem solving and implementing solutions. The PDCA cycle ensures that ideas are appropriately tested before committing to full implementation. Let us look at the specific steps in the cycle.

The Plan-Do-Check-Act Cycle

The PDCA cycle is a four-step model describing the activities a company needs to perform in order to incorporate continuous improvement in its operation. The circular nature of this cycle shows that continuous improvement is a never-ending process. Let us look at the specific steps in the cycle.

- Plan: The first step in the PDCA cycle is to plan. Managers must evaluate the current process and develop a plan for improvement, as well as specific measures to evaluate performance.
- Do: After identifying and analyzing the problem, the next step in the cycle is implementing the plan. During the implementation process, managers document all changes made and collect data for evaluation.

CONCEPT	MAIN IDEA
Customer focus	Goal is to identify and meet customer needs
Continuous improvement	A philosophy of never-ending improvement of the process by which work is accomplished in the organization
Employee empowerment	Employees are involved in and make decisions about their work and take responsibility for staying informed
Use of quality tools	Employee training in the use of quality tools
Product design	Products are designed to meet customer expectations
Process management	Quality is built into the process; sources of quality problems are identified and corrected
Managing supplier quality	Quality concepts must extend to a company's suppliers
Principle-centered leadership	Leadership decisions and actions are based on a set of core principles
Team environment	Promotes the formal and informal joining together of employees at all levels and in all jobs to collectively address business issues and operating processes

Exhibit 6.1 Principles of leadership and management.

- Check: The third step is to check the data collected in the previous phase. Then managers must measure how effective the "test" solution was and analyze whether it could be improved in any way.
- Act: The last phase of the cycle is to implement the "improved" solution fully. Note that this is a cycle; the next step is to plan again. After acting, there is a need to continue evaluating the process, planning, and repeating the cycle again.

TQM has been described as doing the right thing the first time, on time, all the time. The Federal Quality Institute, established to assist federal agencies in their productivity efforts, describes TQM in the following way:

> Total Quality Management is a strategic, integrated management system for achieving customer satisfaction. It involves all managers and employees and uses quantitative methods to improve continuously an organization's processes. It is not an efficiency (cost-cutting) program, a morale-boosting scheme, or a project that can be delegated to operational managers or staff specialists.[1]

Proponents of TQM describe it as a systematic, comprehensive effort to change the way in which organizations operate. TQM focuses on the functioning of the organization as a whole, and not on specific quality programs. TQM is intended to change the way managers, employees, and customers think about an organization, its processes, and its services.

TQM is not without its critics. One concern is that TQM imposes service uniformity. Early TQM efforts involved manufacturing, and in these applications, product variability was considered something to be minimized. The need for objectivity in police work and mandates for equal enforcement of the law can conflict with the philosophy of TQM. Consequently, the application of TQM is hampered in meeting the needs of individual customers. Another concern is that successful implementation of TQM involves a substantial and consistent commitment of the organization's top leaders. In the public sector, leadership in the organization changes so often that even the most consistent TQM organization falters if new leadership is not committed to TQM. Yet another concern for police is regarding the implementation of TQM's principle of customer focus. Police consistently and oftentimes consecutively deal with criminal offenders, victims, witnesses, prosecuting and defense attorneys, judges, jail officials, police in other jurisdictions, the media—the list goes on. Each of these customers impinges upon the criminal justice process and carries their own distinction with regard to requirements placed on police services. So identifying the customer is sometimes a difficult task for law enforcement.

Historical Development of Total Quality Management

The development of the quality movement began with a focus on inspection and postproduction repairs of defective tools. In the 1960s and 1970s, few organizations viewed quality as a responsibility of each and every employee. U.S. companies had developed a tradition of specialization, assigning quality control departments the distinct task of ensuring quality. Products that passed quality control were accepted, whereas others became rework or scrap.[2]

An emphasis on the process by which production occurred came later. With it came efforts to control the variability of those processes and to improve their capability in order to ensure that outputs would consistently conform to the requirements specified for them and thereby eliminate scrap and rework. In the 1980s and 1990s, the inspect-and-repair techniques of U.S. companies began to compare unfavorably with those of their competitors.

With respect to policing, law enforcement agencies are now more than ever focusing on quality as a way of increasing productivity, reducing costs, and meeting the demanding needs of the public. Police managers understand the importance of continuously improving the quality of police services as a way of achieving these goals. Those who begin to learn about quality quickly become familiar with the names of three renowned experts in the field of quality management: W. Edwards Deming, Joseph M. Juran, and Philip B. Crosby.

A Brief on Deming, Juran, and Crosby

In Chapter 2, we introduced W. Edwards Deming, considered to be the founder of TQM. Deming was a statistician and consultant, best known for leading Japanese businesses on the course that made them leaders in quality and productivity throughout the world. U.S. recognition of Deming's methods of quality improvement came in the 1980s as corporations across the U.S. looked for better ways to compete globally.

In the late 1940s, Deming began teaching Japanese industrialists about a management philosophy that included statistical quality control methods. The Japanese industrialists were receptive to an idea of improving quality because they desperately needed to renew and stimulate their economy, which had been devastated by World War II. Deming taught about problem solving and teamwork, concepts that were new to statistical quality control. In essence, Deming took the idea of statistical control and transformed it into a method of management. Soon Japanese industrialists became committed to the idea of improving quality through Deming's total quality management principles. Subsequently, they set up a work system that involved all employees in the improvement process. These functional teams examined various organizational problems and began to solve them collectively. Gradually, Japanese products improved and eventually exceeded the quality of products manufactured by other countries. Later, Deming shared his management ideas with American managers who were receptive to the ideas that helped the Japanese in their recovery.

Although Deming is the most well-known proponent of TQM, there are others who have contributed significantly to the quality movement. For instance, Joseph M. Juran, like Deming, assisted Japan in their quality improvement efforts following World War II. Juran held degrees in electrical engineering and law. He worked as an engineer, industrial executive, government executive, university professor, corporate director, and management consultant and wrote considerably on quality control.[3] Juran focused on management's impact on quality rather than techniques for improving quality. Like Deming, he advocated the use of statistical process control methods in monitoring processes.

Juran divided quality into two types: fitness for use and conformance to specifications. He maintained that a product could meet specifications yet not be fit for use. Juran believed that quality problems lie in organization, communication, and coordination. His ideas on quality improvement can be described in the ten steps outlined in Exhibit 6.2.

Another influential expert on TQM is Philip B. Crosby, who is best known for popularizing the zero defects concept. For Crosby, zero defects does not mean that the product has to be perfect. It does mean that every individual in the organization is committed to meet the requirement the first time, every time.[4] In Crosby's view, quality improvement begins with four absolutes of quality management, considered by him to be the core concepts of the quality improvement process. The four absolutes are:

1. Quality is conformance to the requirements: All of the actions necessary to run an organization, produce a product and or service, and deal with customers must be met and agreed upon. If

---

1. Build awareness of the need and opportunity for improvement
2. Set goals for improvement
3. Organize to reach the goals (establish a quality council, identify problems, select projects, appoint teams, designate facilitator)
4. Provide training
5. Carry out projects to solve problems
6. Report progress
7. Give recognition
8. Communicate results
9. Keep score
10. Maintain momentum by making annual improvement part of the regular systems and processes of the company

Exhibit 6.2 Juran's ten steps to quality improvement.

management wants people to do things right the first time, they must clearly communicate what the expectations are and help them achieve through leadership, training, and fostering a climate of cooperation.
2. The system of quality is prevention: The system that produces quality is prevention (i.e., eliminating errors before they occur). To Crosby, training, discipline, example, and leadership produce prevention. Management must consciously commit themselves to a prevention-oriented work environment.
3. The performance standard is zero defects ("Do it right the first time"): The attitude of "close enough" is not tolerated in Crosby's approach. Errors are too costly to ignore. Leaders must help others in their pursuit of conforming to requirements by allocating resources for training, providing time, tools, etc., to all employees.
4. The measurement of quality is the price of nonconformance: Nonconformance is a management tool for diagnosing an organization's effectiveness and efficiency.

These absolutes help management focus on quality improvement and, more importantly, help them make the shift from what Crosby calls conventional wisdom (the idea that if quality goes up, so does the cost) to the idea that quality and costs are not in competition with each other. According to Crosby, as quality increases, cost decreases. Thus, quality does not cost. This reasoning led to Crosby's famous phrase: "Quality is free, but it is not a gift."[5]

To implement his quality improvement process, Crosby delineates fourteen steps consisting of activities that are the responsibility of top management but also involve workers. The fourteen-step approach illustrated in Exhibit 6.3 represents Crosby's techniques for managing quality improvement and communicating the four absolutes.

Benchmarking

Benchmarking is a quality tool often used as an integrated tool within TQM. It is the process of identifying, understanding, and adapting outstanding practices and processes from other organizations. For police then, benchmarking is used to improve policing by exploiting top-notch practices used by other police organizations.

William Gay has identified several benchmarking steps or metrics to be used in the process of collecting and analyzing performance information from other organizations. Some of these metrics include the following:

1. Decide what to benchmark. A starting point is to address the needs of the citizens by asking key customer service questions such as:

1. Make it clear that management is committed to quality.
2. Form quality improvement teams with representatives from each department.
3. Determine where current and potential quality problems lie.
4. Evaluate the quality awareness and personal concern of all employees.
5. Raise the quality awareness of and personal concern of all employees.
6. Take actions to correct problems identified through previous steps.
7. Establish a committee for the zero defects program.
8. Train supervisors to actively carry out their part of the quality improvement program.
9. Hold a zero defects day to let all employees realize that there has been a change.
10. Encourage individuals to establish improvement goals for themselves and their groups.
11. Encourage employees to communicate to management the obstacles they face in attaining their improvement goals.
12. Recognize and appreciate those who participate.
13. Establish quality councils to communicate on a regular basis.
14. Do it all over again to emphasize that the quality improvement program never ends.

Exhibit 6.3 Crosby's ideas on implementing quality improvement.

Who are the major service users and what are their major needs or complaints?

2. Identify organizations with which to partner. Potentially the selection of organizations to participate in an exchange of information could come from (1) different divisions within a large police department; (2) comparisons with agencies of similar size in neighboring jurisdictions; (3) comparisons with agencies with known good reputations; and (4) comparisons with nonpolice organizations that have developed practices that might have applicability to processes in the department.
3. Collect information. Data gathering involves compiling information from three sources: (1) baseline data that exists with the department; (2) information gleaned from a review of the literature and research previous conducted by others; and (3) data collected from other agencies by means of inquiry.
4. Communicating the findings and recommendations. A key element to this metric is to identify stakeholders to whom the findings will be communicated and whose support will be necessary to carry out the recommendations.
5. Monitor implementation. During the implementation and monitoring step, performance information should be reviewed, and progress reports made available.
6. Evaluate results and recalibrate benchmarks. The ultimate question of impact is central to the evaluation of step in benchmarking. That is, have the implemented changes brought about the expected improvement? Next, recalibration is needed to keep pace with the changing work environment. Benchmarking is a continuous quest for best practices.[6]

WHAT IS THE DIFFERENCE BETWEEN A BEST PRACTICE AND EVIDENCE-BASED PRACTICE?

The terms best practices, what works, and evidence-based practice (EBP) are often used interchangeably because they have similar notions. Best practice suggests techniques and processes that are identified through the literature and one's own collective experience and wisdom of the field, but best practices do not necessarily imply attention to outcomes, evidence, or measurable standards. Moreover, a best practice can have excellent research qualities but still not meet practical considerations that determine its applicability to the field. For example, if a best practice requires elaborate training of staff that is costly, the practice may prove to be useless in the field.

Evidence-based practice uses the best scientific evidence available to guide decision making for the purposing of attaining the best outcomes. The practice uses are reflected in policies, practices, and assessment reports. EBP characteristics are: (1) one outcome is desired over others; (2) it is measurable; and (3) it is defined according to practical realities rather than immeasurable moral or value-oriented standards.

The Center for Evidence-Based Crime Policy at George Mason University has developed an EBP policing matrix, which is a three-dimensional research-to-practice tool that organizes studies relating to strategies that reduce crime and disorder in policing. It allows agencies to view the field of research, from its generalizations to its particulars. The matrix is accessible electronically at http://gemini.gmu.edu/cebcp/Matric.html.

Six Sigma

We want to briefly introduce Six Sigma here, which is the structured application of the tools and techniques of total quality management to achieve virtually error free operations. Sigma is a letter in the Greek alphabet used by statisticians to measure the variability in any process. In its broadest sense, Six Sigma measures an organization's performance and is used to improve the output quality of a process.

Six Sigma uses defects per opportunities as a measurement tool. The number of defects per opportunities is a good measure of the quality of a process or product because it correlates to defects, cost, and time. The sigma value indicates how often defects are likely to occur. The higher the sigma value, the lower the likelihood of defects. A defect is anything that results in customer dissatisfaction. Therefore, as sigma increases, cost and cycle time decrease, whereas customer satisfaction increases.

The Six Sigma methodology uses statistical tools to identify the vital few factors, the factors that matter most for improving the quality of processes and generating bottom-line results. It consists of five phases:

- Define: identify, evaluate, and select projects for improvement and select teams
- Measure: collect data on size of the selected problem, identify key customer requirements, and determine key product and process characteristics
- Analyze: analyze data, establish and confirm the "vital few" determinants of the performance
- Improve: design and carry out experiments to establish cause-and-effect relationships and optimize the process
- Control: design the controls, make improvements, implement, and monitor[7]

A Web site for Six Sigma tools and theory can be found at http://www.isixsigma.com.

Applying TQM Methods in Police Organizations

Thinking about modernizing police management by implementing TQM strategies is relatively new. One reason for its newness is that, for the most part, the fundamental expectation of police to protect society has not changed over time. Police are foremost expected to use coercive measures to bring the force of the law to bear on criminal offenders. Consequently, police personnel, their leaders, and their managers have traditionally been more interested in developing techniques to effectively reduce crime and crime victimization. There has been no specific emphasis placed on police personnel to possess a basic understanding of management principles or scientific methods that are congruent with TQM. Similarly, when contemplating the implementation of TQM, viewing police as a production system might seem foreign. Police organizations are departmentalized, having multiple pockets of work. Therefore, the responsibilities of the various divisions within the police agency are often very different with regard to the type of service provided to the public.

Skepticism about implementing TQM may actually be based on failed experiences in other police jurisdictions. Consider for example, an eighteen-month evaluation of the implementation of TQM in the Omaha Police Department. Although the overall planning of TQM implementation was successful, and the amount of TQM training and the extent of exposure to related activities correlated positively with understanding TQM, there was no real sign of a change in the traditional police culture within this law enforcement agency.[8]

Although it is unrealistic to think that TQM may produce dramatic results in helping police reduce crime, it may prove useful toward developing effective ways of redefining police work. By redefining we mean changes in the way the police visualize their work and their methods. In the traditional strategy of policing, the key unit of work is the incident. Police officers respond to a specific incident, and it is the incident that becomes the focus of their work. What is known, however, is that large proportions of incidents emerge from a relatively small number of situations and locations. Moreover, analysis of the problems underlying many incidents reported to the police suggests that the police might be able to conceive and mount different kinds of interventions.[9]

TQM principles may have the most applicability to police work in the area of process orientation. That is, TQM can help law enforcement evaluate the quality of its services to the community in terms of how police go about performing what is expected of them. According to Clifford Simonsen and Douglas Arnold, questions that should be asked about quality performance include:

1. How long do these various processes take to produce a service/product?
2. How much time does it take to pass that service/product on to the next process?
3. How much of the original effort is reworked or completely rejected at a later stage?
4. How would your clients/customers want these processes to be handled?[10]

TQM may also help to ensure that the quality of police service continuously improves. The basic TQM approach to managing quality consists of setting a standard for a work process, measuring variation in the work process in relation to the standard, and then implementing programs to decrease variation and improve end results. Everyone who provides a service becomes involved both in understanding how quality is measured and in discussing how to improve quality. A team approach is adopted, and instead of focusing on poor quality outcomes and how to avoid them, the team becomes involved in setting continuously improving standards for better performance and in finding ways to meet those standards. The objective is to meet or exceed consumer or user expectations.

TQM and Community Policing

Because of its emphasis on quality service to customers and attention to continuous improvement, TQM is useful to police agencies making the

A Business Approach to Policing?

transition to community policing. The Beaufort, South Carolina Police Department, for example, used TQM strategies in 1994 to help develop team policing concepts that were viewed as crucial toward implementing community policing. The entire police department was involved in an incremental step process to change from traditional to community policing. Recognizing the requisite for training, flexibility, and commitment from all participants, the police department initiated a process of team building to ensure that the responsibility for community policing projects did not rest on a single shift or individual police officer. An environment was created that allowed for various approaches to problem solving. In particular, the process action team approach was employed to identify and analyze problems, implement solutions, and evaluate results.[11]

Perhaps the first law enforcement agency to utilize TQM principles was the Madison, Wisconsin Police Department. Then chief of police, David Couper, and his employees worked for years to change the agency from a highly traditional, bureaucratic organization into a quality-oriented organization. The principles of TQM used in transforming the department are found in Exhibit 6.4. The Madison Police Department operated within a strategic planning framework that incorporates many of the principles of TQM. The Madison Police operating philosophy established that:

- We, the members of the Madison Police Department, are guided by the highest ethical standards.
- We provide the highest quality of personalized services to all who live, work, visit, learn, and recreate in our city.

---

1. Believe in, foster, and support teamwork.
2. Make a commitment to the problem-solving process, use it, and let data (not emotions) drive decisions.
3. Seek employees' input before making key decisions.
4. Believe that the best way to improve work quality or service is to ask and listen to employees who are doing the work.
5. Strive to develop mutual respect and trust among employees.
6. Have a customer orientation and focus toward employees and citizens.
7. Manage on the behavior of 95% of employees, not on the 5% who cause problems; deal with the 5% promptly and fairly.
8. Improve systems and examine processes before placing blame on people.
9. Avoid top-down power-oriented decision making whenever possible.
10. Encourage creativity through risk taking, and be tolerant of honest mistakes.
11. Be a facilitator and coach; develop an open atmosphere that encourages providing for and accepting feedback.
12. With teamwork, develop with employees agreed-upon goals and a plan to achieve them.

Exhibit 6.4 Principle of quality leadership in Madison. (Adapted from: David C. Couper and Sabine H. Lobitz, *Quality Policing: The Madison Experience*. Washington, DC: Police Executive Research Form, 1991.)

- We do this by empowering employees, who build partnerships with the community and other service providers to prevent and solve crime, lessen fear, and reduce neighborhood problems.
- We are committed to enhancing our community's safety and quality of life through continuous improvement of our work.
- We are a community-oriented police department as defined by the people we serve.
- We believe in the dignity of all people and respect individual and constitutional rights in fulfilling this mission.[12]

Police departments have traditionally turned to citizen surveys to assess the quality of police service. Mailed questionnaires and telephone surveys are used to gauge customer satisfaction and are often published in department newsletters. For example, the Reno, Nevada Police Department, in cooperation with a local university, conducts citizen surveys semiannually. In Newport News, Virginia, law enforcement officers regularly conduct neighborhood surveys as part of their community policing initiatives, and in St. Petersburg, Florida, the police department conducts annual surveys to measure citizen satisfaction.

ARGUMENTS FOR AND AGAINST TQM IN POLICING[13]

FOR	AGAINST
TQM increases employee performance and thereupon production.	Production is hard to measure because much of what police do symbolically represents such things as social integration, community well-being, and a sense of propriety and security.
TQM encourages more ethical supervision.	Economical benefit and moral values may be incongruous. Policing sustains ethics through a sense of equality of service and civil liberties.
TQM emphasizes service-orientation and attentiveness to customer needs.	Policing necessitates conflict resolution and an emphasis on the public interests, not those of individual citizens.
TQM emphasizes decentralization and seeks to increase managerial flexibility.	Policing involves highly structured, top-down commands that create orders that ensure compliance with political, social, and legal mandates. Adopting TQM is viewed as a managerial decision to organize and control how work will be carried out by the organization.

Reengineering

The term reengineering comes from a contemporary change management school called business process reengineering in which companies replace their old practices with entirely new ones.[14] Reengineering differs from TQM in that it involves more than just improving certain services within the existing organization. Instead, reengineering seeks to radically redesign all processes with the goal of dramatic breakthroughs in performance. Reengineering calls for throwing out everything that exists and recommends reconstituting a workable organization on the basis of completely new ideas.

Reengineering is guided by many principles, of which two of the most important are: process simplification (keeping processes simple and performed in a natural order) and using technology (as the catalyst for change). Let us examine each of these principles.

Process Simplification

Process simplification is the elimination of undesirable complexity from a business process in order to improve productivity and optimize responsiveness to customer requirements. All processes are composed of activities intended to transform a set of inputs into an output that fully meets customer needs. Unfortunately, because of imperfect planning, changing requirements, outmoded technologies, and bureaucratic evolution, many processes contain a large proportion of activities that do not add value to the output. Undesirable complexity is typically measured in terms of wasted cost or time. Although both metrics are useful and can usually be converted to the other, the business community is increasingly emphasizing the power of cycle time reduction as the metric of choice in driving process simplification. Cycle time analysis ensures focus on the work process itself and uses a simple unit of measurement, which every employee can easily measure. For police, the benefits of process simplification include:

1. Improved responsiveness: As each cycle time is completed, processes are refined to improve the output of the next cycle and to continuously increase police service to the community.
2. Reduced costs: By eliminating wasted time, police services can be maintained within existing budgets.
3. Increased employee satisfaction: Reducing process complexities means police personnel will be increasingly empowered to make decisions and take actions at the street level, a key to increased employee satisfaction.

Moreover, redesigned processes are said to bring several benefits to organizations including dramatic reductions in processing time, cost savings, streamlining of organizational structure, and increased client satisfaction. These benefits are extremely important for large police organizations. For example, Los Angeles County consists of approximately fifty law enforcement agencies whose officers are involved each year in more than five hundred thousand misdemeanor and felony arrests, most of which are prosecuted. The county operates its Consolidated Criminal History Reporting System (CCHRS), which allows police immediate access to information in various databases. The CCHRS generates criminal histories, indicates which police agencies are investigating a person, and generates information and precautions to police personnel. The system offers a massive increase in efficiency to such a large and disparate jurisdiction.[15]

Technology

In their book *Reengineering the Corporation*, Michael Hammer and James Champy note that information technology plays a crucial role in business reengineering. Modern, state-of-the-art information technology is part of any reengineering effort because it permits companies to reengineer business processes.[16] Reengineering, unlike automation, is about taking advantage of the latest capabilities of technology to achieve altogether new goals. Consider, for example, the drug confirmation and report reengineering project conducted by the Los Angeles Police Department. Procedures for confirming the presence of controlled substances in urine samples collected from arrested persons were very time consuming. As a result, there were backlogs of up to three hundred samples, and the turnaround time for tests averaged thirty days. Criminalists within the police department used new technologies to develop more efficient urine sample preparation procedures. This project resulted in a reduction of the backlog samples by 90% and corresponding reductions in sample analysis turnaround by 50%.[17]

Applying Reengineering Principles to Police Organizations

Many of the prescriptions of reengineering run counter to traditional approaches to management. For example, one concept of reengineering management is to create five- to ten-person teams to actually carry out the reengineering. These teams require their members to take responsibility for many of the functions that were formerly considered to be exclusively management functions, and they are based on the extensive sharing of knowledge. As such, this structure is very different from the traditional hierarchical command structures of police organizations.

There have been a great number of publications dealing with organizational change and its impact on productivity and quality improvement. Most examples seem to be related to process-focused changes, which are especially found in the total quality management and reengineering movements. Examples of successful application of total quality management to improve

A Business Approach to Policing? 141

public sector organizations have been commonplace in the literature.[18] This is not the case with reengineering, which still seems to be seen with reserve by public sector leaders.

However, in *NYPD Battles Crime*, Eli Silverman provides perhaps the best example of reengineering and police service. Silverman draws insight into how reengineering techniques were used to reorganize the New York Police Department (NYPD). He examines how then police commissioner William Bratton implemented innovative strategies in 1994 to lower crime. Silverman begins with a historical review of the evolution of police reform movements in New York City, showing that the achievements and failures of earlier external and internal initiatives formed the foundation for today's reengineered NYPD. Drawing on privileged access to police documents and meetings, he then examines how the dynamic interaction of specific strategic, organizational, and managerial changes redefined the approach to policing, transforming the department from a reactive to a proactive force. In particular, Silverman focuses on COMPSTAT, a "strategic control system" that compiles crime statistics, as the crucial mechanism for linking the development of new policies with effective tactics to control crime. The up-to-date and accurate information provided by COMPSTAT drives twice-weekly crime strategy meetings that ensure essential planning, coordination, evaluation, and accountability.[19] Let us look more closely at COMPSTAT's potential as a management tool to reduce crime.

COMPSTAT

COMPSTAT, which is short for "computer statistics" or "comparison statistics," is an administrative innovation introduced as part of the reengineering of the New York City Police Department in the mid-1990s. Perhaps the most widely recognized features of COMPSTAT are (1) twice-weekly meetings, with a precinct commander at a podium fielding pointed questions about patterns of crime and the precinct's efforts to address them, and (2) maps projected on a large screen that depict those crime patterns in spatial terms. In application, COMPSTAT enables police managers to track important outcomes. As a system of performance measurement, COMPSTAT focuses attention on outcomes and provides a means of assessing the success with which police units have produced valuable results by choosing effective tactics and deploying resources.[20]

Police departments in such cities as New York, Boston, Philadelphia, Miami, New Orleans, and Newark, New Jersey, have all experienced significant reduction in violent crimes as a result of the implementation of the COMPSTAT crime control model. Although many of these departments have custom tailored the COMPSTAT process to their own department and community needs, the core elements of COMPSTAT have remained the same.

The core elements provide a basic road map for getting police officers back in the business of proactive problem solving rather than just reacting to crime. A vital component of the COMPSTAT philosophy is its emphasis on holding police managers directly accountable for combating the crime in their assigned area and providing them the authority to deploy their resources to achieve the desired results. The San Francisco, California Police Department identifies four distinct principles of COMPSTAT:

- Principle 1: Accurate and Timely Intelligence. Accurate and timely intelligence or information is absolutely essential in effectively responding to any problem or crisis. Because today's policing techniques nearly always consist of vast amounts of information, it is necessary to provide a vehicle where essential information can easily and effectively be shared with all levels of the organization. Oftentimes, detectives have information on suspects or crime trends and patterns, but the actual field patrol officers who may be in contact with potential suspects have no idea of what information detective personnel possess or need to clear a case. Just as important, this principle also provides for an early warning system to identify emerging crime trends and patterns. In today's environment of ever-shrinking resources, being able to apply the necessary resources to an identified problem area is crucial in successfully reducing crime. Historically, marked police vehicles have randomly been deployed in hopes of deterring potential criminals who see the black and white police vehicles on patrol. This principle suggests that intelligence information be used as a radar screen to direct police resources to the exact problem area.
- Principle 2: Effective Tactics. Traditional policing tactics have always dictated that most problems may be solved at a superficial level. In other words, take care of the suspect without worrying about the social or environmental situation that may be adding to or creating the problem. COMPSTAT tactics encourage "thinking outside the box" and mandate that every resource, both internal and external, is considered in responding to a problem. COMPSTAT tactics also provide for a sense of urgency in responding to problems. The old attitude of public entities responding at slow speed are no longer acceptable. Every case or call for service is handled as the traditional "big case" and is thoroughly and rapidly investigated in a systematic manner.
- Principle 3: Rapid Deployment. For decades, police departments have been driven by calls for service and responded with their limited resources in a reactive manner. With COMPSTAT, the police department is now armed with vital intelligence regarding emerging

crime trends or patterns, which allows for a strategic police response. The strategic response can be in many forms: both traditional uniformed and plainclothes officers, as well as nontraditional decoys and sting operations.
- Principle 4: Relentless Follow-up and Assessment. An essential element in any crucial operation is the need to critically assess past tactics and review what was successfully employed and what just did not work. One of the main differences between private enterprise and the public sector is the bottom line of positive returns. The public sector and police departments have rarely been evaluated on their results. On the other hand, if a business implements an unsuccessful strategy or provides an unacceptable level of customer service, it is not long before bankruptcy is filed. The bottom line with COMPSTAT is results. Everything the police department does, no matter whether administrative, operational, or investigative in nature, is evaluated by the results achieved. Static operations that do not provide for successful results are immediately assessed for their value and necessity to the overall operation of the department.[21]

Questions in Review

1. What are the key characteristics of total quality management?
2. What is the PDCA cycle of TQM?
3. Who are W. Edwards Deming, Joseph M. Juran, and Philip B. Crosby?
4. How can TQM help police organizations making the transition to community policing?
5. Which two principles are most important to reengineering?
6. What is COMPSTAT and how is it used in policing?

End Notes

1. Federal Quality Institute, *How to Get Started Implementing Total Quality Management. Federal Total Quality Management Handbook* (Washington, DC: June 1990).
2. *Management Practices: U.S. Companies Improve Performance through Quality Efforts* (Washington, DC: United States General Accounting Office, May 1991).
3. Joseph M. Juran, *Juran on Leadership Quality* (New York: Free Press, 1989); Joseph M. Juran, *Juran on Planning for Quality* (New York: Free Press, 1988); Joseph M. Juran, *Managerial Breakthrough* (New York: McGraw-Hill, 1964); Joseph M. Juran, *Case Studies in Industrial Management* (New York: McGraw-Hill, 1955); and Joseph M. Juran, *Bureaucracy: A Challenge to Better Management* (New York: Harper and Brothers, 1944).

4. Philip B. Crosby, *Quality Process Improvement Management College* (San Jose, CA: Philip Crosby Associates, Inc., 1987).
5. Philip B. Crosby, *Quality Is Free* (New York: McGraw-Hill, 1979).
6. William Gay, *Benchmarking: A Method for Achieving Superior Performance in Law Enforcement Services* (Washington, DC: National League of Cities, 1996).
7. Forrest W. Breyfogle III, *Managing Six Sigma: A Practical Guide to Understanding, Assessing, and Implementing the Strategy That Yields Bottom-Line Success* (New York: John Wiley and Sons, 2000).
8. Jihong Zhao, *Evaluation on the Implementation of Total Quality Management in the Omaha Police Department: An Interim Report* (Washington, DC: U.S. Department of Justice, National Institute of Justice, 1998).
9. Herman Goldstein, *Problem-Oriented Policing* (New York: McGraw-Hill, 1990).
10. Clifford E. Simonsen and Douglas Arnold, "TQM: Is It Right for Law Enforcement?" in *The Police Chief* (December 1993), pp. 21–22.
11. Richard A. Nagy, "Improving the Quality of Life," in *The Police Chief*, Vol. 67, No. 4 (April 2000), pp. 33–44.
12. David Couper and Sabine Lobitz, *Quality Policing: The Madison Experience* (Washington, DC: Police Executive Research Forum, 1991).
13. Adapted from Brian Forst and Peter K. Manning, *The Privatization of Policing: Two Views* (Washington, DC: Georgetown University Press, 1999).
14. Michael Hammer and James Champy, *Reengineering the Corporation: A Manifesto for Business Revolution* (New York: Harper Business Publishers, 1993).
15. Doug Lemov, "Say Cheers in LA: A Consolidated Criminal History Reporting System," in *Court Technology Bulletin*, Vol. 9, No. 2 (1998).
16. Hammer and Champy, p. 83.
17. William Russell, *City of Los Angeles Commission on Quality and Productivity Awards* (Los Angeles, CA, 1997).
18. Mary Walton, *Deming Management at Work: Six Successful Companies that Use the Quality Principles of the World-Famous W. Edwards Deming* (London, UK: Mercury, 1991); Raff, M. and J. Beedon, "Total Quality Management in the West Midlands Employment Service," in *Managing Change in the New Public Sector*, R. Lovell, ed. (Harlow, UK: Longman, 1994), pp. 294–318.
19. Eli B. Silverman, *NYPD Battles Crime: Innovative Strategies in Policing* (Northeastern University Press, 1999).
20. Robert Worden and Sarah McLean, *COMPSTAT in the Granger Police Department: A First-Year Appraisal* (Albany, NY: The John F. Finn Institute for Public Safety, April 2008).
21. San Francisco Police Department Web page: *http://sf-police.org/index.aspx?page=3255*.

Suggested Additional References and Links to the Web

1. *Community Policing: Looking to Tomorrow* is an article by Drew Diamond and Deirdre Mead Weiss that was published by the Police Executive Research Forum in May 2009. The article presents the current state of community policing according to police chiefs and other police leaders. *http://www.cops.usdoj.gov/files/RIC/Publications/e050920207-CommPolicing_Looking2Tomorrow.pdf*.

2. *Intelligence-Led Policing: The New Intelligence Architecture* is an article by Marilyn Peterson published by the Bureau of Justice Assistance in September 2005. Intelligence-led policing is a collaborative enterprise based on improved intelligence operations and community-oriented policing and problem solving, which the field has considered beneficial for many years. *https://www.ncjrs.gov/pdffiles1/bja/210681.pdf*.

Problem Solving 7

Key Individuals, Concepts, and Issues

Discretion
Policy and procedures manual
Decision making
Autocratic decisions
Democratic decisions
Participatory decisions
SARA model
Brainstorming
Delphi Technique
Critical path analysis
Problem-oriented policing
Community policing
Consensus decisions
PERT

Definitions

Brainstorming: A structured method to address problems by asking people to rapidly propose ideas while the group temporarily withholds its comments and criticisms.

Discretion: The power to selectively enforce laws in order to handle situations and problems.

Mission statement: A broad, general statement that describes the operational philosophy of a law enforcement organization.

PERT: A graphical technique that uses a chart to describe a project or program.

Policy statement: A statement of what is to be done in relation to a particular issue. It reflects the philosophy of the organization and defines the purpose(s) for which an action is taken.

Procedures: Detailed descriptions of how policies are to be accomplished. Procedures specify the steps to be taken, the order in which those steps will be carried out, and by whom.

Selective enforcement: Enforcement of the law in an inconsistent or arbitrary manner.

Chapter Objectives

After completing this chapter you should be able to:

1. Distinguish between reactive and proactive discretion
2. Explain the purposes that policies and procedures serve in a police organization
3. Identify the steps involved in the group decision-making process
4. Describe the four general principles of community policing
5. Outline the SARA model of problem-oriented policing
6. Describe the role of police leaders and managers in the community-oriented policing model

Case Study 7.1

A new memorandum from the watch commander has just been posted in the roll call and briefing room at the Cedar Springs Police Department. It reads as follows:

MEMORANDUM
TO: ALL POLICE PERSONNEL
FROM: WATCH COMMANDER ROBERT TYLER
SUBJECT: TRAFFIC STOPS

In the past several months, the police chief has received several complaints from citizens who have questioned the department's policy on traffic stops. A total of seven complaints have been registered within the past month relating to suspected racial profiling. Specifically, criticism has come from parents who report that their teenage sons and daughters are being systematically stopped and questioned simply because they are Hispanic and for no other reason. Nearly all these parents relate that after being stopped their children were questioned about their activities but none received a traffic citation.

Consequently, the department's policy with regard to traffic enforcement will be examined and scrutinized for possible revisions. In the interim, all traffic stops will result in either the issuance of a citation or the completion of a form identifying the nature of the stop and pertinent information with regard to the race and age of the driver and any passengers. These "Traffic Stop" contact forms will be distributed to all patrol officers during briefing.

1. What process should this police department use to examine its policies and procedures relating to traffic stops?
2. Why is periodic review of policy and procedures important?
3. If asked to revise policy and procedures relating to traffic stops, what ideas would you suggest to address concerns about profiling citizens?

Introduction

A stigma attaches to police work because of its connection with evil, crime, perversity, and disorder. Though it may not be reasonable, it is common that

those who fight the dreadful end up being dreaded themselves. Because the police must act quickly and often on mere intuition, their interventions are lacking in those aspects of moral sophistication which only a more extended and more scrupulous consideration can afford.
—**Egon Bittner, 1980**[1]

In February 2000, four white New York police officers were found not guilty of the killing of a West African immigrant from Guinea named Amadou Diallo. The jury, which consisted of four black women, one white woman, and seven white men, deliberated for three days before acquitting the police officers of second-degree murder charges. Evidence at the trial showed that the officers fired more than forty shots at Diallo in a small vestibule adjacent to his Bronx apartment. Diallo fit the description of a suspect sought by police for rape and when confronted pulled from his pocket a wallet that police mistook for a handgun. The police officers made a split-second decision to defend themselves, and after the barrage of gunfire, Diallo lay dead after being struck 19 times.

In May 2011, SWAT team members of the Pima County Sheriff's Office shot Jose Guerena at his home in Tucson, Arizona, while executing a search warrant for suspected drug trafficking based on information obtained from a confidential informant. Guerena, a 26-year-old former U.S. Marine who served two tours in Iraq, had been sleeping with his wife and son, after working the night shift at a local mining and refining company. As police entered the home, Guerena brandished an AR-15 rifle and SWAT members opened fire. An autopsy revealed that Guerena had been shot 22 times by police.

These and many other real-life scenarios portray a situation in which police reacted to various stimuli in a given environment. The officers made a decision to respond in a certain way based on the immediate information available to them and having processed that information through their individual belief systems. Although the outcomes were tragic, the actions by the police are indicative of decisions that can be made when police conceive a situation as life threatening.

Why were the police quick to fire their weapons? Perhaps it was partly because policing in the United States is a dangerous job. The Officer Down Memorial Page reports that since 1791, there have been 20,640 police officers who have died in the line of duty.[2] In 2010, 105 line of duty deaths were recorded in America. For police, therefore, the possibility of being put in a life-threatening situation is real. When this knowledge is mixed with a volatile situation, tragedy can occur. Yet precisely because police officers can and do make mistakes and because they are given the authority to use lethal force, police will always be subjected to intense scrutiny and be held accountable for their discretionary actions.

In this chapter, we explore police **discretion** and the decision-making process. We begin by elaborating on several elements that constitute the definition of police discretion. Next, we explore the nature of policies and procedures and explain how theory and practice work hand in hand to produce the desired results of an organization's **mission statement**. Our attention then turns to the decision-making process, both on an individual basis and by groups. Three important fact-finding techniques are introduced that can be utilized when tough decisions need to be made by personnel in the police agency. The final section of this chapter addresses several key issues relating to community policing. You will recall the introduction to community policing in Chapter 1. In this chapter, our aim is to provide a basic understanding of the principles and core components of problem-solving within the community policing model.

Discretion

Making choices about what action is most appropriate for a given situation is a task that police are constantly asked to perform. Oftentimes it amounts to on-the-job problem solving by means of trial and error. With patience and enough guesses, this process often leads to successful results. However, this form of decision making lacks uniformity in its procedure, is usually very time consuming, and limits what knowledge is gained to the individual who is trying to resolve the problem.

During other times, police must simply react because the situation warrants an immediate response. Here, the demand is for the police officer to possess a repertoire of common-sense reactions, the choice of which one might be appropriate, usually based on the nature and extent of the emergency or crucial situation. Training then becomes an important means of directing police discretion in the sense that reactive behavior involves "decision making on one's feet" with limited thought and without delay.

Several definitions have been given for discretion in the context of police behavior. Here are several interpretations to consider:

- Discretion involves day-to-day decisions of police that involve routine but adaptive choices. These choices reflect a consideration but not necessarily a complete adoption of organizational policies, as well as an operational style of policing.[3]
- The decision whether and how to intervene in a situation while evaluating the costs and benefits of various kinds of action.[4]
- The power to decide which rules apply to a given situation and whether or not to apply them.[5]
- The use of individual judgment by officers in making decisions as to which of several behavioral responses is appropriate in specific situations.[6]

Problem Solving

For our purposes, we define police discretion as the power to selectively enforce laws in order to handle situations and problems. While we attempt to keep this definition simple, there are three important concepts involved here that require elaboration. First, police discretion involves the discriminate use of power legitimized from governmental and legal concepts that have been established over time to provide social control. We understand police power to be necessarily crucial in modern society, and great demands are placed on its use. Consider the following statement by Ben Whitacker, which captures the essence of the public's supposition about police power and its application in order to provide protective services to the community:

> We expect him [the police officer] to be human and yet inhuman. We employ him to administer the law, and yet ask him to waive it. We resent him when he enforces the law in our own case, yet demand his dismissal when he does not elsewhere. We offer him bribes, yet denounce his corruption. We expect him to be a member of society, yet not share its values. We admire violence, even against society itself, but condemn force by the police on our own behalf. We tell the police that they are entitled to information from the public, yet we ostracize informers. We ask for crime to be eradicated, but only by the use of "sporting" methods.[7]

A second concept found in our definition is that we understand discretion to mean **selective enforcement**, which contemplates the influence of police behavior on a given action of power. In other words, police action is often different because discretion is invariably based on individual choice and preference. One's perceptions, belief systems, and other individual personality traits influence a chosen course of action. Likewise, education, special training, and experience bear on police behavior and how an officer prefers to act.

A third concept is that mandatory actions such as the law and departmental policies become powerful determinants of police behavior. Police discretion involves handling situations and problems. Some are critical events that cause police to react to uncertainty in a given circumstance. For example, when police respond to a robbery in progress, discretionary judgments, such as choosing the most direct route to the location and the amount of force that might be necessary to intervene, must be made quickly. Yet at other times, police discretion is more aligned with proactive decision making. For example, police managers having the ability to preplan the most appropriate way to enforce traffic rules at popular civic events. So, the police organization's ability to clearly articulate guidelines that govern behavior becomes a determinate of discretion. The more lackadaisical the guidelines, the more opportunity for individual police to introduce their own biases and legal interpretations into the decision-making process.

Managing Discretion

In police organizations the "street officer" who patrols the community has the most contact with the public and therefore the greatest opportunity to use discretion. Line staff are almost entirely responsible for enforcing those laws that are least precise, most ambiguous, or whose application is most sensitive to the availability of scarce resources and the policies of the police administrator.[8]

The police manager must decide what steps must be taken to affect the way in which the street officer uses discretion. Although it seems plausible that well-established policies and procedures will sufficiently guide police behavior, it is not likely that such protocol can be guaranteed in practice. This is partly because a specific procedure tends to generate a standard to be followed in a given situation, and there are situations in which no standard seems to apply. Consequently, the idea of managing discretion becomes an endless task for the supervisors and managers of police organizations, especially if strict control is a desired goal of the administration.

All law enforcement agencies through the United States are accustomed to establishing a policy and procedures manual to help guide the job performance of their personnel. Policies and procedures are principles that govern a police organization's operation, as well as prescribe processes to be followed to achieve agency goals. A **policy statement** establishes what is to be done in relation to a particular issue. It reflects the philosophy of the organization and defines the purpose(s) for which an action is taken.

Procedures provide details on how policies are to be accomplished by specifying the steps to be taken, the order in which those steps will be carried out and by whom. Together, policies and procedures provide direction to staff by communicating, in writing, the standard practices to follow in certain situations. By standardizing police practices, the policy and procedures manual serves as a valuable tool in promoting consistency and efficiency within the police organization. Moreover, a policy and procedures manual that is thorough, clearly written, and revised as needed:

1. formalizes mechanisms for the transfer of authority and responsibility to line staff
2. provides a basis for staff training and development
3. addresses mandates developed by national and state law enforcement standards and accreditation organizations

Problem Solving

4. helps to provide accountability by protecting against illegal, unprofessional, and ineffectual practices of police personnel
5. provides documentation to help the administration defend the agency in court actions

Controlling Discretion through Professionalism

O. W. Wilson founded the idea of managing discretion under his concept of police "professionalism," which emerged after the 1931 Wickersham Commission described American police as violent, incompetent, and corrupt. In 1956 Wilson wrote:

> Police objectives are achieved by policemen at the level of performance where the patrolman or detective deals face-to-face with the public—the complainants, suspects, and offenders—and the success of the department is judged by the performance of these officers. Decisions that are advantageous to the department are most likely to be made by policemen who have been selected in a manner to assure superior ability, who understand the police objectives and are sympathetic to them, who are loyal to their department and capable of operating effectively, efficiently, and semi-automatically, and who have high morale.[9]

This Wilsonian professional model, as it became known, concentrated on issues of taking the control away from political influences and placing it into the hands of "professional" police. Achieving this shift from political control to an autonomous public agency required that the nature of police service also change from crime prevention to reactive law enforcement. Consequently, police organizations throughout America in the mid-1900s revisited their administrative policies and developed new supervision strategies, with the ultimate objective of gaining administrative control of police behavior.[10]

Of course, those believing that these concepts were too militaristic criticized this ideology of policing. William Bopp described the basic problem of a heavy-handed police administration in the following manner:

> [O. W. Wilson] unswervingly subscribed to the notions of narrow spans of control, a rigid chain of command, the sanctity of written pronouncements on a wide variety of subjects, specialization of tasks, carefully controlled delegation of authority and responsibility, and the close supervision of the troops in the field. It is narrow in the extreme, and has actually retarded professionalism by fostering an administrative attitude that the rank and file police officers are not to be trusted; they must be closely watched, the subjects of massive policy pronouncements limiting their discretion, and consistently threatened with punishment to forestall misbehavior.[11]

Although the nature of police work remains much the same, perspectives about the job have evolved over time. Demonstrations and riots that occurred throughout the United States confirm that to enforce the law is sometimes to create disorder. What these civil actions also indicated was a need for a cooperative rather than a conflict-oriented model of policing.[12] As a result, new perspectives have emerged that draw attention to the need for police to acquire problem-solving skills that can be applied to a wide range of complex situations.

Even though policing has arguably become even more complex in the twenty-first century and the discretion required in today's policing may be widely acknowledged, the impact of this awareness on police practice is not clearly apparent. George Kelling explains that,

> attempts to control and shape police behavior are still largely mired in the organizational and control apparatus that characterized the far simpler, mid-20th century view of policing: command and control, quasi-military training, factory-like models of supervision, and extensive rules and regulations. These control mechanisms, which are irrelevant to street policing, are based on the Taylor model (discussed in Chapter 2) that dominated organizational thinking for most of the 20th century.[13]

The Nature of Decision Making

Good decision making by public officials is judged by whether or not the outcome is in the best interest of society as a whole. Police are often put in situations in which they must consider the good of many, not of a few. This is a big responsibility, and very often the public does not appreciate the potential dilemmas that surface. In fact, many times people get upset at police because of decisions that are made to help the general public. Take for example, the need for traffic enforcement in order to reduce the number of automobile deaths and injuries in America. In 2008, 37,261 people were killed and 2,346,000 were injured in the estimated 5,811,000 police-reported motor vehicle traffic crashes.[14] According to these figures, the police function of traffic enforcement is clearly necessary, yet most people become immediately frustrated and defensive when pulled over for a traffic violation.

Decision making is greatly influenced by the situation and subsequent need for urgency. A decision that must be made quickly, almost instinctively, is more prone to risk than a decision that can be well thought out and pretested. Decision situations can also be distinguished by the repetitive nature of the situation. If the situation occurs many times over, police personnel can follow rules and patterns of behavior that have been established as a result of previous successful experiences. However, approaches to new and unique situations necessitate that much more reliance will be needed on intuition and judgment.

Problem Solving

Decisions are based upon some combination of fact, theory, and alternatives. As such, organizations, individuals, and groups make choices through the process of an initial gathering of facts, the interpretation of those facts and theorizing why a specific decision is best, and choosing a course of action from several alternatives. The initial stage of the process involves data input (i.e., whatever information is present that can be useful information to make a decision). Next, interpreting this information is accomplished by filtering facts through the observer's belief system. Finally, the decision maker makes a choice among alternatives based upon both the observable events and beliefs. This choice is made against a background of the objectives of the decision maker and after as much information has been gathered as seems necessary and as time and available resources allow.

Group Decision Making

The group decision-making process is comparable with that used by an individual decision maker, but it is much more complex. The additional complications arise of course, because the decision is no longer based on individual knowledge and belief. Rather, the decision is now influenced by the presence of several members of a group, each of whom may have somewhat different information about the decision situation. Each may possess past experiences that are different but relative to the present situation under consideration, and whereas all the members might have similar belief systems, there will no doubt be fluctuations. These differences among the group members may bring about altered perceptions of the alternative choices available to the group and consequently the best course of action. Therefore, a major task in the group decision process is to exchange information among the group members.

Effectively communicating is a crucial step toward increasing the individual members' awareness of different comprehensions of the situation in which they are involved. Oftentimes, however, the dynamics that take place in the interaction group process can include one or more members attempting to influence the action of the entire group. That is, some members of the group may feel compelled to use pressure tactics on other members to align their views and preferences with what is perceived as the favorite course of action. Coalitions may also be formed in which benefits or rewards are offered to those participating in return for support of a particular course of action. This kind of interaction is typical, especially when the stakes are high. Consider, for example, the behavior of politicians whose daily activities involve using power to influence people in ways that benefit individuals or groups and not necessarily society as a whole.

The steps involved in the group decision-making process are illustrated in Exhibit 7.1. Some basic concepts that are commonly regarded in

1. IDENTIFYING THE SOURCE OF THE PROBLEM. There are two questions that must be answered: "Who says that a problem exists?" and "What will happen if nothing is done about the current situation?" Once these questions are answered, the task is to take ownership of the problem and to solicit the assistance of others in solving it, rather than implying that it's someone else's problem that they ought to solve.
2. CLARIFYING THE PROBLEM. This is especially important when working with a large group of people. If group members view the problem differently, the result will be that people will offer solutions to different problems. This calls for precise isolation of the most central characteristic of the problem and requires close analysis of the problem to clearly separate the influencing from the non-influencing factors. This second step of the decision-making process generally requires a consideration of the law and the agency's policy, and the use of good judgment. To clarify the problem, the group should answer the following questions: What are the key or critical factors of the problem? Who legitimately or logically should be included in the decision? Are there others who need to be consulted prior to a decision?
3. GETTING THE FACTS. Facts must be gathered for multiple sources. Individuals can often provide information pertinent to the problem. Records and other documents are other valuable sources of information.
4. SOLICITING ALTERNATIVE COURSES OF ACTION. During this process, the group identifies as many solutions to the problem as possible before discussing the specific advantages and disadvantages of each. A pitfall to avoid in problem solving is that the first few suggested solutions may be exhaustively debated, resulting in many worthwhile ideas never being considered. By identifying many solutions, a superior idea often surfaces that reduces or even eliminates the need for discussing details of more debatable issues. These solutions may be logical attacks at the cause or they may be creative solutions that need not be rational. Therefore, it is important at this step to limit the time spent discussing any one solution and to concentrate instead on announcing as many as possible.
5. SELECTING ONE OR MORE ALTERNATIVES FOR ACTION. Before selecting specific alternatives for action, it is advisable to identify criteria the desired solution must satisfactorily fulfill. This typically eliminates unnecessary discussion and helps focus the group toward the solution (or solutions) that will most likely work. During this stage of the process, it becomes necessary to look for and discuss the advantages and disadvantages of alternatives that appear most feasible. The task is for the group members to come to a mutual agreement on which solutions to actually put into action.
6. PREPARING FOR IMPLEMENTATION. This requires developing a strategic plan consisting of the details that must be carried out by members of the organization for a solution to be effectively activated. Once the required steps are identified, it means assigning these tasks to someone for action. It also means identifying what specific resources will be needed and setting a time frame for completion.
7. THE ACTION PLAN. The next process is to implement the course of action. This calls for people assigned responsibility for any part of the plan to carry out their assignments and to keep to established time limits.
8. EVALUATION. Before the plan is implemented, the group should discuss evaluation and accountability. The goal of evaluation is to monitor performance, provide a source of information that can be used to make future decisions, and to provide feedback to the group members. Once the actions have been completed, it is necessary to assess their effectiveness. Did the solution work? If not, can a revision make it work? What actions are necessary to implement changes?

Exhibit 7.1 Attacking a problem.

Problem Solving

a step-by-step problem solving method include: defining the source of the problem, clarifying the problem and fact finding, choosing among alternative strategies, preparing for implementation, executing the action plan, and evaluation. Each of these steps in the process is predicated on the notion that group decision making is a participatory process. It is a method of improving police services by utilizing the abilities, experience, and talents of all personnel levels by soliciting their input and permitting decision making at the lowest levels.

Analytical Tools for Decision Making

Police agencies tackle tough decisions that require fact-finding techniques to be utilized. The objective of using such techniques is to eliminate uncertainty and ambiguity in the group decision-making process. Although there are many different types of analytical tools that can be used to elicit ideas, we have chosen to highlight three of the more popular techniques used in group problem solving. They include brainstorming, Delphi Technique, and critical path analysis.

Brainstorming is one of the oldest methods of gathering information about a particular problem. It works by focusing on a problem and then deliberately coming up with as many solutions as possible. Brainstorming is most effective in generating new ideas and typically involves the following process:

- Facilitation: Initially, a leader takes control of the session, defining the problem to be solved with any criteria that must be met, and then keeps the session on course. The leader tries to keep the brainstorming on task and steers the group toward the development of several solutions.
- Group participation: Participants in the brainstorming process are encouraged to come up with wild ideas. No ideas are criticized or evaluated in any way before all ideas relevant to the problem are considered. Criticism stifles creativity and cripples the free-running nature of a good brainstorming session.
- Recording: Two or more group members are identified as record keepers. Their task is to record all the suggestions in plain sight (using a chalkboard or flip chart) so that the participants can see the proposed ideas and build on them.
- Evaluation: Once the brainstorming session is complete, a follow-up sorting and evaluation of the ideas is conducted. The goal is to identify those ideas that will best provide a solution to the problem at hand.

The RAND Corporation developed the Delphi Technique in the 1950s as a method of predicting the future by consulting experts in the problem area. It has since evolved into a decision-making tool and is particularly appropriate when decision making is required in a political or emotional environment or when the decisions affect strong factions with opposing preferences. The fundamental premise of this decision-making method is that by involving a group of experts in a particular field to independently predict future events and then averaging out their responses, important information can be obtained with regard to best course of action to solve problems.

The general procedures of this method are based on three characteristics: anonymity, statistical analysis, and feedback of reasoning. The RAND Corporation found that in order to provide a reliable forecast, it was necessary to put together a team of professionals. They also found that anonymity was the key to future success. If a team were assembled, there would likely be some members who possessed more experience than other members of the team. The more experienced individuals would also perhaps be widely respected for their work. The problem that this causes within the team is that less experienced team members would rarely challenge the opinions of better known experts. Therefore, the opinion of the team would often reflect the opinion of the dominant team member and would not constitute a true unbiased consensus.

To solve this problem, the Delphi Technique involves a team of experts who are kept in the dark as to the identity of other team members. The team never meets and acts without the influence or interference of other team members. Each individual's forecast is taken and correlated, and a consensus is then determined. Any individual whose forecast falls outside the consensus is then asked to either defend his or her forecast with statistical evidence or rethink the conclusions. This process is repeated several times until a reasonable and usable hypothesis is concluded.

The Delphi Technique illustrates one key problem that can plague an organization. It shows that the best ideas do not always surface from the most experienced members of the team. As for those individuals who are perceived to be the best according to reputation, they are forced to support or conform. In an open group, they would rarely be challenged because of their reputation and stature.

Critical path analysis is an extremely effective method of analyzing a complex project. It helps calculate the minimum length of time in which the project can possibly be completed and prioritizes activities that need to be completed within that certain time frame. Critical path analysis helps management focus on the essential activities to which attention and resources should be devoted and gives an effective basis for the scheduling and monitoring of progress.

The essential concept behind critical path analysis is that some planned activities are dependent on other activities being completed first. For example,

Problem Solving

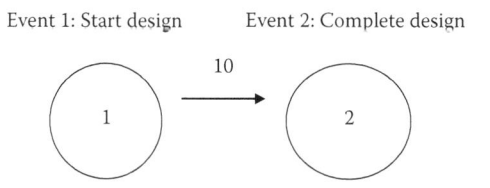

Event 1: Start design   Event 2: Complete design

```
    ①  ——10——▶  ②
```

Activity 1–2: The length of time between the start of the design and the completion of the design.

Exhibit 7.2 Problem solving.

a police manager would not hire additional patrol officers unless money had been previously secured to pay for the new employees' salaries and equipment. These dependent activities need to be completed in a sequence, with each activity being more or less completed before the next activity can begin. Dependent activities are also called "sequential" activities. Other activities are not dependent on completion of any other tasks. These are nondependent or "parallel" tasks.

There are several tools that engage the critical path analysis method to facilitate problem solving. Most are arrow diagrams, such as the decision tree and cause and effect diagram. One of the best methods of engaging critical path analysis is the **Program Evaluation and Review Technique (PERT)**. Through PERT, complex projects can be blueprinted as a network of activities and events (activity network diagram). As such, PERT is a graphical technique that uses a chart to describe a project or program. The basic visual presentation has only two symbols: a circle (event) and an arrow (activity). The events are fixed points in time and represent either the beginning or the completion of an activity. Exhibit 7.2 illustrates the basic event and activity with a time estimate for the activity (i.e., 10 represents hours, days, months, etc.). Exhibit 7.3 is a refined PERT chart that identifies parallel paths that may be performed at any time before or after a particular stage is reached. Note that time estimates are assigned to every activity and then added to estimate the total time for the project. With this simple diagram, if time is registered in days, it is easy to see that the total time for the network is 24 days.

The advantages of using a PERT chart include:

- PERT charts can become very complex if detailed networks exist, but they force the manager to contemplate personnel assignments for the project in detail.
- To demonstrate best- and worst-case project scenarios, most PERT charts identify three time estimates: most optimistic, most pessimistic, and most realistic.
- PERT charts are very useful in large, complex studies where overlooking details may create irresolvable problems.

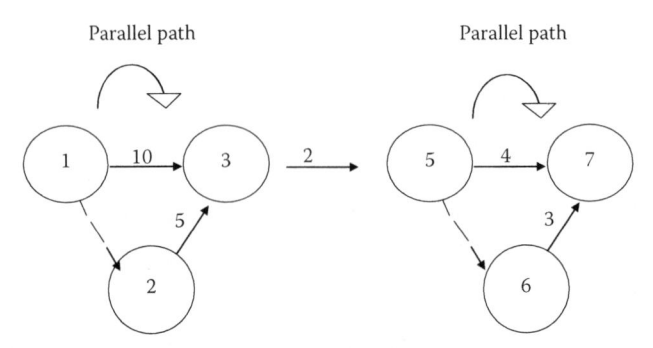

Exhibit 7.3 Refined PERT chart.

- PERT charts are frequently used within an organization for detailed evaluation planning.
- The critical path of a PERT chart highlights important interim deadlines that must be met if the overall evaluation study is to be completed on time.

Community Policing

In Chapter 1, we introduced community policing, which has been arguably the most widely adopted law enforcement reform of the past thirty years. During this period, communities throughout the country have made substantial progress in implementing community policing in large part because of the financial support received through grants allocated by the National Institute of Justice's Office of Community Oriented Policing Services (COPS). Our intention here is to reiterate some of the concepts of community policing with emphasis on several perspectives of problem solving.

Community policing is an organizational philosophy that defines how the goals and objectives of the police agency will be met. Within this philosophy, there are four general principles that guide its use: (1) relies on organizational decentralization and patrol reorientation to facilitate two-way communication between the police and the public; (2) assumes a commitment to broadly focused, problem-oriented policing; (3) requires that police be responsive to citizen demands when they identify local problems and set priorities; and (4) implies a commitment to helping neighborhoods solve crime problems on their own through community organizations and crime prevention programs.[15]

Advocates of the community policing model argue that its proactive nature enables the community to develop strategies that prevent criminal activity before it occurs. The community policing philosophy put into practice is quite different than traditional policing practices that merely

Problem Solving

require police to respond to calls for service that have occurred after the fact. Often, calls for service are related and, if grouped together, disclose a pattern of activity or behavior that presents a more accurate picture of the condition that prompted the calls in the first place. A problem-oriented policing approach offers agencies a model for addressing the underlying conditions that create crime and cause other problems of concern to the community.

- A problem-oriented approach recognizes the expertise of line officers and deputies and allows them to use that expertise to study problems and develop creative solutions to those problems. Experiences in departments around the country have shown that line officers and deputies are capable of contributing much more to the resolution of crime and other community problems than is presently asked of them. Officers and deputies engaged in problem solving have expressed greater job satisfaction and exhibited a keener interest in their work.
- A problem-oriented approach entails greater involvement of the public in police work. Communities must be consulted to ensure that police are addressing the real needs and concerns of citizens. Community involvement and support are key ingredients if law enforcement agencies hope to find long-term solutions to recurrent problems.
- The problem-oriented approach recognizes that much of the information needed to examine and understand a problem is not contained in any law enforcement agency's files. As a result, problem-solving officers and deputies are encouraged to draw on a wide range of sources of information outside of their departments to analyze and address problems.[16]

Within the key components of community policing, problem solving includes the process of engaging in systematic examination of identified problems to develop and rigorously evaluate effective responses. Rather than responding to crime only after it occurs, community policing encourages agencies to proactively develop solutions to the immediate underlying conditions contributing to public safety problems.[17] A major conceptual vehicle for helping officers to think about problem solving in a structured and disciplined way is the scanning, analysis, response, and assessment (SARA) problem-solving model.

- Scanning: Identifying and prioritizing problems.
- Analysis: Researching what is known about the problem.

- Response: Developing solutions to bring about lasting reductions in the number and extent of problems.
- Assessment: Evaluating the success of the responses.

Exhibit 7.4 displays an outline of the SARA model provided by the Center for Problem-Oriented Policing.

Problem solving is based on the assumption that "crime and disorder can be reduced in small geographic areas by carefully studying the characteristics of problems in the area, and then applying the appropriate resources..." and on the assumption that "Individuals make choices based on the opportunities presented by the immediate physical and social characteristics of an

---

Scanning:
- Identifying recurring problems of concern to the public and the police
- Identifying the consequences of problems for the community and the police
- Prioritizing those problems
- Developing broad goals
- Confirming that the problems exist
- Determining how frequently the problems occur and how long they have been taking place
- Selecting problems for closer examination

Analysis:
- Identifying and understanding the events and conditions that precede and accompany the problem
- Identifying relevant data to be collected
- Researching what is known about the problem type
- Taking inventory of how the problem is currently addressed and the strengths and limitations of the current response
- Narrowing the scope of the problem as specifically as possible
- Identifying a variety of resources that may be of assistance in developing a deeper understanding of the problem
- Developing a working hypothesis about why the problem is occurring

Response:
- Brainstorming for new interventions
- Searching for what other communities with similar problems have done
- Choosing among the alternative interventions
- Outlining a response plan and identifying responsible parties
- Stating the specific objectives for the response plan
- Carrying out the planned activities

Assessment:
- Determining whether the plan was implemented (a process evaluation)
- Collecting pre- and post-response qualitative and quantitative data
- Determining whether broad goals and specific objectives were attained
- Identifying any new strategies needed to augment the original plan
- Conducting ongoing assessment to ensure continued effectiveness

---

Exhibit 7.4 The SARA Model. (From the Center for Problem-Oriented Policing http://www.popcenter.org)

Problem Solving

area. By manipulating these factors, people will be less inclined to act in an offensive manner."[18]

Determining the underlying causes of crime depends, to a great extent, on an in-depth knowledge of community. The problem-solving process is explained further:

> The theory behind problem-oriented policing is simple. Underlying conditions create problems. These conditions might include the characteristics of the people involved (offenders, potential victims, and others), the social setting in which these people interact, the physical environments, and the way the public deals with these conditions. A problem created by these conditions may generate one or more incidents. These incidents, while stemming from a common source, may appear to be different. For example, social and physical conditions in a deteriorated apartment complex may generate burglaries, acts of vandalism, intimidation of pedestrians by rowdy teenagers, and other incidents. These incidents, some of which come to police attention, are symptoms of the problems. The incidents will continue so long as the problem that creates them persists.[19]

Supervision and Management in Community Policing

Implementing the principles of community policing requires a change in the organization that must originate at the top and filter down through the organization. It is imperative that the chief executive fully commits to the proactive policing concept and sets the tone for others in the police agency. "The task facing the police chief is nothing less than to change the fundamental culture of the organization. Throughout the period of change, the office of the chief executive is going to be surrounded by turbulence, like it or not. It will require personal leadership of considerable strength and perseverance."[20]

Once the leader of the police agency has committed to adopting community policing, success hinges on how well the staff implements this proactive approach to policing. As such, the police managers and supervisors play an important role in fulfilling the goals of community policing. The effort to collaborate at all levels of the police agency is as critical to successful community policing as the partnership between the officer and the community members. Some of the dynamics pertaining to these interactions include:[21]

- Higher-level managers need to adopt a more strategic outlook to augment or replace the traditional police "command and control" mentality.
- Productivity measures, individual performance appraisals, internal communications practices, and other management systems may also need careful attention and adjustment.

- Supervisors should adopt a "coaching" approach in dealing with subordinates, especially while subordinates learn their new roles of community engagement and problem solving.
- Supervisors will need to assist officers in developing resource contacts in agencies with which they are unfamiliar.
- Management may be called upon to support officers' needs for flexibility in working hours so that they can meet with the community and with members of other agencies and organizations.
- Officers should have access to much of the same information being used by the planning team to improve the chances they will share perceptions of problems and priorities.
- Officer interaction with planning team members should be encouraged, particularly because many team members will be representatives of social service agencies and community organizations.

COMMUNITY POLICING CONSORTIUM TO COMMUNITY ORIENTED POLICING SERVICES

The Community Policing Consortium was created and funded in 1993 as a multi-phased project by the U.S. Department of Justice, Bureau of Justice Assistance (BJA). During Phase I, the consortium was composed of the International Association of Chiefs of Police (IACP), the National Sheriffs' Association (NSA), the Police Executive Research Forum (PERF), and the Police Foundation. These four organizations: (1) researched and produced the consortium monograph entitled, *Understanding Community Policing: A Framework for Action*; (2) provided training and technical assistance to five community policing demonstration sites; and (3) conducted meetings of community policing leaders. During the second phase of the project, the consortium's scope of responsibility was expanded to include the development of community policing curricula and the provision of training and technical assistance to BJA grant recipients, demonstration sites, and comprehensive communities. During the latter part of Phase II, the consortium welcomed the National Organization of Black Law Enforcement Executives (NOBLE). During Phase III, responsibility for the consortium transferred from the BJA to the Office of Community-Oriented Policing Services (COPS).

- **The International Association of Chiefs of Police** is a professional organization comprising more than thirteen thousand top law enforcement executives from the United States and seventy-nine nations. IACP members lead and manage

several hundred thousand law enforcement officers and civilian employees in international, federal, state, and local governments. Since 1893, IACP has facilitated the exchange of information among police administrators, has promoted the highest standards of performance and conduct within the police profession, and has been dedicated to fair and impartial enforcement of laws in accordance with constitutional and fundamental human rights. IACP's police practitioner members enable the association to provide contemporary and innovative information on issues and experiences that form the development of new strategies, tactics, and programs.
- **The National Organization of Black Law Enforcement Executives** (NOBLE) was founded in September 1976 to address crime in urban low-income areas. Recognizing that black law enforcement executives could have a significantly more effective impact upon the criminal justice system through a unified voice, NOBLE was created. NOBLE's membership is located around the country with more than thirty-five local chapters representing state, local, and federal law enforcement executives. NOBLE's mission is to work with communities to foster greater involvement and cooperation with criminal justice agencies, have a positive impact on crime and violence, unify the impact of black law enforcement officers at the executive levels, provide black law enforcement executives with a platform where ideas and opinions can be addressed, and disseminate information pertinent to minority law enforcement executives. NOBLE also provides training, research, and consultation on criminal justice issues.
- **The National Sheriffs' Association** is a nonprofit organization dedicated to raising the level of professionalism among law enforcement leaders across the nation. Throughout its fifty-six years, NSA has been involved in numerous programs to enable sheriffs, deputies, chiefs of police, and others in law enforcement to perform their jobs in the best possible manner and to better serve the people in their counties or jurisdictions. The NSA offers training, information, and recognition to sheriffs, deputies, and other policing officials throughout the nation and has forged cooperative relationships with local, state, and federal law enforcement.
- **The Police Executive Research Forum** is a national membership organization of progressive police executives from the

largest city, county, and state law enforcement agencies. PERF is dedicated to improving policing and advancing professionalism through research and involvement in public policy debate. PERF was incorporated in 1977 to: (1) improve the delivery of police services and crime control nationwide; (2) encourage debate of police and criminal justice issues within the law enforcement community; (3) implement and promote the use of law enforcement research; and (4) provide national leadership, technical assistance, and vital management services to police agencies.
- **The Police Foundation** was established in 1970 with assistance from the Ford Foundation to improve policing and reduce crime in America through research, technical assistance, and communication. The foundation played a pivotal role in the development of community policing, paved the way for the advancement of women in policing, and is breaking new ground with its comparative studies of large urban police departments and technical assistance programs. It provides technical assistance and training to government at all levels and to private institutions concerned with public safety. The Police Foundation has also established a Center for the Study of Police and Civil Disorders.

Questions in Review

1. List several elements that constitute the definition of police discretion.
2. Distinguish between policies and procedures and describe what purposes they serve for a police organization.
3. Identify the steps involved in the group decision-making process.
4. Describe the four general principles of community policing.
5. Outline the SARA model of problem-oriented policing.
6. Define the role of leaders and managers in community policing.

End Notes

1. Egon Bittner, *The Functions of Police in Modern Society* (Cambridge, MA: Olegeschlager, Gunn, and Hain, 1980).
2. Officer Down Memorial Page, Inc. at *http://www.odmp.org*.
3. Michael K. Brown, *Working the Street: Police Discretion and the Dilemmas of Reform* (New York: Russell Sage Foundation, 1981).

4. James Q. Wilson, *Varieties of Police Behavior* (Cambridge, MA: Harvard University Press, 1968).
5. Richard V. Ericson, *Reproducing Order: A Study of Police Patrol Work* (Toronto, Canada: University of Toronto Press, 1982).
6. Steven M. Cox, *Police: Practices-Perspectives-Problems* (Boston, MA: Allyn and Bacon, 1996).
7. Ben Whitaker, *The Police* (Harmondsworth, UK: Penguin Books, 1964).
8. James Q. Wilson, 1968, p. 8.
9. O. W. Wilson, "Basic Police Policies," in *The Police Chief* (November 1956), pp. 28–29.
10. George L. Kelling, and Mark H. Moore, "The Evolving Strategy of Policing," in *Perspectives on Policing*, No. 4 (Cambridge, MA: U.S. Department of Justice and Program in Criminal Justice Policy and Management, John F. Kennedy School of Government, Harvard University, November 1988).
11. William J. Bopp, *O.W. Wilson and the Search for a Police Profession* (Port Washington, NY: Kennikat Press, 1977).
12. Jerome Skolnick, *Justice Without Trial: Law Enforcement in a Democratic Society*, 3rd ed. (Indianapolis, IN: Macmillan, 1994).
13. George L. Kelling, *"Broken Windows" and Police Discretion*, NCJ Document 178259 (Washington, DC: U.S. Department of Justice, October 1999).
14. Fatality Analysis Reporting System. *Traffic Safety Facts, 2008 Data Summary* (U.S. Department of Transportation, National Highway Traffic Safety Administration, May 2009).
15. National Institute of Justice 1998 Annual Report to Congress (December, 1999). Washington, DC: NCJ 177617.
16. *Neighborhood-Oriented Policing in Rural Communities: A Program Planning Guide* (Washington, DC: National Institute of Justice, August 1994).
17. *Understanding Community Policing: A Framework for Action* (Washington, DC, Bureau of Justice Assistance Monograph, August 1994).
18. *Understanding Community Policing.*
19. *Understanding Community Policing.*
20. Malcolm K. Sparrow, *Implementing Community Policing: Perspectives on Policing* (Washington, DC: National Institute of Justice and John F. Kennedy School of Government, Harvard University, 1988).
21. *Neighborhood-Oriented Policing in Rural Communities.*

Suggested Additional References and Links to the Web

1. Ronald Glensor and Kenneth Peak, "Implementing Change: Community-Oriented Policing and Problem Solving," in *FBI Law Enforcement Bulletin*, Vol. 65, No. 7 (1996), pp. 14–21.
2. Rachel Boba, *Problems Analysis in Policing* (Washington, DC: The Police Foundation, 2003). Available at http://www.policefoundation.org/pdf/problemanalysisinpolicing.pdf.
3. *Community Policing Defined* is a publication of the U.S. Department of Justice Office of Community Oriented Policing

Services (Washington, DC). http://www.cops.usdoj.gov/files/RIC/Publications/e030917193-CP-Defined.pdf.
4. The Police Executive Research Forum (PERF) is a national membership organization of progressive police executives from the largest city, county, and state law enforcement agencies. http://www.policeforum.org.

Technology and Management 8

Key Individuals, Concepts, and Issues

Technological change
Computer-aided dispatching
Personal locator system
Automatic transmitter system
Technology Assessment Program Information Center (TAPIC)
President's Commission on Law Enforcement and the Administration of Justice
Vehicle tagging system
Smart gun
National Institute of Justice

Definitions

Automatic vehicle locator (AVL) system: A system that has the capability to track police field units that are in service.

COMPSTAT: An automated crime analysis program that allows for instant statistical updating of all reported crimes, arrests, and other police activities.

Computer-aided dispatch (CAD): A computerized dispatching system used to monitor and better display data, including outstanding calls, ongoing incidents, and patrol unit status and activities.

Crime analysis: The examination and tracking of crime patterns or criminal behavior in a community or a specific geographical area.

Crime mapping: A computerized mapping program that is utilized to solve crimes and to aid in the investigation of crimes.

Mobile data terminals (MDTs): Laptop computers that have been installed in police patrol units and are linked with the CAD system.

Personal locator system (PLT): A system that allows for the dispatchers to communicate with and monitor the locations of officers when they are out of their patrol vehicles.

Smart gun: A handgun that can recognize its user by fingerprint pattern.

Chapter Objectives

After completing this chapter you should be able to:

1. Describe the evolution of police technology
2. Describe the current and evolving state of police technology
3. Identify and describe technologies that will keep officers safer in the field
4. Describe computer-aided dispatch technology
5. Identify and describe technologies that will assist the police in solving crimes and identifying suspects
6. Describe technologies that will assist police management and leadership in administrative tasks
7. Discuss how technology can assist police management in enhancing the delivery of services

Introduction

> We are being swept up into a powerful new technology revolution that offers the promise of a great social transformation, unlike any in history.
> **—Jeremy Rifkin**
> *The End of Work, 1995*

The advancements in policing over the past several decades are grounds for optimism in many respects. There have been groundbreaking changes in virtually every area of the policing profession. It is fair to say that technological change is one of the most powerful forces transforming American policing. Technological change, although not independent of social forces, has had a profound effect on policing. Technology has transformed many skills and eliminated others in today's police organizations.

Did you know that technology has made it possible for more effective decentralization of police operations in the community? For example, computers and electronic mail capacity make it possible for instant communication, which makes it more effective for officers to operate out of satellite offices, storefronts, and substations somewhat autonomously from central police headquarters. Most important, information technology is increasingly making it possible for police departments to operate both nationally and globally. It is undeniable that technology is driving much fundamental change in American policing. The police organization from both an administrative and an operational standpoint has benefited tremendously from technological developments.

This chapter will engage in a broad examination of police technology and how it can specifically assist police managers. First, we will discuss some

Technology and Management 171

of the technological advancements in policing. Second, we will discuss how technology will increasingly assist police executives in more effectively managing police operations. The chapter concludes with a brief discussion on evolving police technology.

Police Technology

Over the years, the policing profession has benefited tremendously from technology. This technology can be seen in terms of modern speed detection devices (radar), mobile data terminals in the police vehicle that enable law enforcement officers to obtain instantaneous record checks on people and vehicles, and the state of the art crime scene detection technologies that assist the police in identifying suspects and solving crimes. If the police are to maintain effective service levels, then it is crucial that they keep abreast of technological advancements in the field.

Historical View of Police Technology

The gradual emergence of police technology can be credited in part to President Lyndon Johnson. In 1966, he chartered the President's Commission on Law Enforcement and the Administration of Justice or, as is often referred to, "The Crime Commission Report." The report was divided into nine areas. Of these, one was titled the Task Force Report on Science and Technology. When the president's commission was formed to study the police, specifically, the police use of technology, their findings illuminated that the police were not using technology at its fullest. The commission also found that United States policing was sorely behind in the use of technology.[1] The commission subsequently recommended the development of law enforcement technology. In 1968, the National Institution of Law Enforcement was created to mainly focus on research and development aimed at improving policing.[2]

The National Institute of Law Enforcement focused on a collaborative effort with federal agencies including the Defense Department, the Department of Transportation, the Department of Commerce, and the National Aeronautics and Space Administration. The National Institute of Law Enforcement is directly credited with advancing technology in the policing profession. For example, the institute worked in cooperation with other agencies in the development of riot control agents, nonlethal bullets, night-vision equipment, and personal communication equipment.[3] It was in 1971 that the Institute established the Law Enforcement Standards Laboratory under the Department of Commerce. The objective of the laboratory was to establish voluntary scientific standards for police agencies. These standards primarily pertained to manufacturing in order for police organizations to develop both effective and high quality equipment that could be purchased by police agencies at a low cost.

The Institute of Law Enforcement issued a report that recommended standards that law enforcement technology should gradually evolve to. By the mid-1970s, the Institute of Law Enforcement's laboratory had completed recommendation for the following standards:

- Portable, mobile, and base station transmitters; mobile receivers; and batteries for portable radios
- Walk-through and handheld metal weapon detectors
- Portable X-ray devices for bomb disarmament
- Communication equipment such as voice scramblers, car locator systems, and radio transmitters, receivers, and repeaters
- Magnetic, mechanical, and mercury switches for burglar alarms
- Handcuffs, riot helmets, crash helmets, police body armor, ballistic shields, and hearing protectors[4]

By the mid-1980s, the Technology Assessment Program Information Center (TAPIC) was created by the National Institute of Justice. The TAPIC had several responsibilities including selecting laboratories to test products, overseeing these testing procedures, and publishing the performance reports to document the results of tests. The National Institute of Justice also established the Technological Assessment Program Advisory Council (TAPAC). The TAPAC consists of more than eighty federal, state, and local law enforcement representatives to confirm that the technology that is being advocated fits the practical needs of police work.[5]

During the summer of 1994, there were significant developments in planning for more effective police technology. The Attorney General of the United States and the Deputy Secretary of Defense signed a memorandum of agreement for the purpose of providing for the joint development and transition of technologies that would be applicable for both law enforcement and the military other than war. Furthermore, the 1995 Defense Appropriations Bill allocated funds to support the dual-use technology program. In essence, the bill defined the essential technological assistance that will be contributed by the Department of Justice and the Department of Defense to police agencies. This bill demonstrated a sound commitment to the development and enhancement of technology for both the police and the military, including:

- Concealed weapons detection
- Authorized-user-only handguns or "safe gun" activities

- Less-than-lethal technologies to halt fleeing vehicles and restrain subjects armed with weapons other than firearms
- Development of personal status monitors
- Interactive simulation trainers
- Explosive ordinance detection and disposal
- Mobile sensor platforms
- Urban mapping and three-dimensional scene generation
- Advanced sensor integration
- Sniper identification
- Response technologies
- Support for National Institute of Justice national law enforcement technology centers[6]

Police chiefs and administrators of small and rural police departments face unique challenges securing technology simply because of budget limitations. Perhaps even large metropolitan police departments face their own set of challenges in identifying and securing technology that will potentially assist in accomplishing police objectives. There is some help available to assist law enforcement in identifying technologies. In 1994, the National Institute of Justice created the National Law Enforcement Technology Center (NLETC). The NLETC was created to serve as a technology and information center for law enforcement. Primarily NLETC disseminates information through Regional Law Enforcement Technology Centers that are collectively known as the Justice Technology Information Network (JUSTNET) and through national and regional conferences. Information is also disseminated to law enforcement organizations by providing access to computer bulletin boards. The JUSTNET can assist police organizations in locating equipment that they may use infrequently but need to use in light of some exigent circumstance. This greatly benefits small and rural agencies that may lack the technological resources to begin with. Through JUSTNET's assistance, a police organization can accurately determine their requirement for technology.[7]

The Current State of Police Technology

Technologies in the policing profession have made great strides in recent years. A technology that is sophisticated today may be outdated and archaic in a few years, as is the case, for example, with computer technologies that most police departments use. To have the most state-of-the-art technology is costly, and many police departments do not have the budget allocations that allow them to frequently upgrade and refine the technology that they use. The use of computer technology within law enforcement communities is now considered a necessity. Likewise, just within the past thirty or so years, there have been significant steps in the advancement of computerization in police agencies. Such steps include:

1. The development of "on-line" or "real time" computing, which allows new items of information to be processed instantly as they are entered into the computer system
2. The gradual movement of computer equipment and expertise from a central data processing department serving the local government to a unit within the police department itself, assisted by outside consultants and vendors
3. The rapid development and spread of personal computers, which gave individual employees access to word processing for personal communication and to departmental databases for information relevant to their professional responsibilities[8]

These changes have required the police to take on additional responsibilities in the training and education of rank-and-file police officers and to not rely solely on computer experts. Today's police officers will have to become familiar with computers and their uses. For example, many police departments now have mobile data terminals (MDTs) in their field patrol units, and we project that by the first quarter of the twenty-first century, the majority will have the terminals in place.

These sophisticated MDT units make it possible for police officers in the field to communicate via the computer to the central communications center and with other officers and enables officers to run records checks and get returns on subjects and vehicles in a matter of seconds. With these cutting-edge developments, police officers are now required to learn basic computing skills and competencies. The use of computers in police departments has improved command, control, and communications systems tremendously. In the following pages, we will examine a few other technological developments in the policing profession and discuss how they foster better operation and management practices, which ultimately lead to better police service.

Computer-Aided Dispatch

Imagine for a moment that you are the victim of a crime and need to call the police. You frantically dial a seven-digit telephone number to your local police department. The police dispatcher answers the phone and you report that you need the police right away! Someone has broken into your home and taken your stereo system, VCR, and other miscellaneous items. The dispatcher then asks for your name, address, and phone number and writes it

Technology and Management

on a small time card. The dispatcher clocks the card in a time clock and forwards it to another dispatcher who then dispatches the police to your address. Not too long ago, this was the normal procedure in communications centers prior to the development of 9-1-1 emergency systems. The emergence of 9-1-1 systems has resulted in a much more efficient system not only in terms of reporting crimes, but also in eliciting police response. Fortunately, the majority of American police departments now have 9-1-1 services for police response.

Computer-aided dispatching (CAD) represents a more efficient way in which to dispatch police units and take incoming 9-1-1 calls. The CAD technology allows for the equal distribution of workloads across many different computers. In contrast to the old dispatching system, when a 9-1-1 call comes in to the communications center, the number the caller is calling from is automatically registered in the computer and in most cases the location of the call. This is advantageous for hang-up calls that the dispatcher may receive. With the CAD technology, they can identify the number and location where the hang-up came from, and police could be dispatched to ensure that there is not a problem. A dispatcher assigned to only one computer workstation can perform multiple tasks that used to take two or maybe three dispatchers twice the time.[9] The CAD work systems can be divided into several full-screen pages. Each page can access different applications. These include calls for service, CAD activity log, electronic activity log, electronic messaging, state and National Crime Information Center (NCIC) interface, and host computer interface. The dispatcher can switch back and forth between applications with a computer keystroke.

The CAD system enables police departments to provide better service to the community by improving the response time of police officers. In the past, police managers have grappled with the question of how to effectively improve the efficiency of police response in the field. In reality, the CAD system has significantly improved police efficiency. The CAD graphic database query and integrated map display with automatic display of incident locations can assist in detection of duplicate or related incidents. The CAD system activity log records every active transaction entered into the system (e.g., date, time, and user identification number). The contents of the CAD activity log can be displayed a number of different ways depending on the needs of the dispatchers, officers in the field, and police supervision or management.

There are three grid systems that CAD utilizes. First, grids are used to determine proper jurisdiction. For example, a call comes into the communication center regarding an injury traffic accident. Information is then fed into the database usually in matter of seconds. The CAD determines whether the police department or sheriff's department should respond and which fire department has jurisdiction to respond (e.g., city or county). Second, when an emergency call is received, a grid system is used to determine the geographical area of the police beat. In essence, the computer assigns the police units based on the geographical grid assignment. Third, the grid system is used to compile statistics for various geographical areas, such as schools, parks, sports centers, and shopping malls.[10]

The benefits of the CAD system for police management are invaluable. The CAD system has allowed police management to more effectively track crime trends with the use of the database. Information as to specific crimes and calls for police service can be extracted from the CAD database. These data are important when making decisions on staffing patterns of field police officers and in identifying those areas of a community where a disproportionate amount of police resources are expended. Furthermore, the CAD system is also an excellent tool for police management to identify specific areas of the community where problem-solving endeavors should be undertaken. Thus, managers can track increases or decreases in police calls to specific areas of the community and have some idea whether problem-solving strategies were effective.

Without the CAD system, data such as this would be very difficult to track, retrieve, and conceptualize. The CAD is increasingly being used throughout the United States for management planning by matching the allocation of police resources in relation to calls for service.[11] There have been many goals regarding the use of the CAD system in police agencies. The following list depicts CAD goals as stated in a survey of 26 cities across the United States:

1. To monitor and better display data, including outstanding calls, ongoing incidents, and patrol unit status and activities
2. To provide better information to personnel, including complaint clerks, dispatchers, and supervisors
3. To help decide which patrol unit(s) to assign to a call for service based on estimated unit locations
4. To reduce response time through reductions in call answering, call processing, unit assignment, and travel times
5. To improve officer safety by more effectively monitoring unit status and responding more rapidly in case of emergency
6. To facilitate access to remote data files, including outstanding warrants, stolen property, and state and national inquiry systems
7. To improve the quality of data maintained from the dispatch process through address verification; automatic assignment of case numbers, dates, and times; elimination of duplicate entries; and so on
8. To better manage police resources through the use of better data and a better understanding of the command and control process
9. To improve service to the public through quicker response time, better dispatch data, and improved management of police resources[12]

Mobile Data Terminals

MDTs are laptop computers that have been installed in police patrol units and are linked with the CAD system. They allow for computer dialogue between police field officers and between officers and the communications center. The communications center sends call data to police units in the field in order to dispatch them to locations where police services have been requested. The officers also have the capacity to log remarks about various calls. This is advantageous for several reasons. For example, let us suppose that police patrol officers working first watch respond to the scene of a domestic disturbance. Once there, they note that one of the parties is very distraught; however, the officers do not have enough evidence to take official action, but they believe that the situation may worsen. The officers can log brief call notes regarding the situation in the event that other police officers, perhaps on another watch, are dispatched to the same address. This is an excellent tool to increase the safety of the officers and citizens because it allows police officers to share information through call notes on persons, places, and events. One other benefit of the MDTs is that they allow field patrol units to run records checks on persons and to run license tag and driver's license information through the NCIC.

The CAD unit is very useful for both line police supervisors and managers. Supervisors can view at any given moment the activity status of field police officers. This is very beneficial in times of massive public emergency when there may be multiple law enforcement agencies involved in the operation. In general, the goals of the MDT system are as follows:

1. To reduce voice congestion and expand the communications capabilities of existing radio channels using digital signals, which have a higher transmission rate than voice signals
2. To increase officer effectiveness through easier access to remote data files, which could potentially result in more "hits" (i.e., apprehensions and recoveries)
3. To increase dispatcher effectiveness by relieving the dispatcher of routine data inquires, patrol status updates, measure repetitions, and/or dispatches of some (noncritical) calls for service
4. To increase officer safety through easier database access, increased communications capability, and an "emergency" button on MDT units
5. To improve message security using digital signals, which are more difficult to decipher than voice messages
6. To improve accuracy and decrease message repetition using mobile digital terminals that can provide hard copies

7. To allow selective routing of messages using terminals that can be addressed either collectively or individually, on a "need to know" basis
8. To allow unattended message reception using terminals that can record messages while an officer is out of a vehicle[13]

Mobile data terminal systems are an effective technological evolution in American policing. These systems have steadfastly improved police field operations and provided a means for police officers to receive the information they need in a more expedient manner. More importantly, the MDTs may allow more time for officers to have greater one-on-one contact with the community and assist officers with a more enhanced problem-solving capability, not to mention increased crime clearance rates. The MDT systems offer the following advantages over the voice dispatching systems.

1. A direct interface between the patrol unit and local county, state, and federal criminal justice information system computers, enabling an officer to query names, license plates, and driver's licenses with almost immediate response and without interfering with radio communications or requesting the services of a dispatcher
2. The elimination of many clerical duties
3. The availability of more detailed information, including addresses displayed with the nearest cross streets and map coordinates (and some cases, even floor plans)
4. Better coordination of all emergency agencies, because their movements can be monitored visually by both officers at the scene and dispatchers
5. Automatic processing of incident information via a preformatted incident form, eliminating the need for the officer to drop off an incident report at the station house and the need for someone to type up a report
6. A dramatic increase in response time as the entire dispatch process, from call to arrival, is fully automated
7. The capability for the accumulation of large amounts of data regarding police incidents and personnel, which can be used in crime analysis and staff allocation planning to assign personnel when and where crime is highest or calls for assistance are heaviest[14]

Automatic Vehicle Locator Systems

An AVL system has the capability to track police field units that are in service. The advantage to the AVL system is that it makes it much easier for the dispatcher personnel to assign the closest police units to an emergency call

Technology and Management

for service. The AVL is also advantageous for supervisors to better track the locations of their officers. The system also enhances the safety of field officers inasmuch that their locations are readily known.

There is one personnel problem that the AVL system presents. Some police officers have not accepted them completely. These officers view the AVL as a threat to their autonomy and feel it will be a mechanism that superiors will use to scrutinize them.[15]

The AVL system has also been criticized by some police executives because a mobile unit might be stationary at a location that is not close to a receiver, which results in the mobile unit disappearing from the system. Furthermore, the AVL system requires a vast amount of expensive equipment and produces results of uncertain reliability. There are several factors other than distance that can have a detrimental effect on the strength of a radio signal. Most AVL systems are designed to poll each mobile unit repeatedly and use the average of several calculations to compute the unit's location. Thus, the calculations are subject to error, especially when a patrol unit is in motion.[16]

There have been attempts to overcome the limitations of the AVL systems. For example, there have been several versions of the AVL that have been introduced that use commercial satellites, in addition to a system operated by the U.S. Air Force using their own satellites. All of the systems function very similarly (e.g., a continuous signal is transmitted from the satellites, whose position in the sky is known). Special receivers in each vehicle receive the satellite signal, and from its strength, direction, or slight variation in frequency, compute the vehicle's position in relation to the satellite.[17] The advantages of the AVL system clearly outweigh the disadvantages. The AVL system is an invaluable aid to dispatchers in keeping track of police in the field.

Automatic Vehicle Monitoring

There have been laudable developments in technology that improve the tracking of police units in the field. Automatic vehicle monitoring (AVM) provides the location and status of the vehicle. The AVM is more inclusive than the automatic vehicle locator system because it can monitor the location and status of vehicle pursuits, burglary in progress calls, and when the officer is en route to scenes.[18] The main difference in the automatic vehicle locator system and the AVM is that the automatic vehicle locator system only provides the location of field patrol units. The location of units is provided by four devices: (1) a navigation (hyperbolic) system that uses a radio location technique called Loran C, a system used by ships at sea; (2) a trilateration system uses radio location from three or more fixed sites; (3) a signpost/proximity system, locating a vehicle through the use of fixed electronic signposts located throughout an area; and (4) a dead-reckoning system where computer-assisted instruments are used to track vehicles on a city map, for example, utilizing an advanced geocoding system.[19]

Personal Locator Transmitter

The PLT system allows dispatchers to communicate with and monitor the location of officers when they are out of their patrol vehicles. The PLT is a device that is worn around the officer's shirt collar. Several years ago, the National Institute of Justice funded the Department of Energy's Idaho National Engineering Laboratory to design the Personal Locator Transmitter (PLT).[20] The PLT uniquely provide the officer with the means of communication during each incident she or he encounters, and if the officer has been injured, her or his exact location would be known.[21] The PLT is currently being refined, and it has not been included as part of the standard equipment of police officers on a large-scale basis.

Remote Control Information System

The remote control information system (RCIS) is along the same lines as the PLT with one distinct difference: the RCIS provides a full-color video and two-way audio communication. This system also monitors an officer's location and vital signs. This would be advantageous in the unfortunate event that an officer is injured in the line of duty; thus dispatchers could monitor vital signs and relay them to emergency medical personnel responding to the incident. Moreover, it would give the dispatcher a glimpse of what is occurring at the scene through the color monitor. It is promising that the RCIS device may replace the handheld portable radio that the majority of police agencies currently utilize.[22]

Crime Detection and Analysis Technology

It is important that police organizations continually seek new and evolving technology for the purpose of crime analysis. Crime analysis is the examination and tracking of crime patterns or criminal behavior in a community or a specific geographical area. With the emergence of community-oriented policing, crime analysis becomes increasingly important. The community policing strategy, as discussed in previous chapters, entails the police being increasingly involved in problem solving. The right technologies can assist the police in problem solving. Questions such as why, how, what, and when are important in the analysis of crime and the problem-solving process. Most American police departments have established some mechanism to track crime. The pin maps that were once a common method of tracking and analyzing crime patterns are now being replaced with sophisticated computerized technology.

One example of the use of technology in tracking of crime and problem solving can be found in the former commissioner of New York City Police Department (NYPD) William J. Bratton's crime tracking program. Commissioner Bratton is credited as having completely reengineered the NYPD to a crime-reducing culture. The underpinnings to Bratton's success with impressive decreases in crime were in large part due to COMPSTAT (COMPuter STATistics). The COMPSTAT system was developed in New York City and serves as a mechanism to ensure command accountability within the NYPD.[23]

COMPSTAT is an automated crime analysis program that allows for instant statistical updating of all reported crimes, arrests, and other police activities. The program is a movie screen-type visual display that provides the framework for the weekly crime analysis meetings at the NYPD headquarters.[24] During regularly held crime analysis meetings, precinct commanders within the NYPD must account for all increases in crimes and provide problem-solving solutions to combat the crime situations. The COMPSTAT system in New York actually shifts the focus to the community, thus requiring police commanders to think about service delivery and problem solving.

The COMPSTAT system, as with any crime analysis technology, requires that specific records and data be maintained. For example, records necessary for an effective database would include: crime description files, known offender files, method of operation data files, criminal history files, property files, and crime location trends.

Crime Mapping Technology

Crime mapping technology is a growing trend in policing and has initially proven to be an effective police strategy. Crime mapping is a computerized mapping program that is utilized to solve crimes and to aid in the investigation of crimes. The crime mapping system is similar to the COMPSTAT system. The National Institute of Justice (NIJ) has advocated the use of crime mapping technology for quite some time. The NIJ advanced the following benefits with the use of crime mapping programs.

> Mapping software has many crime control and preventive applications. In addition to the location of crime, geographical data that can be helpful in crime control and in efforts to apprehend a perpetrator include the perpetrator's last known address, the location of the person who reported the crime, the location of recovered stolen property, and the locations of persons known or contacted by the perpetrator. Geographical information valuable in planning, conducting, and evaluating crime prevention programs includes

locations of crimes committed during the past month; locations of abandoned houses, stripped cars, and other "broken windows" conditions in a neighborhood; and the locations where persons who could benefit from crime prevention and other social programs actually live.[25]

Police departments that utilize the CAD technology may also have crime mapping technology as a feature of the CAD system. One other feature of crime mapping that is available with the CAD system is geocoding. Geocoding is a feature that allows for a records management system with the capability to not only verify addresses as discussed previously but also to associate other geographic information including police reporting areas, beats, and districts.[26]

The Computer and Criminal Investigation

Today, most police departments use computers for many tasks. Computer-aided criminal investigation has the potential to improve the effectiveness of police in solving crimes and identifying suspects. Detailed case notes can also be recorded and stored directly on the computer's database. For example, the Sedgwick County Sheriff's Department located in Wichita, Kansas, has computerized much of their investigative functions. Detectives use case files that are entered into a computer database. Detectives must keep studious case notes about the progress of the investigation in the database. The advantage to computerized investigations is that a supervisor who desires to know what progress has been made in the case can simply access the case via the computer and query the progress. Furthermore, computerizing case notes eliminates the need for volumes of case files.

There are several other advantages to the use of the computer in criminal investigations. One such advantage is computerized mug shots, which make it possible for detectives to quickly access mug shots of suspects through the computer. The New York City police department has an automated mug shot file called CATCH (Computer-Assisted Terminal Criminal Hunt). Using CATCH, detectives enter information such as a description and method of operation of a suspect into the computer. They then receive a computer printout that lists, in rank order, potential suspects. Detectives can then obtain mug shots of the suspects, which can be used to show victims and witnesses in mug lineups.[27]

Evolving Weapon and Crime Control Technology

The advancements in weapons and crime control technology in policing have been enormous. The latest technology has created new pathways for keeping officers safe in the field as well as providing more effective ways to apprehend perpetrators of crimes.

The Smart Gun

A large percentage of police officers each year are killed as a result of firearms. In many of these cases, police are killed with their own firearms.[28] Several years ago, the *New York Times* News Service reported that a New York City police officer was killed when a suspect grabbed a .38 caliber revolver belonging to the officer's partner and shot him four times.[29] Many researchers and practitioners argue that deaths such as this could have been prevented by the use of smart guns. Police management should explore smart gun technology as a way to foster more safety for their personnel.

The smart gun, or the safe gun as it is sometimes called, is a handgun that recognizes its user. The smart gun has a microchip installed in the weapon that stores images of the authorized user's fingerprints. Some smart guns have technology installed that uses radio waves to identify the intended user. In both cases, the smart gun will not fire unless an authorized person's finger is on the trigger. The smart gun has been presented as a way to prevent death and injury among police. Although the smart gun is not presently available for law enforcement use, its potential use is promising. The National Institute of Justice has sponsored smart-gun research, and it is anticipated that in the very near future the smart gun will be available for use in American police agencies.

Fleeing Vehicle Tagging System

The fleeing vehicle tracking or tagging system is a device that consists of a launcher and a projectile with an embedded radio frequency transmitter tag. An adhesive material within the projectile secures the tag to the fleeing automobile. Once attached to the vehicle, officers can track the fleeing vehicle. The obvious advantage of the tracking system is that it reduces the chances of police vehicle accidents that result from a high-speed pursuit. This technology currently is not in widespread use in the policing profession and is being perfected.

Disabling Net and Launcher

Police officers in some cases may be required to restrain a suspect who has attempted to evade or elude. The dangers of these situations for the officer are great. There is always a possibility of a physical confrontation between a suspect and the officers. Whenever possible, it is desired that police avoid a close personal engagement with a suspect to reduce possible injury to officers.

Foster-Miller Inc. has developed a mechanism called the disabling net and launcher system. Foster-Miller Inc. is an independent, privately held engineering and technology development firm that is involved in some research and development for police departments. The disabling net and launching system may in part eliminate a potential dangerous physical confrontation between the officer and a suspect. The disabling net captures a suspect quickly and effectively and can restrict the movement of targets up to thirty feet away. The device can be deployed indoors or outdoors from a 37-mm ammunition or handheld launcher.[30] The net is launched and immobilizes the suspect. According to the Foster-Miller Inc. informational package, the net is the only device that can:

- Capture without pain compliance
- Restrict both fight and flight
- Minimize injury and collateral damage
- Fit a standard weapon or customized, recyclable launcher
- Neutralize threatening animals
- Provide a flash/bang that disorients the target

Mobile Video Recorders

A fair number of U.S. police organizations have mobile video recorders installed in their police field units. Mobile video recorders have the potential to not only support an officer's actions from a legal standpoint but also to provide a means for police management to closely study an officer hurt or killed in the line of duty.

The video recording cameras are mounted in the police vehicle, usually on the dashboard. When the officer activates the emergency equipment, the camera automatically begins to record. Likewise, the officer can self-initiate the camera in the event he or she observes an unusual situation such as a suspected drunk driver. The officer has a small wireless microphone clipped onto his uniform, which then records pertinent information.

The mobile vehicle recorders can serve to protect officers when they are accused of inappropriate conduct. For example, there are many complaints alleging that a police officer was rude and abusive toward a traffic violator. Many of these complaints are proven unfounded after the video is viewed. In some cases, the officer may be accused of excessive force. The mobile vehicle recorder is an excellent tool to see how much force was used and whether it was excessive or within standard operating procedures. The videotape can also sustain complaints of wrongdoing or misconduct on the part of the officer and can assist police management in monitoring those officers. Many civil liberties groups have increasingly called for police organizations to equip all police units with video recorders because they say it will, in part, assist in identifying racially biased police practices such as racial profiling. There have also been incidents where officers have captured on video their own assaults and felonious deaths.[31]

Management and Technology

Computer and other technologies can assist police management in the more effective and efficient management of police resources. However, computer programs are also limited by the extensive manual data preparation that is sometimes required.[32] A concern of police management is the development of a protocol that offers comprehensive guidelines for personnel in the use of police technology. The protocol would include systems planning and implementation, service orientation, and security and privacy issues.

Responsible police managers should strategically develop short- and long-term technological plans. Questions such as what technology does the department anticipate and how that technology will benefit the organization in accomplishing its ultimate mission should be addressed by management and included in the technology plan. As American police agencies gravitate to sophisticated databases, police management will take on a number of important responsibilities. Moreover, police management will be required to answer the following questions:

1. For what purposes does the department collect and store information?
2. What information does the department need to carry out its mission and to support decisions relating to personnel, finances, scheduling, and policing strategies?
3. Where does the information come from? Who will input it into the system? How will it be screened or checked? How will the database be maintained or updated as new information becomes available?
4. What kind of communication links are needed among officers, mobile units, dispatchers, citizens, and so on?
5. Who will have access to information and communications systems? Who will secure the system to prevent inappropriate use?
6. What software and hardware does the department need to achieve its current goals and to maintain flexibility to meet its future needs? Do new components have to be compatible with exiting systems? Does new software have to be tailored to the needs of the department, or will standard packages serve?
7. Based on practical and financial considerations, what components should the department purchase? What ones should it lease? What services should be provided by contractors rather than the department? What vendors and consultants should the department use?[33]

Human Resource Allocations

The tracking and management of human resources is one of the most important tasks of police management. There are some databases that are helpful in assisting police management in the tracking of human resources. The Time Tracker system, developed by Asgard Systems Inc., allows police managers to manage large and complex employee schedules. The Time Tracker software maintains schedules from the past, present, and future. It is an easy and flexible way of defining fair and consistent scheduling patterns. Time Tracker can also track employees vacation time, sick time, lieu time, and user defined other time. It analyzes past activity and prepares data for payroll.[34] Police management is responsible for analyzing large volumes of information in order to make the best decisions for the organization. Computer software can automate this process and identify and warn of inappropriate situations in a wide array of management planning situations. Computer programs such as Time Tracker can provide a wide variety of reports that summarize and analyze activity over time.

Training

Most states require law enforcement personnel to maintain a certain amount of annual in-service training hours to maintain a license to practice law enforcement. For example, the State of Kansas requires law enforcement personnel to obtain forty hours of training annually to maintain a law enforcement certificate. Currently police officers attend training in the classroom setting in order to obtain the required in-service training hours needed.

There are some organizations that provide online in-service training for law enforcement officers. The California Police Officers Standards and Training offers numerous courses online for California law enforcement officers. The idea of offering in-service training through the World Wide Web is not new. For example, colleges and universities across the country offer entire degree programs online. Allowing for some police in-service training hours to be completed online makes good sense for several reasons. First, officers can complete some in-service training without having to be physically present in the classroom. Second, training developed on the computer eliminates the need for classroom instructors and the scheduling of rooms. Training can be completed in fifteen-, thirty-, or sixty-minute blocks. Current computer software has the capability to track an individual officer's time, including the date and time the officer logged onto and off of the training program.

One example of how in-service training can be offered via the Internet is legal instruction. Police officers are required to keep up to date on changes in the law and criminal procedure. This instruction could easily be offered as an online training course. At the conclusion of the course, in order to ensure that the officer has learned the material, they could be required to take an on-line examination. For questions that are missed, the officer would be prompted with the correct answer and directed to review that area of the presentation again. The advantage to this approach is that officers do not have to complete the entire course in one sitting but can break the instruction into different time blocks.

In July of 2000, a group of police practitioners and scholars from around the world met at the FBI Academy in Quantico, Virginia, for the "Futuristics and Law Enforcement: The Millennium Conference." After studying the current and projected state of police training, the group projected that by the year 2020, there is an 84% likelihood that that classroom training for police agencies will be provided on the Internet.[35]

Computer Crimes

It is evident that technology, especially computer technology, has given rise to a host of new crimes that the police had not been accustomed to dealing with in years past. In fact, future acts of terrorism may take place in cyberspace rather than in the physical world. The reason is knowledge, and knowledge is power. The Internet has made the knowledge base both accessible and vulnerable information. Information warfare is the act of attacking data stored in computer databases. Information warfare is not limited to disputes between countries; it can also include corporate and economic espionage as well as bored teenagers looking to make a reputation as a hacker. Although this type of crime takes place in cyberspace, the impact can be felt in the heart of federal, state, city, and county governments because critical infrastructures depend on computer controls to operate effectively.

The increasing sophistication of computer hackers suggests that computer crimes will continue to soar as members of a new generation of criminals are tempted to commit more serious offenses. In addition, traditional barriers to crime faced by former generations of thieves, thugs, and convicts are being obliterated by digital technologies. In a digital world, states or international borders and customs agents do not exist. Bits of information (contraband and otherwise) flow effortlessly around the globe, rendering the traditional concept of distance meaningless. In the past, the culprit had to be physically present to commit a crime. However, this is no longer the case. A computer crimes offender can steal millions of dollars from anywhere on the planet simply by moving electronic ones and zeros into his own bank account.

Information stored in police computer databases may also be vulnerable to attack. Traditionally, police records and information were stored and protected in rooms with limited access and in locked file cabinets and vaults. In the digital world, a police organization's proprietary information may be located on one computer server that is connected to dozens or hundreds of other systems around the country or even the world.

The trends in digital crime appear to be growing more alarming every single year. Police management should ensure that they have the necessary personnel trained in cybercrime and that the data stored in their organization's computer systems are protected from hackers. According to one study, at least twenty companies responding to an annual security survey had suffered losses exceeding $1 million as a result of computer break-ins. The Business Software Alliance estimates the lost revenue resulting from software piracy alone amounts to $2.8 billion per year.

Compared to violent street crime, computer crime is vastly underreported. Underreporting is significant because law enforcement resources are allocated based upon the number of reported crimes. In the past, because police agencies receive few complaints about computer crime, there appears to be no problem.

Training police officers to deal with digital crime is an expensive endeavor. In these times of fiscal constraint, police managers are reluctant to spend limited budgets on anything that will not provide a sure and noticeable return. A properly trained computer crime investigator may require extensive ongoing training and education. Because computer companies introduce many new hardware and software packages each year, staying breast of the educational curve can be a monumental task. Training and equipment are not the only financial impediments to conducting high-technology crime investigations. Such impediments like the physical distance between the perpetrator and the victim also poses special problems for those investigating computer crimes. Thus, this coordination takes time and money. Local and state police agencies will have to build mechanisms to deal with these types of crimes.

In the short term, police management must ensure that the growth in the amount of and personnel dedicated to the problem of computer crimes is addressed. In the long term, police executives have to think strategically about computer crime and must be prepared to allocate the appropriate resources for the recruitment, education, and training of personnel capable of investigating computer crimes.

Future Trends

As discussed previously in the chapter, a few years ago, the FBI released the report from the proceedings of their conference, "Futuristics and Law Enforcement: The Millennium Conference." The purpose of the conference was to take the first step toward producing a vision for policing in the twenty-first century in five areas, one being the future of technology and its effect on law enforcement. The participants not only examined possible futures, but

Technology and Management

they also formulated strategies that police leaders should employ to create the "preferred future" for their agencies and communities. The following strategies were developed specifically addressing the area of technology:

1. Encourage aggressive research and development of nonlethal weapons and apprehension technologies.
2. Form partnerships with academic institutions (in a variety of disciplines) to educate and train personnel in emerging technologies that impact the policing profession.
3. Take a graduated implementation strategy with regard to artificial intelligence, forensic identification, and technology while maintaining and respecting individuals' civil rights.
4. Extensive education and information dissemination is essential to mitigate societal "backlash" in response to new technologies.
5. Because of a lack of knowledge and resources to combat cybercrime, police must seek more funding for education and training to combat these crimes.
6. Law enforcement agencies need to have proactive planning programs to monitor trends, discuss and develop new strategies, and facilitate and respond to emerging trends.
7. Because of a lack of knowledge and resources to combat cyber crime, law enforcement must form a variety of partnerships with both public and private entities.
8. Law enforcement agencies and personnel should be encouraged to further experiment with new artificial intelligence and biometric technologies and should adopt these technologies when they become viable.
9. A proliferation of new benign, mind-altering activities/substances will require the redistribution of certain resources in law enforcement.[36]

Management Considerations

Information technology is now crucial and necessary to support the policies and mission of the police organization. Given evolving technologies, police management will have to consider many perplexing issues, such as training recruit police officers in the skills and competencies required to work in an environment that is becoming more and more technology driven. Will it be appropriate to include instruction in the police academy on computers and databases? Obviously, those agencies that have installed the mobile data terminals in the patrol units will have to ensure that the training is in place to support their use.

As the role of the police manager becomes more complex in addressing how best to deliver police services and how to best manage the human resource needs of the organization, technology will play a major role. There will be an increasing need for police managers to possess the technological skills and competencies that will assist them in their jobs. They will have to become familiar with various databases and how to enter and extract data. Police agencies that have implemented community-oriented strategies within their organizations will rely on technology. Information technology can assist police management in implementing community-oriented policing by making data accessible and thus improving the organization's ability to identify and to respond to problems both within the department and the community.

Organizational Issues

There is a belief that information technology will assist organizations in fostering flatter organizational structures. This has been well established in the private sector. The private sector has experienced praiseworthy results using technology to flatten traditional hierarchies, thus improving the delivery of services and promoting decentralized decision making.[37] Police commanders working in a specific geographical area of a community or precinct can now be empowered to make decisions based on readily available data retrieved from information systems. Technology and data can now be used to drive decisions, thus empowering those performing the service delivery of the organization to make more decisions based on data. Police commanders can then look at first-hand results of field operations based on data retrieved from information services. This is saliently similar to the strategy of community policing, which calls for decentralized decision making and for police organizations to explore more flat organizational structures.[38]

How police management controls the implementation and outcomes of technological change will in large part depend on their capacities and motivation to redistribute decision making and authority in the police organizational structure. Progressive managers will seek to implement the technology necessary so that they may in turn make sound decisions for the good of the organization. If policing is to meet the service demands for an ever-changing society, which is largely technology driven, then they must increasingly explore technological solutions and options.

Questions in Review

1. The Institute of Law Enforcement issued a report that detailed projected standards to which that law enforcement technology

Technology and Management

should gradually evolve. By the mid-1970s, the Institute of Law Enforcement's laboratory had completed their recommendations. What were the institute's recommendations?
2. During the summer of 1994, there were significant developments in the planning for more effective police technology. A 1995 Defense Appropriations Bill allocated funds to support the dual-use technology program. This bill demonstrated a sound commitment to the development and enhancement of technology for both the police and the military. What did these technologies include?
3. In 1994, the National Institute of Justice created the National Law Enforcement Technology Center (NLETC). Why was it created, and what was its role?
4. What is "computer-aided dispatch," and how does it differ from traditional communication systems?
5. How can information services/computers assist police in criminal investigations?
6. How can informational systems/computers assist police management?
7. What are "mobile data terminals"?
8. What are some of the crime control technologies discussed in the chapter?
9. What are the implications that technology will have on the training of police officers?

Biggest Mistakes Police Leadership Makes and How to Avoid Them

Failure to Supervise a Police Lab in Houston, Texas

In October 2003, a grand jury lambasted the Houston Police Department's DNA lab as incompetent and mismanaged but closed out its six-month investigation without indicting anyone.[39] The lab closed its toxicology section after its supervisor failed a competency test. "There seemed to be a total lack of concern about profound errors committed by certain members of the lab's staff," grand jury member Joe King said as he read from a statement on behalf of the panel. "Although seemingly criminal, these acts do not meet the necessary requirements for indictment." The DNA lab has been criticized in recent months because of sloppy work that has resulted in the wrongful rape conviction of at least one man. Josiah Sutton was released on bond in March and is seeking a pardon. He was convicted of rape and sentenced to twenty-five years in prison in 1999.

The police department shut down the DNA section, and independent labs retested three hundred and seventy cases. The results reported by the lab were incorrect in at least twenty-one cases and were inconclusive in many others. The retesting had been ordered after an outside audit of the police lab's DNA section found serious deficiencies in the section. The audit cited the lack of training of the lab's employees, insufficient documentation, and possible contamination of DNA samples.[40]

What Happened?

1. Lack of supervision
2. Budget cuts resulted in hiring poorly trained personnel
3. Political pressures resulted in an attempt to hide the problems

End Results

The public's trust in the justice system and the reputation of the Houston Police Department were damaged.

End Notes

1. The President's Commission on Law Enforcement and Administration of Justice, *Task Force Report: The Police* (Washington, DC: Government Printing Office, 1967).
2. Jeremy Travis, *Criminal Justice Science and Technology Program, National Institute of Justice: Research in Action* (Washington, DC: National Institute of Justice, 1995) p. 1–2.
3. Travis, pp. 2–3.
4. Travis, p. 3.
5. Travis, p. 9.
6. Institute for Law and Justice, *Law Enforcement Options*, Vol. 1, No. 1 (1995), p. 3.
7. *Technology Beat*, National Law Enforcement Technology Center (Rockville, MD, 1995) p. 1.
8. *Local Government Police Management* (Washington, DC: International City Managers Association, 1991) p. 309.
9. Applied Micro Technology, Inc., *Public Safety Products Overview* (Cedars Falls, IA).
10. Applied Micro Technology, pp. 10–11.
11. E. A. Thibault, L. M. Lynch, and R. B. McBride, *Proactive Police Management* (Upper Saddle, NJ: Prentice Hall, 1998).
12. K. W. Colton, M. L. Brandeau, and J. M. Tien, *A National Assessment of Police Command, Control, and Communication Systems* (Washington, DC: National Institute of Justice, 1983).
13. Colton, Brandeau, and Tien, p. 39.
14. Charles R. Swanson, Leonard Territo, and Robert W. Taylor, *Police Administration: Structures, Processes and Behavior* (New York: Macmillan, 1988), p. 367.

15 *Local Government Police Management*, p. 313.
16 Alfred R. Stone and Stuart M. DeLuca. *Police Administration: An Introduction*, 2nd ed. (Englewood Cliffs, NJ: Prentice Hall, 1994), p. 240.
17 Stone and DeLuca, p. 240.
18 Seymour H. Roth, "*History of Automatic Vehicle Monitoring (AVM)*" in IEEE Transactions on Vehicular Technology, Vol. 26, No. 1 (1977), pp. 2–6.
19 Thibault, Lynch, and McBride, pp. 131–132.
20 Lois Pilant, "High Technology Solutions," in *The Police Chief*, Vol. 71, No. 5 (1996), p. 38.
21 Michael J. Palmiotto, *Policing: Concepts, Strategies, and Current Issues in American Policing* (Durham, NC: Carolina Academic Press, 1998), p. 208.
22 Pilant, p. 38.
23 David Anderson, "Why Crime Is Down," in *The New York Times Magazine* (February 1997), pp. 47–62.
24 John S. Dempsy, *An Introduction to Policing*, 2nd ed. (Albany, NY: West/Wadsworth Publishing Co, 1999), p. 338.
25 Thomas F. Rich, "The Use of Computerized Mapping in Crime Control and Prevention Programs," in *National Institute of Justice: Research in Action* (Washington, DC: U.S. Department of Justice, Office of Justice Programs, July 1995), p. 2.
26 Palmiotto, p. 210.
27 Dempsy, p. 118.
28 Palmiotto, p. 217.
29 Anne Eisenberg, "Researchers Aim for 'Smart' Guns," in *New York Times News Service* (New York: September 14, 1998).
30 Foster Miller, Inc., Waltham, MA.
31 Joseph G. Estey, "2000 Survivors Club Hits: In the Past 10 Years, 2000 Officers Have Dressed for Survival," in *Police Chief* (May 1997), p. 19.
32 *Local Government Police Management*, p. 323.
33 *Local Government Police Management*, pp. 324–326.
34 Asgard Systems Inc., Product Brochure (2001).
35 Proceedings from the FBI's Futuristics and Law Enforcement: The Millennium Conference (Quantico, VA, July 10–14, 2000).
36 Proceedings from the FBI's Futuristics and Law Enforcement Conference.
37 Lynda M. Applegate, James I. Cash, Jr., and D. Quinn Mills, "Information Technology and Tomorrow's Manager," in *Harvard Business Review* (November/December 1988), p. 128–136.
38 Michael L. Birzer, "Police Supervision in the 21st Century," in *FBI Law Enforcement Bulletin* (June 1996), pp. 6–10.
39 From an Associated Press Online announcement (October 16, 2003).
40 As reported by the *Austin American-Statesman* (Texas) (November 5, 2003), p. A-1.

Job-Related Issues

9

Key Individuals, Concepts, and Issues

Stress	Police suicide
Occupational stressors	Stress management
Han Selye	Healthy work environment
General adaptation syndrome	Critical incident stress
Levels of stress	America's demographics
Special case stressors	Multicultural diversity
Critical life events scale	Diverse workforce
Hate crimes	Culturally competent
Alcoholism danger signs	Immigration
Distress	Eustress

Definitions

Critical life events scale: Scale developed by John Sewell and identifies critical life events specific to the law enforcement occupation.

General adaptation syndrome: A model designed to describe a person's innate physiological reactions to stressful situations; includes three phases: (1) fight or flight phase; (2) period of repair phase; and (3) exhaustion phase.

Hate crime: A criminal offense committed against a person, property, or society that is motivated, in whole or in part, by the offender's bias against a race, religion, ethnic origin group, or sexual orientation group.

Immigration: Coming into a new country as a permanent resident.

Melting pot: Diverse racial or ethnic groups or both forming a new creation, a new cultural entity.

Pluralism: Mutual respect among the various groups in a society for one another's cultures, allowing minorities to express their own culture without experiencing prejudice or hostility.

Stress: A physical, chemical, or emotional factor that causes bodily or mental tension, resulting from factors that tend to alter an existent equilibrium.

Chapter Objectives

After completing this chapter, you should be able to:

1. Explain the differences between eustress and distress
2. Identify and discuss sources of police stress
3. Identify the three parts of the general adaptation syndrome model
4. Discuss organizational stressors
5. Identify the danger signs of police stress
6. Discuss police management's role in addressing police stress
7. Explain critical incident stress debriefings
8. Discuss factors that may explain why police suicide is higher than other occupations
9. Describe how police management can enhance the cultural competence of officers
10. Discuss the importance of a culturally competent police agency

Introduction

Our purpose in this chapter is to discuss job-related issues that are of concern to police management. As you have read thus far in this text, the task of managing police operations is a complex undertaking. There are many job-related issues that management addresses. Winnowing down a topic such as job-related issues was challenging because there are many. The chapter focuses on three important job-related issues: (1) police stress and stress-management techniques; (2) police suicide; and (3) issues that will impact the police in serving a multicultural society. The chapter presents these important issues with the underpinning of police management's role.

Stress and the Police Occupation

> Police work ranks as one of the most hazardous professions, even exceeding the formidable stresses and strains of air traffic control.
> —Hans Selye

There are many socially redeeming rewards to be gained from a police career—the mere satisfaction of knowing that you made a difference in the community, that you helped a citizen in time of need, or rescued a child in distress. However, there are also those tasks that the police perform that have the potential to cause a great deal of stress. Consequently,

Job-Related Issues

stress over the long term can lead to serious emotional and health-related illnesses. Stress that is left untreated can lead to disastrous social relationships including divorce and other family and job-related problems. The extreme amount of stress experienced by many police officers often goes undetected, or their stress-related behavior is dismissed as an attitude problem or poor performance. Police officers deal with a host of stressful and traumatic incidents by the very nature of the occupation. As a result, they often suffer the effects of stress to a significant degree not found in other occupations.[1]

It is difficult for citizens to imagine what a typical day on the job for a police officer is like. Citizens are often informed about the police by Hollywood and popular television. Many of the popular police television series are far off the mark regarding the realities of police work. Perhaps the following illustration will illuminate to some degree what it is like.

A Portrait of Police Work

Officer Susan Smith is a twenty-five-year-old police officer. She serves in a police department with about seven hundred sworn police officers and in a city with a population of over four hundred thousand citizens. Officer Smith has been employed as a police officer for almost four years and for that entire time has been assigned to second shift field patrol. After daily squad meeting, Officer Smith departs from the police substation at 3:00 p.m. to begin her eight-hour tour of duty.

During the first hour of the shift, she drives around looking things over on the beat. Everything seems relatively quiet. Then, the mobile data terminal in police car flashes her number and assigns her to the scene of a residential burglary. Officer Smith arrives at the burglary scene in a few minutes and is contacted by a visibly upset victim. The victim explains to Officer Smith that her house was broken into and that her computer, television, and some miscellaneous jewelry are missing. The victim explains to Officer Smith that she is renting the property and does not have renters insurance on any of the property that was missing. Officer Smith completes the burglary report, but there is not much evidence left at the scene (she thinks to herself that the chances of catching the perpetrators are not good). In an attempt to calm the victim, Officer Smith explains that the police department will do everything it can to catch the suspects and recover the victim's property.

Officer Smith checks back in service about one hour after she received the initial burglary call. Ten minutes later she receives a call to check a stalled vehicle blocking traffic at a busy intersection. She investigates and cannot locate the owner of the vehicle. Officer Smith calls for a tow truck because the vehicle is creating a traffic hazard. As she awaits the arrival of the tow truck, a citizen approaches the police car and asks for assistance with directions. A few moments later, the tow truck arrives and removes the stalled vehicle from the intersection. Thirty minutes have now passed, and the officer checks back in service. She drives to meet other officers at a local diner for a bite to eat. Officer Smith anxiously anticipates her meal because she has not eaten all day. She spent the entire morning sitting in traffic court, only to be told after three hours of waiting that the defendants in her cases pled guilty and she was free to go.

Officer Smith is ten minutes into eating her meal when her portable handheld radio bellows her number and directs her to proceed to a disturbance with shots fired. The dispatcher instructs that the disturbance is domestic in nature between a husband and wife. Officer Smith leaves her half-eaten meal and drives to the disturbance call. As she drives to the location of the disturbance call, the adrenaline starts to kick in from anticipation of the coming confrontation. Her stomach begins to churn with nervousness, and a hint of anxiety and excitement encumber her. She arrives at the scene of the disturbance and is met by a visibly battered and upset female victim who screams that her husband tried to kill her. A few seconds later, the husband runs out of the house and becomes very belligerent at the site of a police officer. The suspect reeks of alcohol and has to be physically wrestled to the ground and taken into custody.

The fictitious case presented above is indicative of a typical day in the life of many American police officers. Police work can at times be extremely boring and sedentary for hour after hour, and then suddenly, without warning, turn into a life-and-death situation, causing the officer's anxiety level, blood pressure, and demands on the cardiovascular system to increase significantly.

Police officers are called to deal with many complex problems on a daily basis. The police see the best and the very worst in their fellow human beings. They see the child that has been abused by a parent, they investigate the gruesome car accident scene that claimed the life of a young teenager and his father, they see the pain of the poor and homeless on the street corner, they see the disastrous effects of drugs and crime in our inner cities, and they see the terrible scene of a drive-by shooting that has claimed yet another teenager's life and comfort the mother who cries for her loss. Police officers experience the discomfort of having to deliver a death notice to a husband informing him that his wife has been killed in an automobile accident, they see the hopelessness and despair of their fellow human beings, and all too often they hear the cries of the helpless victims of crime who ask the police for justice.

The police are sometimes called upon to make life-and-death decisions in a matter of seconds without the luxury to think about what to do. On any given day, an officer may act as a marital counselor, social worker, attorney, teacher, paramedic, minister, parent, role model, and mentor. Thus, as one might imagine, the job of a police officer carries with it a tremendous responsibility.

The split-second decisions that the police are sometimes called upon to make may at times lead to being second-guessed, critiqued, armchair quarterbacked, dissected, and criticized. Police officers may be required to work on the night shift for many years. For years a police officer may be required to work holidays and weekends away from their families. The years of being assigned to the night shift can result in their missing out on some of the most important stages in their children's lives. The police live in a glass house. It is one of the few occupations where their off-duty activities are restricted, often including where they can live, who they can hang around with, and places they can and cannot frequent.

The police are the gatekeepers of the criminal justice system. Given the discretion powers the police have, they to a large extent control who enters the system. An arrest initiates what can be a lengthy process within the criminal justice system. The police are granted the legal authority to use force, sometimes deadly force, to diffuse a situation. They are legally authorized to arrest, detain, and take someone's freedom and liberty. To some the police represent a love-hate relationship. We love to love them and at other times we love to hate them. When a horrific act of police brutality is caught on video, the police become the villains. Yet recall the September 11, 2001, terrorist attacks and the images we saw on our television sets of police officers and other public safety officials running into the ruble of the twin towers in New York in an attempt to rescue survivors. The police instantly were heroes.

Police officers have awesome responsibilities. In many states you can join the ranks of policing with a minimum of a high school education and as young as nineteen years of age. Few other occupations require the grueling selection process that young men and women aspiring to become police officers go through. This process includes written examinations, physical ability testing, psychological assessments, a polygraph examination, medical examination, urinalysis for drugs, credit checks, and a thorough and revealing background investigation. After being selected, they are then subjected to a rigorous training academy followed by a field training period, to graduate and perform a very complex, dangerous, and stressful job, which may require life-and-death decisions that will often be second-guessed. Not to mention the shift work and being away from their families on weekends and holidays for many years of their careers.

Police Stress

For some time experts have been attempting to reach a consensus regarding a succinct definition and understanding of the effects that stress has on police officers. Sources of stress for police officers are generally placed into five categories: issues in the officer's personal life, the pressures of law enforcement work, the attitude of the general public toward police work and officers, the operation of the criminal justice system, and the law enforcement organization itself.[2]

Hans Selye, who is recognized as a leading authority on stress, defined stress as the "body's nonspecific response to any demand placed upon it."[3] Selye labeled positive stress "eustress" and negative stress "distress." Other experts have defined stress as "a physical, chemical or emotional factor that causes bodily or mental tension, resulting from factors that tend to alter an existent equilibrium."[4] There have been literally hundreds of articles written about police stress. Here is what we generally know about stress:

- Stress in daily life is common, pervasive, unavoidable, and thus to be expected.
- Depending on how one copes with stressful events, the experience of stress can be positive (healthy and happy) or negative (sick and unhappy).
- Because people differ in a variety of ways, each person's means and success in coping with stressful situations will vary.
- There is a mental-physiological mechanism, known as general adaptation syndrome, that assists one in adjusting to demands for change.
- By definition, stress is the nonspecific response of the body to any demand for change. (The demand can be from within or from one's surrounding environment.)
- Police managers are subjected to unusually high demands for change. As a result, they typically experience high levels of stress.[5]

Stress is a condition that may elicit a variety of individual responses to the same stressful condition. Stress does not occur because of a situation a police officer finds him or herself in, but because of an officer's perceived difficulty in handling the situation. For example, when an incident becomes stressful, the officer may not feel capable of coping with the environment or with the situation. In this sense, the officer perceives that he or she cannot handle the situation, which subsequently results in stress. Police officers are frequently exposed to acts that are aggressive, cruel, and violent, and it is situations such as these that create stress on the part of officers. Did you know that a certain amount of stress is required in order to perform our jobs in a productive manner? For example, professional athletes need to have a certain amount of stress in order to function well in a game. An example of this is before the tip-off to a basketball game when the players "pump themselves up."

Recall that Hans Selye identified two types of stress: "eustress," the good stress, and "distress," the bad stress. Eustress is the stress that every one of us

Job-Related Issues

has experienced in our lives. Think about a time when you have been excited about a new event in your life, possibly starting a new job, getting a promotion at work, or buying a new car. Do you remember the way you felt? This is an example of eustress. Eustress is not a threat and we usually experience it as pleasurable stress. A police officer that has recently been promoted or transferred to an elite assignment may experience eustress.

On the other hand, distress is the form of stress that is actually harmful to the individual. This type of stress results from harmful stimuli that can affect the functioning of the individual and his or her inability to cope with the environment. Distress can result from an overworked detective with an overwhelming caseload. Distress can also result from being assigned to, for example, a very high crime area of the community. Every police officer will experience distress throughout their careers.

It is well known to the medical community that stress can impair the social, psychological, and physical functioning of an individual. The immune system of the individual that is exposed to repeated stress is more susceptible to disease, and consequently, these individuals are more likely to have higher absenteeism rates from work. The effects of stress have been linked to hypertension, coronary heart disease, alcohol and drug abuse, migraine headaches, and deterioration in normal interpersonal relations.[6] High levels of stress can be an important determining factor in alcohol abuse among police populations.[7] Some experts have suggested that the effects of stress may be linked to a number of other diseases such as cancer, lupus, and arthritis.[8] Stress may also result in serious psychological reactions including irritability, anxiety, and tension, feeling uptight, or flying off the handle.

Stress results from a poor fit between the individual and the environment. When the environment places high or unanticipated demands on an individual, naturally this results in stress, and when these demands are excessive, debilitating stress results. Hans Selye proposed the general adaptation syndrome (GAS) to describe an individual's innate physiological reactions to stressful situations.[9] The GAS model is composed of three phases. The first phase is the fight or flight response. In this stage, an individual prepares him or herself for action, to either run or fight. The second phase is a period of repair, during which the individual regains his physiological and psychological equilibrium. The final phase, exhaustion, is the result of the individual not regaining his or her physiological and psychological equilibrium.

Although there is a lack of a unified understanding of stress, most experts would agree that the combined physical and emotional demands of police work can create a host of stressful situations that even the most well-adjusted individual may have difficulty managing at times.[10] Stress is the embodiment of conflict resulting from demands for performance of bodily and social (including occupational) functions imposed by any constellation of environmental and psychological factors that either stimulate or inhibit one's ability to satisfactorily perform physiological, psychological, or social functions.[11] The inherent stressful nature of law enforcement requires that fellow officers and supervisors recognize signs of stress and to know when and how to refer officers for assistance. Historically, in the police profession, this has been done in a rather haphazard manner, and often police officers were thought to be weak if they reported a stress-related problem.

It is important to note that those police officers who are experiencing an extraordinary amount of stress may be endangering themselves by becoming more susceptible to alcoholism, drug abuse, and other physical disease. The officer may also be adversely affecting the police organization. For example, the cumulative effects of stress among officers in an organization can lead to:

- Impaired officer performance and reduced productivity
- Reduced morale
- Public relations problems
- Labor-management friction
- Civil suits stemming from stress-related shortcomings in personnel performance
- Tardiness and absenteeism
- Increased turnover because of leaves of absence and early retirements caused by stress-related problems and disabilities
- The added expenses of training and hiring recruits, as well as paying overtime, when the agency is left short-staffed as a result of turnover[12]

Levels of Stress

Stress is an inherent factor in policing regardless of one's position within the organization. Often the stress of the job is identified when police officers answer calls for service and see first-hand the devastation of crime and victimization. In these situations, officers do indeed experience stress; however, stress can be caused by many aspects of policing. Based on the authors' anecdotal accounts from police officers at various ranks, the following is a list of common stressful events in police work.

The Patrol Level

- The stress of shift work
- The stress of working weekends and being away from the family
- The stress of working part-time security jobs to earn a decent living for the family
- The stress of living in a glass house and being held to a higher standard
- The stress of sitting in court many hours during the officer's off-duty time

Job-Related Issues

- The stress of the daily routine of police work (i.e., seeing victims of crime, seeing human behavior at its worst, seeing the homeless and the downtrodden)
- The stress of supervisors continually monitoring and scrutinizing their jobs and the perception that the supervisor has no backbone and does not support the troops
- The stress of being criticized by community groups
- The stress of competing for limited promotional positions

The Supervisor Level

- Having to answer to an immediate supervisor for the purpose of explaining decisions they made in a certain situation
- The stress of having to discipline their subordinates
- The perception of not having any support from the command staff
- The stress of attempting to demonstrate to their subordinates that he is on their side, while at the same time demonstrating to the command staff that he is a company person
- The stress of competing for a limited number of positions at the middle management level

Middle Management Level

- Having to answer to the command staff for problems or incidents within their respective divisions and sections
- The perception that they have no support from the executive command staff
- The stress of having to discipline their subordinates
- The stress of having unrealistic deadlines on reports because of the reactionary nature of policing
- The stress of having to implement new policing strategies

Command Level

- The stress of having to argue for budget allocations to city and county commissions comprised of citizen/politicians who know little about the realities of police work
- The stress of having to answer to community groups (sometimes very hostile groups) for the actions of subordinates
- The stress of getting hit with lawsuits that name the chief or sheriff vicariously for the actions of subordinates
- The stress of trying to stimulate morale within the organization at fiscally devastating times (i.e., no raises for police officers during the next year)

- The stress of having to negotiate with the union for the minor changes within the organization
- The stress of having to deal with officer misconduct within the organization

Professors Thomas Barker and David Carter identified seven categories of police stress:

1. Life threatening stressors: These are characteristics that embody a constant potential for injury or death. A particularly important aspect of these stressors is the knowledge that violent acts against police officers are intentional rather than accidental behaviors. Because the potential of a life-threatening situation is constant, the stressors are inherently cumulative.
2. Social isolation stressors: Included in this category are such factors as isolation and alienation from the community; differential socioeconomic status between the police and their constituency; authoritarianism; cynicism; and cultural distinction, prejudice, and discrimination.
3. Organizational stressors: This source of stress is particularly significant but too frequently overlooked (notably at the practical level). These stressors deal with all aspects of organizational life—both formal and informal. Specific stressors include: peer pressure, role models, performance measures for evaluation, upward mobility, policies and procedures (or the lack thereof leading to inconsistent and/or unacceptable behavior), job satisfaction, training, morale, inadequate supervision and administrative control, inadequate training, internal organizational jealousy (including "empire building"), management philosophy, the organizational structure, and leadership styles. Thus, simply being a member of an organization and trying to succeed can provide a significant amount of stress for the officer.
4. Functional stressors: These are variables specifically related to the performance of assigned policing duties. Included in this category are role conflict; the use of discretion; knowledge of law and legal mandates; and decision-making responsibilities such as the use of force, when to stop and question persons, and how to resolve domestic disputes. If an officer does not have a good understanding of his responsibilities and is ill-prepared to handle them, stress will increase.
5. Personal stressors: These are stressors that have their primary origin in the officer's off-duty life, such as family problems or financial constraints. Particularly noteworthy in this grouping are marital

difficulties, school or social problems of children, family illnesses, and associated personal or family crises. The literature indicates that such stressors clearly influence an officer's on-duty personality, affecting both attitude and behavior.
6. Physiological stressors: A change in one's physiology and general health may also affect one's decision-making capabilities, as well as one's tolerance of others behavior. Fatigue from working off-duty jobs; the physiological impact of shift work (which interrupts the internal clock); changes in physiological responses during critical incidents (i.e., getting an adrenaline rush); and illness or medical incidents are all examples of physiological stressors.
7. Psychological stressors: Most of the stressors discussed above could also be classified in this category. For example, fear that is generated when an officer responds to a dangerous call can be a psychological stressor. The fear may be functional if the officer recognizes it as a warning mechanism and becomes more alert as a result. However, if the officer masks that fear and it becomes internalized, it can upset the officer's psychological balance. Other stress variables in this category include constant exposure to the worst side of humankind and the impact of resolving situations that are of a repulsive nature (e.g., homicides, child abuse, fatal traffic accidents, etc.). These situations can have a traumatic effect on an officer, particularly in a cumulative state. Such stressors may also develop into a psychological condition, such as depression or paranoia, which may, in turn, have significant impact on the abuse of authority.[13]

Special Case Stressors

Some police officers may possess additional levels of stress when compared to other officers. For example, some experts have found that the race and gender of an officer may add to the inherent stressors in police work.

Minority and Female Police Officers

Some research has found that minority and female police officers may experience greater levels of stress when compared to white, male officers.[14] That is, they experience the stressor inherent to the craft of policing like all other officers, but they may also experience several other organizational stress factors. Female police officers may experience stress by having to prove themselves to their colleagues and supervisors because of the heavily male-dominated culture of policing. For many years, the gender disparity in policing has been problematic for female police officers attempting to forge an identity in the profession.

Consider this, from the entry of the first sworn female into policing in 1910 until 1972, women police officers were selected according to a different criterion from men. In many cases, they were employed as policewomen and limited to working with women, children, and typewriters.[15] Historically, female police officers have also had to cope with sexual harassment and public stereotypes. These factors may place an increased level of stress on female police officers.

Minority police officers have experienced many of the same organizational stressors that female officers experience. In addition to the common police stressors inherent with the job, minority police officers have had to endure racial prejudice within the organization, and they are often criticized by some in their own community for joining the ranks of an occupation that many perceive to be in place to control minorities. It is no secret that police-minority relations in the United States have been strained. Many minority communities view the police with considerable suspicion, and unfortunately this suspicion is justified with the prevalence of the known cases of police brutality that have been documented throughout history.

Family Issues

Stress is not just limited to police officers themselves. The police occupation can create a great deal of stress for family members of police officers. Family members have to cope with the shift work, holidays spent without their loved ones, fear of death and injury on the job, along with isolation and low pay. Family members of police officers may also be held to higher standards within the community, especially the children of police officers. Imagine a police officer's son or daughter that has a run-in with the police. Regardless of how trivial the incident, the child suddenly becomes the focal point of whispers, such as, "His mother is a police officer." Just being related to a police officer may at times place family members in the community spotlight.

Communication is another factor that may lead to stress for police officers and their families. Police families sometimes have difficulty figuring out how to effectively communicate with one another. If an officer is experiencing a communication problem within their family, they often exacerbate the problem by retreating to the company of other police officers with the belief that they are the only ones that really understand the job and its problems.

Organizational Stressors

An important and often neglected source of police stress is the stress that can originate from within the police organization. There are several studies that have identified organizational variables as a significant source of stress for police officers.[16]

Some experts have found that the paramilitary and bureaucratic model of organization that is common in police agencies may induce increased amounts of stress. Most police agencies are paramilitary organizations. A paramilitary police organization is one with characteristics similar to the military, such as a rank structure, the technical aspects of the job, a clear chain of command, rigid discipline, and obedience to upper command. Paramilitary police organizations largely inhibit participative decision-making and input from those officers at the bottom of the organizational hierarchy. The paramilitary police organization assumes that every assignment involves skills that do not vary greatly from individual to individual or from setting to setting.[17]

The paramilitary model of policing may create role conflict on the part of police officers. Let us examine the military for a moment. The role of the military in part is fairly clear in the sense that they have an objective to defend the country from foreign enemies. In times of war, the military is generally not bound by constitutional limitations on their actions, for example, searching for enemies and defending and overtaking geographical areas. The military accomplish their mission by working in large teams to achieve their objectives, and usually command and supervision are close at hand.

The police, on the other hand, do not fight wars. The police primarily serve the community. They are bound by constitutional limitations that guide their decision making and actions. In contrast to the military, police officers work relatively alone in the field, use much discretion, and make many decisions without direct supervision.[18] The problem that the paramilitary model creates for police officers is that it advocates an enemy, which may create role conflict. When we think of the military and military action, we think of an enemy. So, who is the enemy of the police? Who do the police fight? The conflict stems from the dichotomy of the crime fighter orientation of policing and the community public service orientation.

Although extremely important for police operations, the chain of command may also create stress on the part of the police officer. The chain of command is used in the military and police organizations. The chain of command is a formal system of communication that allows, for example, a report to travel from a police officer up to the chief of police after it has been reviewed by police personnel within the chain of command (e.g., sergeant, lieutenant, captain, major, and deputy chief). The way in which the chain of command works is that the information or report is supposed to flow expediently and up the chain of command and down the chain of command. This may not always be the case. One of the authors of this textbook recently interviewed a number of police officers serving in several larger police organizations, and one common criticism voiced by these police officers was that communication was a major problem within their organizations. The police officers said that information and reports that were sent up the chain of command sometimes did not get to the chief in a timely fashion. Some officers related that in some cases, they did not receive a reply after submitting a proposed idea to the command staff.

Critical Life Events

James D. Sewell developed a specific critical life events scale that has proven to be a valid and useful tool for identifying stress among law enforcement officers.[19] The scale, which is titled the Law Enforcement Critical Life-Event Scale, identifies one hundred and forty-four critical life events specific to the law enforcement occupation. During Sewell's research, law enforcement officers rated each of the life events on a scale of 1 to 100. The ten most stressful situations, rated by police officers in descending order were: (1) violent death of a partner; (2) dismissal; (3) taking a life in the line of duty; (4) shooting someone in the line of duty; (5) suicide of an officer who was a close friend; (6) violent death of another officer in the line of duty; (7) murder committed by a police officer; (8) duty-related violent injury (shooting); (9) violent job-related injury to another officer; and (10) suspension. Of the one hundred and forty-four critical life events, the least stressful that was rated by law enforcement personnel was the completion of a routine report. Of the police officers who participated in the development of the scale, 52.1% related that they have experienced at least one stress-related illness. The most frequent stress illness given was digestive disturbances, and the second most frequent stress illness cited was the use of alcohol.[20]

End Result of Police Stress

As we discussed previously in this chapter, stress can result from a variety of sources. Stress, from what we know, is the embodiment of conflict resulting from demands for performance of bodily, social, and occupational functions imposed by any constellation of environmental and psychological factors that either stimulate or inhibit one's ability to satisfactorily perform physiological, psychological, social, or occupational functions.[21] As we discuss in the next section, many police officers attempt to manage their stress in unhealthy ways, including substance abuse.

Substance Abuse

In the United States, alcohol is number one in sales and consumption and is the drug of choice for reducing tension and stress.[22] How often have your heard someone you know after a hard day at the office say something like, "I need a stiff drink." Alcoholism in the United States is a significant health-related concern. According to the National Council on Alcoholism and Drug Dependency, 79,000 deaths are annually attributed to excessive alcohol use, and alcoholism is the third leading lifestyle-related cause of death in the nation. Moreover, up to 40% of all hospital beds in the United States (except for those being used by maternity and intensive care patients) are being used to treat health conditions that are related to alcohol consumption.[23]

There is evidence dating back many years suggesting that the high rate of suicide among police officers may be associated with the increased incidence of alcohol abuse problems.[24] Since the mid-1980s, researchers have found a high incidence of alcohol abuse among law enforcement officers. The rates of alcohol and drug abuse among officers range from 20% to over 60%.[25] Some studies have found that substance abuse among younger officers is about 20%, and alcohol abuse among veteran officers was equally about 20%.[26] Substance abuse, particularly alcohol abuse, is often used as a coping device by officers. Some police officers drink together in groups to reduce stress and provide support for one another. For example, officers may meet at a neighborhood bar or at another officer's house to drink and talk shop.

There is an old adage among police officers that no one understands the dilemmas of police work but other cops. Some research has indeed suggested that police officers find it very difficult to socialize outside of police circles.[27] Often the police themselves become a closed society that is suspicious of anyone outside of the policing occupation. A good illustration of this is in Joseph Waumbaugh's classic and bestselling novel *The Choir Boys*.[28] In Waumbaugh's novel, police officers refer to drinking sessions as "choir practice." Choir practice is the ritual where police officers would get together off-duty, consume a lot of alcohol, and talk about the job.

Just how many police officers abuse alcohol is difficult to determine. Studies have produced varying results. Some research suggests that alcohol use among police officers is currently underestimated and may actually be higher than what is believed.[29] One of the problems researchers experience in their attempt to collect more accurate data centers is the fact that many police officers simply will not report their problem for fear of getting into trouble. Therefore the alcohol problem is often hidden until the officer begins to experience more serious psychological and physical problems as a result of the alcohol abuse. Alcoholism over time will usually begin to affect the officer's work habits.

Danger Signs

In the early stages of alcohol abuse, there are usually no outward signs of a problem. This can be problematic for police management, because as noted previously, most employees are reluctant to talk with a supervisor about their alcohol problem. The police officer experiencing alcohol abuse may function normally the majority of the time and only have a few gradual personality changes. For example, some police officers may start to exhibit signs of the inability to deal with stressful situations, which results in increased conflict in their families. Although this in not necessarily always indicative of an alcohol problem, additional signs will be present to others before they are accepted by the problem drinker. Some common signs and symptoms of the officer with a drinking problem may include:

- An increase in the amount of alcohol required to achieve the same effect.
- Lapses in memory or "blackouts" (missing court, increased tardiness in reporting to work, etc.).
- A feeling by the officer that a drinking pattern is getting out of control.
- In the final stage, the officer is unable to stop drinking for any lengthy period of time but derives little or no pleasure from the alcohol consumption.

It is important to point out that an officer may deny that a substance abuse problem exists. Family members may also be in denial and may protect the officer by, for example, calling in sick to cover for a hangover, or they may refuse to acknowledge destructive or unusual behavior. It is incumbent on police managers and supervisors to be aware of the symptoms of substance abuse. Police management and supervision must be willing to take appropriate action and make referrals in order to assist the police officer.

Police Suicide

A study by the National Surveillance of Police Suicide Study found that one hundred and forty-one police officers took their own lives in 2008, and one hundred and forty-three did so in 2009.[30] The rate of suicide among police officers is far greater than in the general population.[31] Although in many cases it may be unexpected, and there is usually no history of counseling beforehand, police suicides have been linked to diagnosable mental disorders, most often involving depression, alcohol, and/or drug abuse. Suicide among police populations seems more prevalent among urban police officers, and the rates of police suicide are continuing in an upward trend.

In the years 1950–1979, a sample of 2,662 police officers averaged one suicide every 2.5 years. From 1980 to 1990, the rate increased to one suicide every 1.25 years.[32] In a 1995 study by the National Fraternal Order of Police that examined life insurance policies of 38,800 FOP members, it was

Job-Related Issues 211

concluded that suicide was the leading cause of accidental death among police officers.[33] Similarly in another study of mortality among Buffalo, New York, police officers it was revealed that officers were eight times more likely to commit suicide than to die in job-related accidents.[34] Other research on police mortality found that when police populations are compared to other working populations, the police rate is almost three times the rate for suicide.[35]

Police suicide is not just a problem in America. Studies of suicides among state police officers in the Federal Republic of Germany found that higher suicide rates were reported for police officers than for comparable age groups in the general population.[36] As we touched on previously, there are several factors that may be related to the high risk of suicide among police officers. These include continual exposure to human misery, an overbearing police bureaucracy, shift work, social strain, marital difficulties, inconsistencies of the criminal justice system, alcohol problems, physical illness, impending retirement, and lack of control over work and personal lives.[37] Many experts report that one of the major causes of police officer suicide is the profound stress of the job, and others have explained their reluctance to seek help voluntarily or in an expedient manner.[38]

Police management should develop guidelines for all rank and file police personnel regarding early warning signals of suicide. This is important so that an officer who recognizes that a colleague may be at risk of suicide can report his observations in a confidential manner. Because police officers generally do not like to show emotion in front of their colleagues, early warning suicide signals may be difficult to identify. The following is a list of early warning signals. Managers should ensure that all police employees are trained to recognize these early warning signals:

- Announce that they are going to do something that will ruin their careers but that they do not care
- Admit that they feel out of control
- Appear hostile, blaming, argumentative, and insubordinate OR appear passive, defeated, and hopeless
- Develop a morbid interest in suicide or homicide
- Indicate that they are overwhelmed and cannot find solutions to their problems
- Ask another officer to keep their weapon OR inappropriately use or display their weapon
- Begin behaving recklessly and taking unnecessary risks on the job and/or in their personal lives
- Carry more weapons than is appropriate
- Exhibit deteriorating job performance (which may be the result of alcohol or drug abuse)[39]

Case Study 9.1

The following fictitious example is presented to further illustrate the complex nature of stress. As you read this case example, we encourage you to think about what you would do if you were a police supervisor.

The Case of Officer Jones

- Officer Jones is a thirty-five-year-old Caucasian male. He is a member of a department with about two hundred sworn police officers. Officer Jones has eleven years of police experience, and he has been a patrol officer for his entire career. Officers Jones always wanted to be a police officer. After graduating from high school, he joined the military to gain some work experience while waiting to reach the minimum age of 21 for joining the police department. He did well in the military, and while not assigned to military police duties, he felt his military experience to be beneficial. Upon discharge from military service, he attended a local community college and applied to the police department and was accepted. He attended the police academy and, within four months after being hired, began his career. Officer Jones continued to take college classes whenever his work schedule allowed. He was married two years after joining the department. The first eight years of his police career were uneventful.
- During the past two years, Officer Jones has received several verbal reprimands by his supervisors for infractions that ultimately resulted in four formal letters of reprimand and the initiation of formal termination proceedings. His performance deteriorated with no apparent incident as the catalyst. Officer Jones denied the abuse of alcohol or drugs to his supervisors. His appearance deteriorated. This was surprising because Officer Jones had always taken great pride to look his very best in uniform. He always maintained a professional appearance with polished boots, clean and neatly pressed uniform, and polished brass. The officers that worked around Officer Jones noticed that he started complaining about the department and the community. His complaints ranged from poor pay to the community's lack of support to the department's inadequate equipment and facilities. Officer Jones quit taking college courses because he viewed them as a waste of time, both personally and professionally. Finally, he separated from his wife and six-year-old daughter, citing financial and relationship problems.
- In the succeeding months, Officer Jones's performance continued to deteriorate. He became confrontational at work with superiors, peers, and citizens. The department received several complaints from citizens regarding Officer Jones's abusive behavior, and several lawsuits were threatened. There was no apparent pattern to his abuse and hostility. Everyone was subject to it. His first formal reprimand resulted from one of the incidents of verbally abusing a citizen. He admitted afterwards that he felt the "department had turned on him and that it was just another example of the department not supporting its officers." His second and third reprimands resulted from an unauthorized high-speed pursuit for an apparent traffic charge. Departmental

Job-Related Issues

policy prohibited pursuits for routine traffic violations without a supervisor's authorization. Whereas Officer Jones acknowledged that he violated the departmental policy, he indicated that he felt "it was bad policy, one that prevented him from doing his job as a police officer." The third reprimand was accompanied by a five-day suspension without pay.
- The fourth reprimand, which led to termination proceedings, involved Officer Jones being arrested for domestic assault. He had gone to his wife's parents' home while on duty and tried to talk with his wife, from whom he was separated, about future visitations with his daughter. This led to an argument, and when his father-in-law tried to intercede, he struck both his father-in-law and his wife. His wife called the police department and reported the incident to a supervisor. Officer Jones was charged with domestic battery, and he was suspended pending termination proceedings. The arresting officer reported that Officer Jones's behavior was erratic, and he suspected that Officer Jones was drinking at the time. Termination proceedings were initiated in accordance with the city's civil service policy.

The above scenario exemplifies the manner in which many law enforcement agencies handle police officers who experience stress-related problems. Traditionally, law enforcement management has been slow to address officer stress, and most attempts to reduce stress have been reactive rather than proactive. That is, the majority of efforts to reduce stress have taken an individual perspective on the problem that usually emphasizes the officer's inability to cope with the stress of policing.[40] Colleagues and supervisors may become aware that a fellow officer is experiencing significant stress but are reluctant to address the problem, either believing it is none of their business or lacking the confidence to address the problem openly. Unfortunately, this could impact the law enforcement agency financially because of turnover and retraining. The Bureau of Justice Statistics estimates that nationwide, it costs about $93,300 per officer to maintain employment with the proper equipment, salaries, and benefits.[41] Given this cost, it behooves law enforcement management to develop strategies to deal with job-related stress.

Managing Stress

There are various approaches to managing police officer stress. Stress management programs are one such approach. These programs assist police officers in managing their stress. With effective stress management, police officers will feel better about themselves and their jobs. By offering a confidential venue for officers to deal with stress, absenteeism because of illness and other factors may be reduced significantly.

Physical Exercise

Not only is exercise beneficial to maintain health, but also a regular physical exercise routine at least three times per week can minimize the effects of stress. Physical exercise improves the body's stamina to deal with stress. There are a number of things that management can do to promote exercise within their police agencies. Some agencies assist their officers with athletic club memberships by paying a certain percentage, whereas others have designated exercise areas and equipment available within police facilities. One other approach is to allow officers flextime to exercise whenever possible, although in large agencies this could be challenging. Flextime might be considered by giving officers extra time for lunch or several hours a week to engage in a physical workout program.

Proper Diet

Proper diet and nutrition can assist in minimizing stress, improving general health, and reducing obesity. Medical evidence is clear that a diet that is high in fat and cholesterol can increase the risk for cardiovascular disease, high cholesterol, and certain types of cancer. As a suggestion, police managers may want to offer courses on proper nutrition as part of in-service training. Police diets tend to be full of fast food and generally poor. This in large part is due to the eat-and-run schedules that police patrol officers frequently work within. Years of eating out in fast-food restaurants while on duty are not conducive to proper diet techniques or good health.

Social Affiliations

Mental health professionals encourage police officers to make friends both inside and outside of the law enforcement profession. Most police officers have a close circle of friends, and they are usually other police officers. Police officers should be encouraged to become active in community service groups or clubs. This is a good way to meet others and develop friendships outside of the policing profession. For those police officers attending college, the college campuses are excellent avenues to make friends outside of the policing profession. Many officers discover that when they talk with others about problems and issues, they feel much better about themselves.

Relaxation Techniques

Relaxation techniques may be beneficial as a stress-prevention or relieving mechanism. The police officer should find a quiet location and relax for short periods of time. The officer should close his eyes, clear all thoughts while taking several deep breaths until he begins to feel his body relax. Soft music playing in the background may help bring on the relaxation state. Studies of police populations in the United Kingdom have found that relaxation techniques were effective in managing stress.[42]

Other Approaches to Stress Management

A Healthy Work Environment

Effective organizations are characterized by fairness, friendliness, and supportiveness, with clear and consistent rules and boundaries.[43] Organizations that exhibit these characteristics provide support to officers and their families, teach stress-management techniques, promote healthy lifestyles, and provide links to outside resources.

Whenever possible, police management should allow for participative decision making. It only makes sense that police management whenever possible should involve those police officers in the field delivering the service to the citizens in the decision-making process. Police officers in the field are exposed to problems on a daily basis and may be in the best position to offer effective solutions. This in and of itself may reduce stress because officers who are involved in decision making have the feeling of being involved and engaged. Most human beings have an intrinsic need and want to be engaged and involved in decisions that will ultimately affect their jobs. Thus, participative approaches within the organization will assuredly foster a healthier organizational work environment for police officers and, in so doing, reduce stress.

Critical Incident Stress Debriefings

Many police departments use stress debriefing sessions for an officer or groups of officers that have been exposed to a critical incident. Critical stress teams are made up of individuals who have received specialized training in mediation and communication techniques. Team members may come from various occupational backgrounds including the law enforcement community, the faith community, the medical community, and other public safety jobs such as emergency paramedics and firefighting services. After an officer is involved in a critical incident such as a significant crime scene, on-the-job injury, or death of a colleague, a trained mental health official leads a critical incident debriefing team with a group discussion that centers on the emotions, thoughts, and reactions of officers who have been exposed to a critical incident. Officers have an opportunity to vent their emotions to the group. Allowing the officer to vent is an important part of the debriefing because it demonstrates to officers that when they talk with others, they are responding very normally to a very abnormal event.

A critical incident is a psychologically distressing experience that is outside the range of usual human experience.[44] For example, the 1995 bombing of the Murrah Federal Building in Oklahoma City, and the September 11, 2001, terrorist attack on the Twin Towers in New York are critical incidents. During the investigation of the Murrah Federal Building bombing in Oklahoma City, critical stress debriefing teams were brought in to provide assistance to first responders.

The Federal Bureau of Investigation (FBI) utilizes stress debriefing teams as part of a confidential effort to assist FBI employees. The FBI's Critical Incident Management Program offers a continuum of interventions and services, providing both immediate and long-term support, including defusing, critical incident stress debriefings, family outreach, manager support, referrals and follow-up, eye movement desensitization and reprocessing treatments, and post-critical incident seminars.[45]

A critical stress debriefing session should usually take place within 24–72 hours after a critical incident. Some officers who have been involved in a critical stress incident would rather not attend the critical stress debriefing sessions. Police management should make the critical stress debriefing sessions mandatory for all officers who have been exposed to a critical incident.

Policing a Multicultural Community

> In a multi-racial society, no group can make it alone.
> —**Martin Luther King, Jr.**
> *March 31, 1968*

The ethnic and cultural diversity of the United States continues to grow at a rapid pace. The United States has welcomed more immigrants than any other country in the world. Early on in our history, it was assumed that immigrants would be assimilated into existing cultural patterns, called the melting pot model. In the twenty-first century, this assimilation model has been recognized as neither a good description of what has happened nor a plausible prediction of what can happen as our population continues to diversify rapidly. The religious and cultural patterns of American society are now more varied than ever. Police management should continue to strive to develop the best methods to police a pluralistic society. Police officers entering the profession today face both a citizen population and a set of professional values that require skills for negotiating cultural difference. Multiculturalism is a definition that has taken on divergent meanings over the years and generally refers

Job-Related Issues

to a society that is made of many different ethnic and racial groups; it does not refer to a movement or political force.[46]

Demographics and Diversity

America's racial composition is changing more rapidly than ever, and the number of immigrants in America is the largest in any post-World War II period.[47] The proportion of African Americans has been rising gradually, and by 2020, African Americans are predicted to comprise about 12.9% of our total population.[48] Similarly, by 2020 Asian Americans will represent about 6.5% of the American population, and Hispanics will comprise more than 37% of our total population.[49] Some suggest that by the year 2030, one out of four U.S. residents will be Hispanic or Asian in ethnic makeup.

Challenges and Opportunities for Law Enforcement

Multiculturalism is an approach to cultural diversity that emphasizes understanding, respecting, and adapting to other cultures and cultural differences. Today, members of different cultures are coming into contact with each other increasingly more frequently. Accepting diversity has always been challenging for many Americans. Some Americans are increasingly uncomfortable with the number of immigrants, refugees, and ethnic minorities in our society in ways that are not much different from times past.[50] Typical criticisms that are common regarding the recent influx of immigrants into the United States include: "they hold on to their cultures, they will not learn our language, their customs and behaviors are strange, and they stick to themselves."[51]

Because of America's growing culture diversity, police management should ensure that they have adequate resources to effectively serve diverse communities. Moreover, it is important that police departments are not only a microcosm of the communities they serve, but also that they accept the values of multicultural diversity.

Hate Crimes

From 2003 to 2009, there was an annual average of about 194,800 hate-crime victimizations and 179,300 hate-crime incidents.[52] In the majority of these attacks, the suspect was motivated by the victim's race or ethnicity. In spite of the rich multicultural diversity in America, there will always be persons or groups who commit crimes against others based their race, religion, or sexual preference. In policing a multicultural society, law enforcement will encounter these types of crimes and the people that commit them. Hate crime is violence of intolerance and bigotry, intended to hurt and intimidate someone because of their race, ethnicity, national origin, religion, sexual orientation, or disability.

In 1990, the Hate Crime Statistics Act was signed into law. It mandates that the U.S. Justice Department collect statistics on crimes against victims based upon race, religion, ethnicity, or sexual orientation. Most states have guidelines in place for police authorities for reporting and investigating hate crimes. Hate crimes demand a priority response from law enforcement because of their special emotional and psychological impact on the victim and the victim's community. The damage done by a hate crime simply cannot be measured solely in terms of physical injury or dollars and cents. Hate crimes intimidate other members of the victim's community, leaving them feeling isolated, vulnerable, and unprotected by the law.

Police managers must ensure that their agencies respond effectively and aggressively to hate crimes. Likewise all personnel within the agency should receive continual training pertaining to hate crime laws and legislation, trends and intelligence pertaining to hate groups, and investigative techniques. Other programs may include community-based education and workshops to ensure that the public is educated on hate crimes. The International Association of Chiefs of Police offered the following recommendations to police departments regarding hate crimes:

- Establish a policy of "zero tolerance" for prejudice throughout the department
- Ensure police are trained to recognize and respond appropriately to hate crimes
- Provide officers with user-friendly hate crime incident report forms that comply with state and national reporting standards
- Sponsor and participate in community events and activities that promote diversity, tolerance, bias reduction, and conflict resolution
- Track the criminal activities of organized hate groups
- Collaborate with community organizations, schools, and other public agencies to develop coordinated approaches to hate crime prevention and response
- Engage the media as partners in restoring victimized communities and preventing bias-motivated incidents and crimes
- Document the positive outcomes of hate crime prevention and response strategies[53]

Building and Supporting a Multicultural Workforce

It is important that police management builds and supports a multicultural workforce. Historically, the policing profession has attracted largely white males from blue-collar backgrounds. It has been difficult for the police to recruit both minorities and females into the ranks of policing.

There are several inherent problems that police managers face when recruiting minorities. The first is the stigma of past injustices and unequal treatment of minorities by the police. To some minority citizens, especially African Americans, the police represent an oppressive force in their neighborhoods. One other concern that has been voiced by some African Americans is that those who enter into policing may be considered sellouts by members of their community. Finally, it may be difficult to recruit minority police officers because minorities may have been exposed to or have witnessed police brutality or unequal treatment at some time during their lives. Police management should meet this challenge head on and develop sound and aggressive recruitment policies to attract and encourage minorities to apply for jobs in policing. As increasing numbers of minorities reach executive positions in police departments, it is anticipated that policy changes will be implemented that directly affect police-minority relations. These policy changes will increasingly address issues such as discourtesy, racial slurs, and aggressive patrol tactics.

Training Officers to Work in a Multicultural Society

Because police officers work in a culturally rich society, quality diversity training programs will continue to be important. Diversity training programs must begin with senior police executives. Training programs should be designed and tailored to challenge stereotypes, to identify and explore groups' similarities and differences; to reduce competitive tensions by facilitating intergroup communication; to impart a sense of value and empowerment in the pursuits of shared organizational goals; and to improve organizational productivity by ridding the workplace of prejudicial and discriminatory behavior. Diversity training in police agencies should be mandated from the recruit to the most senior police officer, and it should not equate to a one-shot training session but rather should be continuous throughout a police officer's career.

Police officers should be culturally competent. To illustrate this point, consider the following. Suppose that a Caucasian police officer patrols an area of the community that is roughly 40% Hispanic and 60% Caucasian. Would it not make sense that in order for the officer to more effectively patrol this area, he or she should learn about Hispanic culture? For example, Hispanic culture is diverse in and of itself. Some fall into the trap of assuming that all Hispanic culture is the same. This is a false assumption. Not all Mexicans, Puerto Ricans, Cubans, and Dominicans share the same culture. There are a host of differences among these groups including different customs, foods, values and behaviors.

It may also be of benefit for the police to have some contextual understanding of those racial and ethic groups represented in the United States. Consider the following recommendations for police authorities pertaining to African Americans:

1. The experience of slavery and racism as well as cultural differences have shaped African American culture.
2. For many African Americans, particularly those in the lower socioeconomic rungs of society, the history of slavery and later discrimination continues to leave psychological scars.
3. There is tremendous diversity among African Americans, which includes individuals of all socioeconomic levels, a number of religions, different regions of the country (rural and urban, as well), and various countries of origin.
4. The changing terms that African Americans have used to refer to themselves reflect stages of racial and cultural growth, as well as empowerment.
5. African Americans react as negatively to stereotypes that they hear about themselves as officers do when they hear such statements as, "Police officers are biased against blacks," or "All police officers are capable of brutality."
6. The predominance of households headed by women, particularly in the inner city, coupled with the myth of women as the head of the household, has created situations where officers have dismissed the importance of the father.
7. Young African American males, in particular, and their parents (of all socioeconomic levels) feel a sense of outrage and injustice when officers stop them for no apparent reason.
8. The use of African American varieties of English does not represent any pathology of deficiency and is not a combination of random errors but rather reflects patterns of grammar from some West African languages.
9. People in positions of authority have often misunderstood aspects of black nonverbal communication, including what has been termed the "cool pose."
10. Cultural differences in verbal communication can result in complete misinterpretation.
11. The existence of excessive force and brutality is still a reality in policing in the United States, even if it is a minority officer who commits these acts. When there is police brutality, everyone suffers, including officers and entire police departments.
12. A dynamic exists between some officers and African Americans, particularly in poor urban areas, whereby both the officer and the citizen are on the "alert" for the slightest sign of disrespect.

13. In areas populated by African Americans and other minorities all over the United States, there is a need for increased and more effective police protection.[54]

Police officers can enhance their jobs by taking the time to learn about various cultures with which they will come into contact within the community. Being aware of minority concerns, diversity, historical backgrounds of the various races, and groups in a community will enhance and facilitate the crime fighting and peace-keeping functions of the police. Consider the case of an officer called to the home of an Asian American family regarding a miscellaneous complaint. In many Asian American families, the relationship and communication patterns tend to be hierarchical, with the father as the identified head of the household. While many of the decisions and activities may appear to be decided by the father, many other people may come into the picture. Generally, if there are grandparents, the father would still act as the spokesperson of the family; however, chances are that he would consult with the grandparents prior to making a decision.[55]

In Middle Eastern cultures, such as that of Arab peoples, the male is overtly the head of the household and his role and influence are strong. The wife has a great deal of influence, too, but it is often behind the scenes.

A few years ago, the Police Executive Research Forum developed an action agenda for police interactions with racial and ethnic minorities. The action agenda included a framework for police to improve the quality of police services in minority communities. Specifically, the following three recommendations were made:

1. First, each law enforcement agency should undertake a critical self-assessment to determine which aspects of its current operations may be the source of tensions with racial and ethnic minority neighborhoods. Where problems are identified, appropriately focused remedies should be developed.
2. Second, leaders of the law enforcement profession should begin to develop a specific package of "best practices" related to the particular problem areas that have been identified. These best practices might include early warning systems, model use of force policies, and model citizen complaint procedures and appropriate procedures for the collection and use of data on traffic stops.
3. Third, research on policing needs to focus on two issues: research on police practices in particular contexts and the extent to which those contexts (e.g., practices by particular units) affect general relations with racial and ethnic minority communities. At the same time, the various best practices need to be subject to independent

evaluation to determine whether they best achieve their intended goals and/or whether some practices are more effective than others.[56]

Multicultural training may reduce the number of lawsuits filed against a police agency, as well as the possibility of civil disorder, but only can succeed with the acceptance and management of cultural diversity. Historically, strategies employed by police in dealing with minorities and minority issues have differed from those of other groups. While improvements in those strategies have occurred in the last decade, further improvements are needed.

There are four primary factors associated with achieving a more culturally aware police organization. First, police officers need to understand how their own cultural background molds their values and behavioral patterns. Second, officers must understand that cultural assimilation no longer is the norm in the United States. Law enforcement officers must learn about the different cultural and ethnic and racial groups in the neighborhoods they patrol. Third, it is critical that officers understand the effective use of cross-cultural communication. Police officers who have a deeper insight into the beliefs, behaviors, and value orientations of various ethnic groups will rely less often on authority and force to resolve problematic situations. Finally, law enforcement officers must develop cross-cultural communicative, analytical, and interpretive skills.

Questions in Review

1. Compare and contrast the two types of stress as identified by Hans Selye: "eustress" and "distress."
2. What effects can stress have on police officers?
3. Discuss what police management can do to assist employees in managing stress.
4. Discuss what police management can do to ensure that their officers are prepared to serve diverse communities.

Biggest Mistakes Police Leadership Makes and How to Avoid Them

Fighting Monsters

> Whoever fights monsters should see to it that in the process he does not become a monster. And when you look into an abyss, the abyss also looks into you.
>
> **—Friedrich Nietzsche**

Job-Related Issues

Thomas J. Cline,[57] President of the International Association of Ethics Trainers, warns us that there is a Trojan horse in law enforcement. Cline states that a law enforcement agency's time and resources are spent showing officers how to stay alive in confrontations with the bad guys, but little or nothing is being spent on how to stay alive in confrontations with ourselves. He notes that too often the attitude is that we know that something is wrong, but no one talks about it, that officers tend to "suck it up and tough it out," leaving them with a feeling of powerless. Cline is talking about the fact that more officers commit suicide than are killed in the line of duty. For example, he notes that in the last decade, about one hundred and fifty-one officers were killed yearly in the line of duty. Cline points out that in 2000, four hundred and eighteen law enforcement officers died by their own hands, about one every 21 hours. Generally, more than two and a half times as many officers take their own lives as die in the line of duty.

All law enforcement departments have regular inspections of equipment and personnel. What inspections can we have to prepare for the inner battles that often result in suicide? Cline advocates to officers

> start building your inner strength today by developing the cardinal virtues: prudence, justice, temperance, and fortitude. Prudence is the umbrella under which the others reside. It is derived from the Latin word *prudentia* and means seeing ahead. We often call it "common sense." Prudence can be learned if a person reminds themselves daily to be docile, open to new learning, especially those things we can learn from others.[58]

Cline contends that our disposition or attitude is critical to learning prudence. Prudence for a police office may include:

- whether or not to arrest
- whether to issue a ticket or not
- whom to assign for a particular task or job
- when to ask your supervisor for vacation, a perk, or a favor
- how to address a problem

Justice is synonymous with law enforcement. It concerns right relations with others in society, giving each person his due, consistently, promptly, and prudently. Commutative justice exists between two parties and requires an absolute fairness in exchanges between two parties in a mathematical way. Distributive justice refers to the relationship between a society and its members. Contributive justice is concerned with what an individual owes his agency and society. A fair day's work is required for each who accepts a position, its pay, and its perks.

Temperance is the virtue of self-preservation and keeps our drives and appetites for pleasure under control. Our drives for pleasure and our appetites can ruin our lives if given free reign. Once the line of temperance has been crossed, the pleasures wane and even turn to disgust. Fortitude is the strength, courage, endurance, resilience, guts, and determination to control our emotions. As Aristotle remarked, fortitude can help us "rule our anger with reason."

One of our problems, according to Cline, lies in keeping passions (emotions) under control, a difficult task, with temptations to do otherwise (what feels good). He contends that this is the reason that we must develop the habitual and firm disposition toward good, becoming virtuous.

End Notes

1. J. M. Brown and E. A. Campbell, *Stress and Policing: Sources and Strategies* (New York: John Wiley and Sons, 1994).
2. P. Finn, "Reducing Stress: An Organizational Approach," in *Stress Management in Law Enforcement*, L. Territo and J. D Sewell, eds. (Durham, NC: Carolina Academic Press, 1999).
3. H. Selye. *Stress without Distress* (Philadelphia, PA: Lippincott, 1974).
4. J. A. De Santo and L. J. Fennelly, "Stress and the Police," in *Law and Order* (February 1979), p. 54.
5. P. M. Whisenard, *The Effective Police Manager* (Englewood Cliffs, NJ: Prentice Hall, 1981), p. 262.
6. L. Territo and J. D. Sewell, *Stress Management in Law Enforcement* (Durham, NC: Carolina Academic Press, 1999).
7. J. M. Violanti, J. R. Marshall, and B. Howe. "Stress, Coping, and Alcohol Use: The Police Connection," in *Journal of Police Science and Administration*, Vol. 13, No. 2 (1985).
8. M. F. Asterita, *The Physiology of Stress* (New York: Human Sciences Press, 1985).
9. Selye.
10. R. H. Anson and M. E. Bloom, "Police Stress in an Occupational Context," in *Journal of Police Science and Administration*, Vol. 16, No. 4 (1988), pp. 229–235.
11. M. I. Kurke, "Organizational Management of Stress and Human Reliability," in *Police Psychology into the 21st Century*, M. I. Kurke and E. M. Scrivners, eds. (Hillsdale, NJ: Lawrence Erlbaum Associates, 1995).
12. P. Finn, "Reducing Stress: An Organization-Centered Approach," *FBI Law Enforcement Bulletin*, Vol. 66, No. 8, (August 1997), pp. 20–26.
13. T. Barker and D. L. Carter, *Police Deviance*, 2nd ed. (Cincinnati, OH: Anderson Publishing, 1991), pp. 204–205.
14. V. Lord, "An Impact of Community Policing: Reported Stressors, Social Support and Strain among Police Officers in a Changing Police Department," in *Journal of Criminal Justice*, Vol. 24 (1996), pp. 503–522.
15. S. E. Martin, "Women on the Move? A Report on the Status of Women in Policing," in *Police Foundation Reports* (Washington, DC: U.S. Government Printing Office, May 1989), pp. 1–8.
16. K. W. Ellison and J. L. Genz, *Stress and the Police Officer* (Springfield, IL: Charles C. Thomas Publishing, 1983).

17 Ellison and Genz.
18 J. H. Skolnick, *Justice without a Trial: Law Enforcement in a Democratic Society* (New York: Wiley, 1966).
19 J. D. Sewell, "The Development of a Critical Life Events Scale for Law Enforcement," in *Stress Management in Law Enforcement*, L. Territo and J. D. Sewell, eds. (Durham, NC: Carolina Academic Press, 1999).
20 H. W. More, *Special Topics in Policing*, 2nd ed. (Cincinnati, OH: Anderson Publishing Co., 1992).
21 Kurke, p. 392.
22 S.A. Maisto, M. Galizio and G.J. Connors, "Drug Use and Abuse, 5th ed. (Belmont, CA: Wadsworth, Cengage Learning Center, 2011).
23 National Council on Alcoholism and Drug Abuse, Inc., *Understanding Alcohol and Alcoholism*, accessed online at: http://www.ncadd.org.
24 J. Schwartz and C. Schwartz, "The Personal Problems of the Police Officer: A Plea for Action," in *Job Stress and the Police Officer*, W. Kroes and J. Hurrell, eds. (Washington, DC: U.S. Government Printing Office, 1976), pp. 130–141.
25 J. M. Volanti, J. E. Vena, and B. Howe, "Stress, Coping and Alcohol Use: The Police Connection," in *Journal of Police Science and Administration*, Vol. 13 (1985), pp. 106–110.
26 P. B. Kraska and V. E. Kappeler, "A Theoretical and Descriptive Study of Police On-Duty Drug Use," in *American Journal of Police*, Vol. 8, No. 1 (1988), pp. 1–36.
27 M. L. Dantzker, *Understanding Today's Police*, 4th ed. (Upper Saddle, NJ: Prentice Hall, 2005).
28 J. Wambaugh, *The Choir Boys* (New York: Dell Publishing, 1987).
29 J. M. Violanti, J. M. Vena, and J. R. Marshall, "Disease Risk and Mortality among Police Officers: New Evidence and Contributing Factors," in *Journal of Police Science and Administration*, Vol. 14, No. 1 (1986), pp. 17–23.
30 A. F. O'Hara and A. M. Violanti, "Police Suicide: A Web Surveillance of National Data," in *Journal of Emergency Mental Health*, Vol. 11, No. 1 (2009), pp. 17–33.
31 E. Hem, A. Marie Berg, and Oivind Ekeberg, "Suicide in Police: A Critical Review," in *Suicide and Life Threatening Behavior*, Vol. 31, No. 2 (2001), pp. 224–233.
32 J. M. Violanti, "The Mystery Within: Understanding Police Suicide," in *Stress Management in Law Enforcement*, L. Territo and J. D. Sewell, eds. (Durham, NC: Carolina Academic Press, 1999), pp. 119–126.
33 *Law Enforcement News, National FOP Looks at Police Suicide and How to Prevent It*, Vol. XXI, No. 422 (April 30, 1995), p. 10.
34 *Law Enforcement News, What's Killing America's Cops? Mostly Themselves*, Vol. XXII, No. 455 (1996), p. 5.
35 Violanti, Vena, and Marshall, pp. 17–23.
36 A. Schmidtke, S. Fricke, and D. Lester, "Suicide among German Federal and State Police Officers," in *Psychological Reports*, Vol. 84 (1999), pp. 157–166.
37 Violanti, Vena, and Marshall, pp. 17–23.
38 P. Quinnett, "QPR: Police Suicide Prevention," in *FBI Law Enforcement Bulletin*, Vol. 67, No. 7 (July 1998), pp. 19–24.
39 K. Mohandie, and C. Hatcher, "Suicide and Violence Risk in Law Enforcement: Practical Guidelines for Risk Assessment, Prevention, and Intervention," in *Behavioral Sciences and the Law*, Vol. 17, No. 3 (1999), pp. 357–376.

40　R. Roberg and J. Kuykendall, *Police Management*, 2nd ed. (Los Angeles, CA: Roxbury Publishing Co, 1997).
41　M. J. Hickman and B. A. Reaves, *Local Police Departments* (Washington, DC: Bureau of Justice Statistics, 2003).
42　J. M. Brown and E. A. Campbell, *Stress and Policing: Sources and Strategies* (New York: John Wiley and Sons, 1994).
43　R. Levering, M. Moskovitiz, and M. Katz, *The 100 Best Companies to Work for in America* (New York: New American Library, 1988).
44　T. Blau, *Psychological Services for Law Enforcement* (New York: John Wiley & Sons, 1994).
45　V. J. McNally and R. M. Solomon, "The FBI's Critical Incident Stress Management Program," in *FBI Law Enforcement Bulletin*, Vol. 68, No. 2 (February 1999), pp. 20–25.
46　R. M. Shusta, D. R. Levine, P. R. Harris, and H. Z. Wong, *Multicultural Law Enforcement: Strategies for Peace Keeping in a Diverse Society*, 2nd ed. (Upper Saddle River, NJ: Prentice Hall, 2002).
47　F. Chideya, *The Color of Our Future*. (New York: William Morrow and Company, 1999).
48　R. W. Judy and C. D'Amico, *Workforce 2020: Work and Workers in the 21st Century* (Indianapolis, IN: Hudson Institute, 1997).
49　Judy and D'Amico.
50　Shusta, Levine, Harris, and Wong, p. 6.
51　Shusta, Levine, Harris, and Wong, p. 6.
52　L. Langton and M. Planty, *Hate Crimes, 2003–2009* (Washington, DC: Bureau of Justice Statistics, 2011).
53　N. Turner, *Responding to Hate Crimes: A Police Officer's Guide to Investigation and Prevention* (Washington, DC: The International Association of Chiefs of Police, 2002), accessed online at: http://www.theiacp.org/PublicationsGuides/LawEnforcementIssues/Hatecrimes/tabid/191/.
54　Shusta, Levine, Harris, and Wong, pp. 188–190.
55　Shusta, Levine, Harris, and Wong, p. 157.
56　S. Walker, "Police Interactions with Racial and Ethnic Minorities: Assessing the Evidence and Allegations," in *Police Executive Research Forum* (2000).
57　T. J. Cline, "Tough and Most Dangerous Battles," in *Integrity Talk* (Chicago, IL: International Association of Ethics Trainers, Spring 2004), pp. 7–8.
58　Cline, p. 8.

Suggested Further References and Links to the Web

1. Robert M. Shusta, Deena R. Levine, Phillip R. Harris, and Herb Wong, *Multicultural Law Enforcement: Strategies for Peace Keeping in a Diverse Society*, 2nd ed. (2002). This book presents practical guidelines on how law enforcement professionals can work effectively with diverse cultural groups, both inside their organizations and in the community. This is an excellent resource for police supervisors and executives.

Job-Related Issues 227

2. Commission on Race and Police-Community Relations: http://www.crpcr.ri.gov/index.htm
3. John P. Crank and Michael Caldero, "The Production of Occupational Stress in Medium-Sized Police Agencies: A Survey of Line Officers in Eight Municipal Departments," in *Journal of Criminal Justice*, Vol. 19, No. 4 (1991) pp 339–349. This study assessed self-reports of occupational sources of stress among line officers in eight medium-sized police departments. In a survey of eight municipal police departments in Illinois, police personnel were asked to identify their principal sources of stress.

Training and Education   10

Key Individuals, Concepts, and Issues

Community policing	Deliberate indifference
Indirect (vicarious) liability	Teacher-centered training
Direct liability	Andragogy
Greason v. Kemp	Educational standards for police
Doe v. Borough of Barrington	Police Corps programs
City of Canton v. Harris	Police education
Failure-to-train liability	Police training
Behaviorist training	August Vollmer
Paramilitary training	Experiential learning

Definitions

Andragogy: The art and science of helping adults learn.

Community policing: A decentralized model of policing in which officers exercise their own initiatives and citizens become actively involved in making neighborhoods safer.

Direct liability: Liability incurred for the actions of supervisors or managers themselves.

Experiential learning: Process whereby knowledge is created through transformation of experience.

Indirect liability: Also called vicarious liability; pertains to liability of supervisors and managers for the actions of their employees.

Chapter Objectives

After completing this chapter, you should be able to:

1. Describe why managers must ensure that proper training is in place within the organization
2. Discuss fail-to-train liability
3. Describe behaviorist training methods

4. Describe the adult learning theory andragogy
5. Discuss various training applications of andragogy
6. Identify and discuss evolving police training curriculum
7. Discuss paramilitary police training

Introduction

> No person, regardless of his individual qualifications, is prepared to perform police work on native ability alone.
>
> *The President's Commission on Law Enforcement and the Administration of Justice, 1967*

Training is the lifeblood of a police organization. It is through training that new recruits learn the craft of policing and veteran officers hone existing skills and learn new ones. The need for police officers to stay abreast with the latest legal decisions, technology, and general advancements in the field are some of the reasons that police officers find themselves in the classroom. Likewise, training is important in order to inform and nurture strategic and operational changes within the police agency. Thus, effective police management and the commitment to effective training go hand in hand.

Police officers are required to complete basic academy training before performing police duties in the community. The number of basic training classroom hours is in no way uniform and varies widely across the United States. Upon graduation from the police academy, police officers in many states are further mandated to receive annual in-service training hours in order to maintain their law enforcement license. For example, the state of Kansas requires all law enforcement officers to receive forty hours of in-service training each year to maintain their law enforcement certificate. If you are a law enforcement officer in the state of Texas, you are mandated to attend forty hours of annual in-service training, and in Arizona, the number of annual in-service hours is eight.

In this chapter, we discuss police training and education in the United States. Specifically, we frame the discussion on what police managers need to know and how training is beneficial for organizational change dynamics. The chapter begins with an examination of the legal requirements that mandate police to train, both preservice and in-service. Next, we discuss evolving themes in police training including teaching and facilitation methods. The chapter concludes with a discussion of police education. Much of the material in this chapter is offered as informational for the purpose of assisting police management in guiding police training and education. Moreover, in the chapter we spend a great deal of time talking about innovations in training. The training academy represents the initial exposure of trainees to the police profession. It is critical that police management stay abreast with the latest trends and developments in training.

There are many factors that impact the training curriculum. These factors may include tactical changes, legal changes, policy and procedure changes, and changes in operating strategy. For example, community policing is one such strategy that if implemented successfully, must be reflected and nurtured through the training curriculum. Community policing has been implemented to some extent in a great many American police agencies. Community-policing strategies represent the most significant strategic change in police operations since the reform era changes that began in the 1930s. With community policing come both internal change (inside of the organization) and external change (service delivery change). With community policing, officers are expected to engage more in proactive problem solving, not totally autonomous from the community, but rather working directly with citizens and other organizations to solve community problems. This differs somewhat from the traditional (professional) model, which advocated the primary role of the police as crime fighters.

Why Train?

Public safety demands that police officers be competent in their job, which is in part nurtured by effective training and development. A police organization that fails to train its officers or does so haphazardly, opens itself up to potential lawsuits. The police operate within a legal vacuum. Put another way, legal ramifications largely dictate the routine of police operations and management decision making. The law and court decisions create this legal vacuum, and management decisions are routinely guided by the sociolegal environment. Almost every new policy, procedure, rule, or regulation is centered on the legal environment.

Police management can be held liable for not establishing appropriate guidelines that dictate the behavior of their subordinates. For example, imagine a police officer who has just been issued a new PR-24 baton by his commander. The officer without any formal training on how to use the baton begins to carry it on duty. While on patrol, the officer receives a call to report to a domestic disturbance and arrives only to meet a very upset and belligerent suspect of a domestic assault. The suspect becomes more upset and angry because of the police officer's presence. The suspect begins to walk toward the officer voicing various and sundry threats while lunging toward the officer. The officer takes out his newly issued PR-24 baton and begins to strike the suspect several times causing serious injury to the suspect. Let us assume that the officer struck the suspect in some vital areas of his body, like the head and neck area. Subsequently, the suspect is taken to the hospital for medical treatment where he remains for several days. Do you see any problem in this case? Undeniably, the officer had a right to defend himself. In fact, that is precisely what he was doing.

The problem centers on the fact that the officer did not know where to properly strike the suspect with the PR-24 baton. In this hypothetical scenario, the police officer and his agency can be held liable for failing to train. If a police officer is issued a piece of police equipment and subsequently is not provided with the proper training on how to use the equipment and uses the equipment in a negligent way (which could have been avoided with proper training), then the officer and police management can be held liable. Can you imagine, for example, a police officer being issued a firearm but not being trained in how to use the firearm? This could potentially be disastrous to the department and the governing body.

Legal Issues

Both federal and state laws hold police officers and police executives accountable for negligence on the part of police officers. The failure of police management to provide police officers with the proper training has resulted in lawsuits, which ultimately cost the police agency and the general citizenry in the form of their tax dollars. Each year in the United States, thousands of plaintiffs file civil suits claiming injury at the hands of law enforcement.[1] Consequently, members of police management are hauled into court to defend against these litigations vicariously because of their positions within the organization.

There are two distinct forms of management liability. The first is direct liability, and the second is indirect liability. Direct liability is liability incurred for the actions of supervisors or managers themselves. For direct liability to exist, managers usually have to engage directly in the activity. The following are ways in which police management can incur direct liability:

1. Supervisors authorize the act. They give officers permission to do something that ultimately results in liability.
2. They participate in the act. They engage in activities with other officers that ultimately result in liability.
3. They direct others to perform the act. They order officers to do something that ultimately results in liability.
4. They ratify the act. Once the act is completed, they fail to admonish or take corrective action when it comes to their attention.
5. They are present when an act for which liability results. They stand by and watch an act occur that results in liability and fail to take corrective action.[2]

Training and Education 233

On the other hand, indirect liability, or vicarious liability as it is sometimes known, pertains to liability of supervisors and managers for the actions of their employees. Let us apply indirect liability to the previous hypothetical case of the officer who was issued the PR-24 baton, not trained on how to use the baton, and as a result seriously injured a suspect with the baton. In this case, police management can be held vicariously liable under indirect liability.

Today most police officers receive formal training in the recruit academy and then in-service training throughout their careers. Training across police departments is in no way uniform and usually varies in length and content. Because of these factors, along with the criticism centering on the adequacy of training procedures, failure to train has been a favored bias of 42 USC (United States Code) 1983 liability;[3] 42 USC 1983 liability is:

> Every person who, under color of any statute, ordinance, regulation, custom, or usage, of any State or Territory or the District of Columbia, subjects, or causes to be subjected, any citizen of the United States or other person within the jurisdiction thereof to the deprivation of any rights, privileges, or immunities secured by the Constitution and laws, shall be liable to the party injured in an action at law, suit in equity, or other proper proceeding for redress, except that in any action brought against a judicial officer for an act or omission taken in such officer's judicial capacity, injunctive relief shall not be granted unless a declaratory decree was violated or declaratory relief was unavailable. For the purposes of this section, any Act of Congress applicable exclusively to the District of Columbia shall be considered to be a statute of the District of Columbia (42 USC 1983).

In cases pursued under 43 USC 1983, deliberate indifference must be alleged connecting the particular violation to inadequate training. For example, in one landmark case, U.S. Supreme Court Justice Byron White, in a rare unanimous opinion, spoke for the court in the City of Canton, Ohio v. Harris succinctly setting forth the issue and the court's disposition:

> [W]e are asked to determine if a municipality can ever be liable under 42 U.S.C. 1983 for constitutional violations resulting from its failure to train municipal employees. We hold that under certain circumstances, such liability is permitted by the statute.[4]

The City of Canton, Ohio v. Harris is an important case regarding management liability and training. Harris was arrested for charges not disclosed by city of Canton police officers. She was carried to the police station in a patrol wagon, and upon her arrival, police officers at the station noticed that she was sitting on the wagon floor. When police officers asked her if she needed medial attention she answered incoherently. While in the police station she slumped to the floor on two occasions, and the police left her lying there to prevent her from falling again. No medical treatment was provided by the police. After an hour she was released from custody to her family, who took her by ambulance to a hospital where she was diagnosed to be suffering from emotional ailments.

Harris sued the city of Canton claiming a violation of her due process rights to receive appropriate medical treatment while in custody. During the jury trial, evidence was presented showing that there was a municipal ordinance authorizing shift commanders to use their discretion and determine whether a detainee required medial treatment. Thus far, do you see any problems with the way the police handled this situation? At trial, it was revealed that the city of Canton police department had not provided special training for police commanders on how to determine who was entitled to medical care. The court rejected the city's argument that only unconstitutional policies can be a basis for an action under the United States Code for civil rights violations (42 USC 1983). Next in the Harris case, the court set forth the degree of fault that must be evidenced by the municipality's inaction before liability can be permitted:

> We hold today that inadequacy of police training may serve as the basis for 1983 liability only where the failure to train amounts to deliberate indifference to the rights of persons with whom the police come into contact.... Thus in the case at hand, respondent must still prove that the deficiency in training actually caused the police officers' indifference to her medical needs. Would the injury have been avoided had he the employee been trained under a program that was not deficient in the identified respect?[5]

Liability for failing train is real. It can be both costly and detrimental for a police organization not only in terms of money, but also in terms of public support and trust. The courts have constructed a three-pronged approach when determining whether police supervisors and management are liable for inadequate training:

1. Whether in failing adequately to train and supervise subordinates he was deliberately indifferent to the plaintiff's constitutional rights
2. Whether a reasonable person in the supervisor's position would know that his failure to train and supervise reflected deliberate indifference
3. Whether his conduct was causally related to this constitutional infringement by his subordinates[6]

In the case of Cooper v. Merrill, the police pursued Cooper, a robbery suspect who was believed to be armed and dangerous. After a car chase, Cooper jumped out of his car, ran, and hid behind some bushes in an attempt

Training and Education 235

to escape the pursuing police officers. During the foot pursuit the police officers fired a number of shots at Cooper, three of which struck him. Cooper filed a lawsuit against the borough police department trainer for, among other claims, a lack of any policy on the use of deadly force, which incidentally the department did not have. The court found that in order to establish such a claim, Cooper would have to show: (1) inadequate training; (2) that the inadequate training represents a policy that reflects a deliberate indifference to plaintiff's constitutional rights; and (3) that the police caused the alleged violation of constitutional rights.[7]

What is further problematic in this case is that other than the use of force statutes of the state, the county had no specific use of force policy. Likewise, there was no evidence that the borough did not provide training either in the field or in the form of a manual or procedure to guide its officers, and therefore the requested summary judgment for the borough was denied.[8] In this case, the decision was based in part because the borough did not have any such training or standard operating procedure that governed the use of deadly force. Therefore, the plaintiff failed to prove what the court suggested he must prove. Nevertheless, the potential problems that failure-to-train liability can create for a police organization should be clear.

One other case that is germane to this discussion is Doe v. Borough of Barrington.[9] In short, this case centered on the issue of police training in the area of contacts with persons infected with acquired immune deficiency syndrome (AIDS). In this case, police officers stopped the plaintiff while he was driving his truck. His wife was a passenger in the truck. The plaintiff informed police as they were about to search him that he had recently tested positive for HIV (the virus that leads to AIDS) and that he had weeping lesions. In another incident later the same day occurring opposite the plaintiff's house, police officers informed the plaintiff's neighbors that he (the plaintiff) had tested positive for AIDS. The neighbors immediately notified others in the neighborhood of the plaintiff's health situation. Many of these same neighbors withdrew their children from the school the plaintiff's children attended. Furthermore, newspaper and media stories soon emerged, and as a result, the plaintiff suffered significant embarrassment, humiliation, and discrimination.

The plaintiff sued and argued that the town (borough of Barrington) was legally responsible because of the lack of training in the proper way to handle confidentiality problems involving AIDS arrestees. The court agreed:

> In light of the duties assigned to police officers, the need for police training about AIDS is obvious.... The failure to instruct officers to keep information about AIDS carriers confidential was likely to result in disclosures and fan the flames of hysteria. [The town's] failure to train officers, therefore was likely to result in a violation of constitutional rights.... knowing that other

communities had taken precautions to protect officers from AIDS, [the town] did not establish its own policy or instruct officers about precautions. As such, [the town] made a conscious decision not to train its officers about the disease.... Clearly [the officers'] ignorance about the disease caused the improper disclosure.[10]

The potential legal liability that police managers may encounter for failing to adequately train their officers should now be clear. Moreover, police management can be held vicariously liable for acts by their officers. Each year the majority of lawsuits filed by citizens against the police allege that they were injured by the police.[11] The law enforcement executive and the officer's immediate command are usually named in the lawsuit because of either personal involvement or from a vicarious standpoint (meaning that he or she was involved because of a policy-making role). Police management should be aware of the potential liability they face in the area of failing to adequately train their employees. It is wise to seek out information about potential civil liability and its parameters, as well as to remain current on litigation in this area.

Training Methods

Police academy training in America is not uniform in either content or the number of hours required for certifying a police officer. The number of weeks required for police recruit training can vary from as little as eight or ten weeks up to a year. For example, the state of Georgia requires four hundred and eight hours or about eleven weeks of training to become a certified police officer, whereas the Los Angeles County Sheriff's Department requires nineteen weeks of training.

The manner in which police training is facilitated is for the most part delivered in the same manner across America. Police training is primarily mechanistic in nature and usually performed in a paramilitary and very structured environment.[12] In fact, it is well documented that police training from the earliest years has been a field dominated by a rigid, militaristic approach.[13] The militaristic environment in policing may be effective when teaching technical and procedural skills, but it does little to promote the acquisition of essential nontechnical competencies such as problem solving, judgment, and leadership.[14]

Behaviorist Police Training

Behaviorism focuses mainly on the hard sciences for an explanation into human functioning, concentrates solely on the objective, and only very rarely recognizes subjective human feeling. Under the realm of behaviorism, the intellect, feelings, and emotions of a person's inner life are not observable or measurable and therefore not investigated.[15] A behavioral police trainer would advocate that learning is a change of behavior and would rely heavily on behavioral objectives that are sometimes referred to as instructional objectives. Advocates of behavioral objectives assert that learning outcomes can be measured objectively and precisely, which will subsequently reveal how much progress has been made by the learner. There are three main components that can readily be found in the behavioral realm of training: the relevant conditions or stimuli under which a student is expected to perform; the behavior a student is to perform, including a general reference to the product of the student's behavior and a description of the criteria by which the behavior will be judged acceptable or unacceptable, successful or unsuccessful.[16]

The behavioral model is commonplace in most police training classrooms. Unfortunately, there is little research regarding how effectively new police officers learn in this type of environment. One problem with the behavioral learning model is that learning constitutes much more than a uniform structured environment. Each individual learner approaches learning from a distinct strategy and style. Learning strategy research has informed us that there are distinct patterns of learning that individuals may use. Conversely, a trainer using a behaviorist approach would argue that all learning should take place in a uniform environment. The content of police training must go beyond merely preparing officers for the mechanical aspects of police work and that training should help them to understand their communities, the police role, police history, and even imperfections of the criminal justice system.[17]

Training should focus on the need for choice in specific, clearly delineated situations, and the reality of police work must be brought into the classroom. Some police observers complain:

> We don't teach young officers the techniques of problem analysis, of identifying and coming up with strategies to problems.... We do not teach recruits how to organize a neighborhood in order to deal with neighborhood problems and that we have to make this a part of everyone's training.[18]

Police training tends to be heavily weighted toward the technical aspects of police work.[19] While this is necessary to a certain extent, these skills should be taught in conjunction with instruction on problem-solving strategies, communication skills, community disorder or quality-of-life issues, and resources available for use in community problem solving. With many of the skills now required of police officers, training must place increasing emphasis on subjects that go hand and hand with community-policing strategies such as problem solving, conflict resolution, working in racially and ethnically diverse communities, and the methods of facilitating community meetings.

New Approaches to Police Training

There is a sizable literature that informs us that adults learn differently than children. However, in thinking back on childhood educational experiences, many readers of this book will find that the same methods of teaching were employed by your high school teachers and by your instructors of classes that you have taken as an adult. For example, the instructor stands in front of the class and lectures for one, two, or three or more hours, and you are expected to take studious notes and then at some time in the future regurgitate the information by a method directed by the instructor. How can we be sure with adult police officers that effective learning takes place in the training environment? How do we ensure that police officers have mastered the material before performing police functions in the community? Does learning in a police training academy really take place using the behavioral model? These are important questions that police managers must investigate.

Andragogy and Police Training

The instruction methods in police training academies should increasingly adapt approaches advocated by adult education scholars. One such approach is a teaching method called andragogy. Andragogy is a teaching method that is vastly in contrast to the traditional models of instruction. The method advocates both the self-directed learning concept and the idea of the instructor as the facilitator of learning.[20] Andragogy is a model that is geared toward working with adult learners. The underlying assumptions of andragogy include:

> As a person matures, (1) his self-concept moves from being a directed to a self-directed human being, (2) he accumulates a growing reservoir of experience that becomes an increasing resource for learning, (3) his readiness to learn becomes oriented increasingly to developmental tasks of his social roles, and (4) his time perspective changes from one of postponed application of knowledge to immediacy of application, and accordingly his orientation toward learning shifts from one of subject centeredness to one of problem centeredness.[21]

Law enforcement trainers are in the business of teaching skills to adults, and to effectively facilitate learning, the instruction should be learner-centered rather than teacher-centered.[22] The advantages to the andragogical approach are that it draws on the trainee's past experience; treats the trainee as an adult; adapts to diverse needs and expectations of participants; and develops critical thinking, judgment, and creativity in the learner.[23]

Police training academies may find it beneficial to highlight self-directed learning on the part of the police officer. This would go hand in hand with community policing. For community policing to be successful, police officers have to be self-directed. When they discover a problem, they will be expected to solve it. What better place to implement the self-directed role of a police officer than in a training academy? Police managers should examine the current methods used in training recruits to see whether they support effective learning.

It is important that specific teaching methods be matched to matter.[24] Within the context of self-directed learning, the trainees do not depend on trainers to meet their specific learning needs but rather can learn at their own pace and determine their level of expertise. This probably works best with veteran officers completing annual in-service training requirements and might not be well suited for new recruits.

Police training sessions can be enhanced through the use of self-directed group discussions and active debate within the context of the training classroom. Police recruits should work out differences and develop personal understandings in the training classroom. When recruits engage in self-directed group discussions with instructors allowing for the airing of many viewpoints, the training classroom should begin to mirror the community with its many voices and perspectives.[25]

Training Applications

Cultural Diversity Training

The changing demographics in the United States make it imperative that recruits and veteran police officers be given diversity training. It is also important for the trainee to become an active participant in diversity training. It cannot be taught very well using strictly a lecture format. This can be accomplished by making use of group exercises and dialogue. The demographics of trainees in the police academy are slowly changing. Police trainees are no longer predominately white or male.[26] The training academy is increasingly becoming a synthesizing process, in which diverse lifestyles and even languages are melding into the police culture. Police trainers should use this academy makeup to their advantage when facilitating cultural diversity. Within the context of cultural diversity training, trainees should be allowed, in small groups whenever possible, to discuss issues pertaining to race with members other than his/her own race or ethnic background. In order to make training as realistic as possible, members of the minority community could be invited to participate with trainees in diversity training. Trainees should have the opportunity to discuss issues centering on race and diversity in the classroom.

Conflict Resolution and Mediation

Police officers perform conflict resolution and mediation on a daily basis. Both new and veteran police officers should receive a sizable block of conflict resolution and mediation training. Police management should, whenever possible, use veteran police officers in conflict resolution and mediation training. Veteran police officers can bring real-life case examples into the classroom. This will assist police trainers when imparting effective mediation and conflict resolution methods. The very nature of veteran officers' past experience in resolving conflict and mediating situations in the field may be advantageous in the process of learning and will make training active and fun. When using andragogy in police training, experience is at the center of knowledge production and acquisition.[27] Veteran police officers usually enjoy sharing their experiences with others. The experiences offered by veteran police officers will add substance and credibility to the topic covered.

Police officers should be allowed, in small groups, to discuss alternative solutions to mediation and conflict resolution. Outside of safety considerations, each crisis has its own specific set of circumstances, thus requiring differing responses. The significance of andragogy is that it allows for many alternatives in mediation, and trainees learn to apply a number of content areas to successfully resolve the conflict.

Criminal Procedure

Teaching criminal procedure, search and seizure, or city ordinances should use a case-study approach. The case-study method is an instructional technique based on real-life examples. Case studies simulate the real world and can be used to orientate trainees to ethical dilemmas of the law enforcement profession. The case-study method was developed at the Harvard University School of Law in the 1880s and later introduced into the Harvard Business School.

Case studies have been used in a wide variety of professional training programs. For example, in law schools, cases are frequently the backbone of a course, with separate cases used throughout the course. Case studies help future lawyers organize complex bodies of facts and information on their own and to inductively arrive at principles and apply them to new situations. The central aim of the case study is to stimulate self-development in a blend of understanding that combines intellectual ability (the power to think clearly, incisively, and reasonably about specific facts and also about abstractions) and to develop practical judgment and social awareness.

Medical schools have also made extensive use of case study approaches in the training of medical students. It is recognized that lectures will still be required to a certain extent when teaching criminal procedure or search and seizure in order for trainees to learn and conceptualize the underpinnings of the exclusionary rule, fruits of the poisonous tree doctrine, and exceptions to the Fourth Amendment's requirement for a search warrant and the like.

The authors have many anecdotal accounts and personal observations that much of the criminal procedure subjects in the police academy are taught almost exclusively using the lecture approach. In many cases, this consists of an assistant district or county attorney lecturing many hours to trainees on the legal aspects of policing with little or no interaction on the part of trainees. A case-study approach may improve the teaching-learning transaction. In law enforcement training centering on legal issues, trainees could be required in small groups to read a case situation and then identify the key issues of the case, present a rationale of why or why not, for example, a warrantless search could be made, and support the rationale with the appropriate search and exception to the search warrant requirement.

Community Survey

One other active teaching technique is to have police trainees conduct a neighborhood survey in a minority neighborhood. The trainees would be required to work in teams when conducting this survey. The objective of the survey is to discover citizen satisfaction with police services, citizen satisfaction with the police, neighborhood problems, and other concerns. The trainees while working in their teams plan and design a survey and then carry out the survey by personally administering it, going door to door in the selected neighborhood.

This training exercise allows trainees an opportunity to practice the skills that they have learned in the academy. For example, the trainees would have to do research on the most appropriate questionnaire design. When conducting the survey in minority neighborhoods, trainees will be exposed to a diverse population of citizens. Thus, trainees will have to learn something about the particular minority group predominant in the neighborhood. If the neighborhood is predominately Hispanic, trainees should study information regarding the Hispanic culture. This may require the trainee to identify resources in the Hispanic community to assist with the questionnaire, perhaps translating the questionnaire into Spanish. The very nature of this activity allows trainees to learn about a culture; perhaps it requires them to practice skills such as communication, problem solving, resource identification, studying survey data, teamwork, and community organization skills. The survey could culminate with trainees facilitating a neighborhood meeting for the purpose of revealing the survey results and brainstorming with citizens on appropriate solutions to problems identified in the survey. Trainees would hold a debriefing meeting with their academy instructor after the neighborhood meeting. The purpose of the debriefing meeting is so that they can share their experiences with other trainees who may have been assigned to another neighborhood.

Within the context of the exercise described above, the instructor plays an important role. The instructor acts as a facilitator or guide in the leaning process. The instructor is also a learner in the sense that he or she may actually learn from the trainees' experiences. This is hand in hand with andragogical teaching approaches, where the instructor provides an environment that is conducive to learning.

Experience and the Classroom

Police training should increasingly bring the past experience of the trainee or in-service officer into the classroom. Experiential learning activities may also be beneficial in the teaching-learning transaction. Experiential learning entails active participation and involvement of students in real-life situations. Experiential learning is defined as "the process whereby knowledge is created through transformation of experience."[28] Experiential learning centers on the belief that complete learning begins with a concrete experience upon which the learner reflects to find meaning. The learner draws conclusions through reflection and discourse and finally enters a phase of active experimentation where ideas and conclusions are tested. Experiential learning is beneficial in minimizing the disconnect that occurs between the academic environment of the police academy and the real world. Seasoned and new police officers alike bring a wide range of individual differences and experiences to the training classroom, and they are a rich resource for learning. Thus, it is important to make training experiential, interactive, and participatory.

Law enforcement training whenever possible should include simulated role-playing exercises and problem-solving activities that help develop communication skills. Police trainers and police officers could be used as actors to construct, for example, a domestic violence situation. Learners would then have to bring their observation and communication skills to solve the problem. Effective scenarios are designed for learners to use their previous knowledge and experiences whenever possible. Role plays are not new, but they are often relegated to one or two hastily conceived practical skills sessions that are poorly performed, monitored, and evaluated.[29] Properly prepared role simulation exercises lead to increased learning and retention.

Training Curriculum

As policing strategies evolve with community policing, so too must what the police are taught in the academy. Research has generally found that police engage in crime fighting for between 10 and 20% of their on-duty time. In other words, most police officers do not spend their tours of duty running from shooting to shooting and from armed robbery to armed robbery. A

Training and Education

sizable amount of time on a tour of duty is spent on service-related functions: that is, taking reports, investigating traffic accidents, responding to calls to assist citizens and the like. The paradox here is that most police academy curriculum is still heavily weighted toward crime fighting.[30] In essence, the majority of police training is geared toward what the police will be doing less than 20 or 30% of their on-duty time.

The President's 1967 Commission on Law Enforcement and the Administration of Justice: Task Force Report on the Police recognized that police training academies for the most part prepare an officer to perform police work mechanically but do not prepare him to understand his community, the police role, or the imperfections of the criminal justice system.[31] Over forty years after the report from the President's Commission, little has changed in the distribution of what is taught to police trainees. For example, some police experts have argued that police training must focus on the need for choice in specific, clearly delineated situations and that the reality of police work must be brought into the classroom.[32] Still others have complained that we do not teach young officers the techniques of problem analysis, of identifying and coming up with strategies to problems; we do not teach recruits how to organize a neighborhood in order to deal with neighborhood problems and that we have to make this a part of everyone's training.[33]

Teaching recruits solely the crime fighting aspects of the job may create a problematic environment for those agencies incorporating community policing. Obviously the crime fighting skills are extremely important; however, police management should undertake a self-study of their training curriculum in order to ensure that topics such as problem solving, community policing, and the service aspects of policing are interwoven into the curriculum.

Historical Underpinnings

An examination of the history of police training in the United States shows that many over the years have advanced the notion of placing more emphasis on the service aspects of policing. For example, one review of early police curriculum found the incorporation of courses in human relations as early as the 1920s.[34] These early police training programs had the following characteristics:

1. They focused on racial, religious, and ethnic conflict.
2. They introduced police officers to the nature of and cases of these sociological problems and their relationship to crime.
3. They stimulated the police to think about crime and social disorders in preventive terms.
4. They often used specially trained police officers as instructors.
5. They mostly disregarded concerns of broad community relations and did not involve community leaders and ordinary citizens.[35]

Many early police training programs were deficient in informing officers on how to respond to and address community-related problems outside of the criminal law or crime fighting role. The crime fighter role that was instilled through traditional police training may not have been the best model to promote police-community partnerships, especially in minority communities, by maintaining that the police should remain aloof from the community they served and that any action outside the legal domain of policing was not a concern of the police.[36]

Professor Herman Goldstein, who pioneered the idea of police as problem-solvers, described major implications for the state of police training programs. He argued that police training programs do a good job at teaching the law, department regulations, and skills (e.g., firearms, defensive tactics, pursuit driving, and evidence gathering) without much attention to how these might apply to specific problems.[37]

Think about this for a moment: Police departments across the United States are mandated to maintain certain proficiencies and competencies. For example, police are required to qualify with their firearms one or more times a year, and they may be required to report for defensive tactics or baton training several times a year. However, when was the last time that police officers were mandated to return to the academy for in-service training to enhance their communication skills or interpersonal communication skills, or to hone up on problem-solving skills, or to learn about different cultures and diversity? We submit that in the majority of police departments across the United States, these subjects are given a back seat to the mechanical or crime fighting skills.

Think about these questions for just a moment. Do police use communication skills on their jobs? Do police work with groups of diverse populations? Do police solve problems in the course of their everyday duties? The answers to these questions are an obvious yes! Are you beginning to see the paradox here?

Evolving Police Training Curriculum

It is important that police training reflect both the changes in operating strategy and the changes in society.[38] This can be a challenging task for police management and training authorities. Police departments that have or are in the process of implementing community policing should examine their training curriculum in order to ensure that the community-policing strategy is supported through training. Even in those police agencies that have not implemented tenets from the community-policing strategy, there should still be periodic reviews of training curriculum to ensure that it adequately represents what police officers need to know to better perform their jobs.

There are some subjects that are not typically taught in most police academies and probably should be. One such subject is police history. Some may question the relevance of teaching such a subject, and some may even argue that police history has absolutely nothing to do with teaching new police officers the craft of policing. We counter such claims and argue that teaching police history is absolutely relevant.

We offer two justifications for the need to teach the history of the police in the police academy. First, if policing is to truly meet the criteria of a "professional status," then police officers should be taught about the history of their profession. Police officers should know the contributions that police reformers such as August Vollmer and O. W. Wilson made to the policing profession. It is important that recruits have some idea of the early roots in the English policing system and contributions of English reformers such as Sir Robert Peel. They need to become familiar with the past in order to understand the future state of policing. Second, police history can provide an overview of the mistakes that the police have made in the past regarding philosophical or strategic implementation. By examining what went wrong, it is then possible to engage in strategic implementation of policy, procedure, and strategy in a different manner.

There are a host of other subjects that should be increasingly included in the police training curriculum. We offer a comprehensive training model developed by Professors Michael J. Palmiotto, Michael L. Birzer, and N. Prabha Unnithan.[39] These authors suggest that the first four weeks of the police training program include the following:

SUGGESTED FIRST FOUR WEEKS OF POLICE TRAINING PROGRAM

FIRST WEEK

Philosophy of police department (training hours: 4)

1. Co-activity with community
2. Trust community
3. Democratic values respected
4. Customer-based policing

Organizational structure of the police department (training hours: 8)

1. Describe organizational structure
2. Be aware of internal communication channels

3. Evolving organizational change to community-oriented policing (COP)
4. Importance of organizational communication with community

Socioeconomic makeup of the community (training hours: 8)

1. Demographic makeup of community
2. Social strata of community
3. Quality-of-life issues
4. Victim characteristics in neighborhoods
5. Political makeup of community

Cultural diversity of the community (training hours: 16)

1. Define cultural diversity
2. Value of understanding cultural diversity
3. Identifying cultural organizations and leaders
4. Hate/bias crimes

Police history (training hours: 4)

1. Understanding historical development of policing
2. Police development in America
3. Modern law enforcement
4. Major law enforcement research findings (e.g., Kansas City Study)

SECOND WEEK

Police operations (training hours: 8)

1. Patrol
2. Investigate
3. Records and communication
4. Police-community relations

Police mission (training hours: 8)

1. Values of policing
2. Mission of policing
3. Long-range goals/objectives of policing
4. Professional orientation

Police culture (training hours: 8)

1. Understanding the police culture
2. Understanding police cynicism
3. Understanding police myths
4. The evolving police culture

Police discretion (training hours: 8)

1. Define police discretion
2. Complexity of police role as it relates to discretion
3. Recent approaches—legal and departmental police-to-police discretion
4. Value and importance of police discretion

Police misconduct (training hours: 8)

1. Define police misconduct
    a. Perjury
    b. Sex on duty
    c. Sleeping on duty
    d. Drinking/drugs
    e. Corruption
    f. Excessive force
    g. Crimes committed by police
2. Internal affairs

THIRD WEEK

Police ethics (training hours: 20)

1. Define terms
2. Morality and the law
3. Morality and behavior
4. Analyzing ethical dilemmas

Problem-oriented policing (training hours: 20)

1. Broken windows
2. Defining problem-oriented policing

3. Problem-oriented policing SARA model (scan, analyze, respond, and assess)
   4. Identification of resources

FOURTH WEEK

Crime prevention (training hours: 20)

   1. Define crime prevention
   2. Environmental design and defensible space
   3. Crime prevention programs
   4. Situational crime prevention

Community-oriented policing (training hours: 20)

   1. Philosophy of community-oriented policing
   2. Fundamentals of COP described
   3. Examination of various COP strategies
   4. Future and long-range implementation of COP

The above training model is designed to provide a foundation for building on community policing. In the model, subjects such as organizational structure and police history are placed early on in the curriculum. Next, the recruit becomes familiar with the community including the social and economic makeup of the community. It is important that police recruits become familiar with the communities they will be serving. As you will note, police misconduct and culture are also depicted in the above training model. Crime prevention and community policing and problem-oriented policing concepts are then covered to provide the framework to incorporate community oriented values early on in the training process.

Caveats for Managers

Many years ago, in 1968, the Urban Task Force in Pittsburgh developed a summary of the shortcomings of training programs that were designed to emphasize more social service aspects such as human relations, community relations, police-minority relations, and intergroup relations. These shortcomings, while published more than forty years ago, are still relevant today. Police executives should be aware of these factors that could impact effective police training.

   1. Imprecisely stated goals and unrealistic expectations
   2. Insufficient active support for programs and programs, goals on the part of high-ranking police officials

Training and Education 249

3. Failure to recognize that a training program requires support from all aspects of organizational philosophy and role conception. Too often, human relations training (as with community relations units) are window dressing, detached from the main thrust of organizational priorities
4. Lack of sophisticated educational technologies
5. Lack of ongoing consultation between police officers and program personnel in planning and implementation
6. Little correlation between curricula and the day-to-day realties of the police function, even in programs with sophisticated techniques
7. Insufficient means for the reinforcement of new learning following the completion of training sessions
8. Little planning for fitting human relations training (or other types of police-community relations for that matter) into changing police agency operations
9. Little use of research findings and observations that appeared in studies of police work and police-community relations, including the pertinent recommendations of federal commissions
10. Basic resistance to organizational change and undue devotion to practices and procedures geared to horse-and-buggy communities
11. Insufficient community participation in planning and implementing training programs
12. Lack of systematic evaluation of the results of training programs[40]

The Environment of Police Training

Police training academies tend to be operated in a paramilitary environment. We define paramilitary as closely resembling the military (i.e., daily inspections, marching, discipline-centered, and clearly designated rank structure). The authors have evidence of this through both anecdotal accounts and direct observations of police training academies across the United States. For example, in one law enforcement training academy in the Midwest, trainees are required to walk against the right side of the hallway at all times while inside the academy building. While in the classroom the trainees are expected to sit with both feet level on floor at all times (e.g., recruits are not allowed to cross their legs or stretch them out in front of them). There is also much emphasis placed on marching and close-order drills similar to the military. One study of police training academies in the state of Illinois found that police trainees were routinely inspected and were taught military protocol such as how to salute and march properly.[41]

Whenever possible, it may be beneficial for police training to move from a paramilitary model to an adult education model. The paramilitary model is problematic when teaching the skills of policing to police trainees. First, the amount of effective learning that takes place in this type of environment is debatable. The paramilitary training model does very little to promote the acquisition of many nontechnical competencies such as problem solving, judgment, and leadership.[42] The paramilitary training model perpetuates a warrior-like mentality on the part of the trainee. With this mentality, there is usually an enemy, and that enemy equates to citizens who have violated the law. We submit that a fair number of police trainees that are entering police service today do not have formal military training. They may gravitate out of the police academy when exposed to this rigid environment, that is, many qualified women and men may leave the police service prematurely. The paramilitary training model that employs the strategy of placing much stress on trainees may prompt trainees to question their self-worth and willingness to follow orders blindly.[43]

The paramilitary model of police training is notorious for training police officers to act in robotic fashion. Undeniably, this is appropriate for many aspects of the crime fighting role but conflicts with what is now desired in today's police officer under community policing strategies. For instance, for many years police were trained to approach a domestic violence situation in a fairly uniform manner. It goes something like this: The officers arrive at the scene, separate the parties, get both sides of the story, and make an arrest if warranted. If an arrest is not made, officers will typically ask one of the parties to leave for the evening until things cool off. The problem here centers on the fact that each domestic violence situation has a distinct set of circumstances. Each situation may require a distinct strategy to resolve the situation. It is generally very difficult to approach a domestic violence in the same uniform manner.

The desired police officer is one who is interested in solving community problems, in working with community members, and in service, and who views formal arrest as only one of a number of options available. Today's police officer is expected to be a resource catalyst for the community and have the desire to work with and interact with many community groups as a routine part of the job. As Michael Charles in his book on police training explains:

> It is critical in the police profession as elsewhere that law enforcement personnel learn how to think critically, conceptually, and creatively when confronted with situations needing analysis and when developing solutions to problems. They must also have the needed skills to learn from their experiences.[44]

Police Education

National study commissions have consistently echoed the theme that many of the problems faced in policing could in part be solved if more qualified persons, particularly those with college degrees, were highly recruited for police work. The idea of the college-educated police officer is not new and can be dated back to 1916, when the University of California at Berkeley established a law enforcement program for police officers.

The initial push for the development of crime-related studies came primarily from August Vollmer, who was chief of the Berkeley Police Department and a faculty member at the University of California at Berkeley. Chief Vollmer devised a law enforcement program in criminology.[45] Through the early and into the mid-twentieth century, the expansion of criminal justice education in the United States was significant. In 1931, the National Commission of Law Observance and Enforcement proposed the application of science to police work with the goal of more effectively dealing with crime. Education became the cornerstone of the movement to professionalize the police.

In 1968, the National Advisory Commission on Civil Disorders discovered that, in many cities, aggressive police patrol tactics and harassment were a result of society's fear of crime and that these aggressive police practices only served to create hostility and conflict between the police and the minority community.[46] President Lyndon Johnson's commission on Campus Unrest advocated higher education for police. The Commission stated that "law enforcement agencies desperately need better educated and better trained policeman.... There should be special monetary incentive for all who enter the police service with college degrees or who obtain degrees while in police service."[47]

The many commissions formed to study the police in the 1960s overwhelmingly recommended that in order to improve law enforcement, the quality of police personnel had to be upgraded through education. The importance of setting educational standards for the selection of police officers has been debated for many years. The National Advisory Commission of Criminal Justice Standards and Goals recommended in the early 1970s that in order for police officers to perform their police duties properly, every police department should establish guidelines for entry level educational requirements. The recommendations made by the commission were:

1. Every police agency should require immediately, as a condition of immediate employment, the completion of at least one year of education (thirty semester units) at an accredited college or university.

Otherwise qualified police applicants whom do not satisfy the condition but have earned a high school diploma or its equivalent should be employed under a contract requiring completion of the educational requirement within three years of initial employment.
2. Every police agency should, no latter than 1975, require as a condition of initial employment the completion of at least two years of education (sixty semester units) at an accredited college or university.
3. Every police agency should, no later than 1978, require as a condition of initial employment the completion of at least three years of education (ninety semester units) at an accredited college or university.
4. Every police agency should, no latter than 1982, require as a condition of initial employment the completion of at least four years of education (one hundred and twenty semester units or a baccalaureate degree) at an accredited college or university.[48]

The educational level of the police in 1966 was 12.4 years. In 1967, the President's Commission on Law Enforcement and the Administration of Justice noted that due to the nature of the police task and its effect on our society, there was a need elevate the educational requirements to the level of a college degree for all future personnel selected to perform the function of police officer.[49] No other document in the history of policing has had such a profound effect on the police as did the President's Commission of 1967 task force report on the police. The recommendation by the Commission for better educated officers, in part, was nurtured through the Law Enforcement Assistance Administration (LEAA). The LEAA, which was established by the Omnibus Crime Control and Safe Street Act of 1968, served until 1978, when it was abolished.

One of the most significant programs of the LEAA was the Law Enforcement Educational Program (LEEP). LEEP provided grants and scholarships to both in-service and preservice police personnel to attend college. There are scores of law enforcement personnel that benefited from LEEP, many of whom are now in executive police positions. The LEEP program played a significant role in increasing the educational levels among the American police.

Despite the recommendations aimed at improving the educational levels and professionalism among police, the majority of the nation's police organizations still only require a high school diploma for employment. It is highly desired that police officers today seek a college education. Police recruitment strategies should target individuals who have college degrees or those who have earned a minimum amount of college credits. Likewise, police management should increasingly move toward college education requirements for police applicants prior to their being admitted into the training academy.

Training and Education

The benefits of a college education for police officers have been well established.[50] These advantages include the following:

1. A college education develops a broad base of information for decision-making.
2. It allows for additional years and experience for maturity.
3. Course requirements and achievements inculcate responsibility in the individual.
4. Both general education courses and course work in the major (particularly a criminal justice major) permit the individual to learn more about the history of the country and the democratic process and to appreciate constitutional rights, values, and the demographic form of government.
5. A college education engenders the ability to flexibly handle difficult or ambiguous situations with greater creativity and innovation.
6. For criminal justice majors, the academic experience permits a better view of the "big picture" of the criminal justice system and provides both a better understanding of and appreciation for the prosecutorial, courts, and correctional roles.
7. The experience of a higher education develops a greater empathy for minorities and their discriminatory experiences through both course work and interaction within the academic environment.
8. It allows a greater understanding, tolerance for other persons, and more effective communication and community relationships in the practice of policing.
9. The college-educated officer is likely to be less rigid in decision-making in fulfilling the role of the police while balancing variable situations and has a greater tendency to wisely use discretion to deal with individual cases rather than applying the same rules to all cases.
10. The college experience will help officers communicate and respond to crime and to service the needs of the public in a competent manner with civility and humanity.
11. The educated officer is more innovative and flexible when dealing with complex police policing programs and strategies such as problem-oriented policing, community policing, task force responses, etc.
12. The college-educated officer is better equipped to perform tasks and make continual policing decisions with minimal, and sometimes no, supervision.
13. College helps develop better overall community relations skills, including the ability to engender the respect and confidence of the community.

14. More "professional" demeanor and performance is exhibited by college-educated officers.
15. The educated officer is able to cope better with stress and is more likely to seek assistance with personal or stress-related problems, thereby making the officer a more stable and reliable employee.
16. The officer can better adapt his style of communication and behavior to a wider range of social conditions and "classes."
17. The college experience tends to make the officer less authoritarian and less cynical with respect to the milieu of policing.
18. A college-educated officer can more readily accept and adapt to organizational changes.[51]

Other advantages of college-educated police officers are:

1. An enhanced understanding of police functions and the police role
2. An increased knowledge of the importance of police in society
3. An improved sensitivity for the problems of people
4. The better ability to communicate
5. The development of critical thinking and analytical skills
6. An improved capability for exercising discretion
7. The refinement of analytical qualities
8. The consideration of moral and ethical implications of police work
9. The development of personal values that are consistent with police organizational goals and objectives in a democracy[52]

Some police organizations have developed educational incentives and standards for their police officers. For example, the Sedgwick County Sheriff's Department in Wichita, Kansas, awards deputies promotional points for possessing a college degree. To be eligible for the rank of captain within the sheriff's department, the deputy candidate must posses a minimum of a bachelor's degree. The Tulsa, Oklahoma Police Department requires their police applicants to have earned a bachelor's degree prior to academy appointment, the San Jose, California Police Department requires a minimum of forty semester hours for employment, and the Dallas, Texas Police Department requires sixty college credit hours.

Starting in the 1990s, federally funded Police Corps programs have increasingly offered educational opportunities for students who desire to enter the policing profession. The Police Corps programs are funded through the Office of Community Policing. Police Corps trainees can obtain their college undergraduate education for free if they work as sworn community police officers for at least four years after they graduate. With that said, the Police Corps participant does not have the luxury of choosing the police agency he works for. Placements in a police agency are usually done based on need, which often equates to those communities that have experienced high crime, along with criteria such as staffing levels within a police agency. The Police Corps program represents a continuing effort to increase the educational levels of American police officers.

Police managers should keep in mind that requiring a college degree as a minimum standard for employment could be discriminatory for minorities. Because of historic discrimination practices, minorities have been at a disadvantage in obtaining a college education. However, if educational and recruitment protocols are properly developed, a higher education requirement should not have an adverse impact on minorities.[53] For an in-depth discussion on this issue, the reader is referred to Chapter 9, which covers recruitment and selection strategies.

Questions in Review

1. Describe how community policing affects the training of police officers.
2. Identify and discuss the traditional training methods in many police academies.
3. What are the assumptions of the andragogical approaches to police training?
4. What subjects are recommended to be included in the training curricula that have historically been missing?
5. Over the past several decades, there have been numerous committees formed to study police training and education. What were the underpinnings of these committees, recommendations as they relate to the educational standards for police officers?
6. Discuss the advantages of college education requirements for police officers.
7. Identify and discuss programs that have been instrumental in assisting police officers financially in obtaining a college education.

Biggest Mistakes Police Leadership Makes and How to Avoid Them

Set forth below are several cases involving police liability and the financial concerns involved. Failure of cities and counties to have an aggressive policy to reduce the potential for lawsuits can be very costly.

City's Insurance Rates Rise: Suit over Police Chase Is Blamed

Bellevue, Illinois, faced a rise in the borough's insurance premium for the year 2003, thanks largely to a lawsuit related to a police chase and a number of accidents on borough sidewalks. According to the mayor, the increase was partly due to the number of claims filed last year. The most significant was for a lawsuit filed against borough police by the mother of Raymond Michelotti, a seven-year-old Brighton Heights boy who was killed in June of 1998 by a driver fleeing Bellevue police.[54]

The driver was chased by police after being involved in an altercation with a pedestrian in Avalon. Although Bellevue police cut the chase short, the driver sped into the North Side and struck Raymond, who was riding his bike. The driver was convicted of a number of charges, including third-degree murder and homicide by vehicle. Raymond's mother sued the borough.

The borough's exact insurance rate for the year hinged upon the outcome of the litigation. "When you have an outstanding situation, insurance companies allocate money in case they wind up losing the lawsuit," the mayor said. "If that case gets settled, our rates could be lowered."

Bellevue officials have not changed their policy on police chases, the mayor said. "I don't think that the Bellevue police did anything wrong in the chase. They called it off when it became too severe," he said. "My understanding was that procedure was followed. The chase was called off well before the accident happened."

Oakland Considers Video Cameras in Police Cars in Reacting to Weight of Recent Lawsuits against City Cops

Fed up with paying tens of thousands of dollars to settle lawsuits filed against the police department every month, the Oakland, California City Council considered putting video cameras in police vehicles to record traffic stops and arrests.[55]

The city agreed to pay $10.9 million to settle a civil suit filed by one hundred and nineteen plaintiffs who claimed they were beaten and framed by a group of officers in West Oakland known as the Riders. The city agreed to spend another $10 million reforming the police department and promised to do a study of the feasibility of installing in-car video systems in the department's fleet.

Because there is no money for any new programs in Oakland's cash-strapped budget, the council members may pay for the test run out of their "pay go" office holder accounts, which they can use for whatever project they wish. "Police liability claims are bleeding badly-needed tax dollars from our city's impoverished coffers that could instead be used to hire new officers, reopen libraries on weekends, or restore our ailing book budget," said the captain of the 42nd Street Neighborhood Alert group. At the last three council meetings, the council voted to pay a total of $271,000 to settle seven cases alleging that Oakland police officers used excessive force.

According to a report compiled by the police department, the cost of installing cameras in the department's two hundred patrol cars could range from $400,000 to $1.8 million, depending on whether a digital system is chosen.

A member of an East Oakland Neighborhood Crime Prevention Council stated, "We need to put that money back in the police department so we can have more police." He said the experience of Newport Beach, California, makes it clear the system would make a huge difference in Oakland. In the decade before installing the system, the Orange County city paid $6 million to settle claims, whereas in the eight years after implementing the system Newport Beach paid less than $600,000 in claims and legal fees.

The system could also be designed to record the officer's comments and interactions up to one thousand feet from the police cruiser. It will be up to the council to decide what to record and how to use the tapes. The report concluded that in-car video systems could offer a potential tool for reducing the number of police misconduct allegations by offering evidence for complaints and encouraging professional conduct.

Supreme Court Examines Police Liability for Faulty Warrant

Federal agents were looking for a rocket launcher and automatic weapons when they pulled up to a house on a rural Montana ranch, but the warrant they carried mentioned nothing about the suspected cache.[56] The omission was a mistake by Bureau of Alcohol, Tobacco and Firearms Agent Jeff Groh, and it could cost him. Unless the Supreme Court says otherwise, Groh will face a lawsuit for damages for violating the constitutional rights of Joseph and Julia Ramirez, who lived on Moose Creek Ranch. The 1997 search followed a tip about illegal grenades and other weaponry. The search warrant should have listed the weapons or other items agents were looking for. Instead, it contained only a description of the Ramirez house.

The Constitution's Fourth Amendment bans "unreasonable searches and seizures" and requires that police have probable cause to get a warrant. Warrants, the amendment says, must be supported by an affidavit and must "particularly describe(s) the place to be searched, and the persons or things to be seized." Law officers are ordinarily immune from suits over their conduct on duty, but the high court has allowed exceptions when the officer violated someone's constitutional rights. The question this time is whether the faulty warrant opened the door for a suit when there was no specific previous case that would have put Groh on notice that he was at risk.

End Notes

1. V. E. Kappeler, *Critical Issues in Police Civil Liability*, 2nd ed. (Cincinnati, OH: Anderson Publishing Co., 1997).
2. R. V. del Carmen, *Civil Liabilities in American Policing* (Englewood Cliffs, NJ: Brady, 1991).
3. C. D. Robinson, *Legal Rights, Duties, and Liabilities of Criminal Justice Personnel* (Springfield, IL: Charles C. Thomas Publisher, 1992).
4. City of Canton v. Harris 489 US 378, 390 fn 10 (1989).
5. City of Canton v. Harris
6. Greason v. Kemp, 891 F2d 829, 836-37 (11th Cir 1990).
7. Cooper v. Merrill, 736 FSupp 552 (D Del 1990).
8. Cooper v. Merrill at 567-568.
9. Doe v. Borough of Barrington, 729 FSupp 376 (D NJ 1990).
10. Doe v. Borough, at 389.
11. W. G. Doerner and M. L. Dantzker, *Contemporary Police Organization and Management* (Boston, MA: Butterworth-Heinemann, 2000).
12. M. L. Birzer, "Police Training in the 21st Century," in *FBI Law Enforcement Bulletin*, Vol. 68, No. 7 (1999), pp. 16-19.
13. S. M. Ramirez, "The Need for a New Learning Culture in Law Enforcement," in *The Police Chief*, Vol. 63 (November 1996), pp. 24-26.
14. M. L. Birzer, "The Theory of Andragogy Applied to Police Training," in *Policing: An International Journal of Police Strategies and Management*, Vol. 26, No. 1 (2003), pp. 29-42.
15. J. L. Elias and S. B. Merriam, *Philosophical Foundations of Adult Education* (Malabar, FL: Krieger Publishing Company, 1995).
16. Elias and Merriam, p. 89.
17. E. Meese, "Community Policing and the Police Officer," in *Perspectives on Policing: National Institute of Justice Report*, No. 15, NCJ 139164 (1993).
18. A. Webber, "Crime and Management: An Interview with New York City Police Commissioner Lee P. Brown," in *Harvard Business Review* (May/June 1991), pp. 17-32.
19. M. L. Birzer (2003).
20. M. Knowles, *The Adult Learner: A Neglected Species* (Houston, TX: Gulf Publishing Co., 1990).
21. M. Knowles, *The Modern Practice of Adult Education: Andragogy versus pedagogy* (New York: Association Press, 1970).
22. S. M. Ramirez, pp. 63 and 24-26.
23. M. L. Birzer and R. Tannehill, "A More Effective Training Approach for Contemporary Policing," in *Police Quarterly*, Vol. 4, No. 2 (2001), pp. 233-252.
24. T. G. Hatcher, "The Ins and Outs of Self-Directed Learning," in *Training and Development* (February 1997), pp. 35-39.
25. M. J. Palmiotto, M. L. Birzer, and N. P. Unnithan, "Training in Community Policing: A Suggested Curriculum," in *Policing: An International Journal of Police Strategies & Management*, Vol. 23, No. 1 (2000), pp. 8-21.
26. K. McCreedy, "Entry Level Police Training in the 1980s," in *The Police Chief* (October 1983), pp. 32-37.

Training and Education

27 B. R. Usher and R. Johnson, *Adult Education and the Post Modern Challenge: Learning beyond the Limits* (London: Routledge, 1997).
28 D. A. Kolb, *Experiential Learning: Experience as the Source of Learning and Development* (Englewood-Cliffs, NJ: Prentice-Hall, 1984), p. 38.
29 K. D. Codish, "Putting a Sacred Cow Out to Pasture," in *The Police Chief*, Vol. 63 (November 1996), pp. 40–44.
30 Birzer and Tannehill.
31 *The President's Commission on Law Enforcement and the Administration of Justice, Task Force Report: The Police* (Washington, DC: Government Printing Office, 1967).
32 G. P. Alpert and R. G. Dunham, *Policing Urban America*, 2nd ed. (Prospect Heights, IL: Waveland Press, Inc., 1992).
33 A. Webber, "Crime and Management: An Interview with New York City Police Commissioner Lee P. Brown," in *Harvard Business Review* (May/June 1991), pp. 17–32.
34 L. A. Radelet, "The Police in the Community," 4th ed. (New York: Macmillan Publishing, 1986).
35 L. A. Radelet, p. 16.
36 Palmiotto, Birzer, and Unnithan, p. 10.
37 H. Goldstein, *Problem Oriented Policing* (New York: McGraw-Hill Inc., 1990), pp. 167–168.
38 J. Connolly, "Rethinking Police Training," in *The Police Chief*, Vol. 75, No. 11, (November 2008), pp. 8–22.
39 Palmiotto, Birzer, and Unnithan, pp. 15–16.
40 Summary developed by Urban Task Force, Episcopal Diocese of Pittsburgh (circa 1968).
41 M. T. Thomas, *Police Training Breaking All the Rules: Implementing the Adult Education Model into Police Training* (Springfield, IL: Charles C. Thomas, 2000), p. 131.
42 P. J. Ortmeier. "Leadership for Community Policing: A Study to Identify Essential Officer Competencies," in *The Police Chief*, Vol. 64, No. 10 (1997), pp. 88–91, 93, 95.
43 W. W. Bennett and K. M. Hess, *Management and Supervision in Law Enforcement* (Belmont, CA: Wadswoth Publishing Co., 2001), p. 261.
44 M. Charles, p. 73.
45 M. J. Palmiottto, *Policing: Concepts Strategies and Current Issues in American Policing* (Durham, NC: Carolina Academic Press, 1997).
46 *Report of the National Advisory Commission on Civil Disorders* (Washington, DC: Government Printing Office, 1968).
47 *U.S. President's Commission on Campus Unrest* (Washington, DC: Government Printing Office, 1968), p. 154.
48 *National Advisory Commission on Criminal Justice Standards and Goals: The Police* (Washington, DC: Government Printing Office, 1973), p. 369.
49 *The President's Commission on Law Enforcement and the Administration of Justice, Task Force Report: The Police* (Washington, DC: Government Printing Office, 1967), p. 126.
50 R. Roberg, K. Novak, G. Cordner, and B. Smith, *Police and Society*, 5th ed. (New York: Oxford University Press, 2012).

51 D. L. Carter, A. D. Sapp, and D. W. Stephens, "Higher Education as a Bona Fide Occupational Qualification (BFOQ) for Police: A Blue Print," *American Journal of Police*, Vol. 7, No. 2 (1988), pp. 16–18.
52 J. W. Sterling, "The College Level Entry Requirement: A Real or Imagined Cure-all," in *The Police Chief*, Vol. 41, No. 8 (1974), p. 28.
53 R. Roberg, K. Novak, G. Cordner, and B. Smith, p. 478.
54 *Pittsburgh Post-Gazette*, North ed. (January 22, 2003), p. A-1.
55 *Tri-Valley Herald* (Pleasanton, CA, January 24, 2004), p. A-3.
56 Groh v. Ramirez, 540 U.S. 551 (2004).

Suggested Additional References

1. Michael J. Palmiotto, ed., *Policing and Training Issues* (2003). This work provides coverage of most police training issues. Each chapter is written by an authority in the field of police training. The volume presents a blend of practical and theoretical experience and provides the most up-to-date information on police training and issues.
2. M. R. Haberfeld, *Critical Issues in Police Training* (2003). This text specifically deals with the complexity and ethical issues associated with the problems of police training. This work provides an analysis of the process of training from historical and conceptual perspectives. The book emphasizes the steps that need to be taken to improve every stage of police training.

Recruitment and Selection

11

Key Individuals, Concepts, and Issues

Recruitment
Police Services Study
Academic curriculum
Americans with Disabilities Act
Davis v. City of Dallas
Minnesota Multiphasic Personality Inventory 2
Griggs v. Duke Power Company
Bona fide occupational qualification
Vanguard Justice Society v. Hughes
Shield Club v. City of Cleveland
Assessment centers

Definitions

Assessment centers: A process in which applicants deal with simulated police officer working conditions and then are evaluated by a team of assessors.

Law Enforcement Management and Administrative Statistics (LEMAS): Every three to four years, the Bureau of Justice Statistics surveys a nationally representative sample of publicly funded state and local law enforcement agencies in the United States.

Minnesota Multiphasic Personality Inventory 2 (MMPI): The MMPI-2 contains 567 psychological test items and is used by some police agencies to gather information on the personality, attitudes, and mental health of its applicants.

Recruitment: A process of identifying and attracting persons to apply for employment with an organization.

Chapter Objectives

After completing this chapter you should be able to:

1. Describe recruitment standards for police officer applicants
2. Describe ways to increase recruitment of minorities and women
3. Explain the stages of the police selection process
4. Identify the impact of Equal Employment Opportunity on police employment practices

Case Study 11.1

The Chief of Police has recently directed that a task force be organized to develop a plan that will increase the number of female and minority employees within the department. Currently, the police department employs only 8% females and 17% minorities. Moreover, of these employees, only 10% actually perform police duties. The latest census report indicates that 47% of the citizens in the city are females and that minorities make up 31% of the total population.

In addition to recruitment issues, the chief also wants the task force to study the relationship between education and professionalism. This request has been made to determine whether upgrading the minimum requirements for entry-level positions within the department will reduce citizen complaints against the department.

The chief has selected you to chair the task force. The chief has given you authority to select the task force members.

1. Would you go outside the police department to find others in the community that would be willing to serve on the task force? If so, who would you approach about serving? Why?
2. What preconceived ideas might some of the task force members have about the influence of education on policing?

Introduction

The Bureau of Justice Statistics reports that an estimated 12,575 local police departments operate in the United States. These agencies employ approximately one-half million full-time sworn officers. From 1987 to 2007, the number of full-time local police employees increased by an estimated 152,000 (34%) or an average of 1.7% annually. The nation's largest local police force, the New York City Police Department, employs 35,216 full-time officers. This is about three times as many as the next largest, the Chicago Police Department (13,336 officers). Forty-six departments employ 1,000 or more officers, and these agencies accounted for about a third of all local police officers.[1]

Every police department recruits for the most qualified people they can find. Most police departments use a variety of recruiting activities, such as advertisements in newspapers, colleges, billboards, television, and radio. Recruiters often attend job and career fairs, and most recruitment efforts include a well-designed department Web page where prospective recruits can find out more about the police department, get information on standards and testing requirements, and determine when applications will be taken. Although few police departments ever face problems in getting enough applicants, the challenge is to select the best and brightest individuals to fill police department positions.

Law enforcement agencies have always placed great emphasis on professional training and higher education for entry-level positions. As early as

Recruitment and Selection

1916, the University of California at Berkeley began to offer law enforcement-related courses after being prompted by August Vollmer, who proposed that police officers have a college degree. Later, in the 1930s, the Wickersham Commission gave national recognition to the need for increased educational standards for the police. In 1966, David Geary, then chief of police in Ventura, California, instituted a four-year college degree requirement. In the 1970s, several studies revealed that officers who had college degrees demonstrated better on-the-job performance, had fewer incidents of misconduct, and took fewer sick leaves than less educated officers. The emphasis on upgrading education requirements continues today. In Atlanta, for example, the starting salary for a police office is dependent upon the level of education of the applicant. Those candidates with a high school diploma or equivalent begin at $39,327.60 per year, compared to $40,704.07 for an officer with an associate's degree and $42,128.714 for an officer with a bachelor's degree.

In contrast, many law enforcement departments require only a high school diploma or its equivalent. This is partly because police leaders worry that higher education requirements may violate Title VII of the Civil Rights Act and Equal Employment Opportunity Commission guidelines. A landmark case in this area was Griggs v. Duke Power Company, 401 U.S. 424 (1971). African-American employees claimed that the requirement of having a high school diploma and passing two aptitude tests discriminated against them. Duke Power Company had openly discriminated on the basis of race in the hiring and assigning of employees at its Dan River plant. The plant was organized into five operating departments: Labor, Coal Handling, Operations, Maintenance, and Laboratory and Test. African Americans were employed only in the Labor Department where the highest paying jobs paid less than the lowest paying jobs in the other four "operating" departments, in which only whites were employed. In 1971, the U.S. Supreme Court ruled that any requirements or tests used in selection or promoting must be job-related.

A similar case occurred in United States v. Paradise, 480 U.S. 149 (1987). In 1972, after a finding in the lower court that the Alabama Department of Public Safety had systematically excluded blacks from employment as state troopers in violation of the Fourteenth Amendment, the U.S. Supreme Court upheld an order imposing a hiring quota and requiring the department to refrain from engaging in discrimination in its employment practices, including promotions. The court ordered that "for a period of time," at least 50% of those promoted to corporal must be black. The department was also ordered to submit a realistic schedule for the development of promotional procedures for all ranks above the entry level. Subsequently, the department promoted eight blacks and eight whites under the court's order and submitted its proposed corporal and sergeant promotional procedures, at which time the court suspended the 50% requirement for those ranks.

Conversely, in Davis v. City of Dallas, 777 F.2d 205 (1985), the Dallas Police Department required applicants to have completed forty-five semester hours of college credit with a C average grade. In this case, the court of appeals ruled in favor of the educational requirement citing that the Dallas Police Department had shown that a high school education today does not represent the same level of achievement that it represented ten years ago. The court also relied on studies that had drawn a connection between higher education and higher performance rates.

Selection is the process of "weeding out" applicants. Although methods of assessing and selecting police patrol officer candidates vary among state and local police departments in the United States, many similarities exist. Most departments use such approaches as written tests, background investigations, physical examinations, and interviews. Generally, police departments emphasize the background investigation because such an investigation can ensure that only the most qualified individuals are recruited and can also indicate an applicant's competence, motivation, and personal ethics. Physical agility testing can test for physical strength and dexterity, qualities necessary in the performance of police patrol officer duties. Some police departments use simulations of real-life scenarios, whereas other police departments use psychological testing, polygraphs, and assessment centers.

In this chapter, we discuss many of the issues relating to the recruitment and selection of police officers. We begin by examining the current status of education and policing. Next, we consider issues that pertain to gender and minority recruitment. Our attention then turns to the selection process. Specific emphasis is given to pre-employment standards and typical hiring practices found in police agencies.

Recruitment

Recruitment is a process of soliciting persons to apply for employment with an organization. In the law enforcement profession, recruitment efforts are extremely important because of the very nature of the job. That is, police work is unique in the sense that the community expects this profession to protect and serve its citizens, even if it means using deadly force to do so. In what other nonmilitary profession do we arm employees and require them to enforce the law? For police organizations then, it is highly desirable to solicit a large pool of applicants to ensure better odds of selecting the right person to carry out the oftentimes stressful and sometimes dangerous duties associated with police work. A study conducted by the *Los Angeles Times* on police recruitment determined that it takes approximately seventeen applicants to hire one officer for the Orange County Sheriff's Department. In Phoenix,

Arizona, the average was twenty applicants per hire. In Memphis, Tennessee, it takes sixteen applicants for one position.[2]

But just what are those characteristics of the right applicant who will best be able to handle the responsibilities of a police officer? We would all agree that, like any other profession, applicants should be intelligent, honest, mature, physically able, and emotionally stable persons. But unlike any other profession, the work that police perform is frequently dictated by the situation. And because the degree in which situations vary is virtually limitless, police officers must be able to wear many different hats to do the job expected of them. Perhaps August Vollmer said it best:

> The citizen expects police officers to have the wisdom of Solomon, the courage of David, the strength of Samson, the patience of Job, the leadership of Moses, the kindness of the Good Samaritan, the strategic training of Alexander, the faith of David, the diplomacy of Lincoln, the tolerance of the Carpenter of Nazareth, and finally, an intimate knowledge of every branch of the natural, biological, and social sciences.[3]

Over the years, recruitment strategies by police managers have changed with the times and in many cases in accordance with applicable laws. The primary goal of recruitment efforts has been to hire persons that will better meet the law enforcement needs of the growing community. A beneficial effect of these efforts has been the steady improvement of the police profession in general. There are, however, several debates within the police profession that have relevance to recruitment. In particular is the dispute regarding educational requirements for police officers. Some have argued that until a standard requiring higher education is universally established, policing will never be fully recognized as a profession. Perhaps equally important is the demographic makeup of the police agency. While there is agreement that police departments should reflect the diversity of their communities, there is considerable disagreement on how to attain a balance, particularly in the areas of race and gender.

Impact of Higher Education on Police Hiring Practices

The debate over higher educational typically involves whether applicants should be required to possess a college education before being hired as a police officer. Those who advocate higher education point to research conducted over the past thirty years showing a positive relationship between higher education and police attitudes and performance. For instance, there is evidence that more exposure to college results in less negative self-esteem and at the same time diminishes hard-line or punitive attitudes toward others.[4] Moreover, college-educated officers are more understanding of social problems within the community and possess greater acceptance of cultural diversity.[5]

There is some indication that requiring a college education for police agencies is beneficial to the level of performance achieved by its police officers. In Virginia, for instance, data from 299 police officers in twelve municipal police agencies were used to determine the relationship between police education and police performance. Police performance was measured by means of supervisor evaluations of each police officer's overall performance, communication skills, public relations skills, report-writing skills, response to new training, decision-making ability, and commitment to the police agency. The results revealed significant correlations between education and most measures of performance. The study also revealed that the benefits of a college education did not become apparent until the police officers gained experience. In addition, police officers with only a high school diploma decreased in overall performance after five years of experience.[6]

Similar connections between education and experience have been made with regard to police corruption. For example, a Mollen Commission (Exhibit 11.1) report of police corruption in New York City found that officers who lack experience and some high education were considered to be more susceptible to involvement in illicit drug-related activities.[7]

Although there is a great deal of evidence to support the notion that higher education is a positive influence on policing, there is opposition to establishing higher educational thresholds for entry-level police positions.

The Commission to Investigate Allegations of Police Corruption and the Anti-Corruption Procedures of the Police Department, commonly referred to as the Mollen Commission, was established in July 1992 by an executive order of New York City Mayor David N. Dinkins. The commission, named for its chairman, Milton Mollen, a former New York judge, was given a threefold mandate: (1) to investigate the nature and extent of corruption in the New York City Police Department, (2) to evaluate the department's procedures for preventing and detecting corruption, and (3) to recommend changes and improvements in those procedures. The commission issued its report in July 1994 and was subsequently disbanded. A few key findings include:

- In New York City's 73rd precinct, between 1988 and 1992, a tightly knit group of 8 to 10 officers who worked together on steady tours of duty routinely conducted unlawful raids on drug locations while on duty.
- In New City's 30th precinct (Manhattan), 30 officers were convicted of primarily drug-related offenses.
- There is a widespread breakdown in field supervision in the NYPD.
- The commission recommends an independent oversight commission with (1) a small permanent staff; (2) the ability and authority to bring on additional staff, as needed, from law enforcement agencies such as the FBI and Drug Enforcement Administration; and (3) subpoena power to enable the commission to carry out its own investigations.

Exhibit 11.1 The Mollen Commission Report. (From *Law Enforcement: Information on Drug-Related Police Corruption*, Washington, DC: U.S. General Accounting Office (May 1998).)

Recruitment and Selection 267

Resistance to raising educational requirements from a high school diploma to a college degree may be with good reason. Consider, for example, a study that examined the relationship between police officers' educational attainment and occupational attitudes and between educational attainment and performance. Data were obtained for the Police Services Study (PSS), which evaluated the impact of organizational arrangements on police service delivery. The second phase of the PSS collected data from twenty-four metropolitan police departments (e.g., Rochester, St. Louis, and Tampa-St. Petersburg). Interviews were conducted with both police officers and citizens in the communities. The results demonstrated that the effects of college education on in-service police officer attitudes were so small that they were not significant. Attitudes of police officers who earned college degrees as preservice students did not differ substantially from those of their less educated peers. Further, when police officers' performance in police-citizen encounters was measured in terms of citizen evaluations, little or no difference between college-educated and less educated officers was detected. Although college-educated police officers may be superior from the perspective of supervisors who find that such officers are more reliable employees and better report writers, they are not superior from the perspective of citizens who are concerned primarily with effective and courteous service. Therefore, the study suggests that police officers' performance and morale will not be affected by policies that encourage in-service education or by college education as an entry requirement.[8]

There is great concern too that highly educated officers will become discontented with the conventional routines often associated with police work and resign their positions. Many of the daily tasks performed by police are somewhat clerical in nature (e.g., issuing traffic citations, writing officer reports, completing automobile accident forms, recording log information). Because law enforcement is a labor-intensive service industry, high personnel turnover rates can prove to be extremely costly. The training of entry-level police officers alone can run into tens of thousands of dollars, not to mention the expense associated with the recruitment and selection efforts that become necessary to replace officers who resign their positions.

Another related issue that often surfaces involves what type of college education is best to prepare a person for police work. Although criminal justice programs in higher education continue to establish a more scholarly approach toward teaching and research, the emphasis on providing technical competence skills continues to be equally as important. The question, however, is how much of the curriculum should be devoted to practical education (e.g., police problems and practices, principles of investigations, tactical and defensive driving, etc.) and how much should emphasize a broader-based curriculum (e.g., psychology, sociology, and human services)?

The undergraduate degree program in the School of Criminal Justice at Michigan State University is designed to provide students with the foundations of criminal justice research and practice. During freshman and sophomore years, students get an overview of criminal justice, criminology, criminal procedure, and research. In the junior and senior years, students focus on specific areas of interest in policing, corrections, juvenile justice, and private security.

Source: http://criminaljustice.msu.edu/academic/bachelors.php
Descriptions of a few selected policing courses that are currently offered to students pursuing a baccalaureate degree in criminal justice at Michigan State University include:

Course: CJ 110 Introduction to Criminal Justice
Description: Description and analysis of agencies and processes involved in administration of justice in the United States.

Course: CJ 220 Criminology
Description: Introduction to the socio-legal foundation of crime. Crime typology and measurement procedures. Theory and public policy. Societal responses to crime and criminals.

Course: CJ 435 Investigation Procedures
Description: Laws of evidence controlling investigative procedures. Crime scene concerns. Multi-agency investigation.

Course: CJ 375 Criminal Law Process
Description: Administration of criminal law. Investigation, prosecution, adjudication, and sentencing. Constitutional safeguards and legal controls on official action.

Course: CJ 421 Minorities, Crime, and Social Policy
Description: A socio-historical analysis of the effects of race and ethnicity on legitimate social opportunities, criminal behavior, victimization, and differential judicial processing. Analysis of the impact of assimilation and acculturation on criminal behavior, victimization, and criminal justice processes.

Course: CJ 434 Police Administration
Description: Organizational theory, leadership, communications, and labor relations in police administration. Historical and legal perspectives.

Exhibit 11.2 Description of the Criminal Justice program at Michigan State University. (From http://criminaljustice.msu.edu/academic/index.php?academic)

Exhibits 11.2 and 11.3 illustrate the nature and scope of two criminal justice undergraduate law enforcement programs. In the first table, Michigan State University's Criminal Justice program is featured because it is representative of a large state university program and also the nation's oldest degree-granting criminal justice program. In the second table, we provide program and course information pertaining to the Department of Criminal Justice at Washburn University, a university with a student population of less than eight thousand, which typifies smaller universities and four-year colleges. Both programs offer introductory courses relating to the criminal justice system, law enforcement, security, juvenile justice, criminology, and the courts. More advanced courses in cultural diversity, administration and management, the law, victimization, and a host of special topic courses then follow. Likewise, they both offer an internship program for students to engage in fieldwork as participant observers in their area of study. It appears that both

The Department of Criminal Justice at Washburn University offers degree programs to prepare students for productive careers in law enforcement, corrections, and security administration. The program is designed to serve both local and distance learning students through web-based and other formats and is intended to produce knowledgeable students who possess analytical and technical skills to compete in today's criminal justice job market. Services are made available to help students reach their full academic potential and prepare them for a lifetime of continuous learning.
Source: http://www.washburn.edu/sas/cj/index.html.

A few policing courses offered to students pursuing a baccalaureate degree in criminal justice at Washburn University include:

CJ 110 Introduction to Law Enforcement
Description: The major functions of modern law enforcement agencies and personnel. Special attention is given to career opportunities and alternatives in the field of law enforcement.

CJ 325 Criminology
Description: Examines various criminological theories including delinquent subculture, differential association, and conflict theory, and their application by criminal justice professionals. In addition, the student will understand and practice the application of criminological theory in dealing with an individual offender.

CJ210/LG345 Criminal Law
Description: Review of substantive criminal law theory and specific elements common to index offenses will be presented. Course will offer a brief synopsis of the historical development of penal codes, as well as application of the Model Penal Code.

CJ230 Principles of Investigations
Description: Principles and procedures used for crime scene protection and search; collection and preservation of evidence; interviewing and interrogation of complainants, witnesses, suspects, and victims; and scientific applications to a variety of investigations conducted in criminal justice setting.

CJ303 Diversity in American Culture
Description: Designed to explore the relationship between culture and the criminal justice system. Emphasis is given to understanding the historical, theoretical, and structural perspectives of racial/ethnic and minority groups in society.

CJ 440 Enforcement Administration
Description: A police administration course with emphasis on principles of leadership and management.

Exhibit 11.3 Description of the Criminal Justice program at Washburn University. (From http://www.washburn.edu/sas/cj/curriculum-CJ.htm#BSCJLawEnforcementDegree)

universities attempt to reach a balanced curriculum that addresses the history, philosophy, and practical approaches to policing.

As noted, the criminal justice programs at Michigan State University and Washburn University each provide broad curriculums to prepare students for a career in law enforcement. Each of these schools offers graduate programs for advanced study of criminal justice. It is reasonable to believe that law enforcement agencies in the locations of these universities are likely to require their candidates to possess some level of higher education.

In Exhibit 11.4, we provide some of the job requirements for entry-level positions for the police departments in East Lansing, Michigan, and Topeka,

East Lansing Police Department	Topeka Police Department
Applicants must:	Applicants must:
• Be a United States citizen.	• Be a United States citizen.
• Be at least twenty-one years of age.	• Be at least twenty-one years of age.
• Possess a Michigan driver's license.	• Possess a Kansas driver's license.
• Have no felony convictions.	• Have no felony convictions.
• Be able to meet physical/essential functions of position.	• Have no health conditions that would restrict the ability to safely complete academy training and to perform all aspects of police work.
• Be C.O.L.E.S certifiable—15-week Police Academy graduate.	
• Associate's degree or equivalent in criminal justice or related field.	• Graduation from a U.S. high school, G.E.D. or equivalent from a U.S. institution that is recognized by the state of Kansas. College is recommended, but not required.

Exhibit 11.4 Job requirements for Police Departments in East Lansing, Michigan and Topeka, Kansas.

Kansas. Note that the East Lansing Police Department requires a two-year associate's degree, but the Topeka Police Department does not require higher education, only recommends it. This minimum educational requirement is common for police agencies across the nation. A study by the Bureau of Justice Statistics of approximately 12,575 local police departments indicates that 82% of these departments require only a high-school diploma. An estimated 16% of departments had some type of college requirement, including 9% with a two-year degree requirement. Only 1% of all local police departments require a four-year college degree.[9]

THE NEW HAVEN, CONNECTICUT POLICE DEPARTMENT

Recognizing that many of their employment candidates will not possess a college degree, some law enforcement agencies have found innovative ways of providing their recruits with the proper educational background necessary to perform police service. The New Haven, Connecticut Police Department, for example, restructured its traditional training academy to form a newly conceived Division of Training and Education. It was charged with the mandate of educating police officers that would work together with neighborhood residents to maintain order legally, humanely, respectfully, and equitably. Some of the educational features include the following:[10]

- A university-styled, community-oriented police academy was developed. The academy is held over a six-month period. It is followed by a sixteen-week field-training officer program, matching new graduates with specially trained veteran officers who act as mentors and on-the-job instructors. The minimum passing grade for all academy examinations, assignments, and projects is 80%, making it the most rigorous and selective school for police officer candidates in the state.
- In addition to a curriculum of traditional subjects such as constitutional law, use-of-force decision making, defensive tactics, firearms, penal code, and motor vehicle law, students learn about the history, culture, and values of New Haven's many different populations. Other courses include Milestones in Civil Rights Legislation, Non-Violent Management of Aggressive Behavior, Alternative Dispute Resolution, HIV/AIDS, the New Haven Needle Exchange Program, Sexual Harassment, Bias and Hate Crimes, and Individuals with Memory, Hearing, and Seizure Disorders. Faculty from the Yale Child Development Community Policing Program helps emphasize the department's commitment to police understanding of child and adolescent behavior.
- There is also an emphasis on experiential learning. This type of learning is a highly participatory instructional method in which students draw on their experience, knowledge, and imagination to solve problems. The conventional classroom setting is not used. Instead, there is free and open exchange of ideas, and the method refocuses the instructor's role from that of deliverer of information to that of guide and coach.

Women in Policing

Prior to the 1950s, the role of women in policing was restricted to social welfare duties. Women were primarily involved with police matters involving female and juvenile offenders. For example, if police were called to a domestic dispute, a policewoman would likely be dispatched to help with the children at the scene. Female police officers were more often than not relegated to clerical work at the police station and called upon to care for any female prisoner that was taken into custody. Amidst the social movements of the late 1950s and 1960s, police departments began to be challenged about the role of women in policing, and with the passage of the 1972 amendments to the Civil Rights Act of 1964, the stereotyping of women police officers as social workers and matrons quickly changed across the country. In 1968,

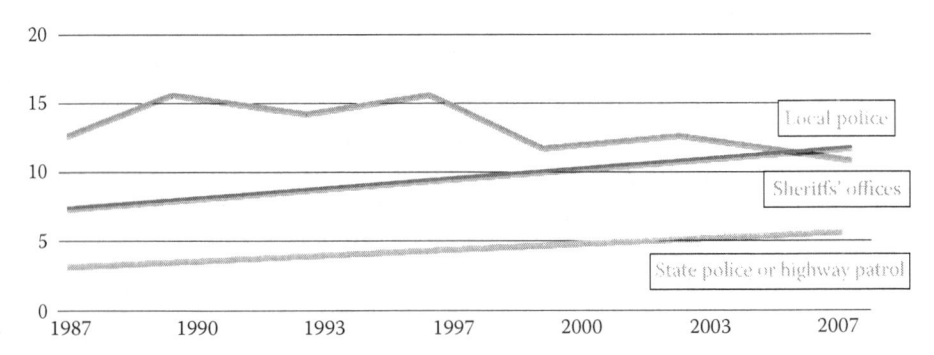

Exhibit 11.5 Percent of officers who are women. (Adapted from Lynn Langton, *Women in Law Enforcement, 1987–2008*. Washington, DC: Bureau of Justice Statistics (June 2010).)

the Indianapolis Police Department made history by assigning the first two women officers to patrol on an equal basis with their male colleagues.[11] By the mid-1970s, police departments nationwide, including New York, Philadelphia, St. Louis, and Miami, had women working in patrol.[12]

In addition to job assignments, police departments are now required by law to eliminate discriminating factors that might hamper the hiring of female officers, yet the number of women in policing has remained modest. The percentage of female officers in local police departments increased steadily over the two decades, from 7.6% in 1987 to nearly 12% in 2007.[13] In Exhibit 11.5, we provide data relating to the percentage of full-time sworn law enforcement officers who are women among state and local law enforcement agencies, 1987–2007.

Problems recruiting women seem to stem from common misperceptions that police officers routinely perform duties that require great physical strength. The media's portrayal of police is in large part responsible for this erroneous public image. Movies frequently depict police as the "good guys" who use force and coercion to get the "bad guys." Consider the police image projected by Hollywood in such movies as *Lethal Weapon*, *Rush Hour*, and *Judge Dredd*. Action films like these give ambiguous meaning to police work. One is led to believe that police work is constant excitement, filled with high-pursuit chases, shooting armed hostage-takers, and uncovering multimillion-dollar drug rings. Male domination is quickly apparent to the viewer because women are rarely the main characters of high-drama, fast-action police movies. When they are, as in the film *Charlie's Angels*, the policewomen are expected to use "smash and crash" tactics to get the job done.

Compounding the problems of public image are the traditional recruitment policies maintained by police departments. Entry level standards for physical agility, for example, may overemphasize physical strength as a prerequisite of police work. It is not unusual for a physical performance test to include such tasks as climbing an eight-foot wall or dragging a 150 pound dummy a distance of one hundred feet. Such activities often have adverse impact against women recruits and may actually not be job-related. Although very young male officers may be able to meet such physical demands, the veteran male officers may no longer be able to scale a high wall or pull a heavy body. Why then are rigid physical performance tests required for all recruits?

The current rate of hiring indicates that women will remain underrepresented within policing unless these types of traditional tests are substituted with more realistic ones that only measure skills and abilities at the minimum level actually needed to be able to perform the job adequately. The good news is that some police administrators have made changes that are having a dramatic impact on the recruitment of women police officers. For example, when the Albuquerque Police Department instituted a range of policies under the "New Workplace Project" funded by the U.S. Department of Labor, the percentage of female recruits increased from 10 to 25%, and they were retained at the same rate as their male counterparts. Similarly, the Tucson Police Department increased their percentage of female recruits from 10 to 29% by implementing active strategies to retain women. Based on both research and practical experience, there is every reason to believe that such changes will yield benefits to women within the police profession.[14]

ADVANTAGES FOR LAW ENFORCEMENT AGENCIES THAT HIRE AND RETAIN MORE WOMEN[15]

1. Female officers are proven to be as competent as their male counterparts: A number of evaluations have been conducted to determine the effectiveness of male versus female officers in law enforcement. Results in agencies in Washington, DC; St. Louis; New York City; Philadelphia; Denver; Newton, Massachusetts; California; and Pennsylvania clearly indicated that men and women were equally capable of police patrol work. Similar research conducted in other countries has reached the same conclusions that no meaningful difference between male and female officers occurs:
   - in their activities or productivity on patrol
   - their commitment to law enforcement organizations
   - their response to violent confrontations
   - their performance evaluations received both at the academy and on the job

   In fact, some studies indicate areas of police performance in which women excel. In one study, female police executives were found to be more flexible, emotionally independent,

self-assertive, self-confident, proactive, and creative than their male counterparts. Other research consistently demonstrates that women in law enforcement have more education than their male peers. Clearly, the body of evidence suggests that male and female police officers are equally capable to successfully meet the demands of the law enforcement profession.
2. Female officers are less likely to use excessive force:

> Police work used to be like a laborer's job...the only requirement was that you had to be tough. Now...[the job] is all about knowing how to talk to people. We screen for drug use, criminal background, but we don't do much screening for people who can get along with other people....A good cop knows how to defuse the situation by talking it out. (Timothy Egan, "Image of 'Man' Behind Badge Changing," *New York Times*, April 25 1991, A14.)

As this quote indicates, a "good cop" uses communication skills in every aspect of the job and can often reduce the need for force by de-escalating potentially violent situations. By this criterion, women clearly make "good cops," as demonstrated in research both in the United States and internationally over the last twenty-five years. To date, there are a number of studies demonstrating that female officers utilize a less authoritarian style of policing that relies less on physical force, despite research showing women respond to similar calls and encounter similar dangers on duty and are as effective as their male counterparts in performing police duties. Other recent research finds no difference in the level of force used by male versus female officers during the course of routine professional duties. Additionally, women are less likely to engage in high-risk pursuits that may harm individuals involved. Regardless of whether female and male officers use comparable levels of force during routine activity, it is clear that women are significantly less likely to be involved in employing both deadly force and excessive force.

- The question of force and physical strength: The question of force lies at the heart of the traditional reluctance to hire women into policing. A number of studies document that both police officers and community members are concerned that women are not strong enough or aggressive enough for police work. However, physical strength has not been shown to predict either general police effectiveness or the ability to successfully handle dangerous situations. In fact, there are no documented cases of negative outcomes caused by the lack of strength or aggression exhibited by a female officer. Rather, some have suggested that alternative characteristics might be preferable to physical strength, such as the ability to defuse potential violence and maintain composure in situations of conflict. It is therefore important to note that female officers not only exhibit more reasoned caution than their male counterparts but also that they increase this tendency in their male partners. Given that an estimated 80–90% of policing involves noncriminal or service functions, the emphasis in traditional policing on physical strength might actually serve as a liability to police departments seeking to successfully meet the demands of their community. In addition, it serves to "weed out" women (and men) who could potentially implement an alternative model of policing that focuses less on physical force and more on interpersonal communication.

- An emphasis on communication: A shift away from an emphasis on physical force is likely to capitalize on the interpersonal skills that female officers possess, not only in equal measure to their male counterparts but often to a greater degree. Unfortunately, these interpersonal skills have not traditionally been emphasized in selection standards and background investigations. In fact, a history of perpetrating violence has often been ignored when screening potential candidates. However, in today's environment of ever-increasing litigation, law enforcement agencies cannot afford to overlook any means of reducing their risk of excessive force in favor of a more service-oriented style of policing. By hiring and retaining more women, departments can go a long way toward transforming their focus to one that emphasizes interpersonal skills and cooperation with the community.

3. Female officers can help implement community-oriented policing: Community policing represents a new approach to modern law enforcement, emphasizing communication and cooperation with citizens as well as informal problem solving. It is therefore important to note that women officers receive more favorable evaluations and fewer citizen complaints than their male counterparts. To illustrate, one study found that male officers were the target of 50% more insults by citizens and almost three times as many threats or attempts at injury in comparison with their female peers. In another study, police training instructors

indicated that female officers have an advantage over their male peers in several areas, including empathy toward others and interacting in a way that is not designed to "prove" something. For their part, female officers are reportedly less cynical in their views of citizens, which is noteworthy because such an orientation is associated with a decreased likelihood of using both reasonable and/or excessive force. Women in law enforcement are also less likely to be involved in misconduct, and they report greater support for the principles of community policing than their male colleagues. It is no wonder, then, that many have suggested hiring more female officers as a way of improving the public image of the police department.

4. The presence of women can bring about beneficial changes in policy for all officers: Lewis Sherman envisioned as early as 1973 that police departments would be held liable for their underrepresentation of female officers and that hiring more women would not only bring them into compliance with the U.S. Constitution but also yield improvements in the procedures for selection, recruitment, and retention of all sworn personnel. As he argued:

> If a woman 5 feet, 3 inches tall can perform the job of patrol, why not a man who is the same height? If a woman needs better physical defense training, might not also a man? If a woman defuses a violent situation without having to make an arrest, shouldn't she or any man who does the same be given a high rating for effective law enforcement performance? Departments could move toward making their selection and training standards job-related, as well as toward development of new measures of police performance. (Lewis J. Sherman, "A Psychological View of Women in Policing," *Journal of Police Science and Administration* Vol. 1, no. 4 (1973): 383–394.)

Improvements such as these would inevitably benefit both female and male employees within law enforcement. The Police Foundation similarly noted in 1974 that:

> The introduction of women will create an incentive…to examine many management practices which are less acceptable now that they must be applied to men and women alike. This may result in the development of improved selection criteria, performance standards, and supervision for all officers.

They further concluded that the expanded supply of police personnel, the reduced cost of recruiting, and better community representation were additional benefits of hiring more female officers.

Having addressed some of the issues pertaining to the recruitment of women, we now turn our attention to the struggles that many law enforcement departments have had with the recruitment of minorities into the police profession.

Minority Recruitment

Police leaders throughout the country have developed affirmative action plans to help with the recruitment of minority employees. In a study of fifty police departments located in the largest cities in America, nearly two-thirds (64%) of the departments reported operating under an affirmative action plan.[16]

When affirmative action is taken to achieve a ratio of minority group employees proportionate to the makeup of the population it serves, police leaders and managers must be sensitive to the impact that it may have on the department. Improving recruitment and hiring practices to ensure equal employment opportunities is a good thing, as long as it is done fairly. Individuals who are not part of an affirmative action plan may feel that the selection and hiring practices are not fair. This can lead to claims of reverse discrimination, and victims may develop resentments toward those who are perceived as receiving preferential treatment because of their race. Moreover, if the agency hires a person who is unqualified but part of a particular ethnic group, only for the sake of getting numbers in line with Equal Employment Opportunity guidelines, problems could occur within the department.

The ultimate goal of an affirmative action plan is to expand employment opportunities for minorities. Most police departments have made modest gains in reaching its goals of recruiting a substantial representation of their ethnic minority population. For example, the Bureau of Justice Statistics, as a part of its Law Enforcement Management and Administrative Statistics (LEMAS) program, surveys a nationally representative sample of state and local law enforcement agencies operating nationwide. In Exhibit 11.6, we provide selected summary data for state and local law enforcement agencies with one hundred or more officers by type of agency as reported by LEMAS. The data from the survey show that 32% of the officers in larger municipal police departments are members of a racial or ethnic minority, compared to 23% in county police departments, 22% in sheriffs' offices, and 16% in state agencies. Overall, 19% of all state and local agencies with one hundred or more officers were racial/ethnic minorities.

The perception of an organization in the labor market has great bearing on recruitment efforts. Law enforcement, by its very nature a public occupation, is constantly under scrutiny by the public. Favorable or unfavorable images are conveyed each day by the media. Publicity, whether in the newspapers, local and national news, or the Internet, far too often depicts

	Local Law Enforcement Agencies				
		County		Municipal	
Primary State Law Enforcement Item Description	Total (N = 755)	Police (N = 32)	Police (N = 501)	Sheriff (N = 222)	Agencies (N = 49)
Number of agencies by number of full-time sworn personnel					
1,000 or more	59	8	39	12	17
500–999	61	4	33	24	17
250–499	159	11	88	60	9
100–249	476	9	341	126	6
Total number of:					
Full-time employees	498,530	31,945	312,201	154,384	87,028
Full-time sworn personnel	346,937	24,345	239,683	82,909	56,348
Uniformed officers assigned to respond to calls for service	200,782	14,419	150,465	35,898	40,387
Overall percent of sworn personnel who were:					
Female	14%	12%	14%	14%	6%
Any racial/ethnic minority	29	23	32	22	16
Black, non-Hispanic	15	11	17	10	8
Hispanic, any race	11	8	12	9	6
Other minority	3	4	3	2	2
Average percent of sworn personnel who were:					
Female	11%	11%	10%	13%	6%
Racial/ethnic minority	19	23	20	16	12

Exhibit 11.6 Selected summary data for state and local law enforcement agencies with 100 or more officers by type of agency, 2000. (Adapted from Matthew Hickman and Brian A. Reaves, *Law Enforcement Management and Administrative Statistics, 2000: Data for Individual State and Local Agencies with 100 or More Officers*. Washington, DC: Bureau of Justice Statistics (April, 2004).)

extreme events. Consider the positive images of the police responding to the September 11, 2001, terrorist bombing of the World Trade Center in New York. Conversely, recall the negative publicity that abounded when police acted in 1991 against Rodney King.

Police leaders must routinely consider the current image of their departments. One significant factor to weigh in the recruitment effort is whether poor images of the police will yield less minority candidates. That is, if minorities perceive that police treat races unfairly, then they will not consider policing as a career. In 1993, Robert Kaminski tested this notion by examining whether attitudes toward the police predicted interest in police work among black and white high school seniors. A survey questionnaire was administered to seniors in Albany Public High School in New York. Responses came from 356 students: 61% were white, 29% were black, 3% were Asian, 1% was

Hispanic, and 5% were of other races. The survey contained seventy-seven questions focusing on attitudes toward the police, exposure to police recruitment efforts, educational and occupational aspirations, and other topics. Regarding the development of a recruitment strategy for black youth, the results indicated that perceptions of unfair treatment of minorities by police did not significantly reduce minority interest in policing. Even though black students were more likely than white students to perceive poorer treatment of minorities by police, this perception had no impact on the likelihood of accepting a job offer.[17]

Selection of New Hires

Police departments employ a variety of screening methods when hiring new officers. The most widely used methods are personal interviews, criminal record checks, background investigations, driving record checks, and medical exams. Many police departments also use psychological tests, drug tests, written aptitude tests, and physical agility tests to screen applicants for sworn positions.

Various aspects of the selection process are continually being revised because of the emergence of affirmative action. To comply with Equal Employment Opportunity Commission (EEOC) requirements and avoid legal challenges, law enforcement agencies must hire personnel to meet very specific standards directly related to the job. The major dilemma in selection is that the best overall predictors of job performance are cognitive skills (i.e., reasoning, judgment, and inferential thinking), which are skills that have the most disparate impact on minorities.[18] Disparate impact is a theory that holds that even where an employer is not motivated by discriminatory intent, Title VII prohibits the employer from using a racially neutral employment practice that has an unjustified adverse impact on members of a protected class.

The roots of the disparate impact standard lie in Griggs v. Duke Power Company 401 U.S. 424, 431-2 (1971). In Griggs, the court interpreted language of Title VII prohibiting employers from adversely affecting employment status "because of" race, color, religion, sex, or national origin to mean that "practices, procedures, or tests neutral on their face, and even neutral in terms of intent, cannot be maintained if they operate to 'freeze' the status quo of prior discriminatory employment practices." The court went on to strike down the power company's use of two generic aptitude tests and a high school diploma requirement. The critical language for future disparate impact case law was contained in the court's statement:

> The Act proscribes not only overt discrimination but also practices that are fair in form, but discriminatory in operation. The touchstone is business

necessity…good intent or absence of discriminatory intent does not redeem employment procedures or testing mechanisms that operate as "built-in headwinds" for minority groups and are unrelated to measuring job capability…. Congress has placed on the employer the burden of showing that any given requirement must have a manifest relationship to the employment in question.[19] (GRIGGS v. DUKE POWER CO., 401 U.S. 424 (1971) 401 U.S. 424.)

The phrases "business necessity," "unrelated to measuring job capacity," and "manifest relationship" have echoed through Title VII court opinions for more than forty years. Griggs has generated an overwhelming number of Title VII cases and subsequent case law, pertaining to practices that may be subject to a disparate impact challenge, which include written tests, height and weight requirements, educational requirements, and subjective procedures, such as interviews. Consider the EEOC guidelines that rule that an adverse impact occurs if members of a protected class are selected at a rate less than four-fifths (80%) of that of another group. If for example, a police department administers a written test and 50% of white applicants receive a passing score on a test but only 30% of African Americans pass, the relevant ratio would be 30/50, or 60%, which would violate the 80% rule. If challenged, the department must demonstrate that the scored test is job-related and consistent with business necessity by showing that the test is "validated," although a formal validation study is not necessarily required.

The EEOC guidelines are applicable to other measures of employee qualifications, such as educational, experience, and licensing requirements. In cases involving clerical or manual labor work, the courts have generally found unlawful educational requirements that have a disparate impact. The higher the professional positions or the greater the consequence of hiring unskilled applicants, the lower the burden upon the employer of proving job-relatedness.[20]

Preemployment Standards

Applicants must be able to meet the occupational qualifications that have been established by the police department. A bona fide occupational qualification (BFOQ) is one that is reasonably necessary to perform a job. An example of a BFOQ in policing might be that the applicant has normal or correctable vision, such as Atlanta Police Department's requirement that, "Visual ability cannot be less than 20/100 in each eye, uncorrected, and must be corrected to 20/20 with glasses, contact lenses or surgery."[21]

Although police departments take a variety of approaches to determine the suitability of an applicant, all departments examine the employment applications to see whether the candidate meets the minimum standards for

Recruitment and Selection

the job. This initial review is commonly referred to as the preemployment screening. The standards, which typically include age, height and weight, physical agility, etc., serve as a threshold to determine which candidates can be eliminated from further consideration. The better the initial screening process, the more economical the selection tends to be. As the candidate continues through the hiring steps, more advanced selection methods such as written tests, backgrounds investigations, interviews, assessment centers, psychological tests, etc., become more expensive to administer.

Consider the eligibility qualifications necessary to be a police officer in Kansas City, Missouri, which are provided in Exhibit 11.7. As with most police departments, the applicant must be at least twenty-one years of age. Some departments allow for recruits to be younger than twenty-one years but usually have some criteria attached to the waiver. For example, the Dallas Police Department maintains an age requirement of twenty-one, unless the

- United States citizen
- 21 years of age upon completion of academy training
- High school diploma or GED equivalent
- Valid driver's license from any state and obtain a Missouri driver's license by the date of appointment
- Live in city of Kansas City, Missouri, within twelve (12) months of employment
- Pass the police officer entrance examination, which measures an individual's ability in arithmetic, reading comprehension, grammar, and writing. A minimum score of 70% in each category is required
- Pass the physical agility test
- Proportional height and weight according to department standards
- A minimum of 20/200 vision uncorrected, correctable to 20/20 with normal color vision
- Ability to communicate clearly and concisely using clear verbal and good writing skills
- Physically capable of operating a department issued handgun and shotgun
- Pass a polygraph examination
- Pass a background investigation
- Pass a psychological evaluation
- Pass a physical examination
- Must meet other requirements as specified by the Kansas City Missouri Police Department during the preemployment process

Disqualifiers

- Dishonesty
- Past pattern of drug abuse and/or use of certain controlled substances
- Excessive traffic conviction history
- Excessive city ordinance, misdemeanor violation convictions, or outstanding warrants
- Felony convictions or misdemeanor convictions directly resulting from felony charges
- Dishonorable discharge from the United States Armed Services

Exhibit 11.7 Minimum Qualifications for K.C.M.O. Police Officers. (Adapted from: Kansas City Missouri Police Department Web page http://www.kcmo.org/police/AboutUs/Departments/Administration/HumanResources/EmploymentSection/Eligibility/index.htm)

applicant is nineteen and a half years of age with at least sixty semester hours with a C average or better.[22]

There have been some legal challenges to age requirements, primarily at the maximum limits. The Age Discrimination in Employment Act (ADEA) offers employment protection to most people forty years of age and older who work for a business that employs twenty or more employees. This, however, is not mandatory. In law enforcement, for example, a provision of the ADEA requires that any newly enacted restrictions establish the mandatory retirement age at fifty-five years or older and that mandatory retirement include a bona fide, nondiscriminatory retirement plan.

As with age requirements, the minimum standards regarding height and weight have been legally contested and found to be discriminating if not justified by the police agency. One of the most notable legal cases is Vanguard Justice Society v. Hughes 471 F. Supp. 670 (1979). In this case, the court concluded that a height requirement of five feet seven inches constituted sex discrimination because the standard excluded 95% of all women and only 32% of men. Today, most police departments make no mention of height or weight requirement. Rather, every applicant is required to successfully pass a rigorous physical obstacle course or other type of agility test.

Historically, the physical agility test consists of completing a certain number of chin-ups, push-ups, and sit-ups within a given time frame. There is also a running requirement, usually in tandem with several obstacles that have to be maneuvered by the candidate. The objective is to measure jumping, climbing, or other tasks that give some insight into the physical fitness of the candidate. For example, the New Jersey State Police Physical Qualification Test consists of a seventy-five-yard run, push-ups, sit-ups, and a one-and-a-half-mile run. An excellent video of these requirements is available at www.state.nj.us/njsp/recruit/pqt.html. However, some physical agility tests are less generic and more specifically tied into some of the physical demands of the job. For example, candidates who receive a tentative offer of employment with the Wisconsin State Patrol must successfully complete four physical agility tests, which include:

1. Obstacle course: The candidate sits behind the steering wheel of a patrol car with hands resting on the steering wheel. At the sound of a whistle, the candidate exits the car and runs a distance of forty yards, makes a left turn, weaves in and out of a series of cones for forty yards, and finishes by climbing a four-foot barrier. The candidate must complete the obstacle course in twenty-nine seconds or less.
2. Traffic hazard removal and aid: The candidate is required to move two objects of different sizes to simulate the removal of a hazard and the ability to render first aid. These must be completed in eighteen seconds or less and include:

- Tire debris weighing approximately sixty pounds that must be lifted, carried, dragged, or pulled a distance of thirty feet
- A first-aid kit weighing approximately thirty pounds that must be lifted and carried a distance of sixty feet

3. Rescue simulation: The candidate stands three feet from a patrol car with the door closed. At the sound of a whistle, the candidate removes a dummy weighing approximately one hundred and sixty-five pounds from the car. The dummy must be dragged, lifted, or carried for sixty feet to a line that is marked by two yellow standards. The dummy's feet must cross the line within forty-nine seconds.
4. Arrest resister: The candidate sits in a car with the door closed. At the sound of a whistle, the candidate exits the car and sprints fifteen yards. From here the candidate pulls the arms of an arrest resister together by grasping the left arm with the left hand and grasping the right arm with the right hand and must hold them together for three seconds. The entire process must be completed in fifteen seconds or less.

Americans with Disabilities Act

The Americans with Disabilities Act (ADA) protects individuals with disabilities from discrimination based on their disability, and the protection of the ADA extends to discrimination in a broad range of activities, including public services, public accommodations, and employment. Although the ADA's prohibition against disability discrimination applies to most private and public employers in the United States, not all individuals with a disability are protected by the act. To be protected, individuals with a disability must demonstrate they are otherwise qualified for the job they seek, can perform essential functions of that job with or without reasonable accommodation, and have a disability that substantially limits a major life activity. However, the ADA does not specifically define the term "reasonable accommodation" but rather provides examples of employer actions that may constitute reasonable accommodation. The Equal Employment Opportunity Commission has established general guidelines on reasonable accommodation.

The ADA prohibits employer discrimination against qualified individuals with disabilities because of their disabilities with regard to application procedures, hiring, promotion, pay, training, termination, and other conditions of employment. Under the ADA, standards and qualifications that screen out individuals on the basis of disability must be related to the job to be performed. An analysis of job qualifications begins with three questions:

1. Do qualifications or standards that screen out persons with disabilities relate to essential functions of the job? Fundamental, not marginal, job functions are considered essential for purposes of the ADA.

Functions are essential when employees are required to perform them and their elimination would alter the job. Even when a function is rarely performed, it may nevertheless be essential. For example, most police officers rarely make forcible arrests, but departments that can demonstrate serious consequences of an officer's inability to do so may establish this ability as an essential function.

2. Are qualifications and standards that screen out persons with disabilities job-related and consistent with business necessity? Under the ADA, standards must be shown to be job-related and consistent with business necessity. Business necessity means that the selection relates to an essential function of the job. Thus, "if a test or other selection criterion excludes an individual with a disability and does not relate to the essential function of the job, it is not consistent with business necessity." However, even if a standard is job-related, it may nevertheless be inappropriate if it does not relate to an essential job function. For example, requiring a driver's license may be job-related for both patrol officers and corrections officers. However, the requirement relates to an essential function of the job of a patrol officer. A corrections officer working in a prison is not required to drive in the course of business. Therefore, if requiring a driver's license screens out a person with a disability, it may be justified for the job of patrol officer but not for a corrections officer because driving is not an essential function of the job.

3. Is there a reasonable accommodation available that enables an applicant, who would not be qualified because of a disability, to meet the qualification standards? Employers have a duty to reasonably accommodate persons with disabilities during the application process to give them an equal opportunity to be considered for the job. Reasonable accommodations during the hiring process can include providing qualified interpreters or readers. It can also mean revising or modifying exams or tests. For example, a candidate who lacks manual dexterity may need assistance in filling out an application form. Without such accommodations, these individuals may have no opportunity to be considered for a job. On the other hand, employers do not have to find a job for a disabled applicant who is not otherwise qualified or consider an applicant for a job for which he or she did not apply.[23]

Drug Testing

Put simply, the reason preemployment drug screenings are commonplace is to decrease the chance of hiring someone who is currently using or abusing drugs. Generally, employers test only for those that are most commonly used and abused: cocaine, phencyclidine (PCP), opiates, amphetamines, and cannabis (marijuana). Some employers also test for alcohol.

Several court cases have molded that standard used by most law enforcement agencies with regard to preemployment drug usage by applicants. In Davis v. City of Dallas, 777 F.2d 205 (1985), for example, the court upheld the Dallas Police Department's policy that applicants could not have recent or excessive histories of marijuana use. Similarly, in Shield Club v. City of Cleveland, 647 R.Supp. 274 (1986), the court ruled that drug testing standards that rejected applicants who tested positive for controlled substances were permissible. In both cases, the courts found that preemployment policy regarding drug history is job-related and nondiscriminatory if applied to all police applicants.

Written Tests

Written tests are very common in the police selection process. The examination itself is used as a means of further screening applicants for the position of police officer. The type of written test varies, but most departments administer an exam that measures general knowledge, intelligence, specific knowledge, or a combination thereof. One written test that is administered by a variety of agencies and municipalities throughout the country is the Police Officer Selection Test (POST), which is made up of four separately timed test sections. POST is an entry-level basic skills test that helps law enforcement agencies select the most qualified applicants by ensuring that candidates possess the basic cognitive skills necessary to successfully perform the job. The first three sections, mathematics, reading comprehension, and grammar, utilize the multiple-choice and true/false formats. The fourth section, incident report writing, requires applicants to provide an essay response. Several companies provide free information and tips on passing the written exam, including example questions.

Psychological Testing

Psychological screening of police candidates is highly desirable, although controversy has emerged regarding the extent and nature of the preemployment screening process for police officers. Issues in preemployment screening focus on cost, local demands, civil rights requirements, and minimum qualifications. Although psychological screening can cost $150 per applicant, training and equipping a police officer can cost between $10,000 and $20,000.[24]

The most widely used test to screen for psychological deviance is the Minnesota Multiphasic Personality Inventory 2 (MMPI-2). The MMPI-2 is a test used to gather information on the personality, attitudes, and mental health of persons aged sixteen or older and to aid in clinical diagnosis. It consists of 567 true/false questions, with different formats available for individual and group use. The MMPI-2 is untimed and can take anywhere from forty-five minutes to two hours to complete. This is normally done in a single session but can be extended to a second session if necessary.

Specific conditions or syndromes that the test can help identify include depression, hysteria, paranoia, and schizophrenia. Raw scores based on deviations from standard responses are entered on personality profile forms to obtain the individual results. There is also a validity scale to thwart attempts to "fake" the test. Because the MMPI-2 is a complex test whose results can sometimes be ambiguous (and/or skewed by various factors), professionals tend to be cautious in interpreting it, often preferring broad descriptions to specific psychiatric diagnoses, unless these are supported by further testing and observable behavior. A sixth-grade reading level is required in order to take the test. Overall, the test can help measure a candidate's emotional suitability for certain positions, cognitive ability, and possible behavioral issues.

Another commonly used psychological written test is the California Personality Inventory (CPI). The CPI was developed over forty years ago as an objective measurement of personality and behavior. The test, which is based on less extreme measures of personality than the MMPI-2, assesses traits, including dominance, responsibility, self-acceptance, and socialization. In addition, some parts of the test specifically measure traits relevant to academic achievement. Another inventory designed to measure a spectrum of personality variables in normal populations is the Personality Research Form, whose measurement scales include affiliation, autonomy, change, endurance, and exhibition.

No matter what psychological test is administered to police applicants, police leaders should consider the personality inventories with particular caution. In sum, any psychological testing must accurately predict an applicant's performance as a police officer before the department can use it as a basis to disqualify an individual. Moreover, it has been suggested that because the best predictor of future behavior is past behavior, greater emphasis should be given to background investigations to identify applicants who may possess a history of disqualifying characteristics, such as emotional instability, violent behavior, etc.

Background Investigation

At some point in the selection process, a background investigation is conducted on the applicant. Many agencies prefer to wait until the initial screening of the applicant pool has been performed and the applicant has successfully passed a written exam and physical agility test. The main reason for delaying the background investigation is that the process is lengthy and expensive.

Background checks generally include contacting former employers and references and also can include financial histories, criminal convictions, education history, prior addresses, and professional licenses. Information about the candidate's possible criminal history is obtained from National Crime Information Center records. A copy of the candidate's fingerprints is also sent to the FBI and state criminal justice records to search for a possible criminal record.

Polygraph Examinations

The purpose of the polygraph is to check the accuracy of background information already gathered during the selection process. Questions involve job-related matters and are administered by a qualified polygraph examiner who is typically an employee of the police department. The major advantage of including the polygraph in the screening process is that applicants who have a history of behavior that may disqualify them from employment are likely not to apply with the police agency. The major disadvantage is that it may put a great amount of stress on the applicant resulting in false-positive readings. Referring again to Bureau of Justice Statistics, of the 12,575 local police departments operating in the United, only 26% of them require a polygraph examination as part of the hiring process.[25]

Interviews

Nearly all police departments use some form of oral interview, which usually occurs near the end of the selection process. The interview allows department managers the opportunity to visit with the applicant, ask direct questions, and draw some conclusions about the applicant's suitability for the job. The face-to-face interview must be conducted with care and an understanding of employment discrimination laws. Thus, it is important for managers who interview applicants to be trained to avoid asking illegal questions or participating in discussions that are potentially illegal. For example, questions regarding race, religion, political associations, etc., should be avoided. Rather, the questions should be phrased to elicit information that will enable the company to determine the applicant's job-related skills and experience, as well as the ability to perform the required work. This is usually accomplished by asking all applicants a standard series of questions and grading their responses. Some questions are open-ended and relate to job interest, as in: Why are you applying for the position of police officer? Other questions involve hypothetical situations, to gauge the applicant's demeanor, as in: How would you react if a citizen got in your face and began screaming racial slurs at you? Still other questions are more job-related and asked to gauge the applicant's ability to think quickly, as in: What actions would you take if, while responding to a medical emergency, you observe a robbery in progress?

Many police agencies have placed a great deal of emphasis on community policing and therefore have developed questions that make inquiry into the applicant's ability to work with all types of people, de-escalate violence, mediate disputes, and engage in problem-solving. Many resources currently exist that can be utilized when refining such interview questions. For example, the Community Oriented Policing Service in Washington, DC, has developed a problem-oriented guide that provides law enforcement agencies with problem-specific questions to assist in identifying potential factors and underlying causes of specific problems, known responses to each problem, and potential measures to assess the effectiveness of problem-solving efforts.[26]

TRAINING ORAL INTERVIEW PANELISTS[27]

The oral interview panel should be diverse in terms of gender and race and should include members of the local community. Sworn and civilian law enforcement employees may also be utilized as interviewers and should be thoroughly trained about the rules of the interview process. At a minimum, training should include:

- An overview of discrimination law and the concept of "adverse impact" as they apply to the oral interview process.
- A discussion of how bias can creep into ratings, even at a subconscious level and the need for consistently applied and objective evaluation criteria.
- A review of the job description for a law enforcement officer and the knowledge, skills, and abilities the interviewers should be looking for.
- Policing philosophy of the agency and the traits desired in a law enforcement officer.
- A review of the questions to be asked and the reasons for each question. Any follow-up questions permitted should be clearly delineated.
- Types of questions that should never be asked. Interviewers should never ask a question not on the interview form.
- Explanation of the rating system and how to assign a score or rating.
- Whether or not interviewers are allowed to discuss their ratings with other panel members.
- The fact that their ratings will be reviewed and evaluated for reliability and possible gender bias.

Assessment Centers

The use of assessment centers in police agencies continues to increase. The term "assessment center" refers not to a physical location but rather a process of evaluating individuals in an organization. According to the International Congress on the Assessment Center Method,

> An assessment center consists of a standardized evaluation of behavior based on multiple inputs. Multiple trained observers and techniques are used. Judgments about behavior are made, in major part, from specifically developed assessment simulations. These judgments are pooled in a meeting among the assessors or by a statistical integration process.[28]

Observing candidates' behavior in simulations of on-the-job challenges offers in-depth information concerning candidate strengths and weaknesses. In an assessment center, each candidate participates in a series of exercises that simulate actual situations from the target job. Expert assessors, providing information unattainable from written tests, interviews, or any other source, evaluate the performance of candidates.

All police leaders agree that new recruits should possess interpersonal skills, common sense, and good judgment. Although these things cannot be measured in a multiple choice, paper and pencil test, they are precisely what an assessment center is designed to measure. Another frequently stated advantage of the assessment center methodology is the nearly nonexistent adverse impact these assessments have with regard to minority candidates. Finally, assessment centers can give candidates excellent feedback on their own performance.

The biggest disadvantage of assessment centers is cost. Apart from the fees a consultant may charge to develop and administer assessments, there are assessor fees, costs associated with the location, supplies, video equipment (when exercises are videotaped), as well as role-player fees. Some departments have made arrangements with other agencies to provide assessors at no cost, thereby eliminating one of the most expensive components. In addition, many agencies use their own facilities to conduct the assessment center. The Fort Worth Police Department, for example, implemented an assessment center approach to evaluate police applicants' sensitivity to others, use of good judgment and common sense, leadership ability, and oral and written skills. This was accomplished by means of work-simulated exercises, group discussions, and individual oral interviews between assessors and applicant.[29]

One central principle for a successful assessment center is that all members of the assessment process must work as a team. The assessors should initially meet and review job descriptions and develop procedures to evaluate the candidates. Next, the assessors should meet with candidates to help them understand the assessment process. The next step is to have two or three assessors evaluate the candidates, reach a consensus on each score, and rank the candidates by converting the values into percentage ratings. Assessors should also develop a narrative report about the candidates. They should provide candidates an opportunity to talk to the assessors and to receive feedback.[30]

Questions in Review

1. Identify methods of recruitment and selection used in policing.
2. Why is knowledge of gender and cultural diversity important in policing?
3. What are the stages of the police selection process?
4. What has been the impact of Equal Employment Opportunity on police employment practices?

End Notes

1. Brian Reaves, *Local Police Departments, 2007*, NCJ 231174 (Washington, DC: Bureau of Justice Statistics, December 2010).
2. Max Downs, Francis Kessler, and Ronald Nelson, *Recruiting Qualified Police Applicants: Problems and Responses* (Police Executive Research Forum, 1987).
3. August Vollmer, *The Police and Modern Society* (Montclair, NJ: Patterson Smith Reprint Series in Criminology, Law Enforcement, and Social Problems, 1969).
4. I. B. Guller, "Higher Education and Police-Attitudinal Differences between Freshman and Senior Police College Students," in *Journal of Criminal Law, Criminology and Police Science*, Vol. 63, No. 3 (September 1972), pp. 396–401.
5. N. L. Weiner, "The Educated Policeman," in *Journal of Police Science and Administration*, Vol. 4 (1976), pp. 450–457.
6. S. M. Smith and M. G. Aamodt, "Relationship between Education, Experience, and Police Performance," in *Journal of Police and Criminal Psychology*, Vol. 12, No. 2 (Fall 1997), pp. 7–14.
7. Milton Mollen, *Commission Report to Investigate Allegations of Police Corruption and the Anti-Corruption Procedures of the Police Department* (City of New York, July 7, 1994).
8. R. E. Worden, "Badge and a Baccalaureate: Policies, Hypotheses, and Further Evidence," in *Justice Quarterly*, Vol. 7 (1990), No. 3, pp. 565–592.
9. Reaves.
10. Steven J. Bonafonte, *Informal Site Visitation of Community-Based Law Enforcement Agencies*, unpublished report (Washington, DC: Department of Justice, National Institute of Justice, April 1994).
11. Dorothy Moses Schulz, *From Social Worker To Crime Fighter: Women in United States Municipal Policing* (New York: Praeger Publishing, 1995).
12. L. J. Sherman, "A Psychological View of Women in Policing," in *Journal of Police Science and Administration*, Vol. 1 (1973), pp. 383–394.

13. Lynn Langton, *Women in Law Enforcement, 1987–2008* (Washington, DC: Bureau of Justice Statistics, June 2010).
14. *Recruiting and Retaining Women: A Self-Assessment Guide for Law Enforcement* (Washington, DC: Bureau of Justice Assistance, 2000). Available online: https://www.ncjrs.gov/pdffiles1/bja/185235.pdf
15. Bureau of Justice Assistance *Recruiting & Retaining Women: A Self-Assessment Guide for Law Enforcement.* (1999). Los Angeles, CA: National Center for Women & Policing.
16. Steve Walker, *Employment of Black and Hispanic Police Officers, 1983–1988: A Follow Up Study* (Omaha, NE: The University of Nebraska at Omaha, 1989).
17. Robert J. Kaminski, "Police Minority Recruitment: Predicting Who Will Say Yes to an Offer for a Job as a Cop," in *Journal of Criminal Justice*, Vol. 21, No. 4 (1993), pp. 395–409.
18. Linda S. Gottfredson, "Racially Gerrymandering the Content of Police Tests to Satisfy the U.S. Justice Department: A Case Study," in *Psychology, Public Policy, and Law*, Vol. 2, No. 3/4 (1996), pp. 419–446.
19. See Aguilera v. Cook County Police & Corrections Merit Board, 760 F.2d 844, 848 (7th Cir.), cert. denied, 474 U.S. 907 (1985). Briggs v. Anderson, 796 F.2d 1009, 1023 (8th Cir. 1986). Watson v. Fort Worth Bank & Trust, 487 U.S. 977 (1988).
20. GRIGGS v. DUKE POWER CO., 401 U.S. 424 (1971) 401 U.S. 424.
21. Recruitment information, Atlanta Police Department, 675 Ponce de Leon Avenue, N.E., Atlanta, GA 30308.
22. Dallas Police Recruiting Information Web site: http://www.dallascityhall.com/html/police.html
23. Paula N. Rubin, *The Americans with Disabilities Act and Criminal Justice: Hiring New Employees* (Washington, DC: Bureau of Justice Statistics, 1994).
24. J. Janik, "Why Psychological Screening of Police Candidates is Necessary: The History and Rationale," in *Journal of Police and Criminal Psychology*, Vol. 10, No. 2 (October 1994), pp. 18–23.
25. Reaves.
26. U.S. Department of Justice, Office of Community Oriented Policing Services (Washington, DC).
27. *Recruiting and Retaining Women*, pp. 15–21.
28. Guidelines and Ethical Considerations for Assessment Center Operations (May, 2000) Retrieved from http://www.assessmentcenters.org/pdf/00guidelines.pdf
29. L. T. Francis, "Assessment Center in Police Selection," in *Texas Police Journal*, Vol. 23, No. 4 (1975), pp. 4–7 and 13–16.
30. Thurston Cosner and Wayne C. Baumgart, "Effective Assessment Center Program: Essential Components," in *FBI Law Enforcement Bulletin*, Vol. 69, No. 6 (June, 2000), pp. 1–5.

Suggested Additional References and Links to the Web

1. *Recruitment, Hiring, and Retention Resources for Law Enforcement* (Washington, DC: U.S. Department of Justice, Community Oriented Policing Services). This link provides online resources for recruiting,

hiring, and retaining law enforcement officers: http://www.cops.usdoj.gov/files/ric/CDROMs/RecruitmentHiringRetention/index.htm.
2. *Police Recruitment and Retention Clearinghouse*, RAND Corporation: http://www.rand.org/ise/centers/quality_policing/cops/resources/tools.html.
3. The Civilian Complaint Review Board (NYC, NY), was created in 1995 as a permanent board to monitor and evaluate anti-corruption programs and efforts of the New York City Police Department: http://www.nyc.gov/html/ccrb/home.html.
4. Christopher Koper, Edward Maguire, and Gretchen Moore, "Hiring and Retention Issues in Police Agencies: Readings on the Determinants of Police Strength, Hiring and Retention of Officers, and the Federal COPS Program" (Urban Institute Justice Policy Center, 2002). This report presents a series of papers addressing a number of staffing issues in policing: determinants of police staffing levels, the processes of hiring and training officers, and retention patterns associated with individual officers and staff positions: https://www.ncjrs.gov/pdffiles1/nij/grants/193428.pdf.

Impact of the Courts and Legislation on Police Management

12

Key Individuals, Concepts, and Issues

Arbitration	Bona fide occupational qualification
Closed shop	Grievance
Collective bargaining	Wagner Act
Civil Rights Act	Title VII
Disparate treatment	Retaliation
Constructive discharge	Affirmative Action
Drug testing	Sexual harassment
Labor relations	Police union movement
Professionalism	

Definitions

Arbitration: Referring a decision to an individual or a panel to resolve a conflict between two or more parties.

Bona fide occupational qualification: A job qualification that is reasonably necessary to perform the job.

Civilianization: Refers to the practice of hiring citizens to perform certain tasks normally performed by certified police officers.

Civil Rights Act: An act designed to prohibit discrimination based on race, sex, color, national origin, or religion.

Closed shop: An agreement between the union and employer that prohibits the employer from hiring nonunion personnel.

Collective bargaining: The process whereby representatives of the employer bargain with representatives of the employees over salaries, benefits, working conditions, etc., with the goal of establishing a written contract between the parties.

Grievance: A formal complaint by an employee that the employer has misapplied or misinterpreted a rule or policy contained in the collective bargaining agreement.

National Labor Relations Board: The principal enforcement agency for laws regulating labor relations between employers and unions.

Sexual harassment: The unwanted sexual attention, advances, and or requests for sexual favors, whether verbal or physical, that affect an employee's job conditions or create a hostile working environment.

Union: A group that has been certified to bargain on behalf of a group of employees.

Wagner Act: The National Labor Relations Act of 1935 that established the National Labor Relations Board.

Chapter Objectives

After completing this chapter, you should be able to:

1. Explain the legal restrictions on police.
2. Discuss the rights of police officers to join unions.
3. Explain the concept of Bona fide occupational qualification.
4. Discuss the issue of sexual harassment.

> **Case Study 12.1**
>
> You are a police officer in a small town. The local city council has voted not to give the police a pay raise for the second straight year. There is talk of a strike or sick-out by the police.
>
> Would you go on a strike? A sick-out? Should police be allowed to strike? If you are aware that a fellow police officer is participating in a sick-out as an illegal form of job action, would you report him or her?

Introduction

It is an unlawful practice for an employer, including a police department, to fail or refuse to hire or to discharge a person or to discriminate against any individual with respect to the terms of employment because of such person's race, color, religion, sex, or national origin (protected classes). It is not unlawful to distinguish between employees based on a bona fide seniority or merit system. In addition, employees can be paid differently based on measures of quality or quantity of production, professionally developed tests, or because the employees work in different locations, if the differences are not caused by an intent to discriminate against a protected class.

Suits against a law enforcement agency for unlawful employment practices may be brought either in state or federal court in the court district where the unlawful practice occurred, where the officer or employee would have worked except for the unlawful act, where the administrative records of the agency are kept, or if no other place, within the court district of the agency's headquarters. A disparate violation is where the employee is treated less favorably than his or her peers because of race, sex, etc. Retaliation, like disparate treatment situations, is based on intentional discrimination. In the constructive discharge cases, the individuals claim that their employers intentionally made their working conditions so intolerable that they were forced to quit or resign. Disparate impact claims are those that involve a facially neutral test, requirement, or practice that affects a protected group more than others and cannot be justified by business necessity. Title VII, in prohibiting religious discrimination, defined religion as including all aspects of religious observance and practice, as well as belief.

One key characteristic of police labor relations is the fragmentation of managerial decision making. Often, it is difficult to conceptualize who is the employer (i.e., the mayor, the city counsel, the people). In those cities with strong city council type government, labor relations is a legislative function. In those cities with strong mayor or city manager type governments, labor relations tends to be an executive function. To understand the present state of police labor relations, we need first to examine the police labor movement that started in the 1900s with the evolution of "police associations" and later legitimate police unions. In many aspects, the relationship between the individual police officer and police management is similar to the relationship between an employee and employer in the public and private sector. There are, however, several areas where the employment relationship that exists within law enforcement agencies is unique to law enforcement.

The present trend in police departments is toward increased union representation and more involvement by unions in the labor management process. Most states now have a "Police Officers' Bill of Rights" or similar statutes that provide that police unions as representatives of the police officers have the right to meet and confer with management regarding working conditions and pay. The statutes in most states guarantee to the police employees the right of collective bargaining.

Police union movements grew out of the same problems experienced by other employees (i.e., long hours, low pay, lack of job security, etc.) Police employees did not, however, have the right to strike. By the 1960s, most urban police officers were members of an employee association. Many of these associations were affiliated with national groups such as the AFL-CIO, the International Conference of Police Associations, and the Fraternal Order of Police. It is estimated that approximately ten thousand police officers are affiliated with the Teamsters Union. Starting in the 1960s, police officers demonstrated an open willingness to engage in the use of militant tactics to obtain better working conditions and higher economic benefits.

One by-product of unionization has been the realization by management that human resources (police officers) are scarce commodities and that there is not an unlimited supply of personnel to replace officers who leave the department because of pay and working conditions. A study by Douglas

Yearwood[1] indicated that approximately 10% of police officer positions are vacant at any one time. Although it would be difficult to measure the exact impact of unions on police working conditions and pay, most researchers agree that police unions/associations have resulted in higher pay and better working conditions for the average police officer.

Collective bargaining between police officers and cities or counties is governed by policies, statutes, executive orders, and ordinances. The states with the most favorable status for police officers in collective bargaining include the states in the Northeast and on the West Coast. The states with the least favorable bargaining status are generally those located in the Sun Belt and the Rocky Mountains. Thirty-eight states and the District of Columbia have either statutes or executive orders that permit collective bargaining by the police. In most of the other states, de facto bargaining exists. Most states have statutory limitations on the scope of collective bargaining by public employees, including police officers.

Employment Discrimination

Title VII of the Civil Rights Act of 1964, as amended, prohibits employment discrimination based on race, color, religion, sex, and national origin. Prior to 1972, the act applied only to private employers. The Equal Employment Opportunity Act of 1972, however, amended Title VII to expand its coverage to employees of state and local governments, as well as to employees of the federal government. Accordingly, since 1972, the act prohibits employment discrimination by law enforcement agencies.

Scope of the Act

Title VII makes it an unlawful practice for an employer, including a police department, to fail or refuse to hire or to discharge a person or to discriminate against any individual with respect to the terms of employment including compensation, conditions of employment, or privileges of employment because of such person's race, color, religion, sex, or national origin (protected classes).[2] It is also an unlawful practice to limit, segregate, or classify an employee or applicant because of those factors.

In 1978, the act was amended to make it clear that basis of sex includes discrimination on the basis of pregnancy or childbirth. Basis of sex, however, refers to gender, not sexual activity. Sexual activity is controlled under other statutes.

It is not unlawful to distinguish between employees based on a bona fide seniority or merit system. In addition, employees can be paid differently based on measures of quality or quantity of production, professionally developed tests or because the employees work in different locations, if the differences are not caused by an intent to discriminate against a protected class. For example, it is permissible to pay officers who work in one section of the community higher pay than other officers if there is a logical reason (e.g., degree of danger involved). It would be an unlawful employment practice, however, to provide pay incentives to those officers assigned to a SWAT team and then not allow females the opportunity to be assigned to the team.

Title VII Suits

Suits against a law enforcement agency for unlawful employment practices may be brought either in state or federal court in the court district where the unlawful practice occurred, where the officer or employee would have worked except for the unlawful act, where the administrative records of the agency are kept, or if no other place, within the court district of the agency's headquarters.

Only a person who has been the object of discrimination may bring a Title VII suit. In cases involving nonpublic employees, the Equal Employment Opportunity Commission (EEOC) may bring suit on behalf of an individual or as a representative of a class. The EEOC cannot sue a state government or political subdivision thereof. In the latter cases, only the individual aggrieved or the attorney general of the United States may bring suit under Title VII. Note that in many states the state's attorney general may also bring an employment discrimination suit under a state act.

Types of Violations under Title VII

Prohibited practices under Title VII generally fall into one of three classes: disparate treatment, retaliation, and disparate impact. Each of these are discussed in this section. In addition, religious discrimination and affirmative actions programs are also addressed.

Disparate Treatment

A disparate violation is where the employee is treated less favorably than his or her peers because of race, sex, etc. For example, there would be illegal disparate treatment if during a layoff of police personnel, the criteria used to select the officers to be laid-off was based on race or another protected classification. Disparate treatment requires an intent to discriminate. Intent has been inferred, however, in cases involving subconscious sex stereotyping. For example, disparate treatment was found in one case where a female was not promoted because she did not dress "like a woman should."[3] One form of disparate treatment is the "pattern and practice" form, where a department has systematically engaged in disparate treatment of a specific race, sex, etc. In these situations, the disparate treatment is a standard operating practice.

Retaliation

Retaliation, like disparate treatment situations, is based on intentional discrimination. In this case, the complaining individual alleges that he or she engaged in a statutorily protected activity and as the result suffered an adverse employment action. The adverse employment action must be made with a retaliatory motive. The retaliatory motive, however, does not need to be the sole cause of the adverse employment action. For example, if a marginal police officer was fired because the officer attempted to organize a police union within the department, the officer is the victim of an unlawful retaliation. Note that one court allowed a former police officer to sue a police department because he was given an adverse employment reference. The court found that the adverse reference was primarily based on the fact that the officer was actively involved in union activities while a member of the police department.

Constructive Discharge

In the constructive discharge cases, the individuals claim that their employers intentionally made their working conditions so intolerable that they were forced to quit or resign. Several cases have held that to constitute a constructive discharge, there must be a denial of an individual's reasonable expectation for working conditions, benefits, or future promotions.

Disparate Impact

Disparate impact claims are those that involve a facially neutral test, requirement, or practice that affects a protected group more than others and cannot be justified by business necessity. Note that the discrimination in these situations may be unintentional. For example, if a police department required all cadet applicants to be capable of lifting two hundred and fifty pounds, the lifting requirement may unfairly eliminate more females than males. Accordingly, the lifting requirement would be subject to disparate impact claims unless the department can establish that it is a bona fide job requirement.

Religious Discrimination

Title VII, in prohibiting religious discrimination, defined religion as:

> The term "religion" includes all aspects of religious observance and practice, as well as belief, unless an employer demonstrates that he is unable to reasonably accommodate to an employee's or prospective employee's religious observance or practice without undue hardship on the conduct of the employer's business.[4]

> The movie *Chariots of Fire* concerned a track star who refused, because of religious beliefs, to compete in a race on Sunday. Accommodations were made for this athlete. If a police officer has religious problems regarding working on Wednesdays, is the police department required to make accommodations for him or her? Would it matter if the police officer was a ten-year veteran or only an applicant for employment?

The U.S. Supreme Court has held that Title VII requires an employer to make only those accommodations to an employee's religious belief or practices that do not impose more than a de minimis cost to the employer.[5]

Affirmative Action Programs

Affirmative action programs are programs that are designed to give minorities a preference based on the concept that affirmative action is needed to remedy the continuing effects of past discriminatory practices. There are possible legal problems with affirmative action programs that discriminate in favor of minorities. Any time that one protected class is given preference over another, a police department is taking a chance. The present trend by police departments is to obtain court approval before establishing affirmative action programs.

Drug Testing of Police Officers

The widespread use of illegal drugs is apparent in every segment of American life, including police employees. Because police work can be stressful and traumatic, it is no surprise that a few officers may use drugs as a means of coping. Accordingly, illegal drug use by police officers is a concern of every police chief. Approximately 73% of police departments conduct drug screening of applicants. In addition, most departments have written policies and procedures for conducting drug screening tests when there are reasons to suspect that an officer has been using illegal drugs.

> **MODEL DRUG TESTING POLICY (INTERNATIONAL ASSOCIATION OF CHIEFS OF POLICE)**
>
> The International Association of Chiefs of Police has developed a model drug testing policy. The policy recommends:
>
> - The testing of all applicants for drugs and narcotics use

- Testing present employees who are having performance difficulties or other indications of a potential drug problem
- Testing employees when involved in the use of excessive force or who suffer or cause on-duty injury
- Routine testing of all employees assigned to "high-risk" assignments such as narcotics and vice[6]

One issue regarding drug tests is whether the establishment of a drug testing program is a change in working conditions and therefore subject to collective bargaining. The union concerns in this area include:

- The standards for drug concentration levels present in the urine
- The confidentiality of results
- Procedural safeguards

When an officer tests positive and further investigation determines that the officer is a drug abuser, the question then is should the officer be treated for the abuse problem, fired, or both. If the police keep a known drug abuser as a police officer, there is a potential for civil liability if the officer is involved in misconduct or an accident. If the drug use is caused, however, by job stress, is it fair to fire the officer? The present trend in handling this situation appears to be that taken by the city of Boston. In that city, assistance programs are available for officers who have problems with drugs. Employees who voluntarily enter the program are provided confidential counseling, and their participation in the program is also confidential. If the officers do not voluntarily seek assistance, they may be fired. Other cities have similar programs. For example, the city of New York has a drug awareness program and a drug awareness workshop included in their training programs. The police employees' association in Philadelphia (Fraternal Order of Police) has produced a videotape program that encourages officers with drug or alcohol problems to seek professional help. In addition, the association provides limited counseling in this area.

Should the police hire individuals who have used drugs in the past? There appears to be no uniform treatment by departments regarding the handling of applicants who either admit or are discovered to have used drugs. Almost all departments screen out individuals who have had serious past drug incidents. Individuals who have only experimented with drugs are screened out in some jurisdictions and not in others. The trend appears to be against automatic exclusion of applicants who have only experimented with drugs. Most departments who accept applicants with a history of drug incidents conduct more in-depth background investigations on those applicants than they do on other applicants. In addition, even the experimental use of drugs is considered as a negative factor in evaluating a person's application.

Sexual Harassment

Another form of employment discrimination that has received a lot of publicity lately is sexual harassment. Sexual harassment is a form of sex discrimination that violates Title VII of the Civil Rights Act of 1964. Sexual harassment can occur in a variety of circumstances. Listed below are some of the key points that the EEOC list regarding sexual harassment:

- The victim as well as the harasser may be a woman or a man. The victim does not have to be of the opposite sex.
- The harasser can be the victim's supervisor, an agent of the employer, a supervisor in another area, a co-worker, or a nonemployee.
- The victim does not have to be the person harassed but could be anyone affected by the offensive conduct.
- Unlawful sexual harassment may occur without economic injury to or discharge of the victim.
- To be harassment, the harasser's conduct must be unwelcome.

Sexual harassment has been a constant area of concern for employers.

THE REASONABLE WOMAN

In one case, the U.S. Court of Appeals for the Ninth Circuit held that in order to evaluate whether a female employee has been sexually harassed, the proper legal standard to use is that of the "reasonable woman." Accordingly, the courts should view the challenged conduct through the eyes of a "reasonable woman." The court stated that using the gender-neutral standard of a "reasonable person" tends to be male-biased and tends to systematically ignore the experiences of women. The court also ruled that in order to avoid liability, employers must take strong and effective steps to remedy sexual harassment in the workplace, even if that involves permanently removing the harasser. [*Ellison v. Brady*]

The newspaper columnist Art Buchwald, in one of his sarcastic columns, advised job applicants to specify whether or not they wanted to be sexually harassed on the job and by whom. This is not a joking matter, because studies indicate that about 50% of all female employees have at one time or another been sexually harassed on the job. The courts often hold employers liable for allowing or permitting sexual harassment.

In cases of sexual harassment by management or supervisory personnel, the employer is normally accountable under the theory that the employer has placed the supervisor or manager in the position of authority. The employer should have a standing policy putting employees on notice that sexual harassment will not be tolerated by any employee.

In one case, a female employee failed to get promoted because the employee who was promoted was willing to have a sexual affair with the supervisor. A Delaware federal court judge held this to be a form of unlawful sex bias and, indirectly, sexual harassment. This case points out that the sexual harassment guidelines are broadly interpreted by the courts. The employer should establish procedures whereby employees who feel that they are being sexually harassed by managerial employees may report the matter to a manager at a higher level without fear of reprisal.

BUNDY V. JACKSON (U.S. COURT OF APPEALS, D.C. CIRCUIT)

Sandra Bundy was employed by the District of Columbia Department of Corrections. She contended that she received and rejected sexual propositions from a fellow employee who later became her supervisor. In addition, she claimed that she received sexual propositions from other supervisors. When she was not recommended for promotion, she complained to the EEOC and later filed her claim in court.

The Court of Appeals held:

- Sexual harassment includes psychological work conditions as well as physical abuse.
- The employer is accountable for the acts of managers and supervisors.
- The employer should have established specific procedures to help prevent sexual harassment.

Labor Relations

One key characteristic of police labor relations is the fragmentation of managerial decision making. Often, it is difficult to conceptualize who is the employer (i.e., the mayor, the city counsel, the people). In those cities with strong city council type government, labor relations is a legislative function. In those cities with strong mayor or city manager type governments, labor relations tends to be an executive function.

To understand the present state of police labor relations, we need first to examine the police labor movement that started in the 1900s with the evolution of "police associations" and later legitimate police unions. In many aspects, the relationship between the individual police officer and police management is similar to the relationship between an employee and employer in the public and private sector. For example, police officers, like other employees, have a need to be involved in determining their conditions of employment. In addition, as with most unionized employees, the major power bases or spokespersons for officers are the unions. Another similarity shared by private and police officer negotiations is that the collective bargaining settlement will often be influenced by the personalities of the negotiators and their negotiating abilities.[6]

> **MANAGEMENT: LABOR'S MOST EFFECTIVE ORGANIZER, BY WALT H. SIRENE**
>
> Employee organizations are made, not born. Rarely does the seed of organized labor sprout in a well-managed organization which has as one of its major objectives the welfare of its employees.... The question is posed, "How can this occur?" [referring to the Teamsters bid to organize law enforcement]. Can we learn from the history of law enforcement labor relations or must we repeat the mistakes which have been made from city to city ... since the Boston police walkout in 1919? How many times must city officials and police managers be reminded that bad faith bargaining with local, independent police associations will lead to the introduction of organized labor unions...?[8]

There are, however, several areas where the employment relationship that exists within the law enforcement agencies is unique to law enforcement. The differences include:

- Police unionism is primarily a local phenomena. National organizations do not play a major role in local police labor relations.
- Police unions, unlike other labor unions, generally do not advocate actions that support strikes of other unions. Police tend to cross picket lines of other unions.
- The collective bargaining arena for police unions is local political units.
- Normally, collective bargaining in the private sector involves two parties: the employer and the union representatives. In police collective bargaining, however, the management is often fragmented by the lack of a single employer who can approve or ratify agreements.
- In private collective bargaining, the parties must normally bargain within the constraints of fixed economic market conditions. Failure to remain within those constraints can result in employers being

priced out of the market, and thus the employees lose their jobs. In police collective bargaining, although the parties are not constrained by fixed market conditions, they are competing with other functions of the city government for scarce tax monies.
- Police economic benefits is often a political issue. Accordingly, it is not unusual for police unions to be actively involved in local political elections by lobbying and other political activities. For example, in some cases, special tax proposals are placed on the ballot as a method to support increased compensation for police officers.

The present trend in police labor relations is toward increased union representation and more involvement by unions in the labor management process. Most states now have a "Police Officers' Bill of Rights" or similar statutes that provide that police unions as representatives of the police officers have the right to meet and confer with management regarding working conditions and pay. The statutes in most states guarantee to the police employees the right to organize, and many guarantee the right of collective bargaining. The typical state statute provides that officers have the following rights:

1. To join or refrain from joining employee organizations
2. To bargain in good faith on issues affecting working conditions, wages, and benefits
3. For mediation when the union and management cannot agree on certain issues

The Police Union Movement

Police union movements grew out of the same problems as those experienced by other employees (i.e., long hours, low pay, lack of job security, etc.). Police employees did not, however, have the right to strike. It was not until recent years that other public employees gained the right to strike in most states. In general, police are usually prohibited from striking or taking part in related job actions.

REFLECTIONS OF A RETIRED POLICE OFFICER

One retired police executive related the working conditions for police officers and the attitudes of police administrators during the 1940s and 1950s as follows:

> In the 1940s, whether you retained your job and or received a promotion depended on politics and who you knew. It helped to be a

> friend of the mayor or one of the city council members. Even job assignments depended on politics. In the 1950s, with the many veterans returning from the military services, there was an ample supply of qualified persons to recruit from. Police officers, to keep their jobs, were often required to work over 48 hours per week with no pay for over-time, to be on call during off-duty hours, to buy their own equipment, and had little job security. Many police departments had the attitude that if you did not like the job, you could quit.
>
> Hervey A. Juris and Peter Feuille, (1973) Police unionism: power and impact in public-sector bargaining. Lexington, MA: Lexington Books, p. 9.

After World War I, police organizations in many cities affiliated with the organized labor movement. The notoriety of the 1919 Boston Police Strike ended for several decades, however, most attempts at affiliation with organized labor. The strike had a chilling effect on labor's efforts to organize the police.[9] Despite the notoriety of the strike, police officers continued to form local associations.

By the 1960s, most urban police officers were members of an employee association. Many of these associations were affiliated with national groups such as the AFL-CIO, the International Conference of Police Associations, and the Fraternal Order of Police. The largest police employee association is the Fraternal Order of Police with approximately two hundred thousand members. The first police group to affiliate with a private sector labor union was the International Union of Police Associations (IUPA). The IUPA, with approximately forty thousand members, is affiliated with the AFL-CIO. It is estimated that approximately ten thousand police officers are affiliated with the Teamsters Union.[10]

Several factors that encouraged police officers to join employee associations included:

- Police dissatisfaction with the increased public hostility toward police that became prevalent in the 1960s
- The court decisions that decreased the discretion of police officers
- The growth of civilian complaint boards to review police officer conduct
- Increased perception of danger to the officers while the economic rewards did not increase commensurately
- The dissatisfaction with personnel practices within many departments that provided no grievance procedures, no overtime pay, and no pay for attending court during off-duty periods
- Poor management by some law enforcement administrators

Starting in the 1960s, police officers demonstrated an open willingness to engage in the use of militant tactics to obtain better working conditions and higher economic benefits. In addition to the above listed factors, three other factors contributed to the emergence of police militancy. Those factors are as follows:

- The confrontation tactics of the civil rights groups, students, and other organized groups demonstrated to the police the advantages of using confrontation tactics. The police had observed, firsthand, the success of those groups in using confrontation tactics.
- The urban police associations had a higher proportion of young officers who appeared to be more willing to engage in overt actions to obtain their goals.
- The high degree of occupational cohesion among police officers contributed to their propensity to be more aggressive in the pursuit of group goals.

Impact of Unionization on Professionalism

Does the unionization of police have a negative impact on the movement toward greater professionalism? The term "profession" is an abstract ideal occupational model.[11] To be considered as a professional is an ideal status that most occupational groups, including the police, strive toward. The concept of striving toward "professionalism" refers to: (1) the extent to which the focus of specialization is occupational as opposed to individual or organizational; (2) the extent to which the occupation stresses the process by which the ends are achieved as well as the final ends themselves; and (3) the extent to which there is a body of codified knowledge that can be transmitted abstractly.[12] The status of professionalism includes autonomy, professional authority, and the power to determine the character and curriculum of the education process. For example, many consider a professional police department as one in which management efficiency and rationality are emphasized, and politics are excluded.

> Does the presence of a union prevent the movement of a police department toward professionalism? Often, unions are considered by the public as "blue collar" activity.

Unionization has been blamed for causing conflicts between police officers and managerial personnel that hamper the movement toward professionalism. The quotation below expresses commonly held thoughts on the dilemma involving police unions and the movement toward police professionalism:

> The power of union organization could replace the appeal of increased education as a means to improve the lot of the rank and file. A socially dangerous isolation of rank-and-file officers could be the result of their seeking refuge in politically active unions. An occupational group which exercises the legal power of physical coercion, even to the point of decisions about the life and death of citizens, must not be forced into alienation, either from the public they are supposed to protect and serve, or from those officially responsible for their supervision and control.[13]

Impact of Unions on Pay and Working Conditions

One by-product of unionization has been the realization by management that human resources (police officers) are scarce commodities; there is not an unlimited supply of personnel to replace officers who leave the department because of pay and working conditions. Some of the improvements that unions take credit for include: paid lunch time, paid roll call time, premium pay for court time during off-duty periods, and increased employee benefits.

Police unions have been unsuccessful in most cities in preventing one-officer police cars and the use of seniority in making job and shift assignments. Unions have apparently contributed toward the movement for increased individual safeguards in police discipline cases.

EDUCATION REQUIREMENTS FOR PROMOTION

One year, New York City Police Department management announced that officers seeking promotion would be required to have at least two years of college level course work. Approximately eighteen thousand police officers planning to take the sergeant's exam would be affected by this new requirement. The Patrolmen's Benevolent Association obtained a court order requiring the city to show cause why the new policy should be implemented. The union contended:

1. That the need for the new requirement should have been negotiated with the association prior to a decision being made as to its necessity.
2. That there was no rational relationship between a college education and the ability to be an effective police sergeant.[14]

Collective Bargaining

Collective bargaining between police officers and cities or counties is governed by policies, statutes, executive orders, and ordinances. The states with the most favorable status for police officers in collective bargaining include the states in the Northeast and on the West Coast. The states with the least favorable bargaining status are generally those located in the Sun Belt and the Rocky Mountains. Thirty-eight states and the District of Columbia have either statutes or executive orders that permit some form of collective bargaining by the police. In most of the other states, de facto bargaining exists. Most states have statutory limitations on the scope of collective bargaining by public employees, including police officers. The general statutory limitations involve management rights discussed in a later section.

In most jurisdictions, police officers' associations may bargain on behalf of their members over wages, hours, terms of employment, and working conditions. Several recent court decisions have allowed the police to bargain about safety problems. For example, the Washington, D.C., police union was allowed to bargain over (1) better marksmanship training and (2) deadlier, "all-lead semi-wadcutter" bullets.[15] Thirty-five states have legislation defining unfair labor practices by public employees and their bargaining representatives.

JOB ACTIONS

The National Advisory Commission of Criminal Justice Standards and Goals includes the following police standards. Every police executive should immediately prepare his agency to react effectively to neutralize any concerted work stoppage or job action by police employees. Any such concerted police employee action should be prohibited by law.

1. Every state...should enact legislation that specifically prohibits police employees from participating in any concerted work stoppage or job action.
2. Every police agency should establish a formal written policy prohibiting police employees from engaging in any concerted work stoppage or job action.
3. Every police agency should develop a plan to maintain emergency police service in the event of a concerted employee work stoppage.
4. Every police agency and all police employees should be allowed ... to engage in collective negotiations in arriving at terms and conditions of employment that will maintain police service effectiveness and insure equitable representative of both parties.[16]

Police Strikes

Although police officers have constitutional rights of free speech and freedom of association, the U.S. Supreme Court has upheld restrictions on the rights of public employees, including police officers, to strike. Laws prohibiting police strikes have not prevented them. Thirteen states have affirmatively sanctioned strikes by pubic employees but have excluded police officers. Eight states statutorily prohibit strikes by any public employee. The justification for prohibiting police strikes normally is based on the concept that police services are necessary for the health and safety of the community. A state supreme court in upholding the right of public employees to strike stated that strikes by public sector employees are not illegal under common law; a public employee's right to strike is not unlimited. The legislatures may, however, prohibit strikes by certain public employees if their striking would invariably result in imminent danger to the public health and safety.[17] Several labor relations experts contend that anti-strike laws make no difference at all.[18] In many situations, in lieu of striking, the officers call in sick with "blue flu."

> **POLICE PROTECTION**
>
> In one city, a police strike resulted in no increase in the area's crime rate. One theory to explain this lack of increased crime is that the criminals fear irate citizens more than they fear the police. One veteran police officer remarked, "Hoods have no rights without police protection. Shop owners will use their shotguns."[19]
>
> During one confrontation between the police union and the city, rather than strike, the New York City Police planned to distribute pamphlets at city airports, railroad stations, and bus terminals featuring a human skull in a shroud with the caption "Welcome to Fear City." A New York court, however, issued a restraining order holding that the distribution of the pamphlets endangered the lives of citizens and threatened the economic well-being of the city.

In some states, to offset the prohibition against police strikes, procedures have been established to handle those situations where collective bargaining fails and an impasse occurs. A common solution is the use of binding arbitration to resolve impasses. In binding arbitration, both sides are required to accept the decision of the arbitration panel. Binding arbitration has been a mixed blessing for some cities. On one hand, it reduces the chance of a police strike. On the other hand, often if parties know that any impasse will be referred to arbitration, they may be less likely to bargain in good faith.

Management Rights

The union and management normally bargain over pay and working conditions. Certain items are traditionally considered by management as management prerogatives and therefore not subject to negotiation. Although management prerogatives vary, the most common ones include:

- The right to determine the mission of the department
- Setting the procedures and standards for promotions
- Maintaining the efficiency of the department
- Directing employees
- Determining job classifications

Memoranda of Understanding

In most police departments, agreements between labor and management have been developed into formal documents called "Memoranda of Understanding." The memoranda is a written agreement agreed to by both management and union as a statement of understanding of the agreements reached at the bargaining table between management and police employees. The standard memoranda is for a duration of one to three years. It is very similar to agreements entered into between private sector employers and their employees.

Normally after an agreement is reached between the union and management negotiators, the agreement must then be ratified by union members and approved by management. Union ratification is usually by secret written ballot. Approval by management requires that the mayor, city manager, and/or the city council approve the agreement. If an agreement is not ratified by union members or is disapproved by management, the negotiators usually go back to the bargaining table to attempt to work out a new agreement that is acceptable to both sides.

FORCED ARBITRATION: ONE CITY'S EXPERIENCE

Oakland, CA was faced with a budget deficit. The city council ordered all city departments to submit budgets designed to reduce city services by 15%. For the fire department, this meant the loss of thirty-six sworn positions. The union protested and took the issue to forced arbitration. The city's planned budget reductions were overruled, and the additional problems noted below were encountered:

- The prior bargaining between the city and the employee associations was negated. All issues, including those agreements that were tentatively settled, were decided again.

- Under its charter, Oakland was required to grant all city employees a 5.88% raise. The arbitrator gave the firefighters an additional 3% hike. This additional raise upset the city pay schedules and came at a time when the city was preparing for negotiations with the police officers association and put the firefighters' salaries ahead of the police officers'.
- Although manning requirements had been a prerogative of management, and the issue had not been raised during contract negotiations, the arbitrator changed the manning conditions to make the city the only one in the state mandated to maintain five-man crews.
- The arbitrator also reduced the firefighters' workweek by four hours. The city estimated that the award cost the city over $4 million additional cost per year during a period of time that the city was involved in fiscal problems.

Off-Duty Employment of Police Officers

In recent years, there has been a substantial growth in off-duty employment of police officers. For example, it was estimated that 47% of the Seattle police officers and 53% nonsworn personnel had off-duty work permits to allow them to work off-duty in uniform.[20] The off-duty employment of officers causes significant concerns by police management. The three most common concerns are listed below:

Conflicts of interest between the official duties of the police officer and those of his off-duty employer:

- Risk of city/departmental civil liability for the actions of the off-duty officer
- Risk of injury that would prevent the officer from assuming regular duties
- Threats to the dignity and status of the department

Conflicts of Interests

Any time a police officer is involved in off-duty employment, there is a risk that his or her authority as a police officer may be used to serve the best interests of the private employer at the expense of the public. For this reason, most departments restrict officers from working as bill collectors, process servers, pre-employment investigators, bail bondsman, or employment with a company affected by a strike or labor problem. A second type of restriction on off-duty employment based on conflict of interest involves locations or establishments. For example, police are normally restricted from employment in gambling establishments and bars. In addition, most departments prohibit police from working in businesses that directly compete with the police such as private security agencies.

Other Limitations

Other general limitations normally placed on off-duty employment include limits on the number of hours of off-duty hours that can be worked, on the amounts of compensation that can be earned, and risks that an officer may take during off-duty employment. In addition, work that is demeaning or affects the dignity of the department is also banned. In some departments, the off-duty employer must provide disability insurance for the officer during off-duty employment to ensure that the public will not be required to pay any compensation for injuries suffered during off-duty employment.

Models for Off-Duty Employment

There are three general models that police departments follow regarding approved off-duty employment: the officer contract model, the union brokerage model, and the department contract model.

In the officer contract model, the individual officer finds his own employment position. The officer independently contracts with the off-duty employer regarding conditions of employment and pay. The officer then applies for departmental approval. This model is used in Atlanta, Charlotte, Cincinnati, and Minneapolis.

The union brokerage model involves those cases where the union or association finds paid details for its members. The union then assigns officers who have volunteered to these details. The union establishes standards for working conditions and pay. The union then bargains with the department over status and conditions of employment. This model is used in Seattle.

Under the departmental contract model, the department contracts with employers regarding paid details. The department then assigns officers who have volunteered to the details. The department negotiates with the union regarding pay and working conditions and then sets off-duty employment standards. In many departments, there is an off-duty employment coordinator who receives requests for police details, issues off-duty permits, and assigns officers to the details. This model is used in Boston, Colorado Springs, and St. Petersburg.

Police Response to Special Populations

In this section, we will examine police response to problems relating to special populations (e.g., mentally ill, public drunks, and the homeless). Police are increasingly requested by the public to handle cases involving people who are mentally ill, drunk in public, and/or homeless. For example, in one study it was estimated that 8% of all police-citizen encounters in one urban police department involved dealing with mentally ill people.[21] In many of those cases, the police officers found themselves saddled with the sole responsibility for mentally ill persons whose public conduct indicated some form of social intervention.

Police are often called to remove homeless people from the streets and local parks. Often these people are a danger to themselves, particularly in cold weather. Like with the mentally ill, there are only limited options for dealing with the homeless. A similar problem involves the public inebriate (drunk). Jail is an inappropriate place to take either the homeless or the inebriate, and there are few other alternatives.

Most researchers will agree that handling the mentally ill, public inebriate, and homeless is not a problem that the police are well equipped to handle. The police, however, are repeatedly called by the public because they provide free around-the-clock service and have a legal obligation to respond to requests for assistance. The helplessness of the situation and the unpleasant nature tends to add additional stress on the individual police officers.

POLICE DUTY TO RENDER ASSISTANCE

There is much concern by police officers regarding dealing with the potential threat of AIDS. As a police officer, can you ethically refuse to help a person with an infectious disease? A New York Police Department manual states: "Police officers have a professional responsibility to render assistance to those who are in need of our services. We cannot refuse to help. Persons with infectious diseases must be treated with the care and dignity we show all citizens."

Questions in Review

1. As chief of police of a small police department, you discover that one of your officers is a drug abuser. Your department is too small to have available professional counseling. What are your options? Would you treat the drug abuser any different from an officer with an alcohol problem?
2. You are a police officer on a patrol assignment. The manager of a local store complains to you regarding two public inebriates who are sitting on a public bench across the street from the store. The merchant complains that the individuals are accosting passers by for "spare

change." How would you handle this situation? Would it make any difference to you if the two individuals are not violating any laws?
3. Jack Ryan, a twenty-one-year veteran FBI agent, informed the FBI that because of religions beliefs, he could no longer carry a firearm. He was then fired. He files suit against the FBI alleging that he was fired because of his religious beliefs. If Ryan was a veteran police officer in your department, how would you handle the situation? [Presently, Ryan is spending his time at a homeless shelter where he lives, ladles soup, and helps jobless people find work.]

Biggest Mistakes Police Leadership Makes and How to Avoid Them

Do Police Officers Accused of Sex Offenses Get Only Slaps on the Wrist?

Yes, reports Nicole Egan in her February 2004 report.[22] It was alleged that a state police major named the breasts of two female employees "Vanilla" and "Strawberry" and groped them whenever he got the chance. He forced a third to submit to oral sex in his locked office and raped her in her home, according to released state police records. Despite the offenses, the commissioner let him use vacation time instead of a forty-five-day suspension without pay so he could retire with full benefits. He was later sentenced to probation and fined for indecent assault.

When one major's girlfriend, a civilian state police employee, broke off their affair, he stalked her and tried to run her off the road, according to state police investigators. He tormented the woman and her co-workers with harassing hang-up phone calls for months. He was neither prosecuted nor suspended from his job. His bosses allowed him to retire with full benefits.

It was reported that another major often groped his secretary's breasts, buttocks, and thighs at work, according to state police records. As head of the state police Bureau of Professional Responsibility, he was in charge of investigating misconduct allegations like the ones eventually lodged against him. Although the charges against him were upheld by internal investigators, his secretary wouldn't press criminal charges. He later retired with full benefits. It was also alleged that for years, the majors' behavior and the lack of consequences they faced were the department's dirty little secrets. The details only became public because of a federal lawsuit against the agency by victims of an ex-trooper who is serving a prison term for sex crimes.

Each of the state police force's seventeen majors oversee a region of Pennsylvania or an administrative bureaucracy. They rank just below deputy commissioner in the 6,100 member force and are among the most powerful commanders in the agency. That top cops preyed on their female civilian employees on and off the job, committing sordid offenses, and faced little or no consequence shows a deep state police culture of tolerating sexual misconduct, experts said. "The discipline for the majors was much too light and sends a message all the way down the ranks," said Samuel Walker, one of the nation's leading experts on police corruption.

Egan stated that the wrist-slap state police response to the trio has shocked law enforcement experts and mocks the State Police Commissioner's claim that every sexual misconduct complaint against state troopers from 1995 through 2001 was properly handled. Without specifically mentioning the cited cases, the commissioner stated that he had reviewed all one hundred and sixty-three cases of state police sexual misconduct unearthed in personnel files between 1995 and 2001 and that all of the cases were properly handled. A spokesperson for the state police stated that there was nothing the department can do to prevent an employee from resigning before being dismissed.

An attorney for one of the victims noted that "What is apparent from all these misconduct cases is that the police are not properly policing themselves. If this were an average citizen, he'd be prosecuted and he'd be going to jail." The attorney stated that it was outrageous that state law allows those convicted of sexual assault to collect a full pension and retire rather than be fired. "If there's loopholes [sic], they need to implement legislation to close them," he said.

The governor, after the report was printed, appointed an international security company to monitor whether the state police adopt forty scandal cleanup suggestions made by the state inspector general. It appears that reforms in the Pennsylvania State Police will prevent a reoccurrence of this magnitude. An active anti-sexual harassment program probably would have prevented many of the abuses reported with the state police.

End Notes

1 Douglas Yearwood (2004, March) Analyzing Concerns among Police Administrators: Recruitment and Retention of Police Officers. *The Police Chief*, vol. 71, no. 3.
2 42 U.S. Code 2000.
3 Hopkins v. Price Waterhouse, 825 F. 2d 458 (D.C. Circuit Court, 1987).
4 42 U.S.C. Sec 2000e-2(c).
5 Trans World Airlines v. Hardison, 432 U.S. 63 (1977).
6 J. Thomas McEwen, Barbara Manili, and Edward Connors, National Institute of Law Enforcement and Criminal Justice Research Project, "Employee Drug Testing Policies in Police Departments: A Summary Report" (Washington, DC: Government Printing Office, October 1986).

7. William H. Holley and Kenneth M. Jennings, *The Labor Relations Process*, 4th ed. (Chicago, IL: Dryden Press, 1990).
8. Walt H. Sirene, "Management: Labor's Most Effective Organizer," in *FBI Law Enforcement Bulletin*, Vol. 52, No. 1 (January 1981).
9. For an excellent but dated study on police unions, see: Hervey A. Juris and Peter Feuille, U.S. Department of Justice Research Project, "The Impact of Police Unions: A Summary Report" (Washington, DC: Government Printing Office, December 1973).
10. Sirene.
11. Juris and Feuille, p. 7.
12. Juris and Feuille.
13. Terry Cooper, "Professionalization and Unionization of Police," in *Journal of Criminal Justice*, Vol. 2 (Spring 1974), pp. 33–34.
14. *Law Enforcement News* (October 15, 1988).
15. *The Wall Street Journal* (April 8, 1975), p. 1.
16. National Advisory Commission on Criminal Justice Standards and Goals, *Police* (Washington, D.C.: Government Printing Office, 1973).
17. Los Angeles County Sanitation Workers v. Los Angeles County Employees Association, 214 Cal. Rtp 424 (1985).
18. Robert E. Doherty, "Trends in Strikes and Interest Arbitration in the Public Sector," in *Labor Law Journal*, Vol. 37 (August 1986), pp. 473–475.
19. *Miami Herald* (July 20, 1975), p. 15-A.
20. Albert Reiss, Jr., National Institute of Justice Research in Brief, "Private Employment of Public Police" (Washington, DC: Government Printing Office, December 1988).
21. Peter E. Finn and Monique Sullivan, National Institute of Justice Research in Action, "Police Response to Special Problems" (Washington, DC: Government Printing Office, January 1988).
22. *Philadelphia Daily News* (February 10, 2004), p. A-1.

Homeland Security and Policing

13

Key Individuals, Concepts, and Issues

Aiding terrorists
First responder
Homeland security
Terrorism

Terrorist organizations
Incident
Incident action plan
Situation assessment

Definitions

Aiding terrorists: Soliciting an act of terrorism, providing support for an act of terrorism, making a terrorist threat, hindering the prosecution of alleged terrorists, and providing funds to a terrorist organization.

Assessment: The evaluation and interpretation of measurements and other information to provide a basis for decision making.

Components of terrorist acts: Intent and act. Intent means to intimidate or coerce a civilian population; influence the policy of a unit of government by intimidation or coercion; or affect the conduct of a unit of government by murder, assassination, or kidnapping. Act means commits, conspires, or attempts to commit a designated felony per statute, in furtherance of terrorist intent.[1]

Emergency: Absent a presidential declared emergency, any incident(s), human-caused or natural, that require responsive action to protect life or property. Under the Robert T. Stafford Disaster Relief and Emergency Assistance Act, an emergency means any occasion or instance for which, in the determination of the president, federal assistance is needed to supplement state and local efforts and capabilities to save lives and to protect property and public health and safety or to lessen or avert the threat of a catastrophe in any part of the United States.

Emergency Operations Centers (EOCs): The physical locations at which the coordination of information and resources to support domestic incident management activities normally takes place. An EOC may be a temporary facility or may be located in a more central or permanently established facility, perhaps at a higher level of organization within a jurisdiction. EOCs may be organized by major functional disciplines (e.g., fire, law enforcement, and medical services), by jurisdiction (e.g., federal, state, regional, county, city, tribal), or some combination thereof.

Emergency operations plan: The "steady-state" plan maintained by various jurisdictional levels for responding to a wide variety of potential hazards.

Emergency public information: Information that is disseminated primarily in anticipation of an emergency or during an emergency. In addition to providing situational information to the public, it also frequently provides directive actions required to be taken by the general public.

Emergency response provider: Includes federal, state, local, and tribal emergency public safety, law enforcement, emergency response, emergency medical (including hospital emergency facilities), and related personnel, agencies, and authorities. See Section 2 (6), Homeland Security Act of 2002, Pub. L. 107-296, 116 Stat. 2135 (2002). Also known as "emergency responder."

Homeland Security Advisory Codes: Red, severe risk; orange, high risk; yellow, elevated; blue, guarded; and green, low risk.

Incident: An occurrence or event, natural or human-caused, that requires an emergency response to protect life or property. Incidents can, for example, include major disasters, emergencies, terrorist attacks, terrorist threats, wildland and urban fires, floods, hazardous materials spills, nuclear accidents, aircraft accidents, earthquakes, hurricanes, tornadoes, tropical storms, war-related disasters, public health and medical emergencies, and other occurrences requiring an emergency response.

Incident action plan: An oral or written plan containing general objectives reflecting the overall strategy for managing an incident. It may include the identification of operational resources and assignments. It may also include attachments that provide direction and important information for management of the incident during one or more operational periods.

Incident command post (ICP): The field location at which the primary tactical-level, on-scene incident command functions are performed. The ICP may be collocated with the incident base or other incident facilities and is normally identified by a green rotating or flashing light.

Incident command system (ICS): A standardized on-scene emergency management construct specifically designed to provide for the adoption of an integrated organizational structure that reflects the complexity and demands of single or multiple incidents, without being hindered by jurisdictional boundaries. An ICS is the combination of facilities, equipment, personnel, procedures, and communications operating within a common organizational structure, designed to aid in the management of resources during incidents. It is used for all kinds of emergencies and is applicable to small as well as large and complex incidents. An ICS is used by various jurisdictions and functional agencies, both public and private, to organize field-level incident management operations.

Major Disaster: As defined under the Robert T. Stafford Disaster Relief and Emergency Assistance Act (42 U.S.C. 5122), a major disaster is

any natural catastrophe (including any hurricane, tornado, storm, high water, wind-driven water, tidal wave, tsunami, earthquake, volcanic eruption, landslide, mudslide, snowstorm, or drought), or, regardless of cause, any fire, flood, or explosion, in any part of the United States, which in the determination of the President causes damage of sufficient severity and magnitude to warrant major disaster assistance under this Act to supplement the efforts and available resources of States, tribes, local governments, and disaster relief organizations in alleviating the damage, loss, hardship, or suffering caused thereby.

Mobilization: The process and procedures used by all organizations—federal, state, local, and tribal—for activating, assembling, and transporting all resources that have been requested to respond to or support an incident.

Terrorism: Use of force or violence against persons or property in violation of the criminal laws of the United States for purposes of intimidation, coercion, or ransom.

Chapter Objectives

After completing this chapter you should be able to:

1. Explain how the Department of Homeland Security operates.
2. Explain the issues involved in preventing or mitigating terrorists' attacks.
3. Explain the various duties of the first responders.

Acronyms Used in Homeland Security

ALS: Advanced Life Support
DOG: Department Operations Center
EMAC: Emergency Management Assistance Compact
EOC: Emergency Operations Center

EOP: Emergency Operations Plan
FOG: Field Operations Guide
GIS: Geographic Information System
HAZMAT: Hazardous Material
HSPD-5: Homeland Security Presidential Directive-5
IAP: Incident Action Plan
IC: Incident Commander
ICP: Incident Command Post
ICS: Incident Command System
IC or UC: Incident Command or Unified Command
IMT: Incident Management Team
JIG: Joint Information Center
JIS: Joint Information System
LNO: Liaison Officer
NDMS: National Disaster Medical System
NGO: Nongovernmental Organization
NIMS: National Incident Management System
NRP: National Response Plan
PIO: Public Information Officer
POLREP: Pollution Report
PVO: Private Voluntary Organizations
R&D: Research and Development
RESTAT: Resources Status
ROSS: Resource Ordering and Status System
SDO: Standards Development Organization
SITREP: Situation Report
SO: Safety Officer
SOP: Standard Operating Procedure
UC: Unified Command
US&R: Urban Search and Rescue

INDIRECT OUTCOME OF 9/11

Long-distance driving increased during the three months after September 11, 2001, and an additional 353 Americans died in highway crashes according to an analysis of U.S. traffic data.[2] Many people concluded that flying was too risky. As the number of air travelers dropped during the three-month period, the deaths on our highways went up. The additional traffic and additional traffic deaths added to the additional requirements of our police departments either directly or indirectly as a result of 9/11.

Homeland Security and Policing

Introduction

> The enemies of freedom have no regard for the innocent, no concept of the just and no desire for peace. They will stop at nothing to destroy our way of life, and we, on the other hand, we stop at nothing to defend it.
> —**Secretary Tom Ridge, Department of Homeland Security**
> *Remarks celebrating the 213th birthday of the United States Coast Guard*

This chapter looks at terrorism, homeland security, and disasters. Our purpose is to acquaint the reader with the basic concepts and provide a general framework for law enforcement involvement. This is a rapidly developing area of study, but an important one. September 11, 2001, changed the American way of life. The impact on law enforcement was significant.

As noted by Jonathan White, many law enforcement agencies have yet to define their role in homeland security.[3] White notes that we assume that law enforcement agencies will play an important role in homeland security, and we tend to forget that the local agencies are consumed with local politics, budgets, and other local issues. As one veteran police officer noted, "Their plate is already full."

White notes that there are more than six hundred thousand law enforcement officers in the United States and thousands of state and local police departments, but their roles in homeland security are unclear. Traditionally, we have attempted to suppress police activities intended to collect information on political movements and activities, but the success of the terrorists on 9/11 has been described as an intelligence failure. White indicates that we should develop a mind-set that allows the six hundred thousand officers to become the eyes and ears of intelligence agencies. He notes that most officers on the streets have little incentive to think beyond the immediate need for fresh information and cannot picture themselves as playing a role in national defense.[4]

Some of the problems involved in changing the role of police to include homeland security are the rivalries between local and federal police, the advocates of local control of the police, and the problems caused by the legal bureaucracy. Presently, each entity in the criminal justice system is independent, although they interact with other parts, and there is no overall leader. Any effort to increase homeland security will need to understand these relationships.

Although the role of local law enforcement agencies in homeland security has not been completely developed, it is apparent that local officers will more likely encounter increased violence from terrorists. Many of these terrorists will be better trained than any subjects the officers have encountered in the past.

Homeland Security Act of 2002

In January 2003, the Department of Homeland Security (DHS) became the nation's fifteenth and newest cabinet department, consolidating twenty-two previously disparate agencies under one unified organization. Prior to the formation of the DHS, no single federal department had homeland security as its primary objective. Its most important job is to protect the American people and our way of life from terrorism. It is expected that the DHS, through partnerships with state, local, and tribal governments and the private sector, will work to ensure the highest level of protection and preparedness for the country and the citizens it serves.

DHS BUDGET IN BRIEF, FISCAL YEAR 2005

The Fiscal Year 2005 budget for the Department of Homeland Security builds upon the significant investments to date that improve our safeguards against terrorism, while also sustaining the many important departmental activities not directly related to our fight against terrorism. The president's budget clearly demonstrates the continuing priority placed on Homeland Security in requesting total new resources for FY 2005 of $40.2 billion. This is an increase of 10% above the comparable FY 2004 resource level. This includes all sources of funding, such as discretionary and mandatory appropriations, offsetting collections from user fees, and trust funds. [Comments taken from Department of Homeland Security Budget in Brief for FY 2005.]

The Homeland Security Act, passed in 2002, was a direct result of the terrorist acts of September 2001. The act was perhaps the biggest "change management" challenge since the establishment of the U.S. Constitution.[5] As noted by Secretary Ridge:

> Homeland security is about the integration of a nation—diverse individuals and institutions united behind a single cause, pledged to freedom's advance and protection. The terrorists are determined and coordinated. Ladies and gentlemen, we must be more so.[6]

Section 102(a) of the act states: "There is established a Department of Homeland Security, as an executive department of the United States within the meaning of title 5, United States Code."

The primary mission of the DHS, as set forth in Section 102(a) of the act, is to prevent terrorist attacks within the United States; reduce the vulnerability of the United States to terrorism; and minimize the damage, and assist in the recovery, from terrorist attacks that do occur within the United States.

Components of the DHS

The major components that report to the DHS include:

- Office of State and Local Government Coordination, which facilitates the coordination of DHS-wide programs that impact state, local, territorial, and tribal governments.
- Office for Civil Rights and Civil Liberties.
- National Infrastructure Advisory Council. The National Infrastructure Advisory Council provides the president through the secretary of the DHS with advice on the security of information systems for critical infrastructure supporting other sectors of the economy: banking and finance, transportation, energy, manufacturing, and emergency government services.
- Chief Privacy Officer. Information and documents are available from the Chief Privacy Officer Homepage.
- US-VISIT Program. The goals of the US-VISIT Program are to facilitate trade and travel, secure our nation, and combat terrorism by improving and standardizing the processes, policies, and systems utilized to collect information on foreign nationals who apply for visas at an embassy or consulate overseas, attempt to enter the country at established ports of entry, request benefits such as change of status or adjustment of status, or depart the United States.
- The DHS is comprised of five major divisions or "directorates": Border and Transportation Security; Emergency Preparedness and Response; Science and Technology; Information Analysis and Infrastructure Protection; and Management. Besides the five directorates of DHS, several other critical agencies are folding into the new department or being newly created.
- Homeland Security Advisory Council. The Homeland Security Advisory Council provides advice and recommendations to the DHS secretary on matters related to homeland security.

Agencies of the DHS

The agencies that became a part of the Department of Homeland Security are housed in one of four major directorates: Border and Transportation Security, Emergency Preparedness and Response, Science and Technology, and Information Analysis and Infrastructure Protection.

The Border and Transportation Security directorate includes the major border security and transportation operations under one roof, including:

- The U.S. Customs Service (Treasury)
- The Immigration and Naturalization Service (part) (Justice)

- The Federal Protective Service
- The Transportation Security Administration (Transportation)
- Federal Law Enforcement Training Center (Treasury)
- Animal and Plant Health Inspection Service (part) (Agriculture)
- Office for Domestic Preparedness (Justice)

The Emergency Preparedness and Response directorate oversees domestic disaster preparedness training and coordinates government disaster response. It brings together:

- Federal Emergency Management Agency (FEMA)
- Strategic National Stockpile and the National Disaster Medical System (Department of Homeland Security)
- Nuclear Incident Response Team (Energy)
- Domestic Emergency Support Teams (Justice)
- National Domestic Preparedness Office (FBI)

The Science and Technology directorate seeks to utilize all scientific and technological advantages in securing the homeland. The following assets are part of this effort:

- CBRN Countermeasures Programs (Energy—chemical, biological, radiological, and nuclear)
- Environmental Measurements Laboratory (Energy)
- National BW Defense Analysis Center (Defense)
- Plum Island Animal Disease Center (Agriculture)

The Information Analysis and Infrastructure Protection directorate analyzes intelligence and information from other agencies (including the CIA, FBI, DIA, and NSA) involving threats to homeland security and evaluates vulnerabilities in the nation's infrastructure. It brings together:

- Critical Infrastructure Assurance Office (Commerce)
- Federal Computer Incident Response Center (General Services Administration)
- National Communications System (Defense)
- National Infrastructure Protection Center (FBI)
- Energy Security and Assurance Program (Energy)

The Secret Service and the Coast Guard are also located in the Department of Homeland Security, remaining intact and reporting directly to the secretary. In addition, the Immigration and Naturalization Service adjudications and benefits programs report directly to the deputy secretary as the U.S. Citizenship and Immigration Services.

Strategic Goals of the DHS

The strategic goals of the Department of Homeland Security are:[7]

- Awareness: Identify and understand threats, assess vulnerabilities, determine potential impacts, and disseminate timely information to our homeland security partners and the American public
- Prevention: Detect, deter, and mitigate threats to our homeland
- Protection: Safeguard our people and their freedoms, critical infrastructure, property, and the economy of our nation from acts of terrorism, natural disasters, or other emergencies
- Response: Lead, manage, and coordinate the national response to acts of terrorism, natural disasters, or other emergencies
- Recovery: Lead national, state, local, and private sector efforts to restore services and rebuild communities after acts of terrorism, natural disasters, or other emergencies
- Service: Serve the public effectively by facilitating lawful trade, travel, and immigration
- Organizational excellence: Value our most important resource, our people; create a culture that promotes a common identity, innovation, mutual respect, accountability, and teamwork to achieve efficiencies, effectiveness, and operational synergies

The DHS and Cyber Security

The National Cyber Security Division (NCSD) is part of Information Analysis and Infrastructure Protection in the Department of Homeland Security. The NCSD is charged with coordinating the implementation of the National Strategy to Secure Cyberspace and serves as the single national point of contact for the public and private sector regarding cyber security issues. The NCSD is also charged with identifying, analyzing, and reducing cyber threats and vulnerabilities; disseminating threat warning information; coordinating incident response; and providing technical assistance in continuity of operations and recovery planning. The NCSD's United States Computer Emergency Readiness Team (US-CERT) serves as a focal point—bridging public and private sector institutions—to advance computer security preparedness and response.

One goal of DHS is improve our cyber security preparedness. To accomplish this goal, the department has established the National Cyber Alert System, which is an operational system delivering to Americans timely and actionable information to better secure their computer systems.[8]

As part of the program, Homeland Security is making available a series of information products targeted for home users and technical experts in businesses and government agencies. These e-mail products will provide timely information on computer security vulnerabilities, potential impact, and action required to mitigate threats, as well as PC security "best practices" and "how to" guidance.

"The development and initial operating capability of the National Cyber Alert System elevates awareness and helps improve America's information technology security posture," said Amit Yoran, director of the National Cyber Security Division. "We are focused on making the threats and recommended actions easier for all computer users to understand, prioritize, and act upon. We recognize the importance and urgency of our mission and are taking action."

The National Cyber Alert System is America's first coordinated national cyber security system for identifying, analyzing, and prioritizing emerging vulnerabilities and threats. Managed by the US-CERT, a partnership between NCSD and the private sector, the National Cyber Alert System provides the first infrastructure for relaying graded computer security update and warning information to all users.

The system provides actionable information to empower all citizens (from computer security professionals to home computer users with basic skills) to better secure their portion of cyberspace. The National Cyber Alert System is designed to provide credible and timely information on cyber security issues and allows DHS to provide both technical and easy to understand information on a timely basis.

The security suite of products includes:

- Cyber security tips: Targeted at nontechnical home and corporate computer users, the biweekly tips provide information on best computer security practices and "how-to" information. How to access: sign up at http://www.us-cert.gov.
- Cyber security bulletins: Targeted at technical audiences, the bulletins provide biweekly summaries of security issues, new vulnerabilities, potential impact, patches and work-arounds, as well as actions required to mitigate risk. How to access: sign up at http://www.us-cert.gov.
- Cyber security alerts: Available in two forms: regular for nontechnical users and advanced for technical users, cyber security alerts provide real-time information about security issues, vulnerabilities, and exploits currently occurring. Alerts encourage all users to take rapid action. How to access: sign up at http://www.us-cert.gov.

All of the information products are available on a free subscription basis and are delivered via push e-mail. Home users can also access cyber security tips and cyber security alerts from US-CERT affiliates including StaySafe Online (http://www.staysafeonline.info).

Law Enforcement and the DHS

The Department of Homeland Security absorbed many different law enforcement resources and organizations. The resources and organizations involved include customs enforcement, Federal Law Enforcement Training Center, Federal Protective Service, immigration-related law enforcement and border patrol, maritime enforcement, and drug interdiction.

Maritime Drug Interdiction

The Coast Guard is the lead federal agency for maritime drug interdiction and shares lead responsibility for air interdiction with the U.S. Customs Service. As such, it is a key player in combating the flow of illegal drugs to the United States.

Treaty Enforcement

The United States Coast Guard is the nation's leading maritime law enforcement agency and has broad, multi-faceted jurisdictional authority. The Coast Guard has had this law enforcement mission throughout its two-hundred-year history and continues to enforce all U.S. maritime law, as well as enforcing international maritime treaties.

Living Marine Resource

Protecting the key areas of the high seas is a mission for the Coast Guard. The Coast Guard enforces fisheries laws at sea, as tasked by the Magnuson-Stevens Fisheries Conservation and Management Act.

National Incident Management System (NIMS)

The DHS has established a NIMS, which is considered to be the nation's first standardized management plan that creates a unified structure for federal, state, and local lines of government for incident response.[9] DHS Secretary Tom Ridge stated,

> NIMS gives all of our Nation's responders the same framework for incident management and fully puts into practice the concept of, "One mission, one team, one fight."
>
> I recognize the efforts of the dedicated professionals from state and local governments, law enforcement, the fire and emergency management communities, emergency medical services, tribal associations, public health, the private sector, public works, and non-governmental organizations across America who teamed together in a collaborative effort to create NIMS. This unique system

provides all of our Nation's first-responders and authorities with the same foundation for incident management, in terrorist attacks, natural disasters, and other emergencies. From our Nation to our neighborhoods, America is safer.[10]

NIMS is designed to strengthen America's response capabilities by identifying and integrating core elements and best practices for all responders and incident managers. Through a balance between flexibility and standardization and use of common doctrine, terminology, concepts, principles, and processes, execution during a real incident will be consistent and seamless. Responders should be able to focus more on response, instead of organizing the response, and teamwork and assignments among all authorities will be clearly enhanced.

Incident Command System (ICS)

NIMS outlines a standard incident management organization called ICS that establishes five functional areas: command, operations, planning, logistics, and finance/administration, for management of all major incidents. To ensure further coordination and during incidents involving multiple jurisdictions or agencies, the principle of unified command has been universally incorporated into NIMS. This unified command not only coordinates the efforts of many jurisdictions but provides for and assures joint decisions on objectives, strategies, plans, priorities, and public communications.

Preparedness

Responder readiness to manage and conduct incident actions is significantly enhanced if professionals have worked together before an incident. NIMS recognizes this and defines advance preparedness measures such as planning, training, exercises, qualification and certification, equipment acquisition and certification, and publication management. Preparedness also incorporates mitigation activities such as public education, enforcement of building standards and codes, and preventive measures to deter or lessen the loss of life or property.

Communications and Information Management

Standardized communications during an incident are essential, and NIMS prescribes interoperable communications systems for both incident and information management. Responders and managers across all agencies and jurisdictions must have a common operating picture for a more efficient and effective incident response.

Joint Information System (JIS)

NIMS organizational measures further enhance the public communication effort. The Joint Information System provides the public with timely and accurate incident information and unified public messages. This system

Homeland Security and Policing

employs Joint Information Centers and brings incident communicators together during an incident to develop, coordinate, and deliver a unified message. This will ensure that federal, state, tribal, and local levels of government are releasing the same information during an incident.

NIMS Integration Center (NIC)

To ensure that NIMS remains an accurate and effective management tool, the NIMS NIC will be established by the secretary of the DHS to assess proposed changes to NIMS, capture and evaluate lessons learned, and employ best practices. The NIC will provide strategic direction and oversight of the NIMS, supporting both routine maintenance and continuous refinement of the system and its components over the long term. The NIC will develop and facilitate national standards for NIMS education and training, first responder communications and equipment, typing of resources, qualification and credentialing of incident management and responder personnel, and standardization of equipment maintenance and resources. The NIC will continue to use the collaborative process of federal, state, tribal, local, multi-discipline, and private authorities to assess prospective changes and assure continuity and accuracy.

The completion of NIMS followed the October 2003 nationwide deployment of the Initial National Response Plan (INRP), which represented the first step in aligning incident management response and actions among all federal, state, tribal, local, and private communities. A final National Response Plan is under development and will eventually replace the INRP, whereas NIMS will continue to provide the nation's doctrinal guidance for incident management for acts of terrorism, natural disasters, and other emergencies.

General Police Duties after a Terrorist Act

Cliff Mariani in his guide on the prevention of terrorism and response to terrorist acts lists the general duties of police officers after a terrorist event.[11] According to Mariani, the officers as the first responders should:

- Observe, witness, and report
- Provide ample information to dispatcher
- Request supervisor and back-up personnel
- Recognize signs and symptoms of biological, chemical, and radiological poisoning
- Request presence of appropriate agencies
- Protect life and property
- Evacuate injured and endangered persons
- Minimize personal risk and contamination
- Be alert for secondary attack or device

- Isolate and contain the area
- Preserve the crime scene
- Detour pedestrian and vehicular traffic
- Apprehend violators
- Cooperate with other agencies working at the scene
- Keep dispatcher informed of developments

Guide to Personal Emergency Preparedness

A comprehensive guide to personal emergency preparedness for terrorism and other disasters is published by the FEMA. The guide "Are You Ready?" is designed to help individuals prepare themselves and their families for disasters. Revised in September 2002, "Are You Ready?" provides a step-by-step outline on how to prepare a disaster supply kit, emergency planning for people with disabilities, how to locate and evacuate to a shelter, and even contingency planning for family pets. Man-made threats from hazardous materials and terrorism are also treated in detail. The guide details opportunities for every citizen to become involved in safeguarding their neighbors and communities through FEMA's Citizen Corps (http://www.citizencorps.gov) initiative and Community Emergency Response Team training program.

Copies of "Are You Ready? A Guide to Citizen Preparedness" are available through the FEMA Publications warehouse (800-480-2520), FEMA publication H-34. For large quantities, your department may reprint the publication.

Coping after a Terrorist Event

The Office for Victims of Crime of the U.S. Department of Justice has developed a guide for citizens for coping with a terrorist attack, "Coping after Terrorism."[12] The guidelines set forth in this section were adapted from this publication. A similar program should be developed for each police department for police officers because the officers will not only have to cope with the attack themselves but will be expected to be leaders in helping citizens cope with it. The guide notes that the terrorists' acts of September 2001 have deeply shaken our sense of safety, security, and emotional well-being. It also notes that all of us have been changed as the results of this tragedy, and we must be resilient and strong in our patriotism and determined in our resolve to find ways to cope with terrorist acts.

Reactions to a Terrorist Act

There is no right or wrong way to react to a terrorist act. Everyone reacts differently, but it will help your recovery process if you do not expect too much of yourself and others. The common reactions include shock and numbness, intense emotion, fear, guilt, anger and resentment, depression and loneliness, isolation, physical symptoms of distress, panic, an inability to resume normal activity, and a delayed reaction.

Generally, the first reaction is a feeling of shock and numbness. The individual may also feel detached, as if he is watching a movie or is having a bad dream that does not end.

The individual may feel overpowered by sorrow and grief as the shock begins to wear off. It is not unusual for individuals to feel intense grief and cry uncontrollably. Some individuals will attempt to hold back their feelings or "swallow" their pain. Most researchers contend that holding back the reaction increases the length of the grieving process. Other individuals, because of the tendency of society to frown on emotional behavior, feel uncomfortable with having expressed emotion and sorrow. These individuals may benefit by seeking help from a counselor or other victims who understand what they are experiencing.

A feeling of fear and being easily startled is a common reaction. Often the individuals will become extremely anxious when they leave their homes or are alone. Violent crimes and especially terrorist acts shatter our normal feelings of security and trust and the sense of being able to control events. The event happens suddenly, and an individual has no time to prepare psychologically for it and therefore generally feels intense anxiety and horror. Once a person has been harmed by a violent act, it is natural to be afraid and suspicious of others. In most cases, the feelings will lessen or go away over time.

Many persons in an attempt to understand why the act occurred and why they lost loved ones find it easier to accept what happened if they can blame themselves in some way. This is a common way of trying to regain control over their lives. In addition, they will often feel guilt and regret for things they did or did not say or do and that they should have protected a loved one better or have done something to prevent his harm. Individuals who are suffering guilt need to find a way to forgive themselves. The feelings of guilt are often increased by others who point out what they should have done differently in the same situation. Individuals who make such statements are generally trying to convince themselves that such a disaster could never happen to them. This reaction is very similar to many rape situations where individuals make statements that she should not have worn that short skirt or been in that area alone.

The feelings of anger and resentment toward the person or persons who caused the tragedy or someone who could possibly have prevented it are very common. This was a general reaction for many Americans after 9/11 toward individuals of certain racial origins. The feeling of anger and resentment may be very intense and may come and go. It is a common reaction to dream about revenge, which may be useful in helping release rage and frustration as long as it goes no further than dreaming about revenge.

It is not unusual for victims of a trauma to be depressed and feel alone. The feelings often develop into a belief that it is too painful to keep living, and victims may often think of suicide. The danger signals that victims should watch for include (1) thinking about suicide often, (2) being alone too much, (3) not being able to talk to other people about their feelings, (4) sudden change in weight, (5) continued trouble sleeping, and (6) using too much alcohol or other drugs, including prescription drugs. Because the feelings of depression and loneliness are increased when individuals are alone, support groups for victims are necessary to help individuals cope.

Terrorism is an abnormal and unthinkable act that horrifies individuals. It often leaves its victims with a feeling that they are different from everyone else and that others have abandoned them. Often other individuals care, but find it hard or uncomfortable to be around victims because it reminds them that anyone can be the victim of trauma.

The common physical symptoms of distress after a traumatic event include headaches, fatigue, nausea, sleeplessness, loss of sexual feelings, and weight gain or loss. Other physical symptoms include a feeling of the lack of coordination, lower back pain, chills or sweats, twitch/shake, and the grinding of teeth.

Feelings of panic are common and are often hard to cope with. The feelings may be so strong that the individual is frightened. In this situation, often the best treatment is to discuss the problem with other individuals who have experienced similar trauma.

The inability to resume normal activity is a common reaction. Some individuals will be unable to return to even the simplest activities in their lives. Often life seems flat and empty, and the things that were enjoyable may now seem meaningless. Individuals may be unable to laugh and feel guilty when they do laugh. Frequently, these feelings surface months after the event. Tears often come and go without warning. Friends and co-workers may not understand the grief that comes with these types of events and the length of time it takes for some individuals to put it behind them and get on with their normal lives.

Practical Coping Ideas

Practical suggestions for coping with traumatic disasters suggested by the Office of Victims of Crime include:

- Remember to breathe. Often when individuals are afraid or upset they stop breathing.
- When possible, delay major decisions. Major changes will not necessary make an individual feel better. Give yourself time to get through

the most hectic times and to adjust before making life-altering decisions.
- After a disaster, simplify your life for a while.
- Take care of your mind and body. Eat healthy and exercise regularly.
- Restrict the use of alcohol and drugs. Although these substances may temporarily block the pain, they keep you from healing.
- Keep the number of a person nearby to call when you need someone to talk to.
- See a counselor.
- Begin to restore order in your world by reestablishing old routines.
- Ask questions. Find out what types of assistance are available.
- Talk to your children and significant other who may be silent victims and make sure they are part of your reactions, activities, and plans.
- Organize and plan how you will deal with the media.
- If necessary, seek the help of an attorney.
- Rely on people you trust.
- Avoid doing upsetting things right before bed if possible.
- Find small ways to help others, as it will help you.
- Ask for help from families and friends.
- Think about the things that give you hope. Make a list of them and turn to them on bad days.

Questions in Review

1. What constitutes a terrorist act?
2. How is homeland security different from standard policing?
3. What is the mission of the DHS?
4. How can the local police act as intelligence-gathering agents for the homeland security programs?

Biggest Mistakes Police Leadership Makes and How to Avoid Them

In the area of homeland security, the biggest problem is the failure to plan for terrorist acts or other disasters. Law enforcement agencies should develop detailed plans and conduct training exercises based on those plans.

End Notes

1 Cliff Mariani, *Terrorism Prevention and Response* (Flushing, NY: Looseleaf Law Publications, 2003) pp. 1–2.

2. As reported in *The Wellness Letter* (Berkeley, CA: University of California, April 2004), p. 1.
3. Jonathan R. White, *Defending the Homeland* (Belmont, CA: Wadsworth, 2004).
4. White, p. 7.
5. As reported in Remarks by Secretary of Homeland Security Tom Ridge at the American Association of Port Authorities Spring Conference, Washington, DC, at the American Association of Port Authorities (AAPA) Spring Conference (March 23, 2004).
6. Remarks by Secretary of Homeland Security Tom Ridge.
7. As taken from the Homeland Security Strategic Plan (February 24, 2004).
8. Press release from the Department of Homeland Security, January 28, 2004.
9. Press release from the Department of Homeland Security, March 1, 2004.
10. Press release from the Department of Homeland Security, March 1, 2004.
11. Mariani, pp. 11–12.
12. "Coping after Terrorism: A Guide to Healing and Recovery" (Washington, DC: U.S. Department of Justice, Office for Victims of Crime, NCJ 190249, September 2001).

Ethics

14

Key Individuals, Concepts, and Issues

Ethics	Morality
Muraskin	Kant
John Stuart Mill	Aristotle
Epicurus	Utilitarianism
Jeremy Bentham	Happiness
Moral development	Kohlberg
Values	Personal gratuities
Leadership	Internal affairs

Definitions

Departmental values: The values that are expressed though the actions of the department.

Ethical egoism: The view that human conduct should be based exclusively on self-interest.

Ethics: A philosophy that examines the principles of right and wrong, good and bad.

Moral development: The theory that we develop morally similar to our physical development and that because we are not born with the ability to understand and apply moral standards to our actions, we develop them similar to the manner in which we learn to do physical things such as ride a bicycle.

Morality: A practice of moral principles on a regular basis.

Utilitarianism: A theory that attempts to answer what makes an action good by evaluating the sum total of the pleasure and pain that a course of action would bring.

Values: Those concepts we value.

Chapter Objectives

After completing this chapter you should be able to:

1. Discuss what constitutes ethics.
2. Discuss the moral development theory.
3. Explain how values are developed.
4. Discuss what constitutes morality.

Introduction: What Is Ethics?

Ethics examines issues involving right and wrong, good and bad, virtue and vice. Ethics has also been defined as standards of fair and honest conduct. To many, the word ethics suggests a set of standards by which a particular group or community decides to regulate its behavior to distinguish what is legitimate or acceptable in pursuit of their aims from what is not.[1] For example, the American Bar Association has ethical standards for attorneys.

The terms morality and ethics are frequently used interchangeably. According to Muraskin, ethics is a philosophy that examines the principles of right and wrong, good and bad. Morality, on the other hand, is a practice of these principles on a regular basis, culminating in a moral life. Accordingly, morality is conduct that is related to integrity. Under this definition, a person may be viewed as ethical by virtue of knowing the principles of right and wrong, but only those who internalize the principles and faith and fully apply them in their relationships with others should be considered moral.[2] Based on the these definitions, consider the following questions: Can a law enforcement officer be ethical and immoral or can a law enforcement officer be moral without understanding the ethical issues involved? In the latter situation, would the officer be considered unethical and moral? Although many writers, like Muraskin, make a distinction between ethics and morality, the two terms are used interchangeably in common practice and are treated as equivalent in this chapter.

Our purpose in this chapter is to introduce the reader to the issues involving ethics and to provide a basic framework to help the reader understand ethical issues and choose courses of action based on those principles. There are two basic questions involving ethics: What should I do? How should I be? Under this approach, ethics involves the evaluation of actions and lives, choices and characters. This orientation is toward rational argument, toward the production of reasons to support one's choices of action.[3] The use of the rational argument approach indicates that the individual should develop his or her own moral reasons to guide their conduct rather than merely parroting the views of others. For example, why is stealing unethical or immoral? The rational approach would use rational arguments to support answers to this question. To state that stealing is unethical because it is a violation of the law would be to parrot the views of the lawmakers.[4]

The problems of ethics are problems about human conduct at the individual level. Not unlike other members of our society, law enforcement officers have obligations that need to be considered in formulating choices of action. Some of these obligations are placed on the officer by being a member of society. Some are placed on the officer based on ethical decisions that the officer has made. In addition, many obligations are placed on the officer by accepting the position of law enforcement officer. When a person enters into a marriage arrangement, the person promises to perform certain obligations. The law enforcement officer promises to support and enforce the laws of the government when the officer accepts his position. These obligations place additional restrictions on our choices of ethical courses of action.

What are the consequences of our actions that should be considered in determining the ethical course of action? A central feature of ethics is that it should make us consider the results of our chosen course of action and the effects of that action on others. Accordingly, the welfare of others is critical in our ethical evaluations. For example, a law enforcement officer, deciding whether to fire his weapon at an escaping criminal, must also consider whether innocent bystanders will be harmed by the discharge of his weapon. If it is likely that his weapon will hurt some innocent person, would it be ethical to ignore that risk and fire into the crowd?

> Anatole France in *Le Lys Rouge* (*The Red Lily*) stated that Ain law, in its majestic equality, forbids both the poor man and the rich man to sleep under the bridge, to beg in the streets, and to steal bread.[5] What does France mean by that statement? Would it be immoral for a mother to steal bread to keep her children alive? Would it make any difference if the mother did or did not understand ethical principles?

Too often the problems that law enforcement personnel get involved in are not recognized as ethical issues until it is too late to consider the appropriate course of action. One street-wise police officer once remarked that the overriding ethical framework that a police officer should use is to ask the rhetorical question: "Would I be ashamed to explain my actions to my grandmother?"

What Constitutes Ethical Behavior?

John Stuart Mill contended that it was the business of ethics to tell us what our duties are or by what test we may know them, but no system of ethics requires that the sole motive of all we do shall be a feeling of duty; on the contrary, ninety-nine hundredths of all our actions are done from other motives, and rightly so, if the rule of duty does not condemn them.[6] Everyone has an opinion as to what constitutes ethical conduct. As Aristotle stated centuries ago: "It is hard to be accounted an expert in ethics because every person seems to think he knows something about it. In fact, everyone does."

Ethics is not considered as the practice of telling or counseling people how to act. Ethics is not meant to instruct people on how to act and is not concerned with values clarification. The real concern of ethics is not what one values, but with what one should value.[7] Ethics' immediate goal is knowledge, not forcing, causing, or encouraging people to act in certain ways.[8] Once a person has the knowledge then that knowledge can serve as a guide to help program our behavior.

The traditional approach to ethics is an individualistic one. Our notions of good and bad, moral and amoral are based primarily on our considerations of a person as an individual. Accordingly, the morality of any profession, including policing, cannot be separated from the morality of the individuals who constitute that entity, and therefore the entity and the individuals who make up that entity need to be studied together.

Ethics as a Restriction on Behavior

It is often stated that ethical restrictions on behavior are unconscious (i.e., when we alter our behavior for ethical reasons, often we do not realize that it is our values and morals that guide our action). Does it matter that our values and moral guidelines are unconsciously held? According to one philosopher:

> Ethics, like metaphysics, is no more certain and no less dangerous because it is unconsciously held. There are few judges, psychoanalysts, or economists today who do not begin a consideration of their typical problems with some formula designed to cause all moral ideals to disappear and to produce an issue purified for the procedure of positive empirical science. But the ideals have generally retired to hats from which later wonders will magically arise.[9]

One of the important questions that should be examined in any study of ethics in the law enforcement context is: "Is ethics a fundamental component of the decision making or only a narrowly defined constraint on individual conduct?"

Ethical egoism describes the view that human conduct should be based exclusively on self-interest. This concept is a normative statement regarding the best way to lead a life and what makes human conduct good or bad. Ethical egoism implies that the right thing to do is to always pursue self-interest. Can people ever act on motives other than those of self-interest? Can a police officer ever act on motives other than those of self-interest? The Greek philosopher Epicurus (341–270 BCE) taught that human beings come to exist simply as parts of nature and like other natural things seek their own

Ethics

self interest.[10] According to Epicurus, self-interest is self-pleasure and is naturally desirable. He also taught that true pleasure was achieved with peace of mind and that other things such as wealth, political power, or fame do not guarantee pleasure.

Utilitarianism is another ethical theory that among other things attempts to answer the question: What makes an action good or bad? The classical utilitarian Jeremy Bentham attempted to provide an objective means for making value judgments. According to him, two important questions face utilitarianism: (1) good or bad consequences for whom and (2) how do we calculate the value of the consequences. Two classical theories of utilitarianism have developed. The first, by Jeremy Bentham, holds that pleasure is the only thing of intrinsic value to people and thus worthy of pursuit. The second, developed by John Stuart Mill, states that happiness is the only thing of intrinsic value and that happiness is not merely the sum total of our pleasures of whatever variety.

Under Bentham's system, also referred to as "hedonistic utilitarianism," actions and practices are right if they lead to pleasure or prevent pain. They are wrong if they lead to pain or prevent pleasure. The measure to use in calculating pleasure and pain depends on their intensity and duration. The present-day approach using Bentham's theory would be to use a cost-benefit analysis of proposed conduct.

According to Mill, the good that is happiness is not merely the sum total of pleasures because there are important qualitative as well as quantitative differences among pleasures. Accordingly, two lives of equal quantitative pleasures may have different values because one may include pleasures of a higher quality. Mill contended that higher pleasures, e.g. intellectual or spiritual pleasures, were preferable to the more sensual pleasures such as eating and sex.

Kantian Ethics

One popular approach to solving ethical problems is that popularized by the eighteenth-century German philosopher Immanuel Kant. This approach focuses on principles to define what is permissible and what is prohibited. To Kant, the essence of morality is strict respect for certain duties and such respect supersedes any other goal. Kant contends that one's duty in a given situation could be deduced from fundamental a priori principles that were open to the careful inquirer, and such principles were independent of experience. According to him, duty is distinct from pleasure, moral virtue is the supreme good, and moral worth is measured neither by the consequences of a person's actions nor by his or her benevolence but rather by the person's intention to obey the moral laws. Accordingly, certain self-evident truths provide "the categorical imperative" for moral behavior.[11] An examination of Nash's approach to solving ethical behavior presented later in this chapter indicates that her approach is a Kantian approach. A similar influence can be noted in the approaches recommended by Benson and Gilbert discussed later in this chapter.

SOURCES OF ETHICAL PROBLEMS

- Personal gain involving activity of a dubious nature
- Individual values in conflict with departmental goals
- Competitive pressures
- Cross-cultural considerations

Laura Nash, in a widely read *Harvard Business Review* article, lists twelve questions that supervisors should pose in examining the ethics of a decision. She contends that the guidelines are a practical approach to considering ethical dimensions of a decision.

1. Have you defined the problem accurately? Obtain a clear understanding of the problem. The more facts that are collected and the more precise the use of the facts, the less emotional your approach to the problem will be.
2. How would you define the problem if you stood on the other side of the fence? Look at the issue from the perspective of those who may question your conduct or those who are most likely to be adversely affected by your decision.
3. How did the situation occur? Look into the history of the situation and make certain that you are dealing with a problem not a symptom.
4. To whom and what do you give your loyalties as a person and a member of the organization? Individuals and supervisors must ask to whom or what they owe the greater loyalty.
5. What is your intention in making this decision? Ask yourself, "Why am I really doing this?" If you are uncomfortable with the answer, do not make the decision.
6. How does this intention compare with likely results? Often, regardless of the intent, the results are likely to be harmful. Accordingly, it is important to think through the likely outcome.
7. Whom could your decision injure? Even though an action may have a legitimate use, what is the likelihood that it could cause harm to someone?
8. Can you discuss the problem with the affected persons before making a decision? If your decision will harm others, can you discuss it with them first and obtain their views on it?
9. Are you confident that your position will hold up in the long run? Will today's decision be tomorrow's bad decision?

Ethics   341

10. Could you disclose without qualm your decision or action to your boss? Would you be comfortable in seeing your action reported on television?
11. What is the symbolic potential of your action if misunderstood? How will others perceive your actions?
12. Under what conditions would you allow exceptions to your stand? What conflicting principles, circumstances, etc., provide a morally acceptable basis for making an exception to one's normal institutional codes.[12]

Moral Development

An awareness of the patterns of moral development may help one understand what is involved in developing a moral position and how to formulate one's own moral positions. We develop morally in a manner similar to our physical development. Because we are not born with the ability to understand and apply moral standards to our actions, we develop it similarly to the manner in which we learn to ride a bicycle or play baseball. Lawrence Kohlberg, after years of research, devised a sequence of six stages in the development of a person's ability to reason regarding moral matters.[13] He grouped the maturation of moral development into three levels, each with two stages. A summary of the six stages follows:[14]

- Level One: Preconventional Stages. These are the first stages, and they are characterized by unquestioning obedience and the gratification of one's own needs.
  - Stage One: Punishment and obedience orientation. At this stage, the physical consequences of an act wholly determine the goodness or badness. The operative rule may be stated as: "Do the right thing and defer to the superior physical power of authorities in order to avoid punishment."
  - Stage Two: Instrument and Relativity Orientation. This is the stage whereby the child identifies right and wrong according to whatever satisfies the desires or needs that the child cares about. The operative rule may be stated as "Respect the needs and desires of others in order to get what is best for you."
- Level Two: Conventional Stages. At the conventional stages, the individual recognizes that meeting expectations of others, e.g., family, peer groups, friends, or employees, is valuable in its own right.
  - Stage Three: Interpersonal Concordance Orientation. The right conduct at this stage is that conduct is viewed as what pleases and helps others and/or elicits social approval (i.e., being the "good

son or good daughter"). This can be seen as the Charlie Brown of *Peanuts* approach.[15] The operative rule for this stage is "Do the right thing to please others in order to be good in your own eyes."
- Stage Four: Law and Order Orientation. The perceived conduct explained in stage three is broadened to include one's own nation. At this stage, the individual is still authority-oriented but also recognizes a personal stake in the maintenance of law and order. The operative rule for stage four should be "Be duty bound to society's norms and respect the law in order to maintain social harmony."
- Level Three: Postconventional Stages. These stages represent the higher level of values. These stages are the autonomous or principle stages. At this level, there is a questioning of the existing social and legal system in the light of social utility and abstract principles (e.g., justice and human dignity). At this stage, we no longer accept the values and norms of our group but attempt to view situations that impartially take into consideration everyone's interest.
  - Stage Five: Social Contract Orientation. This stage is characterized by the recognition of the social contract, an implicit agreement between individual and society. Accordingly to Kohlberg, stage five is expressed in the U.S. Constitution and represents the "official morality" of the U.S. government. He believes that the majority of people never reach this level.
  - Stage Six: Universal Ethical Principles Orientation. The final stage of Kohlberg's moral development includes the formulation of abstract moral principles. Right action is viewed in terms of universal ethical principles because of their logical comprehensiveness. At this stage, the individual acts in a certain way because the action is perceived as conforming to moral principles that he believes are the legitimate criteria for evaluating all other moral rules and arrangements. According to Kohlberg, few individuals reach this stage.

The six stages according to Kohlberg are sequential in that people must pass though each of the earlier ones before advancing to the next higher level. According to Kohlberg, the majority of American people never advance beyond stages three and four.

Values

The term "value" is used in many different ways. Some of its meanings are subjective and some are objective. For example, in economics, value refers to the utility or usefulness of something or some person. Value also has subjective meanings in philosophy. Philosophical values are judgments about classes of objects or phenomena. Philosophers debate whether the value of truthfulness is absolute or situational; that is, it is good to be truthful, but are there situations where the truth might do more harm than good? There is one common core to the various uses of the term "value." Value refers to the "worth" to a system, object, etc.[16] In this chapter, when we speak of values, we are referring to moral values.

Arnold Mitchell states that values more than anything else are what we believe, what we dream, and what we value.[17] Values are those concepts that we hold dear. They act as filters, standards of behavior, and conflict resolvers. Values are also the forces that cause or motivate us to act. Values underpin our attitudes.

Our values are primarily derived from our early formative years. They do, however, change over time. Most people believe that our moral values are learned and that we generally acquire them from our parents, teachers, clergy, and peers. The learning process may be formal, as in school, or informal.

Conflict among values is inevitable. Our innate values often conflict with one another. In order to resolve value conflicts, we prioritize our competing values. For example, we may value life, but our values regarding our duties as a police officer may require us to place our life in danger in order to perform our duties. Accordingly, we must prioritize our conflicting values of continuing life and providing police protection to the public.

Paul Whisenand lists the following general propositions regarding human values:

- The actual number of values that we possess is relatively small when compared to our interests, attitudes, and motives.
- Human beings tend to have similar values.
- Values are organized into hierarchical "value systems."
- The origin of our values can be traced back to our formative years, our culture, institutions, and society.[18]

THE VALIDITY OF THE VALUES OF OTHERS

The focus should not be so much on how to change other people to conform to our standards, our values. Rather, we must learn how to accept and understand others in their own right, acknowledging the validity of their values, their behavior. American Indians believed that "to know another....you must walk a trail in his moccasins." This is a classic challenge for understanding others. If we can understand and respect other people and their values, then we can interact with them in a more effective manner.[19]

Law Enforcement Values

In discussing values and police officers, often the comment is made that the occupational experience of police officers affects their value judgments and that police in general have different values from other citizens. Milton Rokeach conducted a research project on the possible value gap between police and citizens. One hundred and fifty-three midwestern police officers were asked to rank certain values. Their rankings were compared with those of a sample of adults with no connection to law enforcement. Four of his hypotheses and some of his conclusions are set forth below:

- Police have value systems that are distinctly different than those of other groups in American society. Rokeach concluded that this hypothesis was false. That in regards to the thirty-six values considered in this research, police officers are not distinctly different from other groups in American society.
- Police value systems are highly similar to value systems of those with comparable backgrounds. He concluded that this second hypothesis was true and that police have values similar to other adults with comparable backgrounds.
- Police values are a function of personality predispositions. He concluded that this hypothesis was true and that personality rather than occupation tends to account for the selection of guiding principles.
- Police values are a function of occupational socialization. He concluded that this hypothesis was false and that occupational experience did not change the way officers used values as guides.[20]

Departmental Values

Values are beliefs that guide a person's or organization's behavior. All organizations have values. The values are expressed through the actions of the organization. For example, actions or conduct that a police department considers as serious misconduct form a statement of that department's values in that area.

A police department's values can be ascertained by studying its administration and its policing style. For example, how does an administrator react to internal and external police ethical problems? A department that independently adopts an aggressive tactical orientation has a different set of values from the department that actively engages citizens in the crime prevention planning. Often values are taken for granted until a public crisis focuses on a police department. The crisis may indicate that there is a disparity between publicly stated values and actual workplace values.

Management Tools

Organizational values can be important management tools in three circumstances:

1. When management's values are incorporated into the administrative systems and culture of the organization and thereby become work ethics for the organization
2. When management values are suited to the challenges and tasks facing the organization and thereby lead to organizational success
3. When the management, through values, is superior to any other kind of management control[21]

Organizational Culture

Organizational culture in a police department represents a complex pattern of beliefs and expectations shared by its members. It is often defined as the shared philosophies, ideologies, values, beliefs, assumptions, expectations, attitudes, and norms.[22] The dimensions of an organizational culture include:

- Behavioral regularities that are observable: commonly used language, rituals, and ceremonies
- Shared norms
- Dominant values
- Accepted rules of the game that newcomers must learn
- The feeling or climate conveyed by the physical manner in which the organization interacts with outsiders

---

INDIVIDUAL POLICE CONDUCT

To guide police officers in the conduct of their duties, an ethical code was developed. The first code was developed 1956 by the Peace Officer's Research Association of California and Douglas Kelly of the University of California.

Movies like *The Big Easy* and the books like *The Cops Are Robbers* and *Buddy Boys* paint the picture of corrupt police officers who started ignoring little things until the distinction between right and wrong became blurred and the officers became criminals. These scenarios point out the need to stress individual values and ethics and "to thine own self be true." According to Vane King, ethical issues and values are most certainly not a new concern in law enforcement. However, they have never been so publicized, nor have the stakes involved ever been so high.[23]

Personal Gratuities

> Our problem is not to find better values but to be faithful to those we profess.
>
> —John Gardner

A constant ethical problem faced by police officers involves the question of personal gratuities. According to some researchers, the fact that free coffee is being accepted by the police reveals only the surface problem. Many contend that police who become dirty get their start by accepting small gratuities and through the failure of police administrators to take a strong position against "acceptable" gratuities.[24]

IS IT OKAY TO ACCEPT FREE COFFEE?

Is it okay to accept rewards for an act you are being paid to do (e.g., help people)?
Is it okay to take police department pens home?

Personal gratuities also create an unfavorable public perception of police. In the popular song "Walk Like an Egyptian," the Bangles sang: "If you want to find all the cops, they're hangin' out in the doughnut shop." In the movie *Raising Arizona*, a businessman's son was kidnapped. An outlaw contacts him and offers to find his son. The outlaw states he can do what the police cannot. The outlaw states that to find an outlaw, you hire an outlaw. Then he asserts that to find a doughnut, you hire a cop.

The two examples indicate that many people believe that officers spend most of their time in restaurants and doughnut shops drinking free coffee and eating free or discounted food. Citizens who observe the police abuse their power for a free cup of coffee are likely also to believe that the same officers will be willing to take payoffs. Benson and Gilbert advocate that the solution to this problem is to: first, require that every supervisor demand completely and unequivocally that any personal gratuity is wrong and second, that all officers must be educated in skills to avoid offered gratuities and the accompanying embarrassments.[25]

Individual Guidance

There are some basic ethics tests that individual officers may use for guidance in questionable situations. The tests recommended by Benson and Gilbert include:

Ethics

1. Common sense test: Does the questioned act make sense?
2. Publicity test: Would you be embarrassed if the conduct was reported on the front page of your paper?
3. One's best self test: Does the conduct fit your concept of your best self?
4. Most admired personality test: What would your father or mother do in this situation?
5. Hurting someone else test: Does your conduct cause "internal pain" to someone else?
6. Foresight test: What are the long-term effects of your conduct?

If your proposed conduct fails any of the above tests, then do not take the action.

Some commonsense recommendations for avoiding offered gratuities include:

- Vary your habits and places. If you are regularly observed in the same restaurant all the time, people will assume that you are receiving gratuities.
- Develop a set response without fanfare to avoid the offer of free coffee or food. Know the price of the food and on your way out, leave that amount with the cashier with a smile and a thankyou.
- Develop a set of responses to insist that the bill be paid. Explain to the cashier that you appreciate her thoughts but you would feel better if you paid for the food.
- Explain that accepting free meals or coffee is against departmental policy.

Steven Brenner and Earl Molander list the factors that contribute to unethical behavior in business.[26] The same factors appear to be valid for police work. The factors are as follows:

- The behavior example set by superiors in the department
- The behavior of fellow employees
- The ethical climate of the profession
- Society's moral climate
- Organizational policy or lack thereof
- Personal financial needs or desires

Leadership Roles

Most researchers contend that police supervisors set the moral tone of the department and that top management serves as a key reference point for all subordinates.[27] If that is so, then supervisors are obligated to set an ethical example for other officers to follow. In addition, top administrators should be willing and able to discipline violators of ethical standards. Often inaction by those in key positions is considered as approval of the conduct in question. A key duty of police executives is to evaluate what the public expects of its police and then communicate clearly and inculcate values, such as fairness, honesty, reliability, and accountability, to the others in the department. Police leaders have the responsibility to develop an ethical environment that eliminates public suspicion and lessens the temptations toward unethical conduct.

Internal Affairs Unit

Most researchers agree that the effectiveness of any police department depends greatly on its internal integrity and external reputation in the community. Accordingly, it is important that any allegations of police misconduct be investigated quickly and efficiently. Failing to investigate citizen complaints or requiring citizens to prove acts of misconduct before taking action can lead to a loss of public confidence in the department. In addition, the department has a duty to do more than just investigate citizen complaints. When there is reason to believe that police misconduct has occurred, the department has the responsibility to initiate its own investigation. To establish and maintain public confidence, all investigations of police misconduct must be objective, thorough, and fair to all concerned.

The standard unit for the internal investigation of police misconduct complaints is the internal affairs unit. In large departments, this may consist of several full-time officers. In a small department, it may consist of the part-time assignment of one officer. In most departments, to insure that the chief is responsible for and kept current on matters involving internal discipline, the unit reports directly to the chief of police.

The internal affairs unit should be concerned with serious violations on the part of police officers. It should not become involved in issues properly belonging to command. For example, it should not be concerned with issues that can be resolved by supervisors (e.g., reports of tardiness, improper dress, and absenteeism). The unit should conduct all investigations impartially, objectively, and with integrity. The activities of the unit should be well documented for the benefit of both the public and the officers.

Ideally, the department will have a clear, comprehensive written directive that delineates the process and procedures to be used in investigating police misconduct. All complaints, even those determined to be unfounded, should be recorded. The recording also helps the police department refute any claims that complaints are being ignored. Each complaint, whether in person, by telephone, or in writing, should be taken courteously and recorded.

Most departments retain their records of internal investigations for two to five years, purging the files if no subsequent complaints are filed within that period.

Two difficult questions in dealing with police misconduct investigations are how much of the information is to be released and to whom. On one hand, does the person who filed the complaint have the right to know how the complaint is being handled, and on the other hand, are the confidentiality rights of the officer being investigated. Records of internal investigations should not be retained with individual personnel records. The segregation of the files helps strengthen the confidentially of the internal affairs records. The separation also makes the records more difficult to obtain in civil court actions, in that the party requesting the records in a court action has the duty to establish the necessity for their disclosure.[28]

The ideal internal affairs department carefully observes the rights of the principals involved. When an officer is being interviewed, the International Association of Chiefs of Police recommends the following conditions:

- The interview will be conducted at a reasonable hour and unless immediate action is required, while the officer is on duty.
- The officer should be informed prior to the interview who will be present at the interview and the name of the officer in charge of the investigation.
- The officer should be informed of the nature of the investigation and the names of the complainants.
- The interview should be held during a reasonable period, allowing time for personal necessities and reasonable rest periods.
- The interview should be recorded, and all persons participating in the interview should be aware of the recording.
- The officer should be afforded the assistance of counsel or other representative of his choice, at all times during the interview.[29] (Note that in most states there are state statutes that provide protection for the officers similar to those noted above.)

Whether or not the officer may be required or pressured to take a polygraph exam or ordered to appear in a lineup depends on state law. State law must also be considered in determining whether an officer may under threat of firing be required to take physical tests such as voice-print analyses or providing hair samples. In most states, officers may be ordered in administrative investigations to answer questions and incriminate themselves. Such forced statements, however, may not be used in criminal proceedings. Volunteered statements are generally admissible in criminal proceedings, if the requirements of the Miranda rule have been followed. Generally under federal law, police officers may not be forced into making statements to be used in criminal proceedings under threat of losing their jobs.

The citizen who made the complaint has a right to make the complaint anonymously. The citizen should receive acknowledgment that the complaint was received and that appropriate action will be taken. The citizen should also be advised of an officer that he may contact for more information regarding the complaint.

LAW ENFORCEMENT CODE OF ETHICS

As a law enforcement officer, my fundamental duty is to serve mankind; to safeguard lives and property; to protect the innocent against deception, the weak against oppression or intimidation, and the peaceful against violence or disorder; and to respect the constitutional rights of all men to liberty, equality, and justice.

I will keep my private life unsullied as an example to all; maintain courageous calm in the face of danger, scorn, or ridicule; develop self-restraint; and be constantly mindful of the welfare of others. I will be honest in thought and deed in both my personal and official life. I will be exemplary in obeying the laws of the land and the regulations of my department. Whatever I see or hear of a confidential nature or that is confided to me in my official capacity will be kept ever secret unless revelation is necessary in the performance of my duty.

I will never act officiously or permit personal feelings, prejudices, animosities, or friendships to influence my decisions. With no compromise for crime and with relentless prosecution of criminals, I will enforce the law courteously and appropriately without fear or favor, malice or will, never employing unnecessary force or violence and never accepting gratuities.

I recognize the badge of my office as a symbol of public faith, and I accept it as a public trust to be held so long as I am true to the ethics of the police service. I will constantly strive to achieve these objectives and ideals, dedicating myself before God to my chosen profession...law enforcement.

Ethics in Review

As noted earlier, ethics is the normative study of individual conduct. Ethics has also been defined as a set of rules that define right and wrong conduct. Ethics deals with fundamental human relationships. Accordingly, ethics help us to know when our behavior is acceptable and when it is disapproved and considered wrong.

Often ethics is erroneously considered the practice of telling or counseling people how to act. Ethics, however, is not designed to instruct people on how to act. Ethics is also not concerned with values clarification. The real concern of ethics is not what one values but what one should value. Ethics' immediate goal is knowledge, not forcing, causing, or encouraging people to act in certain ways. Once a person has the knowledge then that knowledge can serve as a guide to help program our behavior.

The traditional approach to ethics is an individualistic one. Our notions of good and bad, moral and amoral are based primarily on our considerations of a person as an individual. It is often stated that ethical restrictions on behavior are unconscious, that is, when we alter our behavior for ethical reasons often we do not realize that it is our values and morals that guide our action.

Ethical egoism describes the view that human conduct should be based exclusively on self-interest. This concept is a normative statement regarding the best way to lead a life and what makes human conduct good or bad. Ethical egoism implies that the right thing to do is to always pursue self-interest.

Utilitarianism is an ethical theory that among other things attempts to answer the question: What makes an action good or bad? The classical utilitarian Jeremy Bentham attempted to provide an objective means for making value judgments. According to him, two important questions face utilitarianism: (1) good or bad consequences for whom and (2) how do we calculate the value of the consequences?

We develop morally similar to our physical development. Because we are not born with the ability to understand and apply moral standards to our action, we develop it similar to the manner in which we learn to ride a bicycle or play baseball.

The term "value" is used in many different ways. Some of its meanings are subjective and some are objective. For example, in economics, value refers to the utility or usefulness of a thing or person. Value also has subjective meanings in philosophy. Philosophical values are judgments about classes of objects or phenomena. Philosophers debate whether the value of truthfulness is absolute or situational, that is, it is good to be truthful, but are there situations where truth might do more harm than good. There is one common core to the various uses of the term "value." Value refers to the "worth" of a system, object, etc.

All organizations have values. The values are expressed through the actions of the organization. A police department's values can be ascertained by studying its administration and its policing style. How an administrator should react to internal and external problems are examples of police ethical problems. A department that independently adopts an aggressive tactical orientation has a different set of values from the department that actively engages citizens in the crime prevention planning. Often values are taken for granted until a public crisis focuses on a police department.

Ethical Exercises

1. Your personal hall of fame: Make a list of the ten people that you admire most. Then make a list of qualities that you admire most in the persons listed. Examine the list. The items listed probably reflect character traits, abilities, etc., that you admire and therefore place a high value on.
2. Make a list of the ten things that you enjoy (value) most. Rank the list from 1 to 10 with 1 being your most valued activity. Next, place the letter "a" by those activities that you have done in the last two weeks, a "b" by those you have done within the last three months, a "c" by those things that you have not done within the last year, and a "d" by those things that you have not done within the past two years. Examine the list. How does the assigned letter compare with the assigned number (e.g., do 1 and 2 in your list have an "a" designation)? Are there any patterns in your list? Do you need to reassign your rankings? What does the list demonstrate regarding where your values lie?

Questions in Review

1. Discuss why departure from ethical conduct on the part of one police officer can affect all the officers in the department.
2. Is it ever permissible for a police officer to give false testimony in court to ensure that a dangerous criminal goes to jail?
3. Explain the differences between ethics and values.
4. Review Professor Nash's twelve questions. Which of them can be helpful in assessing the ethics of a law enforcement course of action?
5. Officer West reported to internal affairs that Officer White, a ten-year veteran, had a habit of eating in the nicer restaurants in the city and leaving without paying the ticket. What do you think of Officer West's conduct? Is he a snitch? Would you blow the whistle on Officer White?

Biggest Mistakes Police Leadership Makes and How to Avoid Them

More police careers are destroyed because of ethical issues than any other reason. As noted by many researchers including Neil Trautman, founder of the International Association of Ethics Trainers, "Ethics training is the greatest need in law enforcement." As noted by Samuel Johnson in 1750, "Men more frequently require to be reminded than informed."

The authors recommend at least one member of each law enforcement agency be a member of the International Association of Ethics Trainers. The association was founded in 1991 to assist those interested in promoting high ethical standards. It provides information and resources to educators, trainers, administrators, and leaders primarily in but not limited to law enforcement. The address of the association is P.O. Box 388191, Chicago, IL 60638-8191.

End Notes

1. Anthony Flew, *A Dictionary of Philosophy*, 2nd ed. (New York: Gramercy, 1999).
2. Roslyn Muraskin and Matthew Muraskin, *Morality and the Law* (Upper Saddle River, NJ: Prentice-Hall, 2001).
3. Kevin Ryan as reprinted in Muraskin and Muraskin (2001), pp. 7–8. Also see: R. Dworkin, *Taking Rights Seriously* (Cambridge, MA: Harvard University Press, 1977).
4. Muraskin and Muraskin.
5. Anatole France, *The Red Lily*, translated by Winifred Stephens (New York: Mead, 1927).
6. John Stuart Mill, *Utilitarianism* (1863) as republished in *The Utilitarians* (New York: Dolphin Books, 1961), pp. 419–420.
7. Peter A. Facione, Donald Scherer, and Thomas Attig, *Values and Society* (Englewood Cliffs, NJ: Prentice-Hall, 1978).
8. Facione, Scherer, and Attig, p. 10.
9. Felix S. Cohen, *Ethical Systems and Legal Ideals* (Ithaca, NY: Great Seal Books, 1959), p. 3.
10. Facione, Scherer, and Attig, p. 39.
11. Clarence C. Walton, *The Moral Manager* (New York: Harper & Row, 1988).
12. Laura L. Nash, *Ethics without the Sermon* (Cambridge, MA: Harvard Business Press, (1981).
13. Lawrence Kohlberg, "Moral Stages and Moralization: The Cognitive-Development Approach," in *Moral Development and Behavior: Theory, Research, and Social Issues*, Thomas Lickona, ed. (New York: Rinehart & Winston, 1976), pp. 31–52.
14. Manuel G. Velasquez, *Business Ethics: Concepts and Cases* (Englewood Cliffs, NJ: Prentice-Hall, 1982).
15. Vincent Barry, *Applying Ethics: A Text with Readings*, 2nd ed. (Belmont, CA: 1985), p. 15.
16. Lane Tracy, *The Living Organization* (New York: Prager, 1989).
17. Arnold Mitchell, *The Nine American Lifestyles* (New York: Macmillan, 1986), p. 33.
18. Paul Whisenand, *The Effective Police Manager* (Englewood Cliffs, NJ: 1982).
19. Morris Massey, *The People Puzzle: Understanding Yourself and Others* (Reston, VA: Reston, 1979), pp. 79–80.

20 Milton Rokeach, Martin G. Miller, and John A. Snyder, "The Value Gap between Police and Policed," in *Journal of Social Issues*, Vol. 27 (1971), pp. 155-171.
21 Robert Wasserman and Mark H. More, "Values in Policing," in *Perspectives on Policing*, No. 8 (Washington, DC: U.S. Department of Justice, November 1988).
22 Don Hellriegel, John W. Slocum, Jr., and Richard W. Woodman, *Organizational Behavior*, 5th ed. (St. Paul: West, 1991), p. 302.
23 Vane R. King, "Rededicating Ourselves to Leadership and Ethics in Law Enforcement," in *FBI Law Enforcement Bulletin* (January 1991), p. 24.
24 For an excellent discussion on this problem see Bruce L. Benson and Gilbert H. Skinner, "Doughnut Shop Ethics: There Are Answers," in *The Police Chief* Vol. 55, No.12 (December 1988), pp. 32-33.
25 Benson and Skinner, p. 33.
26 Steven Brenner and Earl Molander, "Is the Ethics of Business Changing?" in *Harvard Business Review* (January/February 1977), pp. 48-54.
27 King.
28 For an excellent discussion on the confidentiality of internal affairs records see Frankenhause v. Rizzo, 59 R.F.D. 339 (E.D. Pa., 1973).
29 International Association of Chiefs of Police, "The Disciplinary Process-Internal Affairs Role." in Training Key, Issue 299 (1980), full issue.

Index

A

Achievement-oriented leadership, 91
Administrative management
    Chester Barnard, 50
    Henri Fayol, 48–49
    Mary Parker Follett, 49
Administrative science, 48
Affirmative action programs, 299
AFL-CIO, 295, 305
Aiding terrorists, 317
Alcoholism, danger signs of, 195, 209–210
Americans with Disabilities Act, 283–284
    assessment centers, 289–290
    background investigation, 286–287
    drug testing, 284–285
    interviews, 287–288
    polygraph examinations, 287
    psychological testing, 285–286
    written tests, 285
America's demographics, 195
Andragogy, 229, 238
    and police training, 238–239
Applied strategic planning model, 111
    contingency planning, 115
    gap analysis, 114
    implementation, 115–116
    integrating action plans, 114–115
    mission formation, 113
    performance audit, 113–114
    planning to plan, 111
    strategic business modeling, 113
    value scan, 111–112
Arbitration, 293
    forced, 310–311
"Are You Ready?" FEMA guide, 330
Aristotle, 338
Assessment centers, 261, 289–290
Authoritarian, leadership styles, 93–95
Autocratic, leadership styles, 93–95
Automatic vehicle locator (AVL) systems, 169, 178–179
Automatic vehicle monitoring, 179–180

B

Barnard, Chester, 50
"Behavioral Dimensions of Charismatic Leadership" (Conger and Kanungo), 98
Behavioral science model, 25–26
Behavioral systems, 53–54
    Kurt Lewin, 53–54
Behaviorism, 236–237
Behaviorist police training, 236–237
Benchmarking, 125, 132–133
Benevolent-authoritative system, 56
Bentham, Jeremy, 339, 351
Best practice vs. evidence-based practice, 134
The Big Easy (movie), 345
Blanchard, Ken, 90
Bobbies, 8, 9
Bona fide occupational qualification, 280, 293
Brainstorming, 147, 157
"Broken windows," 38
Buddy Boys, 345
Budget plans, 118–119
Bundy v. Jackson, 302
Bureaucracy, 35
Bureaucratic management, 44–47
Business approach to policing, 126–127
    applying reengineering principles to police organizations, 140–141
    applying TQM methods in police organizations, 135–136
    basic elements of total quality management, 127–128
    Plan-Do-Check-Act cycle, 128–129
    COMPSTAT, 141–143
    historical development of total quality management, 130
    benchmarking, 132
    brief on Deming, Juran, and Crosby, 130–132
    Six Sigma, 134–135

process simplification, 139–140
reengineering, 138–139
technology, 140
TQM and community policing, 136–138

C

California Personality Inventory (CPI), 285
CATCH (Computer-Assisted Terminal Criminal Hunt), 182
Chain-of-command, 83, 94
The Challenge of Crime in a Free Society, 16
Charisma, 97
Charismatic leaders, leadership styles, 94, 97–99
  vs. noncharismatic leaders, 98
Citizen advisory board, 64
Citizen input on police management, 64
Civil Rights Act, 293, 296. *See also* Title VII suits
  scope of act, 296–297
Classical management vs. humanistic management, 39
Closed shop, definition, 293
Collective bargaining, 293, 296, 308
College education benefits, for police officers, 253–254
Community policing, 1, 16, 17–18, 38, 103, 108, 110, 160–163, 229, 231
  affecting role of police supervisor, 19
  consortium to community oriented policing services, 164–166
  every officer as leader, 73–74
  principles, 18
  problem-oriented approach, 161
  role of police supervisor, 19
  structure and, 73
  supervision and management in, 163–164
  TQM and, 136–138
  traditional vs., 19–21
Components of terrorist acts, 317
COMPSTAT, 125, 141–143, 169, 181
  principles of, 142–143
Computer-aided dispatching (CAD), 169, 174–176
  goals, 176
Computer and criminal investigation, 182
Computer-Assisted Terminal Criminal Hunt (CATCH), 182
Computer crimes, 187–188
Conduct, individual police, 345

Connecticut Police Department, 270–271
Consolidated Criminal History Reporting System (CCHRS), 140
Constructive discharge, 298
Consultative system, 57
Contingency approach, 90–92
Contingency planning, 115
Contingency theory, 26, 91
The Cops Are Robbers, 345
Courts and legislations impact on police management, 294–296
  affirmative action programs, 299
  drug testing of police officers, 299–301
  employment discrimination, 296
    scope of act, 296–297
  labor relations, 302–304
    collective bargaining, 308
    impact of unionization on professionalism, 306–307
    impact of unions on pay and working conditions, 307
    police strikes, 309–310
    police union movement, 304–306
  off-duty employment of police officers, 311
    conflicts of interests, 311–312
    models for off-duty employment, 312
    other limitations, 312
  police response to special populations, 312–313
  sexual harassment, 301–302
  Title VII, types of violations, 297
    constructive discharge, 298
    disparate impact, 298
    disparate treatment, 297–298
    religious discrimination, 298–299
    retaliation, 298
  Title VII suits, 297
Crime analysis, 169
Crime control technology, evolving weapon and, 182–183
  disabling net and launcher, 183–184
  fleeing vehicle tagging system, 183
  mobile video recorders, 184–185
  smart gun, 183
Crime detection and analysis technology, 180–181
Crime mapping, 169
  technology, 181–182
Criminal Justice Program
  at Michigan State University, 268
  at Washburn University, 269

Index

Critical incident stress debriefings, 215–216
Critical life events scale, 195
Critical path analysis, 157, 158, 159
Crosby, Philip B., 130, 131
Crosby's ideas on implementing quality improvement, 131
Cultural diversity training, 239
Culturally competent, 219

D

Davis v. City of Dallas, 264, 285
Decision making, 150, 154
    nature of, 154–155
        analytical tools for decision making, 157–160
        group decision making, 155–157
Decoy and sting operations, 70
Deliberate indifference, 233
Delphi technique, 157, 158
Deming, W. Edwards, 59–61, 130
Democratic (participative), leadership styles, 94, 95
Demographics and diversity, 217
Departmental values, 335
Department of Homeland Security (DHS), 322
    agencies of the, 323–324
    budget, 2005, 322
    components of, 323
    and cyber security, 325–326
    law enforcement and, 327
        living marine resource, 327
        maritime drug interdiction, 327
        treaty enforcement, 327
    strategic goals of, 325
Differential response to calls, 63, 67
Directed patrol, 63, 67
Directive leadership, 91
Direct liability, 232
Disabling net and launcher, 183–184
Discretion, 147, 150–152
    controlling discretion through professionalism, 153–154
    definitions in context of police behavior, 150
    managing, 152–153
Disparate impact, 298
Disparate treatment, 297–298
Distress, 200, 201
Diverse workforce, planning, 119
Division of labor, 35, 46, 105

Doe v. Borough of Barrington, 235
Drucker, Peter, 57–59
Drug testing of police officers, 299–301

E

Education, training and, 230–231
    behaviorist police training, 236–237
    environment of police training, 249–250
    legal issues, 232–236
    need for training, 231–232
    new approaches to police training, 238
        andragogy and police training, 238–239
    police education, 251–255
        benefits of college education for police officers, 253–254
        National Advisory Commission of Criminal Justice Standards and Goals, recommendations, 251–252
    police training program, suggested first four weeks, 245–248
    training applications
        community survey, 241–242
        conflict resolution and mediation, 240
        criminal procedure, 240–241
        cultural diversity training, 239
        experience and classroom, 242
    training curriculum, 242–243
        caveats for managers, 248–249
        early police training programs, 243
        evolving police training curriculum, 244–245
        historical underpinnings, 243–244
    training methods, 236
Emergency Operations Centers (EOC), 317–318
Emergency operations plan, 318
Emergency public information, 318
Emergency response provider, 318
Employment discrimination, 296
    scope of act, 296–297
English Police Forces, development of established, 7–9
Environment of police training, 249–250
Envisioning, 119
Epicurus, 338, 339
Equal Employment Opportunity Commission (EEOC) requirements, 279, 283

Ethical behavior, 337–338
Ethical egoism, 335, 338
Ethical problems, sources of, 340
Ethics, 335, 336–337, 338
    ethical dimensions of decision, 340–341
    Kantian ethics, 339–341
    as restriction on behavior, 338–339
    in review, 350–351
Eugenics, 83
European Police System, 13
Eustress, 200–201
Evaluation, 120–121, 157
Evidence-based practice vs. best practice, 134
Evolving weapon and crime control technology, 182–183
    disabling net and launcher, 183–184
    fleeing vehicle tagging system, 183
    mobile video recorders, 184–185
    smart gun, 183
Exception, principle of, 41
Experiential learning, 229, 242
Exploitive-authoritative system, 56

F

Failure-to-train liability, 235
Fatigue Study (Gilbreth and Gilbreth), 43
Fayol, Henri, 48–49
Female police officers, 205–206
    critical life events, 208
    family issues, 206
        communication, 206
    organizational stressors, 206–208
FEMA's Citizen Corps, 330
Fiedler, Fred, 91
Fingerprinting, 88
Fleeing vehicle tagging system, 183
Follett, Mary Parker, 49
Forced arbitration, 310–311
Force field analysis, 35, 53, 54
    use of, 54
Functional relating, 49
Functional stressors, 204
Functions of the Executive (Barnard), 50
Futuristics and Law Enforcement: The Millennium Conference, 187

G

Galton, Sir Francis, 87
Gantt, Henry, 41–43

Gantt chart, 35–36, 41, 42, 43
Gap analysis, planning, 114
General adaptation syndrome (GAS), 195, 201
Gilbreth, Frank Bunker, 43
Gilbreth, Lillian Moller, 43
Goals, 103
    and objectives, 107, 109, 120–121
Goode, Cecil, 88–89
Great Depression, 14
Grievance, definition, 293
Griggs v. Duke Power Company, 263, 279
Gulick, Luther, 49, 105

H

Hackers, computer, 187
Happiness, and utilitarian ethics, 339
Hate crimes, 217–218
    recommendations, 218
Hawthorne effect, 36, 51
Hawthorne studies, 50
Healthy work environment, 215
Hedonistic utilitarianism, 339
Hersey, Paul, 90
Hierarchy of Needs, Maslow's, 52
Historical time lines in policing, 27–28
Hollander, Edwin, 92
Homeland security, 321
Homeland Security Act of 2002, 322
    agencies of the DHS, 323–324
    components of the DHS, 323
    DHS and cyber security, 325–326
    strategic goals of the DHS, 325
Homeland Security Advisory Codes, 318
Homeland security and policing, 321
    coping after terrorist event, 330
        practical coping ideas, 332–333
        reactions to a terrorist act, 330–332
    general police duties after terrorist act, 329–330
    guide to personal emergency preparedness, 330
Homicides, variables affecting clearance of, 69
House, Robert, 91
Humanistic management approach
    behavioral systems, 53–54
        Kurt Lewin, 53–54
    human relations movement, 50–53
        Abraham Maslow, 51–53
        Elton Mayo, 50–51

Index

human resources perspective, 54–57
   Douglas McGregor, 54–56
   Rensis Likert, 56–57
systems approach, 57–61
   Peter Drucker, 57–59
   W. Edwards Deming, 59–61
Humanistic management vs. classical management, 39
Human relations model, 25
Human relations movement, 50–53
   Abraham Maslow, 51–53
   Elton Mayo, 50–51
Human resources model, 26–27
Human resources perspective, 54–57
   Douglas McGregor, 54–56
   Rensis Likert, 56–57
The Human Side of Enterprise (McGregor), 54

I

Immigration, 195
Implementation, 115–116
Incident, definition, 318
Incident action plan, 318
Incident command post (ICP), 318
Incident command system (ICS), 318, 328
Indirect liability, 233
Information warfare, 187
Institute of Law Enforcement, 172
Integrating action plans, 114–115
Internal affairs unit, 348–350
International Union of Police Associations (IUPA), 305
Investigation process, 68–69

J

Job analysis process, 77
Job characteristics important for employee motivation, 77
Job design, 75–76
Job enrichment, 76–77
Job-related issues, 196
   building and supporting a multicultural workforce, 218–219
   challenges and opportunities for law enforcement, 217
   danger signs, 209–210
   demographics and diversity, 217
   end result of police stress, 208
   hate crimes, 217–218
   managing stress, 213
      critical incident stress debriefings, 215–216
      healthy work environment, 215
      physical exercise, 214
      proper diet, 214
      relaxation techniques, 214–215
      social affiliations, 214
   minority and female police officers, 205–206
      critical life events, 208
      family issues, 206
      organizational stressors, 206–208
   police stress, 199–202
      categories of, 204–205
      command level, 203–204
      levels of stress, 202
      middle management level, 203
      patrol level, 202–203
      special case stressors, 205
      supervisor level, 203
   police suicide, 210–213
   policing multicultural community, 216–217
   stress and police occupation, 196–197
      portrait of police work, 197–199
   substance abuse, 208–209
   training officers to work in multicultural society, 219–222
Joint Information System (JIS), 328–329
Juran, Joseph M., 130, 131
Juran's ten steps to quality improvement, 131
Justice of peace, 6
Justice Technology Information Network (JUSTNET), 173

K

Kansas City Study, 66
Kant, Immanuel, 339
Kantian Ethics, 339–341
K.C.M.O. Police Officers, qualifications for, 281
Kohlberg, Lawrence, 341, 342

L

Labor relations, 295, 302–304
   collective bargaining, 308
   education requirements for promotion, 307

impact of unionization on
    professionalism, 306–307
impact of unions on pay and working
    conditions, 307
management, 303
police strikes, 309–310
police union movement, 304–306
Laissez-faire, leadership styles, 94, 95–97
Law enforcement
challenges and opportunities for, 217
code of ethics, 350
and the DHS, 327
    living marine resource, 327
    maritime drug interdiction, 327
    treaty enforcement, 327
values, 344. *See also* Ethics
    departmental, 344
    individual guidance, 346–347
    leadership roles, 347–348
    management tools, 344
    organizational culture, 345–346
    personal gratuities, 346
Law Enforcement Assistance
    Administration (LEAA), 252
Law Enforcement Educational Program
    (LEEP), 252
Law Enforcement Management and
    Administrative Statistics
    (LEMAS), 261
Law enforcement training/trainers, 238, 242
Lawlessness in Law Enforcement
    (Wickersham Report), 14
Leadership, 1, 3–5, 83, 86
    maturity level style and, 91
    principles of leadership and
        management, 128
    process of, 4
    traits important for successful, 88–89
Leadership approaches, 85–86, 87
    Cecil Goode, 88–89
    contingency approach, 90–92
    leadership styles, 93, 99
        authoritarian (autocratic), 93–95
        charismatic leaders, 97–99
        democratic (participative), 95
        laissez-faire, 95–97
    Ralph Stogdill, 88–89
    Sir Francis Galton, 87
    situational approach, 89–90
    trait approach, 87
    transactional approach, 92–93
Leadership behaviors, 90, 91–92

Leadership Challenges (Kouzes and Posner), 85
Leaders vs. managers, 86
Legal issues, training, 232–236
Legalistic style, policing styles, 22
Legislation and court's impact on police
    management, 293–296
    affirmative action programs, 299
    drug testing of police officers, 299–301
    employment discrimination, 296
        scope of act, 296–297
    job actions, 308
    labor relations, 302–304
        collective bargaining, 308
        impact of unionization on
            professionalism, 306–307
        impact of unions on pay and working
            conditions, 307
        police strikes, 309–310
        police union movement, 304–306
    off-duty employment of police officers, 311
        conflicts of interests, 311–312
        models for off-duty employment, 312
        other limitations, 312
    police protection, 309
    police response to special populations,
        312–313
    sexual harassment, 301–302
    Title VII suits, 297
    types of violations under Title VII, 297
        constructive discharge, 298
        disparate impact, 298
        disparate treatment, 297–298
        religious discrimination, 298–299
        retaliation, 298
Legitimacy of position, 83
Le Lys Rouge (The Red Lily), 337
Lewin, Kurt, 53–54
Liability, 234
Licors, 5
Life threatening stressors, 204
Likert, Rensis, 56–57
Linking pin, 36, 56
Living marine resource, 327
Long-term plans, 103
    vs. short-term, 116–117
Lynch, Ronald, 107

M

Major disaster, 319
Management, 1
    Deming's management principles, 59–60

Index

features of effective, 57
functions of, 48
principles of, 48–49
principles of leadership and management, 128
Management, technology and, 170–171
  computer and criminal investigation, 182
  computer crimes, 187–188
  crime detection and analysis technology, 180–181
  crime mapping technology, 181–182
  current state of police technology, 173–174
    automatic vehicle locator (AVL) systems, 178–179
    automatic vehicle monitoring, 179–180
    computer-aided dispatch, 174–176
    mobile data terminals (MDT), 177–178
    personal locator transmitter (PLT), 180
  evolving weapon and crime control technology, 182–183
    disabling net and launcher, 183–184
    fleeing vehicle tagging system, 183
    mobile video recorders, 184–185
    smart gun, 183
  future trends, 188–189
    management considerations, 189–190
    organizational issues, 190
  historical view of police technology, 171–173
  management and technology, 185
    human resource allocations, 186
    training, 186–187
  police technology, 171
  remote control information system, 180
Management by objectives (MBO), 26, 36, 58
  steps in process, 58
Management liability, 232
Management theory, 37–40
  administrative management
    Chester Barnard, 50
    Henri Fayol, 48–49
    Mary Parker Follett, 49
  bureaucratic management, 44–47
  humanistic management approach
    behavioral systems, 53–54
    human relations movement, 50–53

human resources perspective, 54–57
systems approach, 57–61
scientific management
  Frank and Lillian Gilbreth, 43–44
  Frederick Winslow Taylor, 40–41
  Henry Gantt, 41–43
Managers vs. leaders, 86
Managing criminal investigations (MCI), 68
Maritime drug interdiction, 327
Maslow, Abraham, 51–53
Maslow's Hierarchy of Needs, 52
Maturity level style and leadership, 91
Mayo, Elton, 50–51
McGregor, Douglas, 54–56
Melting pot, 195
"Memoranda of Understanding," 310
Mill, John Stuart, 337, 339
Minnesota Multiphasic Personality Inventory 2 (MMPI-2), 261, 286
Minority and female police officers, 205–206
  critical life events, 208
  family issues, 206
  organizational stressors, 206–208
Mission, 103
  formation, 113
  statement, 113, 147
Mission Statement of The Madison, Wisconsin, Police Department, 19
Mobile data terminals (MDT), 169, 177–178
Mobile video recorders, 184–185
Mobilization, 319
Model drug testing policy, 299–300
Modern police agency, 2–3
  community policing, 17–18
    role of police supervisor, 19
  development of established English police forces, 7–9
  development of police management theory, 23
    behavioral science model, 25–26
    contingency theory, 26
    human relations model, 25
    systems theory, 26
    traditional management model, 23–25
  evolution of modern police department, 5
    early English law enforcement, 5–7
    early policing, 5
  human resources model, 26–27

management and leadership, 3–5
organizational culture, 29
police reform era, 12
   professionalism, 13
   progressive era, 12–13
policing in American Colonies, 9–10
policing in 1950s and early 1960s, 15
policing in Urban America, 10–11
policing styles, 21
   legalistic style, 22
   service style, 22–23
   watchman style, 21–22
state police, 12
War on Crime Era, 15–17
Wickersham commission, 13–14
Modern police department, evolution of, 5
   early English law enforcement, 5–7
   early policing, 5
Mollen Commission Report, 266
Moral development, 335, 341–342. *See also* Ethics
Morality, 335
Multiculturalism, 217
   multicultural diversity, 217
   multicultural society, training officers to work in, 219–222
   multicultural workforce, building and supporting, 218–219
   recommendations pertaining to African Americans, 220–221
   recommendations pertaining to racial and ethnic minorities, 220–221
Multicultural training, 222
Muraskin, 336

N

National Advisory Commission of Criminal Justice Standards and Goals, 251–252
National Advisory Commission on Civil Disorders, 251
National Crime Information Center (NCIC) interface, 175
National Cyber Alert System, 326
National Cyber Security Division (NCSD), 325
National Incident Management System (NIMS), 327–328
   communications and information management, 328
   Incident Command System (ICS), 328
   Joint Information System (JIS), 328–329
   NIMS Integration Center (NIC), 329
   preparedness, 328
National Institute of Justice, 172, 173, 180, 181, 183
National Labor Relations Board, 293
National Law Enforcement Technology Center (NLETC), 173
Nature of policing, principles, 3
Negative stress. *See* Distress
New Patterns of Management (Likert), 56
The New State: Group Organization the Solution of Popular Government (Parker Follett), 49
Nightwatch (Carpentier and Cazmian), 78
NIMS Integration Center (NIC), 329
NYPD Battles Crime (Silverman), 141

O

Off-duty employment of police officers, 311
   conflicts of interests, 311–312
   models for off-duty employment, 312
   other limitations, 312
On the Art of Cutting Metals (Taylor), 41
Operational management of police agency, 64
   basic functions of police agency, 65
      decoy and sting operations, 70
      investigation process, 68–69
      patrol operations, 65–68
   organizational development, 74–75
   organizational structure and design, 70–71
      differentiation, 71
      spans of management, 71–72
      structural design, 72–73
      structure and community policing, 73
   personnel
      commitment, 78–79
      job description, 75
      job design, 75–77
      shifts, 77–78
      public satisfaction increases with general perception of police performance, 80
Operational plans, 103
   vs. strategic plans, 116
Order maintenance, 22, 29
Organizational culture, 29

Index

Organizational development (OD), 63, 74–75
Organizational stressors, 204
Organizational structure and design, 70–71
   differentiation, 71
   spans of management, 71–72
   structural design, 72–73
      functional structure, 72–73
      line and staff structure, 72
      matrix structure, 73
   structure and community policing, 73

P

Paramilitary model of policing, 207, 250
Paramilitary training, 250
Participative, leadership styles, 92, 94, 95
Participative group system, 57
Path-goal theory, 91–92
Patrol operations, 65–68
   differential response to calls, 67–68
   directed patrol, 67
   split force patrolling, 67
PDCA cycle. *See* Plan-Do-Check-Act (PDCA) cycle
Peel, Sir Robert, 8, 65, 245
Performance audit, 113–114
Personal gratuities, 346
Personal locator transmitter (PLT), 169, 180
Personal stressors, 204–205
Personnel, police
   commitment, 78–79
   job description, 75
   job design, 75–77
   shifts, 77–78
Personnel allocation and staffing plans, 117–118
Personnel plans, 118
PERT (Program Evaluation and Review Technique), 147, 159–160
   advantages, 159
Physical agility tests, 282–283
Physiological stressors, 205
Plan-Do-Check-Act (PDCA) cycle, 128–129
Planning, 103, 105
   applied strategic planning model, 111
      contingency planning, 115
      gap analysis, 114
      implementation, 115–116
      integrating action plans, 114–115
      mission formation, 113
      performance audit, 113–114
      planning to plan, 111
      strategic business modeling, 113
      value scan, 111–112
   budget plans, 118–119
   diverse workforce, 119
   evolving themes, 108
   factors in, 119
      envisioning and planning, 119–120
      evaluation, 120–121
      planning diverse workforce, 119
   implementation
      and evaluation, 104–105
      need for, 107–108
      personnel allocation and staffing plans, 117–118
   personnel plans, 118
   strategic planning, 109–111
   traditional planning, 105–107
   training plans, 118
   types of plans, 116
      operational plans vs. strategic plans, 116
      short-term vs. long-term plans, 116–117
      single-use plans, 117
   use of research in, 108–109
Pluralism, 195
Police Administration (Wilson), 38
Police agency, basic functions of, 65
   decoy and sting operations, 70
   investigation process, 68–69
   patrol operations, 65–68
Police Corps programs, 254
Police departments, job requirements (East Lansing, Michigan and Topeka, Kansas), 270
Police discretion, 151
Police education, 251–255
   benefits of college education for police officers, 253–254
   National Advisory Commission of Criminal Justice Standards and Goals, recommendations, 251–252
Police Executive Research Forum, 221
Police management theory, development of, 23
   behavioral science model, 25–26
   contingency theory, 26
   systems theory, 26
   traditional management model, 23–25
"Police Officers' Bill of Rights," 295, 304
Police Officer Selection Test (POST), 285

Police organizational chart, 47
Police Planning (Wilson), 104
Police response to special populations, 312–313
Police Services Study (PSS), 267
Police suicide, 210–213
Police supervisory styles influence patrol officer behavior, 95
Police Systems in the United States, 13
Police technology, 171
    current state of, 173–174
        automatic vehicle locator (AVL) systems, 178–179
        automatic vehicle monitoring, 179–180
        computer-aided dispatch, 174–176
        mobile data terminals (MDT), 177–178
        personal locator transmitter (PLT), 180
    historical view of, 171–173
Police training. *See* Training and education
Police union movement, 295, 304–306
Police work, portrait of, 197–199
Policing, homeland security and, 321
    coping after terrorist event, 330
        practical coping ideas, 332–333
        reactions to a terrorist act, 330–332
    general police duties after terrorist act, 329–330
    guide to personal emergency preparedness, 330
Policing multicultural community, 216–217
Policing styles, 21
    legalistic style, 22
    service style, 22–23
Policy and procedures manual, 152
Policy statement, 152
Portrait of police work, 197–199
POSDCORB, 49, 105–106
Positive stress. *See* Eustress
The Practice of Management (Drucker), 59
Praetorian guard, 5
Preservation of peace, 2
President's Commission on Law Enforcement and Administration, 16, 171, 252
Principle-centered leadership, 128
Principle of exception, 36
Principle of quality leadership in Madison, 137

The Principles of Scientific Management (Taylor), 41
Problem-oriented policing, 161, 162
Problem solving, 148–150, 159
    attacking a problem, 156
    community policing, 160–163
        supervision and management in community policing, 163–164
    discretion, 150–152
        controlling discretion through professionalism, 153–154
        managing discretion, 152–153
    nature of decision making, 154–155
        analytical tools for decision making, 157–160
        group decision making, 155–157
    process, 163
Procedures, 147, 152
Process improvement, 125
Process simplification, 139–140
Professionalism, 13, 153, 306
    impact of unionization on, 306–307
Program Evaluation and Review Technique (PERT). *See* PERT
The Protestant Ethic and the Spirit of Capitalism (Weber), 46
Psychological job requirements, 77
Psychological stressors, 205

Q

Qualifications (minimum) for K.C.M.O. Police Officers, 281
Quality improvement
    Crosby's ideas on implementing, 131
    Juran's ten steps to, 131
Quality leadership in Madison, principle of, 137
Questers (trackers of murders), 5

R

Raising Arizona (movie), 346
Rattlewatch, 10
Recruitment, 261, 264
Recruitment and selection, 262–264
    Americans with Disabilities Act, 283–284
    assessment centers, 289–290
    background investigation, 286–287
    drug testing, 284–285
    interviews, 287–288

Index

polygraph examinations, 287
psychological testing, 285–286
written tests, 285
recruitment, 264–265
impact of higher education on police hiring practices, 265–270
minority recruitment, 277–279
women in policing, 271–277
selection of new hires, 279–280
preemployment standards, 280–283
Reengineering, 125, 138–139
principles to police organizations, applying, 140–141
Reengineering the Corporation, 140
Reflections of a Retired Police Officer, 304–305
Religion in Title VII, 295
Religious discrimination, 298–299
Remote control information system (RCIS), 180
Retaliation, 298

S

SARA Model, 161–162
Scientific management
Frank and Lillian Gilbreth, 43–44
Frederick Winslow Taylor, 40–41
Henry Gantt, 41–43
Selection, recruitment and, 262–264
Americans with Disabilities Act, 283–284
assessment centers, 289–290
background investigation, 286–287
drug testing, 284–285
interviews, 287–288
polygraph examinations, 287
psychological testing, 285–286
written tests, 285
recruitment, 264–265
impact of higher education on police hiring practices, 265–270
minority recruitment, 277–279
women in policing, 271–277
selection of new hires, 279–280
preemployment standards, 280–283
Selective enforcement, 147, 151
Service style, policing styles, 22–23
Sexual harassment, 294, 301–302
"reasonable woman" standard, 301
Shield Club v. City of Cleveland, 261

Shire reeve, 6
Short term plans, 103, 116
vs. long-term plans, 116–117
Single-use plans, 117
Situational leadership theory, 89, 90
Situational variables, 83, 89
Six Sigma, 134–135
phases, 135
Smart gun, 169, 183
Social isolation stressors, 204
Span of control, 71
Spans of management, 63, 71
The Speaker of the House of Representatives, (Parker Follett), 49
Special case stressors, 205
Split force patrolling, 63, 67
State police, 12
Stogdill, Ralph, 88–89
Strategic business modeling, 113
Strategic planning, 103, 109–111
vs. operational planning, 116
Stress, 195, 200
end result of, 208
levels of, 202
command level, 203–204
middle management level, 203
patrol level, 202–203
supervisor level, 203
Stress and police occupation, 196–197, 199–202
categories of, 204–205
portrait of police work, 197–199
special case stressors, 205
stress, managing, 213
critical incident stress debriefings, 215–216
healthy work environment, 215
multiculturalism, 217
physical exercise, 214
proper diet, 214
relaxation techniques, 214–215
social affiliations, 214
Structural design, 72–73
Studies in Crime and Law Enforcement in Major American Cities, 16
Styles of policing. *See* Policing styles
Substance abuse, 208–209
danger signs, 209–210
signs and symptoms, 209
Suicide, police, 210–213
Supervisors, 19, 163
Supportive leadership, 92

Systems approach, 57–61
  Peter Drucker, 57–59
  W. Edwards Deming, 59–61
Systems theory, 26

T

Task Force Report: Science and Technology, 16
Task Force Report: The Police, 16
Taylor, Frederick Winslow, 40–41
"Taylorized occupation," 76
Team environment, 128
Technological Assessment Program Advisory Council (TAPAC), 172
Technological change, 170
Technology and management, 170–171
  computer and criminal investigation, 182
  computer crimes, 187–188
  crime detection and analysis technology, 180–181
  crime mapping technology, 181–182
  current state of police technology, 173–174
    automatic vehicle locator (AVL) systems, 178–179
    automatic vehicle monitoring, 179–180
    computer-aided dispatch, 174–176
    mobile data terminals (MDT), 177–178
    personal locator transmitter (PLT), 180
  evolving weapon and crime control technology, 182–183
    disabling net and launcher, 183–184
    fleeing vehicle tagging system, 183
    mobile video recorders, 184–185
    smart gun, 183
  future trends, 188–189
    management considerations, 189–190
    organizational issues, 190
  historical view of police technology, 171–173
  management and technology, 185
    human resource allocations, 186
    training, 186–187
  police technology, 171
  remote control information system, 180
Technology Assessment Program Information Center (TAPIC), 172
Terrorism, 319
Terrorist acts, components, 317
Texas Rangers, 12
A Theory of Leadership Effectiveness (Fiedler), 91
Theory X and Y, 55
Title VII suits, 263, 295, 296, 297
  types of violations under, 297
    constructive discharge, 298
    disparate impact, 298
    disparate treatment, 297–298
    religious discrimination, 298–299
    retaliation, 298
Total quality management (TQM), 27, 60, 125, 127–128
  arguments for and against, 138
  and community policing, 136–138
  historical development of, 130
    applying methods in police organizations, 135–136
    benchmarking, 132–133
    brief on Deming, Juran, and Crosby, 130–132
    Six Sigma, 134–135
  Plan-Do-Check-Act cycle, 128–129
  process, key characteristics, 128
Traditional management model, 23–25
  administrative management, 24
  bureaucratic management, 23–24
  leadership, 24–25
  scientific management, 23
Traditional planning, 105–107
Training
  multicultural, 222
  officers to work in multicultural society, 219–222
  oral interview panelists, 288
Training and education, 230–231
  behaviorist police training, 236–237
  effective police training, 247–248
  environment of police training, 249–250
  legal issues, 232–236
  need for training, 231–232
  new approaches to police training, 238
    andragogy and police training, 238–239
  police education, 251–255
    benefits of college education for police officers, 253–254
    National Advisory Commission of Criminal Justice Standards and Goals, recommendations, 251–252

police training program, suggested first four weeks, 245–248
training applications
  community survey, 241–242
  conflict resolution and mediation, 240
  criminal procedure, 240–241
  cultural diversity training, 239
  experience and classroom, 242
training curriculum, 242–243
  caveats for managers, 248–249
  evolving police training curriculum, 244–245
  historical underpinnings, 243–244
training methods, 236
Training methods, 236
Trait approach, 87
Trait theory, 88, 89
Transactional approach, 92–93
Treaty enforcement, 327
Twentieth-century management movement, 39

U

Undercover operations, 63, 65
Union, 294
42 USC 1983 liability, 233
US-CERT (United States Computer Emergency Readiness Team), 325, 326
Utilitarianism, 339, 351

V

Values, 112, 335, 342, 351. *See also* Ethics
  conflict among, 343
  validity of values of others, 343
Value scan, planning, 111–112
Vanguard Justice Society v. Hughes, 282
Vertical differentiation, 71
Vicarious liability. *See* Indirect liability
Vollmer, August, 13, 14–15, 263, 265
Volstead Act (National Prohibition) (1920), 13

W

Wagner Act, 294
War on Crime Era, 15–17
Watchman style, policing styles, 21–22
Weber, Max, 44–47
Weberian bureaucracy, 45–46
Wickersham commission, 13–14
Wilson, Orlando W., 13, 24, 38, 104, 106, 107, 112
Wilsonian professional model, 153
Wolfgang, Marvin, 68
Women in policing, 271–277
  advantages for law enforcement agencies, 273–276
Workplace culture. *See* Organizational culture

Z

Zero defects, 131, 132